Saddam's Secrets

THE HUNT FOR IRAQ'S HIDDEN WEAPONS

Tim Trevan

HarperCollins*Publishers*

HarperCollins*Publishers*
77–85 Fulham Palace Road,
Hammersmith, London W6 8JB

A Paperback Original 1999
1 3 5 7 9 8 6 4 2

Copyright © Tim Trevan 1999

The Author asserts the moral right to
be identified as the author of this work

A catalogue record for this book
is available from the British Library

ISBN 0 00 653113 X

Set in Sabon

Printed and bound in Great Britain by
Caledonian International Book Manufacturing Ltd, Glasgow

'There is surely no greater wisdom than well to time the beginnings and endings of things.'

FRANCIS BACON

'Reasons are not like garments, the worse for wearing.'

ROBERT DEVEREUX, LORD ESSEX

'Plus ça change, plus c'est la même chose.'

FRENCH PROVERB

Contents

List of Maps and Diagrams

Author's Note

I shall start with what this book is not.

It is not an exhaustive academic study of the UN's efforts to disarm Iraq. I have interviewed only a few people in preparing this book, and have sought out little more documentation than that which I had while I worked with the UN Special Commission. My principal sources have been openly available UN documents, the few interviews I conducted and my own diary notes. Where the memories of two or more individuals differ, I have gone with the version that chimes with my own memory, even if this may be wrong.

Nor is it meant to be an impartial, objective account. I do not believe in objectivity. We all approach each issue from within the prison walls of our own culture, our previous experience and our current knowledge. I have not sought out people to get 'the other side of the story'. My apologies go to those who might feel that they should have had the chance to balance this account, particularly my friends at the International Atomic Energy Agency (IAEA).

Rather, this book is meant to be a frank account of what I knew at each stage of the unfolding saga of the search for Iraq's biological weapons, with all the institutional biases and prejudices of the time. The aim of recording the prejudices is not gratuitously to harm, but only to tell what is relevant to understanding the decision-making process from the UNSCOM perspective as I saw it. Others in UNSCOM may well have seen it differently. Others outside UNSCOM most certainly did.

It is also meant to be a tribute to the hard work of the entire biological team: Dick Spertzel, David Kelly, Gabriele Kraatz-Wadsack, Terry Taylor, Hamish Killip, Nikita Smidovich, Roger Hill, Annick Paul-Henriot, Ray Zalinskas, Amelia Jones, and the many others who worked on the subject.

My thanks and admiration go out to everyone at UNSCOM – those still there and those who have moved on to other things. I learnt a lot from working with you. In particular, I learnt so much about so many aspects of diplomacy from watching Rolf Ekéus at close quarters. He, more than anyone else, showed me what strategy is and the importance of using psychology to plan and implement it. Thanks to all at UNSCOM who gave their time in interviews – they know who they are – and to other interviewees no longer with UNSCOM or the IAEA – David Kay, Scott Ritter and Johan Molander.

My thoughts are also with those who did not live to see the full story unfold – Annick Paul-Henriot and Achim Biermann. Annick died of heart failure in January 1995, just months before the final breakthrough; Achim doing what he loved best, driving his motorcycle.

Thanks, too, are due to Richard Butler for agreeing to let me interview UNSCOM staff and for releasing the photographs used in this book and to Ewan Buchanan and Rachel Davies for making the copies for me.

My thanks go also to Sophie Hicks and Charlotte Spencer at Ed Victor Associates, who helped get the book published, and Richard Johnson and Sophie Nelson, who edited it. Special thanks go to Philip Hand, Damien Lewis and Terry Taylor for reading the first draft of the text and for their encouraging and useful comments on it.

There are three people without whom this book would never have been written: Johan Molander, who recruited me to

Right: Map 1: Iraq and the Middle East

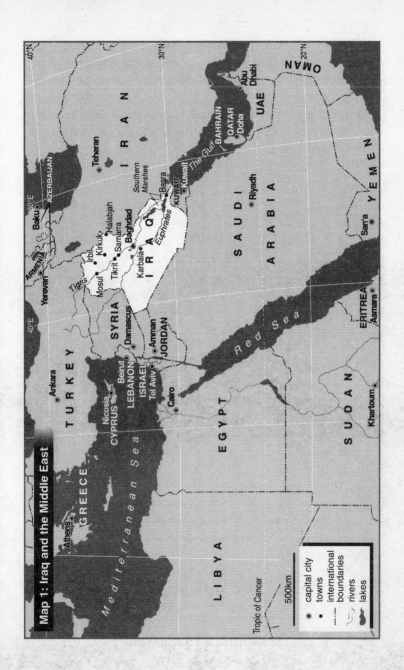

Map 1: Iraq and the Middle East

UNSCOM; William Shawcross, who bullied and finessed me into getting an agent and encouraged me during the writing; and my agent Graham Greene, whose faith in me and my story gave me the confidence to write it.

Last, but in no way least, I should like to thank John Scott for his constant friendship and calm advice during my nearly four years at UNSCOM.

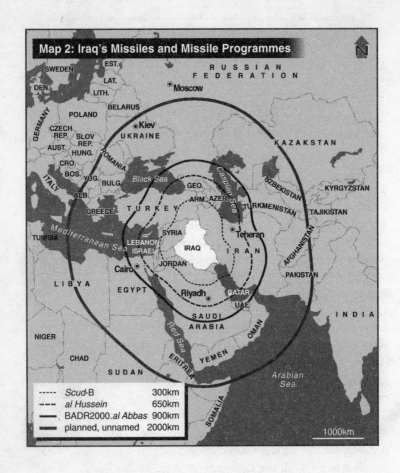

Map 2: Iraq's Missiles and Missile Programmes

Iraq imported SCUD B missiles from the Soviet Union throughout the 1980s. However, these missiles could not hit Tehran, so Iraq developed the al Hussein missile. Iraq was also working on longer-range missiles.

PROLOGUE:

First Impressions, 21 February 1992

The wheels of the plane touched down heavily on the tarmac at Habbaniyah air base. After a series of lurches to and fro, it straightened out and the air brakes went on heavily. We all tipped towards the front of the plane, our seat belts holding us in. The plane was a C-160 Transall, a troop- cum cargo-transporter with canvas and steel-tubing seats arranged sideways along the fuselage. 'We' were a high-level delegation of the UN Special Commission for Iraq (UNSCOM; the 'weapons inspectors'), sent to try to resolve the latest crisis between the UN and Iraq. There were also some thirty or so members of a Bundeswehr helicopter detachment flying into Baghdad to replace the existing contingent. I looked anxiously over my right shoulder at the cargo stowed at the rear of the plane – supplies for the support staff permanently based in Baghdad – to make sure that it was not sliding forward to crush us. It was fine, and I saw to my surprise the ramp doors opening even as we were still rolling down the runway. This was my first flight with the Luftwaffe. I would soon become blasé about these oddities of travel with UNSCOM.

After a short while the aircraft turned around, taxied back to the apron area and came to a halt. The propellers were baffled. Once they had stopped turning the front door was opened by the German aircrew and the steps slid down to the ground. We all unbuckled our belts, stood up stiffly and picked up our briefcases.

The high-level delegation comprised five members: Rolf Ekéus, Executive Chairman of UNSCOM, a senior Swedish diplomat, tall, distinguished-looking, almost avuncular, with a shock of white hair; John Scott, legal counsel to UNSCOM, British, a retired deputy legal adviser at the UN; Stefan Noréen, a Swedish diplomat on six-month secondment to UNSCOM as Rolf's special adviser (the position I was to inherit); Olivia Platon, Rolf's personal assistant, a Filipina member of the UN Secretariat seconded to UNSCOM; and myself, the novice, the only one who had not yet been to Baghdad.

Rolf was the first to step out into the white of the doorway, followed by John, Stefan, Olivia, and then me. The light was blinding after the dimness of the aircraft. After my eyes had adjusted I saw the flat, dusty landscape scarred by cracked-open aircraft bunkers and the twisted remains of Russian aircraft of various descriptions, the results of the coalition's round-the-clock bombing of Iraq's airports. Below me to my left was the reception line of Iraqi officials being buffeted by a hot dry wind typical of this part of Iraq. There was also the ever-infectious smile on the face of Kevin St Louis, UNSCOM's field director in Baghdad. I could feel the hot air rising up my trouser legs in a way that only happens when you step off an air-conditioned plane into a very hot environment.

So this was Iraq.

After perfunctory handshakes and nodding of heads (conversation was impractical over the noise of the aircraft engines) we were efficiently bustled into waiting air-conditioned cars from the Iraqi Ministry of Foreign Affairs' Protocol Department. Rolf and the Iraqi Foreign Minister's adviser, Wissam al Zahawi, took a black Mercedes bearing the AAA insignia I later learned was the monogram of the leading Mercedes dealer in Kuwait, a sure sign that the car was war booty. Olivia and Stefan, with a Protocol 'minder', took a white Chrysler. John and I sat in the blue Chrysler with a cracked windscreen with Saeed al Musawi, the head of the Disarmament Section of the Iraqi Ministry of Foreign Affairs.

The procession drove slowly around the perimeter of the entire airfield – a deliberate ploy to rub in the fact that Iraq had recently made life tougher for our inspectors. This they had done by forcing the UNSCOM aircraft to park on the opposite side of the airfield from the Immigration Office and refusing to allow UNSCOM vehicles to drive across to them (it was therefore impossible for inspectors to unload the cargo directly into waiting vehicles). Instead, UNSCOM was forced to hire an Iraqi Airways bus, unload the cargo into this, drive around the perimeter of the airfield, as we were doing, to the Immigration Office (a drive of some two miles instead of the 400 yards across the runway), unload the bus and reload the vehicles. This bus frequently broke down and was always late. This meant that inspectors had to spend an extra hour in the blazing sun after a gruelling journey before they could set off for Baghdad and their hotel rooms. This might seem a petty gripe, but it was indicative of the Iraqi regime's determination not to cooperate with us but to make our task as hard and as unpleasant as possible.

We arrived at the Immigration Office. Clearly, Habbaniyah air base had long since ceased to be a civilian airport, let alone an international one used to handling immigration visas. The building was little more than an oblong brick barrack. Plaster was peeling off in places, the paintwork was grubby. An unmistakable odour wafted into the corridor from behind the door incongruously labelled in Roman script 'WC'. We were shepherded into the VIP room, where we sat in large, overly ornate sofas which looked totally out of place against the plain, painted walls. Everything smelt of dust, of disuse. Sweet lemon tea was served as we waited for our UN laissez-passers to be stamped. Wissam al Zahawi was talking to Rolf about how sanctions were affecting him, about how he missed flying to Vienna for a weekend to catch an opera and a meal. I looked around and marvelled again at the incongruity of it all. After an eternity, our documents were stamped and we got back into our cars to race away to Baghdad.

In the car John Scott was talking with al Musawi. After eliciting the likely schedule of meetings and Iraq's initial negotiating position, John asked how the Third River Project was proceeding. I admired his stamina: he had some twenty-five years on me but was still going strong when I was on the point of shutting down.

The Third River Project was Iraq's plan to build a huge irrigation channel between its two great rivers, the Tigris and the Euphrates, ostensibly to alleviate arable land shortages and salination problems with the soil. Certainly, looking out of the window, one could see a white layer of salt on nearly all the ground near the road. But in my mind the sub-text was also running – Saddam's desire to drain the marshes in the south of Iraq so that his troops could root out the opposition forces that hid in them, regardless of the untold environmental damage this would cause, in addition to the loss of the entire Marsh Arab culture. Al Musawi suddenly became more animated and enthusiastic, talking in detail and with pride about the project. Despite my tiredness, I struggled to participate in this diplomatic small talk and to absorb as much as possible of the scenery that sped past us. In later visits I found that sleep was the best way to pass this tedious part of the trip. As it was, my mind wandered to thinking about the meetings ahead and what I had learnt about Iraq during the previous six weeks.

My recruitment to UNSCOM was both pure serendipity and seeming preordination. It came about through a chance meeting in August 1991 with a Swedish former colleague of mine, Johan Molander, at the Auberge de Lyon in downtown Geneva. The dinner had been arranged by a mutual friend, Geoff Weir, a Canadian diplomat at the Conference on Disarmament, to celebrate his birthday. Johan and I had both been at the conference, as diplomats, until recently. I had left the conference and the Foreign Office in January 1990 to gain an MBA at INSEAD, a business school hidden in the forests of Fontainebleau, and was now on holiday from my job in Paris, which I was hating. Johan had also left Geneva to join up with his former ambassador there, Rolf Ekéus, who had been appointed Executive Chairman of the UN Special Commission for Iraq, established to get rid of Iraq's weapons of mass destruction in the aftermath of the Gulf War.

Johan was Rolf's special adviser – his political adviser and strategist – and had just returned from a trip to Baghdad where, with the second chemical inspection team, he had been invest-igating how to destroy Iraq's vast stockpiles of chemical weapons. He had stopped off in Geneva to attend to some personal matters before returning to UN headquarters in New York. Despite days of gruelling travel and work, Johan was his usual debonair and lively self – immaculately presented, all Cheshire cat smiles and Richard Burton voice booming outrageous stories, the life and soul of the party.

Late in the evening I contrived to sit next to Johan to catch up on old times. I also seized the opportunity to ask whether there were any jobs going at UNSCOM. He told me that there were only vacancies for technical experts. UNSCOM had no money, no budget – all the staff were either provided by the UN or on loan from governments who paid their salaries. But having dashed my hopes of a job, Johan immediately suggested that I might replace him, as he was due to return to Stockholm soon to take up a senior position in the Swedish Foreign Ministry. He said he would talk to Rolf about this possibility.

I reminded him that I had a particularly apposite résumé – I had graduated in Cellular Pathology in 1980 and joined the Foreign Office, where I had been put on the chemical and biological weapons desk in the Arms Control and Disarmament Depart-ment, and then sent to learn Arabic at London University's School of Oriental and African Studies (SOAS). After that, I had spent three years in Yemen doing political and military work, two years in London dealing with Rules of War and other issues in the UN Department, and two years in Geneva negotiating the global chemical weapons ban. While that did not make me a technical expert, it did seem that everything on my CV was merely preparation for UNSCOM.

I left the matter for a fortnight or so and then called Johan in New York. He said he had not yet had occasion to raise it with Rolf, but promised to do so. He was as good as his word. A month later, at the end of September 1991, while I was visiting my mother in Plymouth, there was a television news report about the stand-off in the parking lot between UN inspectors and Iraqi officials over whether the UN could remove documents about Iraq's nuclear programme. I had made some disparaging remarks about David Kay, the chief inspector: it seemed to me that he lacked the diplomatic skills needed to resolve the situation in his favour without such confrontations. The telephone rang and my mother answered. It was the Foreign and Commonwealth Office. Rolf Ekéus had spoken to the British ambassador to the UN, Sir David Hannay, about the possibility of recruiting me, and he in turn had lobbied on my behalf. The Foreign Office were ringing to ask my mother if she had a contact number for me; they wondered whether I might be interested in a short-term contract with UNSCOM. I leapt at the chance.

About a week later, once it was clear that the Foreign and Commonwealth Office would recruit me, I called Johan in New York to thank him for his help. He shrugged it off, warning me that all the interesting part was over. Iraq had been forced to admit it had a nuclear programme. Implementation was likely to become dreary routine. I have remembered this warning with a wry smile on many occasions in the intervening years. Every Friday that we spent in New York Rolf Ekéus (dry gin martini, straight up with a twist), Rachel Davies (head of the Information Assessment Unit (IAU) in UNSCOM – gin and tonic or a Heineken), Olivia Platon (whisky sour or frozen margarita) and myself (dry gin martini, straight up with olives) would unwind from the week with drinks at the Ambassador's Grill bar in the UN Plaza Hotel across the street from UN headquarters. Rolf would always remark that it had been an extraordinary week, only to remember immediately that every week with UNSCOM was extraordinary. Johan came to mind each time Rolf went through this routine.

In any case, Johan obviously does not think that UNSCOM has become boring yet: upon Rolf's departure from the commission to take up the position of Swedish ambassador in Washington in July 1997, Johan took over as the Swedish member of the commission.

I arrived in New York on 16 January 1992. It was something of a homecoming for me because UNSCOM was staffed with so many of those who had served with their national delegations or the UN in the Conference on Disarmament in Geneva. Despite Johan's words, I discovered that UNSCOM was once again embroiled in a clash with Iraq. It had been set up under the terms of the ceasefire to supervise the elimination of Iraq's weapons of mass destruction – its chemical and biological weapons and long-range missiles – and to monitor its industry to ensure that this was not used to rebuild the banned weapons. By the time I joined UNSCOM there were some twenty-five staff in New York, mostly seconded from the UN, NATO governments or Russia, about twenty in Bahrain operating the transport aircraft into and out of Iraq, and about fifty support staff in Baghdad running the field office there and supporting inspections.

It had taken the summer of 1991 for UNSCOM and the International Atomic Energy Agency (IAEA) to write and harmonise plans for the 'ongoing monitoring and verification' of Iraq's industry, and these plans had been adopted by the UN Security Council in October 1991. Iraq was required, within fifteen days, to make declarations about its 'dual-purpose' capabilities (i.e. the materials and equipment in its legitimate industries that could also be used for building banned weapons). Instead, on 19 November 1991, Iraq's Foreign Minister, Ahmed Hussein, sent a diatribe to the Security Council President asserting that the Council had acted illegally in adopting the resolution, and stating that Iraq refused to be bound by the proposed monitoring regime.

As he did each time he was confronted with Iraqi obstruction, Rolf Ekéus considered how this latest setback could best be presented to the Council. Clearly, UNSCOM could not afford to run to the Council each time Iraq obstructed its work in the slightest way. It must first prove that it had exhausted all other, diplomatic attempts to gain Iraqi acquiescence. Rolf had therefore planned a multi-staged approach. First, he called together to New York analysts from the intelligence communities of five of the key countries at the UN – the US, UK, France, Russia and Germany – to share with UNSCOM their assessments of what Iraq had yet to declare. On the basis of this assessment, which bought four of the Council's five permanent members into the game plan (China being the odd one out), he dispatched a high-level team to Iraq, headed by two members of the commission (John Gee of Australia and Peter von Butler of Germany), to demand that Iraq accept the monitoring regime for its industry and give a full account of past programmes. If that failed, he would report to the Council and have them send him to Baghdad seeking Iraq's compliance with a strongly worded demand. He would, if necessary, supply the Council with the wording for that demand. This far-sighted approach also gave warning to Council members that enforcement actions might be necessary should the stratagem fail.

Sitting in on the meeting of intelligence analysts was, for me, a surreal experience. During my ten years as a British diplomat the KGB had been the enemy. On a more personal level, Nikita Smidovich, who was now my colleague in UNSCOM, had been my principal opponent when we were both negotiating the chemical weapons ban in Geneva just two short years previously. Now, the KGB's post-communist successor, the FIS (Foreign Intelligence Service), was not only sitting in a room with its American, French, British and German counterparts, openly sharing assessments; it was doing so in front of UN officials who included Nikita, Scott Ritter (a US marine) and myself.

Quite apart from the politics of the New World Order, the substance of the exchanges was equally eye-opening. Iraq had claimed that it had no biological warfare programmes or activities whatsoever. After the first inspection team's discovery of vials of anthrax, botulinum and gas gangrene, the story had changed, and the Iraqis were now saying that they had had a small, purely defensive research programme that had been inefficiently run and had not met with much success.

None of the intelligence analysts bought this latest Iraqi story. Concerns centred around four issues; these would eventually be backed up by some new hard evidence to seal the case against Iraq, but at this stage they remained frustratingly unsubstantiated:

- **Destruction of evidence.** The Salman Pak site (about 25 kilometres south-east of Baghdad), which, the intelligence communities suspected, had been the centre and birthplace of the Iraqi biological weapons programme, had previously contained a fermenter and an incinerator. Broken remains of inhalation chambers were also found scattered around the site during the first inspection. Fermenters can be used to grow bacteria in large quantities; incinerators are needed to get rid of highly toxic waste materials (clearly essential in a biological warfare laboratory); inhalation chambers are used to test the toxicity and infectiousness of bacteria – another key piece of equipment when trying to identify the most effective biological warfare agents. Furthermore, Iraq had razed the Salman Pak facility to the ground only one week before the first inspection of the site. These facts begged the questions, What was Iraq trying to hide by doing so? and Why?
- **Reconfiguration of facilities.** A second facility, the al Hakam plant, looked as if it might have been built for the manufacture of biological weapons. The high, double security fences around it indicated that it was a secret military facility. The fact that it was built quickly and lacked any building documentation showed that it was a high-priority government project and thus beyond the reach of local planning authorities. Its links to the Salman Pak site and the attempts by personnel there to buy three large fermenters made its activities suspicious.

But, most damning of all, the buildings were designed for

high degrees of containment – i.e. to stop bacteria and viruses escaping from the laboratory into the surrounding environment. This is essential if one wants to work safely or secretly with biological warfare agents – it is hard to keep biological warfare research a secret if one has to explain frequent outbreaks of unusual diseases in the communities around the laboratory. At al Hakam there was evidence that it had high-performance air conditioning and filtration for scrubbing the air leaving the building clean of bacteria and viruses; there was also evidence that, prior to the inspections, decontamination shower units between the laboratory area and the outside world (to ensure that scientists do not bring deadly bacteria out of the laboratory on themselves or their clothing) had been removed. All that remained of them were marks on the floor where the walls used to be. Again, these changes to the buildings' structure and removal of bulky equipment such as the air conditioning begged the question: Why were the changes made and why was the equipment removed – what had changed about the nature of the activities taking place at the facility which meant that the earlier, high-containment features were no longer required?

- **The materials acquired and the work undertaken.** The strains of bacteria acquired by Iraq were ones most suited to warfare purposes (they were resistant to high temperatures). The experimentation undertaken (including aerosolisation – creating a cloud of droplets hanging in the air, each containing a number of bacteria or viruses) indicated research not into how to defend against biological weapons but into how to disseminate them, i.e. how to weaponise stocks of bacteria and viruses. Taken in conjunction with the equipment observed (fermenters, air conditioning and filtration, inhalation chambers), this pointed to an offensive, not defensive, bent to Iraq's biological warfare research.

- **The people and their skills.** The biological research programme in Iraq had recruited mechanical and process engineers, indicating that it was more than a research programme, that work had moved at least into production development, and perhaps into pilot plant and weaponisation stages.

Armed with these assessments, the John Gee and Peter von Butler team left for Baghdad, arriving on 27 January 1992. They returned a week or so later, virtually empty handed. Despite a new man in charge on the Iraqi side, British-educated General Amer Rasheed al Ubeidi – who was not without a certain roguish charm – very little new was learnt. The team had received a flat refusal on monitoring and, on the basis of the joint intelligence assessments received before the trip, became convinced that Iraq was not telling the truth about its biological, or other activities. Instead of the 'full, final and complete disclosures' required by the ceasefire, Iraq had provided incredible accounts which insulted the team's intelligence. In the UNSCOM meeting following the team's return to New York, Johan Santesson, a Swedish chemical weapons expert and another former colleague from Geneva days, described the new Iraqi declarations, in his slow heavily accented English, with the straightest of faces and the maximum of irony in his voice, as 'full, final and complete fairy tales'. Within UNSCOM this nickname stuck for those, and subsequent, Iraqi declarations.

On the basis of this team's evidence, John Scott and Stefan Noréen prepared a special report to the Security Council on Iraq's non-compliance. This was circulated on 18 February 1992, and the Council met the next afternoon. Rolf Ekéus, as he had planned, was sent by the Council to Iraq that evening with a strongly worded message addressed to the Iraqi regime.

The new team, comprising Rolf Ekéus, John Scott, Stefan Noréen, Olivia Platon and me, was on a plane from New York at 7.30 p.m. I was quickly to learn what a hard task master Rolf was, and how determined he was to lead from the front. We arrived in London at just after six the next morning (the 20th) and caught the 10 a.m. flight to Bahrain. We landed at 9.30 p.m. to be informed that our flight to Baghdad would leave at 6 a.m. on the 21st, which meant a 5 a.m. departure from the hotel. Rolf negotiated that back to 5.30 a.m. We landed at Habbaniyah airfield at around 10.30 a.m. on the 21st. After tea in the VIP room there, we drove to Baghdad, and arrived in our hotel rooms at around 1.15 p.m. Rolf gave us fifteen minutes to freshen up before we gathered to prepare for the meetings with the Iraqis that afternoon. We also had five hours of meetings (and several more hours of waiting for meetings) on the 22nd, and three hours on the 23rd. We then left the hotel at around midday on the 24th, took off from Habbaniyah at about 1.30 p.m., arriving in Bahrain at 6.30 p.m., where we ate a meal and got some sleep. The next two days were spent drafting our report to the Security Council, and meeting Bahraini ministers, officials and local ambassadors. We left the hotel at 11 p.m. and caught the 12.45 a.m. flight to London on the 27th, arriving at 6.30 a.m. We caught the 10.30 a.m. flight to New York and then drove straight to a meeting of the Security Council to report on the outcome of the trip. In eight days I had had twenty-four hours' sleep – I had not yet mastered the art of sleeping in planes and cars.

Our arrival at the Rasheed Hotel in central Baghdad on 21 February 1992 was, as always, met with a crush of journalists and TV camera crews trying to talk to Rolf as he walked purposefully in the direction of the lifts at the far end of the hotel lobby. This process was dubbed by John Scott the 'Baghdad Shuffle' – tens of journalists facing Rolf, thrusting microphones and cameras in his face while simultaneously bombarding him with questions and shuffling backwards as he moved forwards. Rolf stopped for a short while and briefly stated the purpose of our visit: to deliver a message to the Iraqi government from the Security Council, demanding Iraq's acknowledgement of its obligations under two resolutions (707 and 715); and to obtain Iraq's commitment to deliver 'full, final and complete disclosures' of its weapons programmes and its acceptance of the monitoring and verification of its dual-purpose industry. He then resumed his march, fielding the questions in a terse fashion. When we reached the lifts, some of the journalists tried to get in too, but were pushed back by the Iraqi Protocol officers accompanying us.

Upstairs, we were shown to our rooms. The hotel is shaped like a long, thin cigarette packet. The lifts are in the middle, and so the corridors that lead to the rooms either side of the lift shaft are long, narrow and dark. The darkness is enhanced by the wood panelling. Our rooms were at the end of the corridor furthest away from the street, on the fourteenth floor. Inside, the rooms are like any other businessman's hotel – spacious, with double beds, a desk, marbled bathroom and large panoramic views of Baghdad. A complimentary basket of fruit awaited each of us, including succulent Iraqi dates – something to be treasured, given the limited fare available in the restaurants.

A quick freshen up, unpacking of clothes, and we met up again in Rolf's suite. Here we exchanged information gained from our conversations with our Iraqi counterparts during the drive in from Habbaniyah airfield. Protocol had assured us that there would be a meeting at three o'clock that afternoon. Aware that our rooms were likely to be bugged, we took a stroll through the large hotel gardens to fine-tune the arguments. Rolf was meticulous in his preparation for such important meetings – repeating the arguments over and over again with his aides, bouncing ideas off them, reformulating the words until he was happy and comfortable with them.

The hotel had been built to host delegations to the Non-Aligned Movement summit conference in the late 1970s, cancelled following Iraq's invasion of Iran. It is a fifteen-storey modern tribute to grey marble, black glass and concrete, cold and heartless. Its gardens are admittedly splendid but, prison-like, they are surrounded by high-security walls with watch towers and machine-gun stands; they also contain a helicopter pad with a mini control tower. However, the gardens provided a place to talk and almost the only daylight we saw on this and similar trips down the years.

Before three o'clock we were back in Rolf's suite waiting for

Protocol to come and pick us up for the meeting. At 3.30 we went looking for them. No sign. Regular forays into the lobby failed to track anyone down until about 4.30, when we were told that the meeting would be at six. Six came and went. Eventually we were contacted and told the meeting would be at 7 p.m.

The Iraqi side was headed by Mohammed al Sahaf, Iraq's Minister of State for Foreign Affairs, a bluff Shia Moslem who had previously been ambassador in Sweden. He was dressed in green battle fatigues, back ramrod straight, mouth fixed in a stern smile. With him was the surprisingly tall and thin General Amer Rasheed al Ubeidi, at that time vice-chairman of the Military Industrial-isation Corporation (MIC), also in battle fatigues. What struck me about him was that, although in no way good looking, he was curiously attractive: his face was very mobile and his grey-tipped moustache did not look quite standard Iraqi issue; his eyes, from behind his steel-framed glasses, were quick and sparkled with intelligence and humour. Also present were Dr Human Abdul Khaliq Ghaffour, chairman of Iraq's Atomic Energy Commission, Saeed al Musawi and a few other suits.

The meeting opened with a forty-minute exposition by Rolf of the message from the Security Council, with added explanations why UNSCOM needed the 'full, final and complete disclosures' of Iraq's weapons programmes, why monitoring was required, and how sanctions would be lifted once all this was provided. This was followed by an hour-long diatribe from al Sahaf about how Iraq had already given UNSCOM everything, how the more UNSCOM was given the less satisfied it was, how Iraq did not believe that the UN would lift the sanctions (there was therefore no incentive to cooperate with UNSCOM), and how there was a need for an end to this process. Rolf then responded, provoking interventions and further responses, but no yielding on the UN demands.

The highlight of this meeting was the biggest and most bare-faced lie I ever heard, delivered without a hint of humour or embarrassment. To counter claims by Rolf that Iraq had been less than honest in its declarations in the past and had withheld information from inspectors, Dr Human Abdul Khaliq stated categorically that that was not true. Iraq, he said, had volunteered everything – it had even given UNSCOM 60,000 documents about its nuclear research. The 60,000 documents he was referring to had been at the centre of the parking-lot stand-off with David Kay and Bob Gallucci. UNSCOM, acting on very good intelligence, had launched an inspection specifically to track down Iraq's archives about its nuclear programmes. This intelligence had been so accurate that it led the inspection team to stashes of documents in two different buildings. In the first building the Iraqi officials accompanying the team had confiscated the documents at gunpoint. At the second site they had tried the same thing but the team refused to relinquish the documents. Armed Iraqi soldiers then prevented the inspectors from leaving the site with these documents; the team refused to leave without them, resulting in a stand-off. The inspectors and the documents stayed in the parking lot for four hot days, surrounded by Iraqi soldiers. The situation was resolved only when the US threatened to resume military action against Iraq. Iraq had yielded those documents at gunpoint; it had not given them up voluntarily in the spirit of cooperation. When I heard Dr Human say that Iraq had given UNSCOM all those documents, I could not believe my ears. Fortunately, there was no video recording of this meeting. I am sure my jaw must have hit the table.

The meeting ended with no agreement on substance, but with a promise of a meeting with the Deputy Prime Minister, Tariq Aziz, at his villa the following day at 9 a.m. We went back to our hotel, exchanged notes on the meeting, ate and went to sleep. We met again for breakfast at eight the next morning, rehearsed the line to take with Aziz, and then waited, and waited, and waited for the Protocol people to appear. The meeting was delayed for thirty minutes, and then another thirty. We finally left the hotel at around 11.30 and were whisked, again at high speed, to Tariq Aziz's villa. The villa was one of those that had been built for heads of state and government visiting the Non-Aligned Conference but, like the hotel, had never been used for that purpose; instead it had been given to Tariq Aziz. It was near a walled complex of similar villas opposite the Ba'ath Party headquarters, also used by Ba'ath officials. So far, I had seen little damage resulting from the war. Here the destruction was near total. The Ba'ath Party building had been hit by Tomahawks. Its outer walls showed dangerous cracks and it was unoccupied. The villas in the complex had all been hit several times, but there was no collateral damage outside the walls.

Much was said during the Gulf War about the accuracy of the American smart weapons that was subsequently found to be more propaganda than truth. Much is now being said about the thousands of civilians who were killed by these weapons. The truth may lie somewhere in between, but as far as I could see on that drive to Tariq Aziz's house, the bombs were accurate. And it is worth remembering that Iraq could show journalists only two major sites where large numbers of civilians were killed by military action: the bunker and the market at Fallujah – one a targeting error, the other a faulty fin on a smart bomb.

The semi-circular ramp outside the villa swept the cars up to first-floor level. We were led through an austere hallway into a long, narrow sitting room. Sofas and armchairs were lined up against the walls. Tariq Aziz welcomed us, and sat down at the far end of the room. Unlike the others, he was comfortably dressed in a safari suit. We sat along the wall to his right, with the other Iraqis facing us. The team of the previous night was joined by the Minister for Foreign Affairs, Ahmed Hussein, and the chief of the International Organisations Department, Riyadh al Qaysi. But the arrangement of the furniture ensured that attention inevitably focused on Aziz, who clearly enjoyed the limelight. Sweet Arabic tea was served in glasses with glass saucers, the bottom half-inch pure sugar.

The meeting followed a similar format to the previous day: Tariq Aziz talked for some forty-five minutes first, then Rolf responded for about forty minutes. The same points were made on both sides, albeit with somewhat refined arguments. Aziz made it clear that, in his view, there should be an end to the investigation into past programmes. Iraq's declarations had been muddled, but could be reformulated to make them more consistent. UNSCOM should draw up a definitive list of questions it needed resolved and there should then be a seminar, at which UNSCOM and Iraqi officials could resolve them, whereupon UNSCOM should report to the Council that its task was complete and sanctions should be lifted. Iraq accepted the principle of future monitoring of its industry to ensure it was not used to rebuild banned weapons under resolution 687, but objected to the inspection powers given to UNSCOM by resolution 715. This resolution extended the intrusive, 'anytime anywhere with no delay' UNSCOM inspections indefinitely, beyond the elimination of the banned weapons until such time as the Security Council decided that they were no longer needed. It would also extend these rights to the monitoring of Iraq's dual-purpose industry – factories which have legitimate purposes but which could also be used to make the banned weapons. These rights were an affront to Iraq's sovereignty, national security, territorial integrity and dignity: Iraq would not accept resolution 715. Rolf countered each of these points, explaining how, with Iraqi cooperation, all remaining issues could be clarified quickly, but that Iraqi information would have to be supported with evidence and verified. The meeting ended with an agreement that both sides would put their views and interpretations of the situation on paper and exchange these that evening. The purpose would be to present the two views to the Security Council in preparation for Aziz's visit to New York.

We rushed back to the hotel, grabbed a bite to eat in the cafeteria and launched into writing the UNSCOM paper. The menu in the cafeteria was comprehensive, but experience proved that omelettes and meat were the safest bets. We developed a routine of eating omelettes for breakfast and lunch, and a meat dish for dinner. For a while after each trip to Baghdad my diet was egg-free.

A further meeting was held that evening. The Iraqis had not

completed their paper, and so the time was spent discussing the details of ours. It was not until the next evening, presumably after Aziz had been informed of the content of the UNSCOM paper and had had time to brief Saddam on it, that the Iraqi side produced their paper.

A quick reading of it proved that our mission had failed on both key points. Iraq did not acknowledge either resolution 707 or 715: it would not give the full, final and complete disclosures of the past programmes, including the biological weapons programme, that we sought. Nor would it accept the plans for ongoing monitoring and verification of its dual-purpose industry in the form dictated by the Council. Iraq was trying to set up Aziz's address to the Security Council as a trial of UNSCOM and its competence, instead of a trial of the Iraqi government and its failure to comply with the terms of the ceasefire. It was aiming to get the Council to rein in UNSCOM, and call off its bloodhounds.

This refusal to accept monitoring was to hamper the biological weapons investigation for a further twenty months. It was only when Iraq withdrew its fundamental opposition to monitoring that UNSCOM could get the new leads that enabled it to crack the case.

When I started writing this book in February 1998, it was six years since I had first met Tariq Aziz. Looking at the issues then separating the UN and Iraq, nothing had changed. Iraq was still claiming, as it did in 1992, that it was in full compliance with the ceasefire terms, having declared all its programmes and destroyed all its banned weapons. Iraq was still claiming, as it did in 1991, that the teams were unbalanced, with too many Americans in them. Iraq was still complaining, as it did every year that I worked with UNSCOM, that UNSCOM was overstepping its mandate and was acting unprofessionally. Iraq is still trying to block access to certain sites, as it did in 1991 and 1992. Iraq was still trying to discredit any UNSCOM report that countered any of these claims, just as it tried to rewrite UNSCOM reports, and even IAEA resolutions, in 1991. And Iraq was still demanding that the UN live up to its obligations and lift the sanctions; otherwise Iraq would end its 'cooperation' with the UN, as it had threatened to do in 1991, 1992, 1993, 1994, 1995, 1996, 1997, 1998 ...

And Iraq was lying yet again. But several things had changed: for one thing, Iraq's biological weapons programme was out in the open, successfully uncovered, at least in part, by the UN inspectors.

Back in February 1992 we did not know whether we could ever get Iraq to agree to reveal its hidden weapons and to accept monitoring of its industry. We knew we had to try, or there would be another war. We knew, too, that tracking down biological weapons programmes would be hard: biological weapons can be produced with very compact equipment, which can easily be moved from place to place and stored almost anywhere.

By the end of the visit I had begun to realise how difficult the task ahead would be. Faced with shameless lying by an entirely cynical and ruthless opponent, how could one proceed? Such regimes are impervious to normal diplomatic pressures. I had clearly underestimated the task and had to admit to myself that I had previously unfairly maligned some of the inspectors, David Kay in particular, for being unable to resolve matters through diplomacy. I now had immense respect for what he did in the parking lot during those four days in September 1991. Many of my cosy ideals about international law and the efficacy of diplomacy had been shattered in the face of uncompromising evil.

During that short trip I did a lot of growing up. Like most others who have served with UNSCOM, I have had my views of the world indelibly altered by the experience. We learnt so much about ourselves, about realpolitik, and about how to stand up for what we believed in.

So this is the story of one of the greatest detective investigations of all time – how UNSCOM uncovered Iraq's hidden biological weapons programme. The stakes were high and were played out under the glare of international scrutiny. At times the inspectors were ridiculed by their erstwhile supporters. At times their commitment to the objective was questioned. But they stuck to the task and won.

The story is a fascinating one. But I hope that it will also provoke the reader to think about how democracies and liberal regimes can protect themselves against the absolutely ruthless, determined dictators of the world.

CHAPTER 1

Chances Missed

'What I tell you three times is true.'
   LEWIS CARROLL, 'The Hunting of the Snark'

*'On doit des égards aux vivants; on ne doit
aux morts que la vérité.'* (We owe respect to
the living; to the dead we owe only the truth.)
   VOLTAIRE

David Kelly arrived in Baghdad for the first time on 2 August 1991. He was chief inspector of UNSCOM7/BW1 – the seventh UN team of weapons inspectors to go to Iraq, the first to look for biological weapons. His team comprised twenty-eight members, a mixture of nationalities and specialities. Some were micro-biologists, medical or biotechnology experts; others were munitions and safety experts; and yet others were special forces or intelligence types. The aim was to meet up with various logistics personnel from the UN's office in Baghdad and inspect six sites suspected of being used by Iraq to build biological weapons.

Everything about David Kelly speaks of attention to detail. He stands erect, sports a neatly trimmed salt-and-pepper beard and looks out at you sternly from behind rather large glasses. His normal dress consists of sharply pressed trousers and shirt, tie and jacket. He speaks with a clear, clipped English accent. He is an expert in biological weapons defence from Britain's Chemical and Biological Defence Establishment at Porton Down on Salisbury

Plain. His duties there had involved conducting biological weapons inspections at certain Russian factories and laboratories as part of a then still secret trilateral Russo-Anglo-American arrangement following the demise of the Soviet Union.

The biological weapons inspection had been long in the planning. Five weeks earlier David had flown to New York at the suggestion of Professor Bryan Barrass, a retired expert on protection against chemical weapons who is the epitome of a kindly English gentleman professor of science. Professor Barrass had been named by the UK as its representative on the newly formed UN Special Commission (UNSCOM). He was chosen not only because of his grey hair and his many years of distinguished service at Porton Down; he was an acknowledged expert and possessed the gravitas required for this extremely important and sensitive task. He had, many years ago, invented the CAM – the Chemical Agent Monitor – which was the first 'real-time' sensor for use in the battlefield to detect a chemical attack. He had also been involved in many other programmes to provide physical and medical protection for British and NATO troops against both chemical and biological attacks.

Bryan Barrass had been in New York for some time helping UNSCOM to plan its chemical weapons inspections. When it became clear that someone was needed to plan and lead the first biological weapons inspection, he had not hesitated to suggest David Kelly, whom he knew from their days together at Porton Down to be an expert both on biological weapons and on inspections. The British government were contacted through their Permanent Mission in New York and they agreed to release David from his other duties for two months so that he could go to New York to plan and then lead the inspection.

In New York David set about the difficult task of putting the team together. Everything was new. No one had ever carried out absolutely no-notice UN biological weapons inspections in a country that was hostile to the idea of being inspected. The inspections in Russia had been conducted by British and American national inspectors, not the UN, and they were part of a voluntary trilateral agreement, not a condition imposed following the ending of military actions against a country. The main international treaty dealing with the banning of biological weapons, the Biological Weapons Convention, had no provisions for conducting such inspections. Indeed, there was not even an international body charged with ensuring compliance with its terms – the countries that had signed up to the treaty merely met every five years to review its status.

The first task facing David Kelly was to identify what was known about Iraq's biological weapons capabilities – about the weapons they might possess and about the materials and equipment they might have for making them. The next was to plot the locations of these various assets and obtain maps and line diagrams of the various sites. The third step was to set an objective for the inspection and, from that, to define what expertise would be required in team members. Once individuals with the necessary expertise had been identified, their respective governments had to be contacted: if the individual were a government employee, his release had to be sought to serve with UNSCOM for the duration of the inspection; if he were a civilian, his government was asked to pay for his services to UNSCOM. Once the team members were known, a precise inspection plan had to be drawn up, showing who would be responsible for doing what. Finally, the timing of the inspection had to be planned so that it did not clash with too many other inspections, to ensure that sufficient logistics personnel (medics, communications personnel, translators, drivers) and equipment (cars, radios, satellite telephones) would be available. That said, the team had to move fast to ensure that the intelligence they were acting on did not age – i.e. that Iraq would not have time to remove items before the team got there.

Four weeks after David's arrival in New York this had all been done and the inspection team assembled in Bahrain. At this point, seven days before David Kelly left with his team for Baghdad, Derek Boothby, UNSCOM's deputy director of Operations (an ex-Royal Navy officer and a veteran of the UN's Centre for Disarmament Affairs), announced from his office in Bahrain that David Kelly had arrived to lead a biological weapons inspection team into Iraq the following week. This was a clear breakdown of communications within UNSCOM. David had wanted his inspection to be as much of a surprise for the Iraqis as possible. He did not want them to have any time to organise and prepare themselves for it. Somehow, this fact had not filtered through to Derek who, in addition to being in charge of Operations, was at that time also responsible for conducting UNSCOM's relations with the press and media. For the first nuclear, chemical and missile inspections, which were fairly straightforward inventory-taking inspections to document Iraqi declarations (as opposed to no-notice inspections), the practice had been to announce the teams in advance. Derek had merely followed this precedent.

This was perhaps the first element in a series of events that, with the benefit of hindsight, had they been avoided, could well have meant that Iraq's biological weapons programme might have been uncovered in that hot summer of 1991. As it was, the Iraqis were able to stonewall until July 1995.

David Kelly's team assembled in Bahrain seven days before their flight to Iraq. It was the first time they had all gathered together, and many had never met before. The time was used to make introductions, to clarify the aims of the inspection, and to train in safety procedures. The mission was potentially dangerous. The sites they were to inspect might well be contaminated with biological or chemical agents or unsafe from bombs or mines. Detailed briefings were conducted on a need-to-know basis. When dealing with time-sensitive intelligence the last thing you want is for one of your team inadvertently to let slip your plans. The fewer people know the whole picture, the less likely is the intelligence to be compromised by human error.

That said, everyone on the team knew the overall mission. Iraq was suspected of having a programme to build biological weapons. Under the terms of the April 1991 ceasefire, it was required to declare its biological weapons-building capabilities and to hand over such assets to UNSCOM for destruction. It had declared that it had no biological weapons, and no one in the team believed that to be true. In broad terms, the team had either to force Iraq to admit to the programme and make truthful declarations, or to search for evidence of biological weapons-making at certain sites identified by the analysts.

David Kelly had targeted six such sites within Iraq for inspection. Given Iraq's denial of any military biological programmes, Western intelligence had singled out these sites as likely centres of Iraq's biological weapons programme. In addition, David had used his time in New York to draw up a questionnaire for Iraq to fill out on its holdings of dual-use items – items that Iraq claimed were being used for legitimate purposes but which could, nevertheless, be used to make biological weapons. In writing this questionnaire, David had elicited the cooperation of a Russian diplomat seconded to UNSCOM, Nikita Smidovich.

Nikita is a six-foot bear of a man, with a thatch of black hair, big brown eyes that can reprimand or tease with a glance, and a huge Cossack-style moustache that dominates his face. He is remarkably astute and adaptive. He spent many years with the Russian delegation to the Conference on Disarmament in Geneva, specialising first in the Biological Weapons Convention and later in the negotiations to ban chemical weapons globally. With UNSCOM, he was to go on to become an expert on missile systems too. Nikita's performance in Geneva was so outstanding that he was, on 16 June 1991, one of the first disarmament experts to be recruited by Rolf Ekéus when he was appointed chairman of UNSCOM. It was only after several months that someone found out that the Russian government had stopped paying Nikita's salary. Rolf so valued his input that a way was quickly found of putting Nikita on a UN contract to ensure that he could stay. Nikita was able to help formulate a suitably worded questionnaire

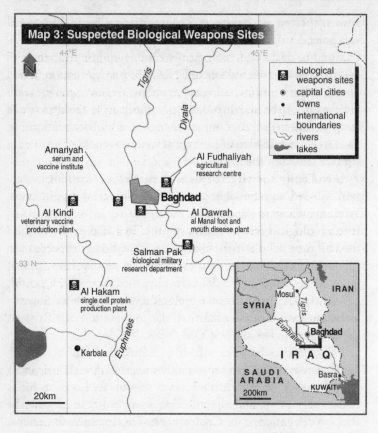

Map 3: The Suspected Biological Weapons Sites

The sites suspected by Western intelligence of being part of Iraq's biological weapons programme were all within 30 kilometres of Baghdad. Al Hakam was added because Iraq had listed it in its declarations as a warehouse where biological equipment was stored.

aimed at eliciting important information from the Iraqis without alerting them to the fact.

Consequently, the first order of business upon arriving in Baghdad would be to hold a meeting with the Iraqis, question them about their declarations, receive their filled out questionnaire, and plan the inspection activities (without giving away the details of the sites to be inspected). The first site on the list was the al Manal Foot and Mouth Disease Plant at al Dawrah, 5 kilometres south-west of Baghdad. Others included the al Fudhaliyah Agricultural Research Centre, for which it was known that the Iraqis had, in the mid-1980s, tried to buy industrial-scale fermenters, the al Kindi Veterinary Vaccine Production Plant, the Serum and Vaccine Institute at Amariyah, and a set of buildings at the base of the Salman Pak peninsula to the south-east of Baghdad, suspected of being the headquarters of the Iraqi biological weapons effort. All these facilities were within a 30-kilometre circle around Baghdad (see Map 3). The inspection was planned to last two weeks. Events did not quite work out like that.

The practice was for teams to get up very early in the morning so that the two-and-a-half-hour flight from Bahrain to the Habbaniyah air base in the Iraqi desert, some 120 kilometres to the north-west of Baghdad, could be accomplished before the real heat of the day started. The team gathered in the lobby of the Holiday Inn at 5.30 a.m., were transported by bus straight onto the tarmac at Manama airfield in Bahrain and loaded their equipment and luggage directly onto the C-160 transport aircraft operated by the German Luftwaffe. At Habbaniyah the team was met by Kevin St Louis, the head of the UNSCOM field office in Baghdad. The Iraqis had yet to start their games with incoming flights: the aircraft pulled up to the apron immediately in front of the administration buildings and the team unloaded their equipment straight into UNSCOM four-wheel drives. They then sat and waited some sixty minutes while their UN laissez-passers were

stamped. During this time their Iraqi counterparts (the minders)
tried to pump David Kelly and other members of the inspection
team for details of their plans. The team kept quiet, although a
kick-off meeting was arranged for that evening.

It was held in the conference room on the ground floor of the
Palestine Hotel. Across the road was the Ishtar Sheraton, where
UNSCOM had its field office. UNSCOM's permanent Baghdad
staff and transient inspectors tended to stay in one of these two
hotels for convenience and safety. (The Rasheed was the hotel
generally used for hospitality by the Iraqi government.)

Brigadier Hossam Amin led the Iraqi delegation. Hossam is a
soft-spoken, shortish man, with a permanently worried look on
his face, who never seemed quite to fit his favoured pale blue safari
suits. He shifted uncomfortably in his chair during the
interminable meetings between UNSCOM and the Iraqis, and
always looked as if he would much prefer to be somewhere else –
far, far away. He was then the most senior Iraqi minder, and would
later be appointed director of Iraq's National Monitoring
Directorate. Before the Gulf War he was a middle-ranking official
within Iraq's Military Industrialisation Corporation (MIC), the
vehicle that had been responsible for all Iraq's chemical, biological
and missile programmes, and much more besides.

Almost from the outset it was clear that the Iraqis knew that
they had to change their tune. Hossam Amin admitted that Iraq
had conducted 'biological research activities for military
purposes' under the auspices of the Technical Research Centre
(TRC), without further specifying what military purposes meant
(i.e. whether it was a military programme to develop protection
against biological weapons – such as vaccines or protective
clothing and filters – or one to build biological weapons for
offensive use). He handed over a one-page summary, which
detailed a research programme, based at Salman Pak, of some ten
people working on anthrax, botulinum toxin and *Clostridium
perfringens* (gas gangrene) and headed by Dr Rihab Taha al Azawi.
A direct question from David Kelly elicited the response that Dr

Ahmed Murtada (now Iraqi Minister for Communications) was the director-general of the TRC. Hossam Amin also handed over the completed questionnaire on the current disposition of dual-purpose equipment in Iraq. This document indicated that a number of fermenters were being stored at the 'al Hakam warehouse'.

These revelations changed everything. The team now needed to document as much evidence as possible on this new declaration. They would now split up. Everyone would visit the Salman Pak site, but the senior members would interview Dr Rihab Taha and Dr Murtada, while the others conducted a survey of the site. Once the work at Salman Pak was completed, the team would revert to the original plan of inspecting the other five sites. In addition, David contacted New York seeking authority to inspect the al Hakam site, which had previously been unknown to Western intelligence.

The team met at six the next morning in the lobby of the Sheraton Hotel, boarded the bus and four-wheel drives and drove down to Salman Pak in convoy with their Iraqi minders. There, Dr Rihab Taha was presented to the team as the sole driving force of the biological programme. She was a fairly plain, nondescript woman, in her mid-thirties, with a broad forehead, wide-set eyes and a triangular chin framed by bouffant, dark, shoulder-length hair. Her dress – usually a jacket over a blouse and knee-length skirts – was conservative and frumpy. Forceful is not an adjective that comes to mind. Taha vacillated between nervous wariness and prickly defensiveness. When put under pressure, she was equally capable of bursting into tears as of launching into an angry shouting match. She was educated in Iraq and Britain, ending up with a PhD in Toxicology from the University of East Anglia. The Western press would later dub her 'Dr Germ'.

From the outset, David Kelly and others in UNSCOM doubted that Dr Taha was in fact the instigator and driving force behind Iraq's biological weapons programme. She had very limited work and technical experience, no military background, and did not

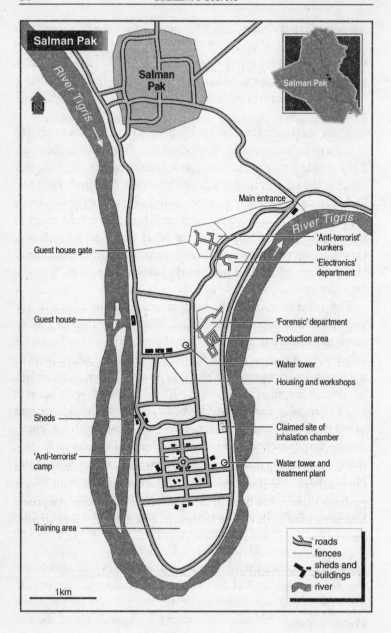

Salman Pak

Salman Pak

River Tigris

N

Salman Pak

Main entrance

River Tigris

'Anti-terrorist' bunkers

Guest house gate

'Electronics' department

Guest house

'Forensic' department

Production area

Water tower

Housing and workshops

Sheds

Claimed site of inhalation chamber

'Anti-terrorist' camp

Water tower and treatment plant

Training area

roads
fences
sheds and buildings
river

1km

Opposite: Diagram 1: Salman Pak

At the start of the first biological inspection, Iraq admitted that it had conducted 'biological research activities for military purposes' at the compound to the south of Salman Pak.

come across as someone who could drive an entirely new programme through bureaucratic red tape. And, while working women are a feature of modern Iraqi life, it was doubtful that a woman would be given such a responsible position within the politico-military establishment of Iraq.

In the talks Dr Taha quickly established the party line. The programme was an entirely exploratory one, aimed at investigating the options for both protection against biological weapons and the development of offensive capabilities. It had started in 1986 and had remained a small and relatively unsuccessful programme. It had ended in autumn 1990 with the autoclaving* of Iraq's entire stock of biological warfare agents (anthrax, botulinum and gangrene). Additional work had taken place on biological warfare simulants.

Dr Taha admitted that, in 1985, the State Establishment for Pesticide Production (SEPP – an organisation known to have purchased materials for the chemical weapons programme) had bought a fermenter on behalf of the programme. This was installed in 1986 in a purpose-built facility, destroyed by the Iraqis days before the inspection, and had been used from 1987 onwards to ferment micro-organisms. Taha stated that only *Bacillus subtilis* (an anthrax simulant) and *Bacillus thurengensis* (an insect pathogen claimed to have been chosen for biopesticide purposes) had been used in this large fermenter. She admitted that smaller devices had been used to ferment botulinum, and that laboratory-scale production of anthrax had taken place. There were conflicting statements about the production of gangrene.

---

* An autoclave is like a pressure cooker. It is used in biological laboratories to sterilise equipment.

In summary, Taha claimed that only ten people had worked on the programme, and only three of them had been research staff with PhDs. During its four years only ten scientific papers had been written and no conclusions on biological warfare had been reached. It was categorically stated that Iraq had never purchased biological weapons, or equipment to defend against them or detect them, and that there were no plans to vaccinate Iraqi military personnel against biological warfare agents.

David Kelly and the other team members found these explanations increasingly incredible: they implied that Iraq had invested heavily in a biological research programme without any clear objective in mind. Taha's response to that was that Iraq's oil wealth allowed it to undertake programmes without regard to cost or return. This despite the fact that it was precisely Iraq's bankruptcy following the Iran–Iraq war that was one of its main justifications for invading Kuwait. In fact, at the time the programme was started, Iraq was still at war with Iran, and was in excess of $100 billion in hock to its creditors. Furthermore, the low price of oil meant that its oil revenues were sinking below the level required to service its outstanding borrowing. It was simply inconceivable that Iraq would, under such conditions, start an expensive military programme without some concept of how the results of the research could be applied to the war at hand.

Meanwhile, the survey component of the inspection team was unearthing disturbing evidence. The Salman Pak site had been organised in three parts: a forensic or chemical and biological area; an electronics research and manufacturing site; and an electronics production and storage area. In addition, there was a guest-house area and an anti-terrorist training centre. All these buildings are located just south of the village of Salman Pak on a low-lying pencil-like peninsula, surrounded on three sides by the Tigris river. The land is flat, covered in large part by reed grasses. The buildings are nondescript – ochre brick, one- or two-storey block buildings that would pass unnoticed in most Middle Eastern countries.

The Iraqis explained that the Forensic Science Biology Building had been erected in 1982 to a high standard as a toxicological animal testing facility. No clarification was offered on how it had interacted with the other facilities and activities at the site before the declared inception of the military biological programme. The team determined that the facility could have been used for testing both chemical and biological weapons materials.

The Salman Pak site had been largely destroyed by the coalition's precision bombing. But as the inspection progressed, it became clear that a good deal of equipment had recently been removed, that some buildings had been torn down, and that a new layer of earth had been laid down on some parts of the site to cover up evidence. All this activity had taken place in the seven days between Derek Boothby's announcement of the impending inspection and the inspection team's arrival at the site. This raised some serious questions about what had been at Salman Pak one week previously.

Nevertheless, some useful evidence was found, including animal cages – some for primates, which indicated that experimentation on animals with biological agents had taken place. Dr Taha admitted that experiments on animals had been conducted to ascertain the toxicity of agents, but denied that any work had been done on primates. Given the presence of such cages and the admission of testing on animals, it was put to Taha that she would have needed an aerosolisation chamber to conduct the experiments. This was acknowledged. It was established that an aerosolisation chamber had been built some time before 1986, probably in 1983, but the site of this chamber 'could not be found'.

Eventually the Iraqis led members of the team some 2 kilometres down the road and showed them a broken aerosolisation chamber. Close observation indicated that the chamber had not been damaged by bombing, but by crushing, suggesting that the Iraqis had sought to destroy this piece of evidence. The fact that it had been removed some distance from its original location heightened this suspicion.

Finally a purpose-built stand-alone cold store was found near the Forensic Science Biology Building. The Iraqis claimed that this was a chemical store, but its configuration was not suited to chemical storage – it was ideal for storing bulk quantities of biological warfare agents. This served only to heighten David's suspicions that bulk production of biological weapons had either taken place or was planned.

On the third day of discussions David received a message over the mobile radio from other members of the team who were surveying the site. They had come across a large radioactive cobalt source, which represented a severe health hazard. David had to contact the IAEA inspection team, as cobalt is usually associated with nuclear activities; he was furious with the Iraqi minders and officials for having put his inspectors in a health-threatening situation.

When he returned to the discussions, David was in an appalling mood. He was certainly not about to take any bullshit from the Iraqis. Dr Murtada now appeared to explain his involvement in the biological programme as director of the Technical Research Council. David's questioning of him was blunt and aggressive. Murtada admitted that the planning had started earlier than the declared 1986. David put it to him that, given the equipment and experiments undertaken at Salman Pak, there was no way that the programme could have been purely defensive. Murtada acquiesced to this statement, implicitly agreeing that there had been an offensive biological weapons programme. A year later this was denied by General Amer Rasheed al Ubeidi, who explained that his friend and protégé had failed to understand the question; his response had been forced out under unbearable pressure from David Kelly. This despite Murtada's excellent English, senior position and presumed experience in dealing with Saddam's regime.

Finally, to explain his own lack of knowledge about the programme, even though it was ostensibly conducted under the auspices of the TRC, of which he was director-general, Dr Murtada stated that the programme was classified as 'private' and that Dr Taha, as director of research, reported directly to Hussein

Kamal Hassan, Saddam Hussein's cousin and son-in-law. Hussein Kamal Hassan had been Under-Secretary at the Ministry of Industry and Military Industrialisation (MIMI, now reorganised as the MIC) when the programme started, but by 1991 was Minister of Defence and responsible for the ruthless suppression of the popular uprisings in southern Iraq and Kurdistan during the spring and early summer of 1991.

As the five days of talks with Dr Rihab Taha progressed, so did the impression that the full story had not been revealed. Answers to questions were inadequate or not credible. She became less cooperative in resolving questions. It was clear she wanted the biological file closed, with agreement from David Kelly that what little Iraq had done on the biological side was ended once and for all and that all the capabilities had been destroyed. To this end, contradicting her earlier statement that all biological cultures from the programme had been destroyed in autumn 1990 when the programme had been wound up, she presented the team with a collection of bacterial seed stocks, which included the warfare agents anthrax, botulinum, gangrene, tetanus, tularensis and others, and warfare agent simulants *Bacillus subtilis*, *Bacillus cereus*, and *Bacillus megaterium*. It did not include *Bacillus thurengensis*, which she had earlier admitted working on at Salman Pak.

In return for handing over the seed stocks, Dr Rihab Taha sought a statement from David Kelly confirming that this represented the full extent of the Iraqi military biological programme and that that was the end of the matter. David wisely declined to make any such statement, but instead accepted them as a symbolic gesture of Iraq's intention to cease research into biological weapons. In fact, he reported to UNSCOM that there was ample scope for Iraq to have retained other seed stocks.

David Kelly had intended to carry on from the Salman Pak inspection to the other sites, and to add the newly declared al

Hakam site to his programme. However, larger issues were afoot. David Kay, from the International Atomic Energy Agency, was conducting his second inspection. Shots had been fired at his team to prevent them from finding physical proof that Iraq had actively been trying to build nuclear weapons, bringing the UN and Iraq to the brink of war again. Resources had to be allocated to the IAEA team to allow it to continue its activities longer than had initially been planned, and also to an incoming missile inspection. This meant withdrawing cars, radios and interpreters from David Kelly's team. Without the logistical support, he had to call a halt to his inspection.

His team had much to be happy about. Iraq had been forced to change its story about the biological programme; it had now conceded that it had a military programme that included most of the agents that intelligence had suggested were part of the programme. It had also been forced to admit that it had deliberately lied. To explain the evidence of tampering with the site observed by the inspectors, David Kelly was told officially that, following the decision to terminate the military biological activities at Salman Pak, an order had been issued from on high to deny the existence of the programme and to remove the evidence from the site. Although it was later decided that an admission should be made, another order had been received just before the inspection to eliminate any evidence that could reveal the progress or size of the programme.

Years later, in meetings with Rolf Ekéus, Tariq Aziz repeated a variant of this explanation. He claimed that Iraq did not view UN Security Council resolution 687 (1991) as the end of the war but merely as a ceasefire. Iraq was petrified that George Bush might resume the war or that Iran, with whom it had recently fought a much bloodier and longer battle and with whom it had yet to negotiate a peace treaty, might take advantage of Iraq's weakened military position. For these reasons (i.e. because they might be required in new hostilities for the defence of Iraq), according to Tariq Aziz, Iraq had decided not to offer up its weapons programmes, except obsolete weapons such as the unreliable sarin and tabun chemical weapons. This, allegedly, also explained why Iraq had only declared half of its SCUD force. Tariq Aziz went on to say that once the Iraqi leadership realised that these fears were unfounded, it was too late to come clean to UNSCOM, and so Iraq unilaterally and clandestinely destroyed its banned weapons and all evidence of the programmes under which they were built. While on the face of it this is a plausible explanation, it was to be belied by Iraq's practice and evidence later gleaned by inspectors.

The first biological inspection left the uncomfortable impression that the full story was not yet told. The team's report to UNSCOM concluded that Iraq had had, at Salman Pak, the capability to produce biological weapons on a limited scale. While it saw no evidence that Iraq had made biological weapons, and while it had not seen any equipment for filling munitions with biological warfare agent, the extensive preparation of the Salman Pak site by the Iraqis before the inspection meant that such equipment could well have been there previously. Orally, David Kelly further expressed his personal conviction – not one shared by the team as a whole – that the programme had been an offensive one aimed at the production of biological weapons. Iraq had also filled out the questionnaire about dual-purpose equipment, and this could be used to plan a second biological inspection.

In short, the feeling was that a good start had been made in uncovering Iraq's biological warfare programme. There was an eagerness to get back to New York, analyse the results of this first inspection, and get on with planning the second.

In fact, as David Kelly now recognises, this was an opportunity missed. Had the team arrived before the clean-up at Salman Pak, they might have been able to learn a lot more about the full extent of the biological programme. Had Iraq provided the completed questionnaire but not owned up to a military biological programme, they would have conducted the planned inspections at all sites within the week, probably including the al Hakam site. And had the IAEA team not been delayed, the resources would have been available and David's team could have stayed the second week and visited al Hakam.

As it turned out, al Hakam was not inspected at that time, and the second team did not manage to return to Iraq until the end of September 1991. By then, Iraq had cleaned up the al Hakam site too, and the door to understanding the full extent of Iraq's biological weapons programme had been slammed shut. It would take a full three years of painstaking work to prise it open again.

CHAPTER 2

Why All the Fuss?

'Making peace is harder than making war.'
ADLAI STEVENSON

'I never wonder to see men wicked, but I often
wonder to see them not ashamed.'
JONATHAN SWIFT

An aircraft goes by at low altitude. It looks as if it is leaking
something from the tanks under its wings, but it does not seem to
be in trouble and it is too high to be crop-dusting. You do not know
it, but you are under attack. Indeed, within an hour of so, you have
forgotten about the aircraft.

The next day you notice that several of your friends at work,
normally good workers, are generally under the weather and
sluggish. You wonder whether there was a big party you were not
invited to. It hits you – and others – two days later. The first thing
you feel is a slight fever, and your chest feels tight. You think you
have a bout of pneumonia. Over the course of the week many others
are complaining of weariness and chest pains. As time goes on, you
all find you have difficulty breathing and develop high fevers. Your
skin is turning a bluish-purplish colour, your neck has begun to
swell and you cannot stop sweating. A day or so later you die.

At microscopic level, your bloodstream has been taken over by
billions of tiny, rod-shaped *Bacillus anthracis* bacteria – they are
only five or ten thousandths of a millimetre long. There are so

many that your blood has become a blackish sludge. And they have released two exotoxins – poisons – into you.

That is what it is like to die of inhalation of anthrax spores – Woolsorters' Disease.

Now imagine another scenario. You are at home with your family. Bombs burst. Your first concern is your kids. You get everyone into the basement – out of harm's way, you think. In fact the bomb has just released the virus that causes haemorrhagic fever. The viruses have drifted around the small village where you live. You cannot see them; they are too small – only 100 nanometres (ten millionths of a centimetre) long. Unbeknownst to you, your whole family is being infected. However, you and your spouse are relatively safe. Adults have a well-developed set of defences against this pernicious virus. But your six-year-old daughter is not so lucky. The bomb dropped near your house was designed to kill children. While both you and your spouse suffer irritating flu-like symptoms over the next few days, you have to watch your daughter going through the agonies of the full-blown fever. It begins after you think the danger has passed. Your daughter develops a sudden high temperature and her face flushes. This lasts two to seven days, during which time she also develops convulsions and starts bleeding internally. After a few more days her fever drops. This is not the good sign you think it is. Your daughter's circulatory system is failing – the virus has damaged her blood vessels so badly that they are leaking. She now has nose-bleeds, bleeding gums and gastrointestinal haemorrhaging. Red blotches appear under her skin as the blood vessels rupture. She dies that day.

But no one would conceive of developing such weapons, would they? Well, Iraq did.

Biological warfare is old – even older than the science of micro-biology.

In medieval Europe land warfare was common and townsfolk

learnt that to survive they had to protect themselves by building massive town walls. This in turn led to siege warfare, where the invading army would simply blockade the town until its inhabitants were so short of food and water that they starved or surrendered. Often, sanitary conditions in the encampments of the besieging army were so bad that many were struck down by diseases such as cholera. At some stage, someone in a besieging army had the bright idea of hurling the dirty clothes of the cholera victims over the town walls to infect the townsfolk. It clearly worked in many cases. Whether it was planned or not, disease is thought to have played a major role in the conquistadors' military successes in Latin America. Whole communities of Amerindians died of the diseases imported by the Spanish from the old continent.

All this happened hundred of years before Robert Koch and Louis Pasteur had worked out the scientific principles of disease and postulated the existence of bacteria as causal agents in the nineteenth century, and while Western medicine still believed that disease was caused by bad humours.

Further east, more progress had been made. In the Turkey of the caliphs, in order to protect against the ravages of smallpox, it was common practice to vaccinate people with attenuated versions of the disease. Thus the first steps in protecting townsfolk against biological warfare had been taken long before Edward Jenner persuaded the stuffy English medical establishment that his work on cowpox did provide effective protection against smallpox at the end of the eighteenth century.

There are many potential biological agents that can be used to make biological weapons. They can either be live organisms, such as bacteria or viruses, or the toxic chemicals released by such organisms in their own evolutionary biological war of survival – toxins. But practicalities have, until the birth of genetic engineering, limited the number of viable agents for full-scale biological warfare to a relatively small number of candidates.

The problem is not how to make the agents in large quantities, nor even their toxicity. It is how to deliver them. Many live organisms are killed off by exposure to light or oxygen. Others need moisture and die if they dry out. Most living organisms and proteins (most toxins are proteins) are susceptible to both heat and shear forces. As a result, the standard munitions of warfare – missiles, rockets, bombs, artillery shells, mortars and grenades – are pretty ineffective ways of delivering biological weapons. They either rely on an explosion to spread the biological agent, probably destroying most of it in the heat and shear forces, or deliver all of the agent in one spot, resulting in a very poor spread and limiting its effectiveness to perhaps less than that of standard explosives munitions.

To be effective as a military weapon, the biological agent must be spread over a large area, in just the right doses to be harmful to human life, and in conditions that ensure the survival of the agent long enough to cause that harm. The optimal solution is to create an aerosol – a suspension of liquid droplets contaminated with the biological agent – which is sprayed at the right altitude over the target site. The droplets have to be of the right weight so that they drift down to the ground rather than hanging indefinitely in the air until they are blown away by the wind. They must also be of the right size so that, once they are breathed in by the targets, they lodge in the lungs and do their damage. But they cannot be too big or they would fall to the ground too quickly – before they were breathed in by the enemy soldiers – and would not penetrate the lungs enough to cause infection.

That said, biological weapons can still be very effective terror weapons even if the problems of effective dissemination are not solved. Terrorists do not have to kill millions to achieve their objectives with biological weapons. They can use biological weapons to contaminate, say, the air-conditioning unit of a government building. Such an act would cause massive panic. Alternatively, they can deliver individual doses of the biological agent to their intended target, as the Bulgarian secret services did to the defector Georgi Markov in London in the 1980s, jabbing him in the leg with an umbrella tip poisoned with a mycotoxin. The bizarreness of the means of delivery makes no difference – the defector died just as painfully as if a more 'professional' means had been used.

Similarly, rogue states, such as Iraq, do not have to have a militarily 'effective' biological weapon to make use of them politically. A ruthless dictator such as Saddam Hussein does not need to prove to his neighbours that he has effective biological weapons which he can deliver on long-range missiles. He only needs to persuade them that he may have them. If only one of the hundred or so SCUDs launched by Iraq in the Gulf War had carried so much as a sniff of biological agent, it would have changed the whole course of the war.

It is the image of whole communities dying prolonged and painful deaths that gives biological warfare perhaps the greatest stigma of any weapon. The soldiers who fought in the First World War were traumatised by the use of chemical weapons, but biological weapons were not used then. The Second World War saw both sides armed with new generations of chemical weapons (including nerve and mustard agents) and biological weapons (Britain, for instance, had anthrax weapons), but they were not used. In contrast, the use of nuclear weapons, despite their known destructive power, was justified on the grounds that it would shorten the war and thus save lives. Despite the resulting radiation sickness and the much increased destructive power of such weapons since, the major world powers still regard the use of nuclear weapons in extremis as justifiable; no such justification is made for biological weapons.

Whatever the reason, biological weapons are regarded by the world community as evil: they were the first class of weapons of mass destruction to be banned globally, by the 1972 Biological

Weapons Convention. This treaty, negotiated in the Conference on Disarmament (CD) in Geneva and open to all countries, bans not only the use of biological weapons, but also their possession. In 1991, 115 countries were signatories to this convention. Iraq had signed the treaty, but not ratified it – meaning that it was bound morally but not legally by the treaty's bans and that it undertook not to do anything to undermine its basic objectives. In contrast, by 1991, twenty years of negotiations in the CD had yet to produce a global chemical weapons ban. That task was not completed until 1993.

The CD was set up as an East–West Europe disarmament forum after the Second World War, with only eight countries participating – four from NATO and four from the Warsaw Pact. Over the years, this conference was broadened from its European theatre origins to become the principal forum in which to negotiate global arms control and disarmament arrangements. As a consequence, by 1991 its membership had expanded to forty countries from around the world. While not a UN body, it is serviced by UN staff, meets in UN buildings, and reports to the UN General Assembly.

Before the Gulf War started, the Western members of the coalition forces were convinced that Iraq had a biological weapons programme. The soldiers they sent to the Gulf to liberate Kuwait were vaccinated against anthrax, botulinum toxin and the plague. The coalition bombed numerous sites around Iraq because intelligence indicated that they had been part of the programme.

When the time came to end the fighting, the senior members of the coalition, led by the United States, wanted to be sure that they would not have to come back to fight the war again. They wanted to ensure that Saddam's regime was so weakened that it could never again pose a threat to the region or the world. In particular, they did not want to run the risk that their soldiers might have to come back to face a Saddam Hussein armed with weapons of mass destruction. Saddam had used chemical weapons in his war against Iran, and against his own people in Halabjah in the Kurdish regions in northern Iraq. He had modified SCUD missiles to deliver these weapons as far away as Tehran. Put the two together and you had a scary combination.

The Americans were so worried about the possibility of chemical weapons being used against their soldiers that they had led the Iraqis to believe that any use of chemical weapons would be met with a nuclear response. During a meeting in Baghdad in 1995 I heard Tariq Aziz explain to Rolf Ekéus why they had not used chemical weapons in the Gulf War. According to his version of his meeting with US Secretary of State James Baker in Geneva in January 1991, during the last-ditch US–Iraqi talks aimed at averting war (George Bush's 'extra mile'), Baker had told him that 'if Iraq uses non-conventional weapons, the US will respond massively and overwhelmingly in a manner from which it would take Iraq centuries to recover'.

Tariq Aziz had gone on to say, 'We are not stupid. We knew what that meant. It meant a nuclear response.'

If this were indeed an accurate portrayal of both the Geneva meeting and the Iraqi reaction to it (and I believe that it was), it meant that the US had exercised a nuclear deterrent successfully against a non-nuclear power in response to a perceived chemical weapons threat. While whatever Baker had actually said to Aziz was clearly successful, threatening nuclear retaliation is a very high-risk policy and one which any responsible leader would wish to avoid where possible.

Consequently, when given the chance to set the conditions for a ceasefire, the US jumped at the opportunity to eliminate Iraq's weapons of mass destruction, the means of their production and long-range delivery. Iraq was to be banned from having nuclear, chemical and biological weapons, and missiles with a range greater than 150 kilometres (coincidentally, roughly the shortest distance between the Iraqi and Israeli borders).

This was formalised in the ceasefire resolution adopted by the

UN Security Council on 3 April 1991 – UNSCR 687 (1991). This resolution is a complex and wide-ranging one, covering many issues – from the demarcation of the Iraqi–Kuwaiti border to the cessation of Iraqi support for terrorism. It is ground-breaking in many ways, not least because it was the first Security Council resolution ever that was also an official ceasefire with the force of an international treaty.

Its terms undeniably constitute a massive ceding of sovereignty by Iraq to the UN, which Iraq was forced to accept, grudgingly, as the price for ending hostilities following the 100 hours of land war. Indeed, Iraq refused to accept its terms until it became evident that the US was prepared to resume hostilities if this refusal continued. Iraq's humiliation was deepened by being forced to accept the terms in writing to the UN Security Council. It responded with an eleven-page diatribe against the iniquities of the resolution, before meekly accepting its terms. The main thrust of the objections were that Iraq was being singled out for special punishment – why should it be punished for having weapons of mass destruction when Israel was not? This was a reference to the widely held belief, neither confirmed nor denied by Israel, that it has nuclear weapons, and probably also biological and chemical weapons. Almost as an afterthought, the letter stated that Iraq was in compliance with its obligations under the 1925 Geneva Protocol (banning the use of chemical and biological weapons) and the 1968 Non-Proliferation Treaty (banning the possession of nuclear weapons). The letter of acceptance, delivered on 6 April 1991, bore the signature of Iraq's Foreign Minister, Ahmed Hussein.

The resolution mandated the creation of a number of new bodies to implement its various provisions. However, there was something of a disagreement between France, on the one hand, and the US and the UK on the other, about who should be responsible for getting rid of Iraq's nuclear capabilities. The first Anglo-American draft of the ceasefire resolution had envisaged the creation of a Special Commission (later to be known as UNSCOM) responsible for all the banned weapons systems. This had caused an uproar at the IAEA, the international organisation established as a result of Eisenhower's Atoms for Peace project of the mid-1950s. France championed the IAEA's cause, and was soon joined by factions of the US administration.

There was a big issue at stake here. The IAEA had been established primarily to promote the spread of peaceful uses of nuclear energy. This, in itself, was something of a deal between the nuclear weapons powers and the non-nuclear weapons states, whereby the latter would forgo the option to acquire nuclear weapons in return for assurances that they would have access to nuclear technology for non-military purposes. Later, once the 1968 Non-Proliferation Treaty had been negotiated, this organisation was also charged with conducting nuclear 'safeguards' – inspections of declared civil nuclear facilities in the signatory countries to ensure that the nuclear fuel in such facilities is not diverted for building nuclear weapons. Safeguards are essentially a method of accounting for weapons-grade uranium and plutonium. Iraq had been a party to the Non-Proliferation Treaty (NPT) and had been subject to Safeguards inspections by IAEA teams for some time.

Certain parts of the US administration were furious that the IAEA inspectors had, in the course of their inspections in Iraq before the Gulf War, failed to notice the huge nuclear weapons programme going on under their noses, details of which were now available from several high-level Iraqi defectors. These critics further pointed out that it was inconsistent to ask the IAEA both to promote the nuclear industry and to police it. It had not done anything to win over its critics by seemingly refusing to admit that anything was wrong with its record in Iraq. The worry was that it had not learned its lesson. The critics concluded that it could not be trusted with disarming Iraq. Some went so far as to suggest that the IAEA had proved itself incapable of being both the salesman and the policeman in the nuclear industry and so should also be stripped of its role in conducting nuclear Safeguards. They proposed that a new agency be set up specifically for that.

The rallying of certain parts of the US administration to the French defence of the IAEA created a split in the government. This was, in itself, a continuation of a longer-term split that went back to the days of the Carter administration in the late 1970s, when a young official by the name of Bob Gallucci was on the staff of Joe Nye in the Politico-Military Section of the US Department of State. Gallucci sought to block the sale of German nuclear technology to Brazil, which was at that time locked in a nuclear arms race with Argentina. This action had brought him into conflict with the IAEA and those who sought to promote the spread of nuclear technology, led within the US administration by the formidable Richard Kennedy, the US representative on the board of governors of the IAEA.

Now the same players were involved again. Gallucci was in the State Department advising on how to deal with the aftermath of the Gulf War – in particular the weapons aspects. Kennedy, while retired, was still an *éminence grise* on US policy towards the IAEA, and dominated the thinking of officials in the US mission to the UN in Vienna, seat of the IAEA's headquarters. Now Hans Blix, a Swedish lawyer-turned-diplomat–turned-politician, was Director General of the IAEA.

The situation was further complicated by the fact that the Non-Proliferation Treaty was a limited-term treaty. Like the IAEA itself, it was something of a bargain struck between the nuclear weapons states and the rest of the world; those states which did not have a nuclear capability had been very reluctant to set in stone for all time the right of the five nuclear weapons states to retain nuclear weapons while the rest of the world signed up to an obligation not to build or buy them. Naturally, many of these states sought a commitment (which was not forthcoming) from those with nuclear weapons to negotiate the full disarmament of their nuclear arsenals. This failure to get a timetable for full nuclear disarmament meant that certain important states would only sign up to a limited term treaty. The term was set at twenty-five years, with the idea that, if nuclear disarmament were not on the agenda by then, the parties could agree to allow the treaty to subside.

The twenty-five-year review was due in 1993. There was still much discontent amongst the non-nuclear states about the fact that full nuclear disarmament was still not being considered. There was a real danger that the treaty would not be extended beyond the twenty-five-year term, which would be a massive blow to the West's main instrument for stopping the spread of nuclear weapons – one of the highest foreign affairs and security priorities of virtually every NATO state.

The Kennedy camp argued persuasively that to deny the IAEA the right to disarm Iraq's nuclear capabilities would be to weaken, potentially fatally, the IAEA at a time when the West needed to rally all its nuclear non-proliferation forces in the run-up to the Non-Proliferation Treaty Review Conference.

Kennedy won the major part of the day. The IAEA was named as the organisation responsible for eliminating Iraq's nuclear weapons capabilities. However, Gallucci did not lose the day entirely. UNSCOM was given the sole right to designate un-declared sites for inspection. Furthermore, the resolution called for the IAEA to conduct its inspections with the cooperation and assistance of UNSCOM. This gave UNSCOM a political *droit de regard* over the nuclear inspections. Gallucci's final success was to negotiate with the UN that the deputy chairman of the UN Special Commission should always be an American, and to get himself appointed to that position.

These, and other personal rivalries were to be a factor in how inspections were conducted, with ramifications beyond the nuclear inspections.

While the overall objectives of the ceasefire resolution were clear, the means to achieving them were not elaborated. Under the resolution, Iraq was to accept the elimination of its nuclear, chemical and biological weapons and long-range ballistic missiles and anything that went into producing, testing, maintaining, repairing or developing them. To this end, it had to submit to the UN, within fifteen days (i.e. by 18 April 1991), declarations on the locations, amounts and types of all banned items and accept on-site inspections by UNSCOM and the IAEA to verify these statements and take possession of the banned items pending their elimination. Finally, Iraq was to accept plans, still to be drawn up, for the future ongoing monitoring and verification of its compliance with these undertakings – particularly its obligation not to rebuild its weapons programmes. This would mean monitoring its dual-purpose industry.

The resolution called upon the UN Secretary-General, 'in consultation with the appropriate governments', within forty-five days (i.e. by 18 May 1991), to:

develop and submit to the Council for approval, a plan calling for the completion of the following acts within 45 days of such approval:

(i)   The forming of a Special Commission, which shall carry out immediate on-site inspection of Iraq's biological, chemical and missile capabilities, based on Iraq's declarations and the designation of any additional locations by the Special Commission itself;

(ii) The yielding by Iraq of possession to the Special Commission for destruction, removal or rendering harmless ... of all items specified ... including items at the additional locations designated by the Special Commission ...;

(iii) The provision by the Special Commission of the assistance and cooperation to the Director General of the International Atomic Energy Agency ...

in consultation with the Special Commission, to develop a plan for the future monitoring and verification of Iraq's compliance ... to be submitted to the Council for approval within 120 days ...

It similarly called upon the director-general of the IAEA to draw up plans for destroying Iraq's banned nuclear capabilities and monitoring its compliance into the indefinite future.

The Secretary-General (then Javier Perez de Cuellar) immediately searched around for a suitable Executive Chairman for the newly created Special Commission. Ideally the person should have a strong background in chemical and biological weapons disarmament and in dealing with highly charged political issues at the highest level. The person should also know how to deal with the UN apparatus and should have experience of Middle Eastern affairs.

This effectively limited the selection to ambassadors at the Conference on Disarmament. The aim was to find a non-NATO person to take the job. Rolf Ekéus was the obvious choice. As the Swedish ambassador to the CD, he had been very active in all areas. He had three times chaired the Chemical Weapons Committee charged with drafting a global ban of chemical weapons. He was the instigator of the 'rolling text' – the document that over some seven years was to evolve into the Chemical Weapons Convention, signed in 1992. For many years he chaired the non-aligned group's meetings on both chemical and biological weapons. He also chaired the meetings on radiological weapons and had a strong personal and professional interest in nuclear disarmament issues. In April 1991 he was the Swedish ambassador in the Vienna-based talks to reduce Conventional Forces in Europe (CFE) – the late 1980s successor to the long-running Mutually Balanced Force Reduction talks (MBFR) of the early 1980s. Interestingly, the original name was to have been Conventional Armed Forces in Europe (CAFÉ), but this was deemed too flippant.

During his Geneva days, Rolf Ekéus had earned a reputation as a hard-working and highly competent diplomat and negotiator. In the 1989 Paris conference, held to reaffirm the commitment of the

States Parties to the 1925 Geneva Protocol that banned the use of chemical and biological weapons in war, he played a pivotal role in avoiding a split between the Arab countries and the rest of the world on the text of the final statement. This statement was originally conceived by the French government as the crowning diplomatic achievement of the conference; it sought to kick-start the stalling negotiations on banning possession, not just use, of these weapons. Failure to obtain consensus on a final statement would have meant diplomatic humiliation for France.

In Vienna, less charitable assessments were made by some NATO diplomats. Rolf Ekéus was seen by some as obstructionist (to NATO objectives) and by others as a bumbling and ineffective chairman. If these critics had looked closer they would have observed how effective such bumbling could be. Rolf would lapse into what some of us at UNSCOM came to refer to as 'Swinglish' whenever he did not want to answer a question or come to an agreement on an issue. With such Swinglish, he could easily filibuster any issue or leave you with the impression that you had received an answer to your question but that somehow it was your fault that you did not understand it. One of my New York banking friends once commented, 'I saw your boss on the news last night. I don't know what he said, but I believed him.'

Rolf was offered the job and, after consultation with his Foreign Minister, quickly accepted it. The first thing he did was to call his deputy from his days in the Swedish mission to the CD, Johan Molander, who was still in Geneva, with an invitation to join him in New York. Having seen the tight timetables for fulfilling the disarmament mandate contained in the ceasefire resolution, and fully aware that with each day that Iraq remained in possession of the banned weapons it lost out on some $25 million of oil revenues,* Rolf rushed over to New York to start his new job,

---

* The ceasefire stated that the oil embargo was not to be lifted until Iraq was disarmed, meaning that, until this happened it was losing profits from being unable to export its OPEC quota of 3 million barrels of oil a day.

abandoning his family and work in Vienna. Indeed, for the next two years, somehow, he managed to do both jobs – Executive Chairman of the Special Commission and Swedish ambassador to the CFE talks – commuting between New York and Vienna.

When Rolf Ekéus arrived in New York in April 1991, it was to an empty office, with a chair, a secretary (Olivia Platon, seconded to UNSCOM from the UN's Centre for Disarmament Affairs, co-located with UNSCOM's new offices on the thirty-first floor of the UN headquarters building), and no phone. He was chairman of an organisation with no money, no budget, no furniture and no people. On the up side, he was bound by no rules and no precedents. He had a broad mandate – a true blue-sky opportunity.

The first task was to call together all the other members of the Special Commission appointed by the Secretary-General (the commissioners) and start turning the directives of the ceasefire resolution into a workable programme of operations. The Secretary-General had appointed twenty-one members to this commission, including Rolf Ekéus as both the Swedish member and Executive Chairman, and Bob Gallucci as both the US member and Deputy Executive Chairman. Most of the members of the commission were either diplomats with experience in arms control issues, or scientists in the various government research institutes responsible for developing protection against chemical and biological weapons. A few were academics with knowledge of relevant disciplines, and others were military officers.

Bryan Barrass was the British member. He is an expert on chemical weapons. Four other members – Peter Dunn of Australia, Paul Aas of Norway, Jack Ooms of the Netherlands and Marjatta Rautio of Finland – were also experts from their respective countries' chemical and biological warfare defence establishments. These five experts agreed to rotate in and out of New York so that one was always available to provide advice for chemical and biological weapons inspectors.

The second task was to start recruiting people to staff this new organisation. Several were offered from the Centre for Disarmament Affairs, including Derek Boothby as deputy director of Operations, Olivia Platon as secretary to the chairman, Agnes Marcaillou to man the chemical weapons destruction operations desk, and numerous support staff. A retired deputy legal counsel for the UN, John Scott, was recruited on 5 May 1991 to provide legal advice on setting up UN operations that would operate under the protection of diplomatic immunity.

The majority of analysts and operations positions were filled by personnel offered by governments – diplomats, civil servants and military personnel with relevant expertise in weapons systems, disarmament treaties and arms controls inspection regimes (such as START or INF*). Two of these early recruits – Nikita Smidovich and Scott Ritter – would become household names.

The third task was to agree with the Iraqis the precise terms under which inspections would be conducted.

With all that in place, planning and conducting inspections in Iraq could start.

---

* The Strategic Arms Reduction Treaty, and the Intermediate-range Nuclear Forces Treaty.

CHAPTER 3

An End to Innocence: Iraqi Lies and Cheating Exposed

'If a man will begin with certainties, he shall end in doubts,
But if he will be content to begin with doubts, he shall end in certainties.'

FRANCIS BACON

'Die breite Masse eines Volkes ... einer grossen Lüge leichter zum Opfer fällt als einer kleinen.' (The broad mass of a nation ... will more easily fall victim to a big lie than to a small one.)

ADOLF HITLER

Iraq delivered its first declarations to the United Nations on 18 April 1991, precisely as stipulated in the ceasefire resolution. However, the timing was just about the only aspect of the declarations that did meet the requirements. Key members of the Security Council soon made it clear to Rolf Ekéus that the declarations were incomplete and misleading.

The assessments made grim reading. In the nuclear area, Iraq had declared the known civil nuclear programme that fell under the IAEA Safeguards regime. However, it stated that there had been no nuclear weapons programme, that all civil nuclear activity had stopped after the Gulf War, and made no mention of any plans to enrich uranium – that is, to isolate the isotope of uranium used in making nuclear bombs. Similarly, there was no mention of pilot fuel production facilities, irradiation facilities or reprocessing facilities. The few declared sites fell far short of the number suspected of being involved, and no mention was made of procurement activities, or foreign suppliers of the technology for Iraq's nuclear activities.

In fact, the intelligence community was certain that there was a military nuclear programme aimed at building a nuclear bomb. Defectors had indicated a full-scale enrichment programme, spread over many sites and linked into an elaborate covert network of suppliers of technology. These sources also indicated that there were pilot fuel production, fuel irradiation and reprocessing plants and that, while the Gulf War had severely damaged the nuclear bomb programme, that work was continuing.

Things were little better in the chemical weapons declarations. Iraq had declared stocks of 280 tons of sulphur mustard (a nasty chemical which blisters the skin with horrific burns and, if inhaled, destroys lung tissue – the victim drowns as his lungs fill up with fluids) and 75 tons of sarin (a nerve agent which can be absorbed through the skin, blocking the transmission of nerve impulse and leading to paralysis of vital bodily functions such as breathing and heartbeat). While Iraq admitted having precursor chemicals (raw materials or intermediate products used for the manufacture of chemical weapons) for another nerve agent, tabun, it claimed that it had not manufactured this agent. There was no mention of either production or possession of precursors for nitrogen mustard, the nerve agents GF and VX, or the choking agent phosgene. Iraq declared only 650 tons of stocks of precursor chemicals and a total stock of some 10,331 chemical weapons munitions (bombs, rockets and artillery shells) and thirty SCUD missile warheads filled with nerve agent.

These declarations fell far short of Western intelligence assessments in every area. Iraq was known to have used chemical weapons in war on many occasions. The UN had sent inspection teams into Iran in 1983 and 1984 at the request of the Iranian authorities to investigate their allegations that Iraq was using chemical weapons against their country. While the UN was unable to state categorically who had used the weapons, it did conclude that mustard agent had been employed on Iranian troops. Iraq again used mustard against Iranian troops in 1987 as part of its successful push to oust them from the al Faw peninsula in the south of Iraq. Finally, Iraq had used chemical weapons, probably tabun or sarin, on its own people in March 1988 during an attack on the Kurdish village of Halabjah – again a well-documented event.

Not surprisingly, no mention was made in Iraq's declarations about these past events. But what was surprising to the intelligence community was that the declarations implied a far smaller Iraqi chemical weapons programme than would have been consistent with such extensive incorporation of these weapons into its military doctrine, and with their extensive combat use. The suspicion was that Iraq was merely offering up its obsolete and dangerous stock for UNSCOM to destroy, and keeping back its more modern and useful weapons and the facilities to make them.

In the missiles area it was the same story. Iraq declared that it had some fifty-two SCUD missiles, either in their original configuration or in the Iraqi modification, the al Hussein (which had an extended range), a total of only six missile launchers, and that only a handful of sites were involved in its missile programmes. It made no mention of the superguns. This, again, did not tally with estimations that Iraq should have up to 350 SCUDs remaining. Given the firing rate of SCUDs in the Gulf War, it was inconceivable that Iraq only had six launchers. It was known to have been working on building superguns – the customs services of various European countries had been intercepting components for them throughout the summer of 1990. Likewise, it was known that Iraq had several major programmes either to develop or to modify a whole range of missiles, including a variant of the defunct Argentinian Condor II missile programme, code-named BADR 2000.

But the situation with regard to biological weapons was by far the worst. Iraq had simply stated that it had no biological weapons programme. According to intelligence assessments dating back several years, however, it had a full-blown programme to manufacture large quantities of biological warfare agents, including anthrax, the plague and botulinum toxin, and perhaps as many as fifteen additional agents. Sources indicated that Iraq had probably succeeded in weaponising biological agents too – putting them into bombs or missiles for delivery as a battlefield weapon. The key site suspected of involvement in all this was Salman Pak, although there was a shopping list of other suspect sites – the ones David Kelly intended to inspect on his first trip to Baghdad.

With neither staff nor means of collecting data independently, there was only one course of action open to Rolf Ekéus – to call a meeting of all the members of the commission to consider the Iraqi declarations in the light of these intelligence assessments, and to plan a series of inspections to seek to verify, or debunk, the Iraqi declarations.

The commissioners met in early May 1991. After being greeted by Rolf Ekéus and reminded of their mandate, they were given the Iraqi declarations and then received an intelligence briefing from a gaggle of intelligence analysts who had flown into New York from Washington DC specifically for the meeting. The briefing did not go down well. According to Johan Molander:

Well, these guys with their dark glasses and briefcases handcuffed to their wrists come into the room. And they start lecturing the commissioners on Iraq's programmes like they were little children who could not really understand nuclear and chemical weapons. And they show their grainy photographs that had clearly been so degraded that you could hardly make out anything. Well, being treated like that did not go down well with some of the experts, like Johan Santesson and Bryan Barrass. It was like being told 'We know best, do as we say.'

That said, the briefing did serve a useful purpose. It put the commissioners on notice that Iraq was not cooperating and that there might be trouble ahead. It also provided imagery of sites that needed to be inspected. When the commissioners split up into various sub-groups, looking into chemical and biological weapons, missiles, nuclear weapons and monitoring of industry, they were able to start planning inspections of some sites other than the ones declared by Iraq, and to draw 'line diagrams' – the all-important maps which enabled inspection planners to communicate clearly and unambiguously to the chief inspector which buildings had to be inspected and what needed to be looked for in each of them. These diagrams were also indispensable to the chief inspectors in orienting themselves on arrival at a site.

The significance of the meeting was not lost on Rolf Ekéus and Johan Molander, either. Both were uncomfortable with the fact that the UN operation was so completely reliant on information coming from one source – a source that might not always provide unbiased information solely for the purposes of the stated UN mandate.

While some of the commissioners were planning the first inspections, Rolf Ekéus was addressing the other matter that had to be resolved before the first inspector set foot on Iraqi soil – the Status Agreement on the facilities, privileges and immunities to be enjoyed by the inspectors while in Iraq on official duties. Privileges and immunities are essential in all diplomatic operations – they are the legal framework that ensures that states cannot take international and national officials prisoner or otherwise harm or obstruct them. There are whole treaties that deal with this subject.

But UNSCOM and the IAEA could not rely on standard diplomatic immunities to ensure that they had the privileges necessary to do their job – their task was not a standard diplomatic one. The ceasefire resolution adopted by the UN Security Council had set up UNSCOM and tasked it with conducting inspections but had not gone into any details.

John Scott was recruited specifically to assist in the writing of the Status Agreement. John is an unassuming character, but a fount of hilarious stories gleaned from over thirty-five years of public service in the highest echelons. At some 5' 8", dressed in the standard male office attire of jacket and tie, he is not an immediately imposing presence. But his sharp mind and encyclopaedic knowledge of the UN and international law made him an invaluable asset at UNSCOM. Not only had he been involved in making the legal arrangements for the establishment in Baghdad of the UN's Economic and Social Council for West Asia, but he also knew many of the senior Iraqi diplomats and legal advisers with whom UNSCOM would have to deal. For me personally, John was often a level head in times of need.

John wrote a first draft, based on the existing international treaties on immunities and privileges, and on the standard UN agreements of this nature. Rolf Ekéus and Johan Molander then added many details, based on their experience of newly negotiated arms control and disarmament agreements – in particular on the Inspection Protocol of the draft Chemical Weapons Convention still being negotiated in Geneva at that time. Bob Gallucci also proposed some amendments based on his experience with START and INF treaties between the US and the Soviet Union. The result was a letter sent from the UN Secretary-General to the Iraqi Foreign Minister on 6 May 1991. This is a truly historic document, in that it provided the first instance of extensive rights required for no-notice disarmament activities since the creation of the UN. The powers it gives to UNSCOM and the IAEA are extraordinary:

- Unrestricted freedom of movement into, out of and (without notice) within Iraq by inspectors, their property, supplies, equipment and materials using their own means of transport
- Unimpeded access to any site or facility in Iraq duly designated by the Executive Chairman of UNSCOM for inspection

- The right to request, receive, examine and copy any record, data or information or examine, retain, move or photograph any item relevant to the disarmament mandate
- The right to conduct interviews of relevant personnel
- The right to put under observation, inspect or monitor any site or activity and to install equipment or construct facilities for this purpose
- The right to choose sites for the storage, destruction or rendering harmless of banned items, or to construct such facilities
- The right to take aerial photographs
- The right to take and analyse samples of any kind, and to remove and export them for off-site analysis
- The right to unrestricted communications by radio, satellite or other means, and to secure mail.

Iraq was to facilitate all this, and to ensure the safety and security of UN personnel involved in the disarmament activities at its own expense. It was responsible for accommodating the inspectors, providing extra transport if needed, along with maps and other assistance as requested.

Not surprisingly, Iraq balked at this. Riyadh al Qaysi, the legal adviser for the Iraqi Ministry for Foreign Affairs and Iraq's top negotiator on both the Iraq–Kuwait border demarcation and the oil-for-food talks being held under UN auspices, was in New York at the time as Iraq's representative on the UN General Assembly's Sixth Committee and he sought to modify these rights with UNSCOM. Rolf Ekéus told him in no uncertain terms that the contents of the Status Agreement were not up for negotiation; it was take it or leave it.

Meanwhile, the first nuclear inspection team (IAEA1) had gathered in Bahrain and was ready to go about its business. The IAEA, as an existing organisation with a ready assembled inspectorate, was ahead of UNSCOM in the inspection process. Hans Blix, Director General of the IAEA, had set up an Action Team comprising some of his more senior and experienced inspectors from the IAEA Safeguards inspections. This team had already studied the Iraqi declarations and intelligence from other sources and was all set to go and check them.

Rolf Ekéus discussed the matter with Hans Blix. He reasoned that the team should wait until the Status Agreement was sorted out. Hans countered that the IAEA did not need a new Status Agreement, it already had one with Iraq under the Safeguards arrangements. Rolf felt that it would be bizarre to have two different inspection regimes in Iraq – a nuclear one constrained by the standards of intrusiveness negotiated with Iraq under the Safeguards arrangements and another, operated by UNSCOM alone, that was more intrusive and overlapped with the nuclear area, given UNSCOM's responsibility for designating additional, undeclared sites for no-notice inspection. Tempers flared, with Rolf threatening to withhold the UNSCOM-flagged aircraft, which the IAEA team needed to reach Iraq from Bahrain, until the matter was resolved.

In the event, the Status Agreement was expanded to include the IAEA and the IAEA team's departure was delayed a day to allow Rolf time to overcome the Iraqi refusal to acknowledge the agreement. In the course of 14 May 1991 a solution was found and the team left for Baghdad. Rolf would write to the Iraqi ambassador to the UN in New York, Abdul Amir al Anbari, explaining how UNSCOM intended to use its extraordinary powers, in order to allay Iraqi concerns that they might be used abusively. This letter was sent on 15 May and an acceptance of its terms received from the Iraqi Foreign Minister on 18 May. The Status Agreement was in place and inspections could proceed.

The first sets of inspections were relatively unconfrontational, but they did vindicate the concerns of the intelligence community.

IAEA1 inspected the vast nuclear research complex at al Tuwaitha. Many of the buildings had been destroyed by coalition bombing, making the task of the inspection team that much more difficult and dangerous. That said, the team was able to conduct a thorough search of the site and to confirm the location of the key item on its agenda, the highly enriched uranium which forms the fuel of both nuclear reactors and nuclear bombs.

But the inspection also proved that all would not go smoothly in the disarmament effort. Iraq had conducted extensive clearing operations before the inspection to remove much of the equipment that had been at al Tuwaitha. It had not declared this equipment, nor given its present location. And while some of the relocated items were shown to the team, Iraq refused to reveal the whereabouts of other equipment.

Most alarming was the discovery of 2.26 grams of plutonium, an artificial element that forms the key component of modern nuclear weapons. States Parties to the Non-Proliferation Treaty are required to declare any work, even at laboratory level, conducted on this substance. Iraq had failed to do so, undermining its claims that the research had been entirely scientific and peaceful.

The first chemical inspection, UNSCOM2, was led by the Australian commissioner Peter Dunn, who had been the head of Australia's Chemical Defence Establishment. His team flew into Baghdad on 8 June 1991 with Rolf Ekéus and Johan Molander, who were making their first introductory trip to Iraq. The chemical team planned to inspect the vast Muthanna State Establishment site out in the Iraqi desert 73 kilometres to the north-west of Baghdad. They were beaten to it by Rolf and Johan by one day.

Muthanna turned out to be a truly massive site, covering some 25 square kilometres; although it had been heavily and accurately bombed by the coalition, it was clear that it had been built for the production and storage of large quantities of chemical weapons. Very little cleaning up had taken place since the bombing, and a thick garlicky smell still hung cloyingly in the air as Rolf and Johan were driven along the long, dusty roads between the various buildings and bunkers that made up the site. This was the first, and hopefully last, time that Johan had smelt mustard agent, the source of the garlicky odour. Leaking chemical weapons and barrels of toxic chemicals were not the only hazards to face the inspectors: unexploded bombs, anti-personnel mines and collapsing buildings conspired to make Muthanna perhaps the most dangerous place on earth in June 1991.

The first missiles team, UNSCOM3, flew into Iraq on 30 June with a mandate to take possession of the missile launchers and missile components that Iraq had declared and destroy them. They were taken to another massive military site, al Taji, which is so big that it would qualify as a town rather than a military camp in most countries. There the teams were shown and subsequently supervised the destruction of sixty-two missiles (ten more than Iraq had declared – they had not mentioned shorter-range, but still banned, al Fahad missiles), ten launchers (four more than declared), thirty-two warheads, support vehicles (e.g. radar trucks), rocket fuel and many other missile-related items.

By now, David Kelly was in New York planning the first biological weapons inspection. But, before this could happen, the big fireworks were to go off during the second nuclear inspection, led by the veteran IAEA Safeguards inspector, David Kay.

CHAPTER 4

The Guns Come Out:
Iraq blocks access, removes items

'Behold, I stand at the door and I knock.'
REVELATION 20

'A few honest men are better than numbers.'
OLIVER CROMWELL

Early on the morning of 28 June 1991 David Kay arrived at the Military Transportation Facility at Fallujah to the west of Baghdad, with his team of inspectors. David was the veteran of many nuclear inspections, all undertaken with the IAEA under its Safeguards procedures. But this was very different. This was the first no-notice inspection he had led to search for evidence of nuclear weapons or equipment for making them. Excitement was running high.

American intelligence had indicated that the Iraqi regime had gathered various items from its nuclear weapons programme at this site. Iraq had, however, denied in its declarations to the UN that it had any plans or capabilities for building nuclear weapons. The team was on the brink of proving the issue one way or the other and was now also armed with experience of how to deal with the Iraqis. On its first two attempts, on 23 and 25 June, to inspect sites not mentioned in Iraq's declarations of its nuclear capabilities, the Iraqis had physically blocked them from entering the sites. This time they were prepared.

As the convoy of vehicles carrying the inspection team and their

Iraqi minders drew up to the site, David Kay informed the chief minder that he wished to inspect the site and that, while he was waiting to gain entrance, no vehicles other than UN ones should enter or leave the site and no equipment should be moved. As a precaution, given the events at the previous two sites, David dispatched a number of his inspectors to 'secure the site' by watching the exits. One inspector climbed the nearby water tower, which gave a splendid view over the entire site.

As half expected, the Iraqis decided to prevent the team from entering the site. While David Kay was dealing with this, trying to persuade the Iraqis at the gate to let them in and reminding them that Iraq was under international obligation to do so, he received an urgent message over the portable Motorola radio from his colleague up the water tower: inside the site the Iraqis were loading onto trucks the very bomb-making equipment that the intelligence reports had said were there. The trucks were getting ready to move out.

The team had struck gold. With one slight problem. They were unarmed, and heavily armed Iraqi soldiers stood between them and the evidence they were looking for.

David Kay made sure that those watching the exits were ready to photograph the events. Rick Lally, an American official loaned to the IAEA for the duration of the inspection, was one of those closest. This was only the second nuclear inspection in Iraq following the war and not all the logistics were in place. Rick had brought his own very new and expensive camera along on the trip.

When the Iraqi trucks started rolling out of the Fallujah camp, Rick snapped away with his camera. He jumped into one of the UN vehicles with some other inspectors and gave chase to the convoy of trucks and equipment, taking more photographs. Suddenly, an Iraqi vehicle raced up alongside and drove the inspectors' car off the road. Rick, thinking quickly, removed the film from the camera and hid it. The Iraqis tried to bully him, at gunpoint, into surrendering the film and the camera. David Kay watched in amazement as Rick refused to hand it over, arguing that it was not a camera but a new type of binoculars. Whatever he said, it worked. He kept his camera.

Later David asked Rick why he had not simply given up the camera, knowing he had already saved the photographic evidence on the film. The IAEA would have paid for a new one. Rick explained that he had brought the camera on the inspection against the express wishes of his wife. He had promised not to lose or damage it. Rick was clearly a man of his word.

Things got worse. Another group of inspectors in pursuit of the fast disappearing evidence had shots fired over their vehicles. With the convoy and the evidence now gone, the team returned to the gates of the site, only to be told by the camp commander that, while he would like to allow them in, he had orders not to do so. David Kay responded that, in this case, he had no option but to report that the team had been denied immediate access to the site, that equipment had been removed contrary to his request, and that he had been obstructed from carrying out his duties in accordance with the ceasefire resolution. He also complained about the use of firearms against his inspectors.

Iraq was now in clear breach of its fundamental obligations – to declare fully its holdings of banned items, to allow access to sites for inspection and to ensure the safety of inspectors. These most serious events needed to be reported to Vienna and New York. The news was greeted in New York with alarm. The UN Security Council met almost immediately to discuss how to react.

Meanwhile, US satellites high above were recording the events on the ground and watching where the Iraqi convoy was headed.

No one quite knew what had been photographed – but the Iraqis had clearly gone to a lot of effort to hide it and so it was probably involved in a high-priority clandestine programme, presumably nuclear. The photographs were analysed in Vienna, New York,

Washington and elsewhere, but no one recognised the items of equipment. Someone suggested that perhaps they were calutrons,* but this was initially dismissed because they were antique technology: no one in his right mind with access to modern methods would use them to separate weapons-grade uranium. The costs and the energy requirements were way too high. However, the photographs were eventually taken to a retired nuclear weapons engineer, living somewhere in the American Mid-West, who had worked on the Manhattan Project. Without any priming, the gentleman immediately diagnosed the items as calutrons.

The focus of the crisis shifted to New York, the seat of the UN Security Council. The Council is in charge of maintaining or restoring international peace and security. It was under this mandate that the Council had sanctioned the coalition's use of military force to remove Iraq from Kuwait, and that it had adopted the ceasefire resolution banning Iraq from keeping weapons of mass destruction. Now that Iraq had refused to comply with the resolution's terms, it was up to the Council to decide on measures to enforce those terms. The threat of resumed military action loomed large.

The Council was predictably outraged by Iraq's actions. The photographs taken by the team were shown in evidence against Iraq. The US tacitly let it be known that it had the satellite photographs of what had gone on. (In fact, this was partly a bluff because the satellite coverage of Iraq on 28 June had been intermittent for some reason. The convoy had been lost somewhere before it reached its destination.) Even those who had had reservations about the ceasefire terms (Yemen – Iraq's friend

---

* Pieces of equipment, used in the electromagnetic isotope separation (EMIS) method of isolating weapons-grade uranium, that employ very strong electromagnetic fields to accelerate particles at high speeds.

during its brief occupation of Kuwait – and Cuba, that old friend of America's enemies) now supported tough UN action to force Iraq to comply.

The anger in the Council was only compounded by Iraq's own efforts to mollify it. The meeting called on 26 June to consider how to react to the blocking of access to David Kay's team on 23 and 25 June heard the Iraqi representative in New York, Abdul Amir al Anbari, brush its concerns aside and aver that Iraq was cooperating with all UN missions. Now, just two days later, they were forced to meet again to learn that Iraq's cooperation with the UN included firing shots at its personnel.

The meeting condemned these actions as flagrant violations of the ceasefire resolution and the Status Agreement. This finding opened the door to military action, but the statement issued by the President of the Council went one step further, noting that any recurrence of non-compliance on Iraq's part would have 'serious consequences' – code for military action.

Iraq was offered a chance to redeem itself before the bombs started falling. The Council demanded that David Kay's team should be given access to the items removed from the Fallujah military camp. It also called on the UN Secretary-General to send a high-level delegation to Iraq to

> convey the Council's urgent demand for unequivocal assur-
> ances that the [Iraqi] Government will take all necessary
> measures to ensure that no hindrances are placed in the way of
> the discharge of the Special Commission's mandate and that
> it will accord full cooperation, including immediate and
> unimpeded access to the inspection teams ...

The Secretary-General immediately summoned Rolf Ekéus to his office to send him on this high-level delegation, which was to comprise Rolf as Executive Chairman of UNSCOM, Hans Blix as Director General of the IAEA, and Yasushi Akashi, the UN's

Japanese Undersecretary-General for Disarmament Affairs. After a brief discussion Rolf asked who was to be the mission's leader and was told that he would be. Foreseeing problems with Hans Blix on this, given that the crisis had wide-ranging implications for the task of enforcing the ceasefire, although it actually centred on a nuclear inspection, Rolf suggested that he might need that authority on paper. The Secretary-General picked up his letter-head notepad and hand-wrote a memo confirming that Rolf was to be leader of the delegation.

Rolf Ekéus, having anticipated the Council's mandate, or perhaps having suggested it, had a packed suitcase in his office, as did Johan Molander, John Scott and Olivia Platon. That same afternoon of 28 June they left the UN headquarters building for JFK Airport and took the red-eye to London to connect with the flight to Bahrain, arriving late in the evening of 29 June. Yasushi Akashi joined them. There they met up with Hans Blix and the Egyptian Mohammed el Baradei (later to succeed Hans on the latter's retirement) from the IAEA. Early the next morning they boarded the flight to Baghdad, arriving in their hotels around midday on 30 June.

The first meeting was held with the Iraqi Foreign Minister, Ahmed Hussein, on the evening of 30 June. He stated that Iraq was willing to cooperate with the mission to overcome the 'bureau-cratic problems that had occurred'. Rolf Ekéus emphasised that the mission was sent by the Security Council, not just by UNSCOM or IAEA. He was required to deliver a message from the Council expressing its condemnation of Iraqi actions in blocking access to sites and shooting at the team members; the Council was seeking unequivocal assurances that access would not be blocked again and that inspectors' safety and security would be guaranteed. He asked what actions Iraq intended to take to ensure that these events did not recur and he pointedly reminded Ahmed Hussein that the Council had sent his mission to try to avoid the 'serious consequences' which might ensue if these demands were not met.

Blix offered the Iraqis a way out of their dilemma: they had been caught lying about the extent of their nuclear activities, but perhaps, he suggested, they had assumed that the ceasefire resolution did not cover certain activities, such as the separation of highly enriched uranium (HEU). If that were the case, Iraq might want to submit a second declaration about its nuclear capabilities, to include any installations or material for the enrichment of uranium such as calutrons or centrifuges, whether intended for civilian or military uses, and to open up the sites where they were located for inspection. That would reduce the need for the Special Commission to designate sites for no-notice inspections at locations undeclared by Iraq.

In response, Ahmed Hussein blamed the access problems on the UN for seeking to conduct inspections over the Eid holiday, when few Iraqis were at work. There are two Eid holidays each year in the Moslem world – Eid al Fitr and Eid al Adhaa. It is true that they are the most sacred days in Islam. However, that clearly was not the real reason why the Iraqis had blocked access at Fallujah and the other sites. There were many people working at each of the facilities – enough at Fallujah to load the trucks immediately the team arrived with large quantities of bulky and heavy equipment and drive it away. Ahmed Hussein blamed the shooting incident on the soldiers' general nervousness in the aftermath of the war.

The next morning, 1 July, the mission met the Iraqi Deputy Prime Minister, Tariq Aziz. Rolf Ekéus reiterated the Council's demands and the threat of serious consequences should the issue remain unresolved. Somehow keeping a straight face, Tariq Aziz replied that Iraq had 'from the beginning cooperated with the inspection teams'. The problems had started because of the Eid holiday. He then laid into the Council for failing to hear Iraq's side of the story before condemning it. He complained that the inspectors had tried to carry out inspections over a holiday and demanded that Iraq should receive advance notice of all inspections so that the government authorities could ensure access. He also complained that David Kay's team was full of Americans and concluded that they were all CIA agents. He insisted that inspectors of other nationalities be used. After this blast he said that the mission should meet the Prime Minister of Iraq, who would give them the assurances of compliance the Security Council sought.

Rolf refuted this tirade. The fact that the Iraqis had removed items from the site under the noses of the inspectors proved that advance-notice inspections would not work. They could simply move items before the teams arrived. The speed with which this had happened also demonstrated why inspections had to be conducted despite holidays – if teams delayed inspections for holidays or weekends, the intelligence on which the inspections were based would be out of date by the time they were carried out. The incident at Fallujah proved that Iraqi countermeasures did not take holidays or weekends off.

On the issue of the nationality of the inspectors, Rolf Ekéus reminded Tariq Aziz that there were only five nuclear weapons states in the world that could provide nuclear weapons experts. Of those, the US was the only one with expertise in electromagnetic isotope separation (EMIS). Given that Fallujah was suspected of hiding calutrons for an EMIS programme, it was natural that the bulk of the inspectors should come from the only country in the world other than Iraq with that expertise. He refuted the claim that the persons in question were CIA; they came from US national laboratories and research institutes.

Tariq Aziz repeated that Iraq had no problems with inspections after appropriate notice, but would insist on such notice. The UN should tell Iraq what it wished to see and it would see it. At this point Hans Blix took out the photographs taken by Rick Lally and said that the inspectors wanted to see the large, cylindrical objects seen on the truck. Aziz dismissed the photographs as US propaganda, but was told that they were taken by the IAEA inspection team. Rolf reminded Aziz that access to the photographed items was an issue on which the Security Council was awaiting a report from the mission. A report that the mission had failed to gain access could have serious consequences.

The meeting ended without further progress at about 1.30 p.m. A further meeting with the Foreign Minister was held that evening. Ahmed Hussein said that he had instructions from Saddam Hussein that the mission must accomplish its tasks and return home satisfied. Iraq was returning the trucks to the designated site for inspection. There would be a further meeting the next day with the Minister of Defence, Hussein Kamal Hassan, and the chairman of the Iraqi Atomic Energy Commission (IAEC), Human Abdul Khaliq, to whom the mission could put its questions about Iraq's nuclear activities.

At that meeting, held on the morning of 2 July, Hussein Kamal Hassan sought to limit UN inspection rights by stating that trucks moved in and out of the Fallujah plant continuously and most of them had nothing to do with the inspection process; the inspectors did not have to see them and could not stop them. He said that there were no materials at Fallujah other than those required for the reconstruction of Iraq. The Fallujah site was an assembly point for efforts and materials for reconstruction engineering projects, and had received some materials from the IAEC's facilities – items no longer needed by the commission which could nevertheless be used in the reconstruction project. He chided the inspectors for trying to force their way into the Fallujah camp on the grounds that it was a military camp which was closed to civilians. He ended by saying that the trucks that had left the site on 28 June were now back at Fallujah and ready for inspection.

Rolf Ekéus pointed out that the inspectors wished to see what had been in the trucks, not just the trucks. Hans Blix stated that the IAEA suspected that the trucks carried components for calutrons, i.e. equipment for the separation of uranium. The inspectors were interested not just in the HEU but also in the equipment used to isolate it. Blix was also looking forward to hearing from the chairman of the IAEC whether there had been a programme to isolate HEU.

Human Abdul Khaliq now spoke up. The materials on the trucks had been taken from the Tuwaitha site (the headquarters of

Iraq's nuclear research and the home of its nuclear reactors) as part of the clean-up operation in the aftermath of the war. The IAEC had given large quantities of materials and equipment to the reconstruction effort. In addition, the commission had delivered to the Ministry of Defence for destruction any items that might be in contravention of the ceasefire resolution. He stated categorically that the IAEC had no programme for uranium enrichment; it had never had one, be it centrifuge or EMIS or any other system. Iraq's nuclear capabilities had, he said, been exaggerated. The inspectors could examine all this material.

Rolf Ekéus reminded Khaliq that the UN inspectors had a great deal of expertise in these matters and that these experts believed that Iraq had an enrichment programme. He warned that it was not an issue that could be taken lightly. The denial of any such programme was a serious matter. Rolf, deliberately giving the Iraqi side a face-saving way of backing down from the egregious lie just uttered by Khaliq, asked whether there was an uranium enrichment programme outside of the IAEC's purview.

But the Iraqis did not take it. Tariq Aziz jumped in with both feet, stating scornfully that Iraq had only one Atomic Energy Commission. The statement just made was Iraq's official position. With a typical rhetorical flourish, he said it was unjust and unacceptable for the mission to expect Iraq to admit to things it had not done and show it things it did not have.

At this point Hans Blix once again showed the Iraqis the photographs taken by Rick Lally, and reiterated that the objects did exist. He welcomed the chance to inspect items removed from Tuwaitha but reminded Iraq that the UN should have been invited in first to supervise and witness the destruction. He asked whether the items that had been removed from Fallujah still existed or whether they had since been destroyed.

Tariq Aziz remained scornful. He said it had not been possible to invite the IAEA to witness the destruction because the cost would have been too high – Iraqi children were starving because of the Security Council's sanctions. Human Abdul Khaliq, in answer to Blix's earlier question, said that the materials had been destroyed in the war. Blix, now exasperated, asked whether he should report to the Security Council that the materials removed from Fallujah on 28 June were now either destroyed or lost. Hussein Kamal Hassan denied that that was what was being said. Some materials had been destroyed on the instructions of Saddam Hussein, other materials had not. The UN could inspect it all. This bizarre meeting ended with an agreement that Hans Blix and Human Abdul Khaliq should visit the Fallujah site with the inspection team that afternoon.

It was a long inspection. Hans Blix did not make it back in time for the meeting that evening with the Iraqi Prime Minister, Saadoun Hammadi. Hammadi reiterated that, while Iraq did not like the ceasefire resolution, it would implement it. Like the others, he blamed the blocked access on the Eid and on the failure of the UN to give notice of the inspection – 'one could not expect an isolated military commander to respond favourably to someone knocking on the door for admission'. That said, he hoped all the problems could be smoothed out soon.

Rolf Ekéus noted that not all had gone smoothly in the talks. The reaffirmation that Iraq intended to implement the ceasefire provisions and to ensure the safety and security of inspection personnel was well received by the mission, but the failure to present the equipment removed from the Fallujah site and the declaration that Iraq, contrary to the evidence collected by the inspectors, had no programme to enrich uranium were both problematic. Rolf read out the conclusions he intended to report to the Security Council, which restated what he had just said. Yasushi Akashi noted that the conclusions read out by Rolf Ekéus were the unanimous conclusion of the high-level delegation. Hammadi's only reaction to this was to reiterate that, in Iraq's view, the Fallujah incident had been blown out of all proportion and that Iraq intended to comply fully.

A final meeting with the Foreign Minister, called at Rolf Ekéus's request, was held late that night of 2 July after Hans Blix's return from Fallujah. Rolf had not wanted to leave before the high-level mission had presented its conclusions to the Iraqi leadership in unison. Now all three senior members of the mission were there and Rolf again read out for Ahmed Hussein the conclusions of their report to the Secretary-General. He said that the mission had not yet come to a final decision on the report. In response to this, Hussein suggested holding a further meeting with experts the next day to iron out any problems the mission might have with the statements of Human Abdul Khaliq. Blix noted that during the inspection that afternoon the team had not been taken to the items removed from Fallujah on 28 June, but to different items taken from the Tuwaitha site; it had therefore done nothing to change the conclusions of the report. Hussein asked whether they could stay on longer but was firmly told that they had to leave the next morning to catch up with the Secretary-General, who was awaiting them and their report impatiently in Geneva.

Attempts by Ahmed Hussein to set up a further meeting at midnight were dismissed. Rolf Ekéus retorted that the mission had been waiting two days for a satisfactory answer on the Fallujah materials and had not received one. It was hard to see what a further meeting could achieve. If Iraq had anything further to add about its nuclear activities or about the location of the items taken from the Fallujah site, it could contact the IAEA in Vienna or UNSCOM in New York. Ahmed Hussein agreed to this.

The team arrived in Geneva on 4 July to update the Secretary-General and to prepare the report to the Security Council. Iraq's reaction to this mission and the events of the next few days was to bring Iraq and the US back to the brink of war – the first of a series of military stand-offs that would become the hallmark of Iraqi–UN relations over the coming years.

CHAPTER 5

Spies and Spy Planes: A New Game Plan

'Speak softly and carry a big stick.'
THEODORE ROOSEVELT

'When peace is broken anywhere, the peace of all countries is in danger.'
FRANKLIN D. ROOSEVELT

The US Fifth Fleet, based out of Manama in Bahrain, is a truly awesome force. It comprises eighteen combat ships, of which seven are armed with Tomahawk missiles. On board are some 2000 marines trained in special operations, and landing ships and helicopters to take them wherever they need to go. But the heart of the fleet is its two aircraft carriers, the *USS Independence* and the *USS George Washington*. Each of these ships carries its own air force. Between them, they have 155 aircraft, including fighters to protect the fleet and the other aircraft, bombers and ground attack aircraft to hit targets in enemy territory, and various surveillance aircraft to gather information in real time so that the control room in the carrier can direct operations effectively. The total hitting power is a staggering 5 million pounds of high explosives, roughly the equivalent of several of the Allies' 1000 bomber-raids on Dresden in the Second World War.

In early July 1991 the Fifth Fleet was on duty in the Gulf. Relations with Iraq remained tense, and the degree of readiness was even higher than normal. It was known on board the ships that if any action were to be taken against Iraq in retaliation for blocking the inspections, they would be involved.

On 4 July the high-level mission completed its report to the Security Council, which met immediately to consider it.

This report noted Saddam Hussein's letter to the Security Council, claiming that he had ordered all Iraqi authorities to cooperate with the UN weapons inspection teams, and his further statement that Iraq had abandoned all banned weapons programmes. It also noted Iraq's assurances that no hindrances would be placed in the way of inspection teams, that teams would have immediate and unimpeded access to all sites, and that they could stop and inspect vehicles in transit. Finally, it noted that Iraq had reiterated its undertaking to guarantee the safety and security of inspectors and that full authority had now been given to the Minister of Foreign Affairs to issue directives to other Iraqi authorities to ensure compliance. The report also described Iraq's objections to the ceasefire resolution, its complaints about the manner in which the inspections had been conducted and its accusations about the composition of the team.

The Council, however, focused on Iraq's failure to provide access to the items that had been removed from Fallujah. Iraq was roundly condemned for this and military preparations were stepped up in Washington DC for an air strike against Iraqi sites that had been involved in the nuclear weapons programme. These preparations were obviously taken seriously in Baghdad. The UN Secretary-General received another letter from Saddam Hussein dated 5 July 1991, repeating previous assurances on compliance and stating that Iraq would draw up a list of all the items of concern for consideration by the inspectors. The list would be ready by the evening of 7 July or the morning of 8 July.

David Kay's team was no longer in Iraq, having left with the high-level mission on 3 July. So a new team was dispatched by the IAEA under the leadership of Dimitri Pericos, another veteran inspector under IAEA Safeguards agreements. Dimitri arrived in Baghdad on the 7th, and Iraq made a new declaration about its nuclear activities, as suggested by Blix during the high-level mission, the next morning.

The new declaration confirmed what had been suspected by David Kay and his team-mates. Iraq had had a full-scale programme to enrich uranium. The deputy chairman of the Iraqi Atomic Energy Agency – now Deputy Minister for Industry and Minerals – Dr Jaffar Dhia Jaffar, was put forward as the leader of the enrichment programme. Incredibly, however, Iraq still insisted that this was not a military programme, that the research into enrichment was being conducted without any intention of using the HEU for developing nuclear weapons.

Dr Jaffar Dhia Jaffar insisted that the primary aim of the programme was to produce fuel for research reactors and a future nuclear power programme. But the evidence belied his explanation. The combination of two types of equipment to separate uranium – equipment which had high capacity and modest separation ability combined with other equipment with low capacity and high separation ability – had all the hallmarks of a specific intention to produce large enough quantities of highly enriched uranium for weapons purposes. The scale of the operation, too, was indicative of a full-blown military programme. There were two sites designed to separate out uranium using the EMIS technique – one at Tarmiya just north of Baghdad, and another at Ash Sharqat, just north of Saddam's home town of Tikrit. Dimitri's team were shown a video of the inauguration of the Tarmiya plant in February 1990. From this and from the blueprints of the plant, they calculated that Iraq could produce up to 15kg of highly enriched uranium (93 per cent) per year at that plant alone. If Ash Sharqat were a replica of Tarmiya (as suspected by the inspectors), rather than a factory for the plastic coating of equipment (as declared by Iraq), that would have given Iraq sufficient HEU to produce two nuclear bombs a year.

In order to hide these activities from the inspectors Iraq had not

Map 4: Iraq's Nuclear Sites

The summer of 1991 revealed some of the extent of Iraq's nuclear activities. Tuwaitha was the main research centre, home of the nuclear reactors. Tarmiya and Ash Sharqat were being built to separate out weapons-grade uranium. Al Jazira provided feed material (uranium fluoride) for this effort. Al Furat was making centrifuges for another method of obtaining weapons-grade uranium – gas centrifuge separation.

only removed key equipment from the Tarmiya and Ash Sharqat sites; they had even laid a fresh cement floor at both sites to cover tell-tale signs of the original layout, such as rails and return irons for the separators.

And the story went on. Iraq admitted that it had investigated other means of producing HEU – gaseous diffusion, gas centrifuge and chemical enrichment. The team left convinced that what they had seen was part of a full-blown nuclear programme, and that they had a lot of work left to do to track down all the equipment and components that had been removed from Tuwaitha, Tarmiya and Ash Sharqat. They were also convinced that the various other enrichment programmes (particularly the gas centrifuge route) were by no means fully explained and were probably far more advanced than Iraq was admitting, and that there were many other undeclared nuclear weapons sites in Iraq that now needed to be inspected.

Dimitri Pericos's team completed its inspection on 18 July 1991 and left for Bahrain to write up its report. Meanwhile, David Kay was organising a fourth nuclear inspection to follow up on the revelations about a centrifuge enrichment programme, to make a detailed assessment of the EMIS programme, and to search for evidence of facilities for weaponisation – putting all the components together into a bomb.

The additional revelations obtained by Dimitri's team had confirmed the worst fears of the Security Council, but had not gone far enough to allay concerns either about Iraq's honesty or about its abandonment of a nuclear weapons programme. Consequently, tensions remained high and the possibility of military action against Iraq imminent. President Bush demanded that Iraq should come clean on the full extent of its nuclear activities by 22 July, leaving the consequences of non-cooperation to Iraq's imagination.

In David Kay's mind, there was no ambiguity. His team stayed in Bahrain an extra night to avoid being in Baghdad, so convinced were they that the attack was coming. But in the course of that day Iraq indicated that it had some new information to divulge. The dogs of war were kept on their leash and David's team set about its business.

When David arrived back in Baghdad with his team on 27 July, he was greeted by a much relieved Dr Sami al Araji, the Iraqi official sent to accompany the team. Dr Sami clearly believed that David's arrival meant that there would be no American bombing for the moment, but he was overly sanguine – he did not know that David Kay was under instructions to report his team's precise location to UNSCOM in New York every three hours in order to 'deconflict' their activities with anything the US military might do – that is, to ensure that they did not become inadvertent targets of US high explosives.

Dr Sami's anxiety of the previous days must, however, have reflected the fact that the Iraqi leadership as a whole perceived the military threat to be real and imminent. The next morning Iraq, as promised, disclosed further information about its nuclear programme, admitting to yet more materials hidden from previous inspections. In particular, it became clear that Iraq had embarked on a clandestine programme to produce natural uranium fuel elements from nuclear materials that it had not declared to the IAEA under the Safeguards Agreement as required. Furthermore, Iraq had conducted two experiments at its Experimental Reactor Fuel Fabrication Laboratory at Tuwaitha to produce fuel elements that contained plutonium. The IRT-5000 reactor core, which was at the centre of this experiment had been subjected to two IAEA Safeguards a year which had not detected this undeclared activity. The evidence all pointed to Iraq having deliberately removed the experimental fuel elements before each inspection to avoid detection.

During the course of this inspection it became ever clearer that Iraq had had a systematic plan to build nuclear weapons and that it had taken measures to prevent their detection by the IAEA's

Safeguards inspections. A no-notice inspection of an undeclared site at al Jizira (the Mosul Production Facility) revealed that this was in fact a site for producing uranium fluoride (UF_6), the feed material for gas centrifuge separation of highly enriched uranium. The team also visited the al Furat complex, a huge facility that Iraq was now forced to admit was built to manufacture centrifuges for the separation of HEU using the gas centrifuge technique. The plans were advanced. They entailed building and operating the centrifuge production plant by the end of 1991, building and operating the first 100-machine centrifuge cascade by mid-1993, and building and operating a 500-machine cascade by early 1996. Such a system would be capable of producing as much as 25kg per year of HEU (uranium containing 90 per cent or more of the weapons-grade isotope U^{235}).

Finally, David Kay and his team visited another site designated by UNSCOM, al Atheer, suspected of being associated with the weaponisation of nuclear materials. At the start of the inspection Dr Jaffar Dhia Jaffar stressed the Iraqi position, which was that no decision had been taken to develop nuclear weapons; he tried to disassociate his staff from any incriminating evidence that might be revealed by, incredibly, stating that any nuclear explosive design activities that had occurred 'had been only individual exercises by interested scientists'.

David Kay's interpretation was somewhat different. His team concluded that the site contained 'remarkable capabilities in relevant technologies'. As they noted in their report,

One of the most visible weaponisation activities is high explosive testing. The most suitable facility for this activity which came to the inspection team's attention was the firing bunker – now heavily damaged – belonging to the Hatheen Establishment at al Musayyib, near the al Atheer materials research centre. The bunker ... has clearly been used a few times for crude testing of conventional explosives. It is capable of supporting significant physics experiments critical to nuclear weapons development ... Some construction work is under way at this site despite the damage, and this suggests that such a facility has very high priority.

Here, as elsewhere in the inspection, there were inconsistencies in the statements of various Iraqi officials about what activities had taken place and for what purpose. Apart from Dr Jaffar Dhia Jaffar, who was spouting the party line, there was also a marked reluctance in the Iraqis who had worked there to speak to the inspectors and explain their actions. Some developed selective amnesia, remembering things only in the vaguest of terms, if at all.

All this convinced David Kay and his team that the true purpose of the site and the activities conducted there were not being revealed. In fact, they concluded in the report they prepared for the Security Council at the end of their inspection on 10 August 1991 that:

Al Atheer and its companion facilities at al Hatheen and al Musayyib constitute a complete and sufficient potential nuclear weapons laboratory and production facility all within one common fence line. This combined facility is so big and well equipped that it can clearly do much more than the limited non-weapons activities that the Iraqis claim as its purpose.

As David Kay's inspection was continuing, news of its findings was leaking piecemeal into the Security Council. The horror with which the findings were greeted cannot be overstated. It was one thing for a Third World country to spout anti-First World rhetoric about the injustice of the split between nuclear-weapons states and the rest enshrined in the Non-Proliferation Treaty. It was another for them to try and partially redress the balance by pursuing the development and production of other non-conventional weapons, such as chemical weapons: some fifteen to twenty states were presumed to have done so already. But it was entirely another –

unacceptable – case, in cynical and flagrant breach of commitments assumed under the Non-Proliferation Treaty and its Safeguards Agreement with the IAEA, to seek to separate out plutonium and to work, in such an obviously singleminded way, on building a Bomb.

The result was the strongest outpouring of vitriol and bile in the history of the UN – resolution 707 (1991), adopted on 15 August. This resolution 'Condemns Iraq's serious violation of a number of its obligations under ... resolution 687 (1991)... which established a ceasefire and provided the conditions essential to the restoration of peace and security in the region.' It also condemned Iraq's violation of its commitments as a party to the NPT and under the Safeguards Agreement. But the really hurtful part for Iraq was contained in the new demands placed upon it – that Iraq:

cease immediately any attempt to conceal any movement or destruction of any material of equipment relating to its nuclear, chemical or biological weapons or ballistic missiles programmes, or material or equipment relating to its other nuclear activities without notification to and prior consent of the Special Commission ... make available to the Special Commission, the IAEA and their inspection teams any items to which they were previously denied access ... allow the Special Commission, the IAEA and their inspection teams to conduct both fixed wing and helicopter flights throughout Iraq for all relevant purposes, including inspection, surveillance, aerial surveys, transportation and logistics without any interference of any kind and upon such terms and conditions as may be determined by the Special Commission and to make full use of their own aircraft and such airfields in Iraq as they may determine are most appropriate for the work of the Commission ... halt all nuclear activities of any kind, except for use of isotopes for medical, agricultural or industrial purposes until the Security Council determines that Iraq is in full compliance with this resolution ... and the IAEA determines that Iraq is in full compliance with its safeguards agreement with that Agency ... respond fully, completely and promptly to any questions or requests from the Special Commission, the IAEA and their inspection teams.

It further determined that Iraq should no longer own nuclear weapons-related items, be it components or the means of their development and production.

Thus, at the stroke of a pen, Iraq had become the first country to be banned from any civil nuclear activity, and the first to be forced to accept aerial surveillance of its entire country at any time.

Iraq sought to call these aerial surveillance flights 'spy planes'. They were not and are not. They were mandated by the highest court on earth – the UN Security Council. They are directed by the Special Commission's Executive Chairman. They are overtly conducted under a UN flag with UN accreditation.

Many journalists still use the misnomer 'spy plane' to describe the U2 aircraft which fly under a UN flag over Iraq, presumably because it sounds better than 'high-altitude reconnaissance aircraft'. Spying is an illegal and clandestine activity: spies can be summarily shot. The irresponsible use of such loose terminology puts the lives of UN pilots in danger.

Neither the operation of high-altitude surveillance aircraft nor the operation of helicopters would go smoothly, however. Iraq could be expected to cause difficulties, but now the US did too.

The planning of the early inspections had made the importance of good aerial imagery (photographic or other) abundantly clear to everyone at UNSCOM. At the same time, it was now evident that the UN's initial estimate of forty-five days to disarm Iraq was wildly short of the mark. The Iraqis were not cooperating: at best they were making false declarations and daring the UN to catch them in the act of lying if it could; at worst, they were shooting at UN inspectors and denying them access to sites and vehicles when they got close to physical evidence of these lies. UNSCOM needed to hunker down for the long haul. And this meant that it had to develop more and better means of surveilling Iraq.

Another issue had also emerged during the first intelligence briefing. UNSCOM would only remain credible in the eyes of the international community if it were seen to be truly independent of any outside interference from governments (particularly the US). For that, it had to ensure that new surveillance assets would be under its own control and that it could assess and interpret intelligence in-house in order to protect itself against abusive intelligence reports. That is, it should itself be able to determine whether any information it received was sufficiently reliable and unbiased to act upon, and assure itself that the information was being provided and acted upon in the interests of the mandate to disarm Iraq of weapons of mass destruction, and not for any other extraneous purpose or hidden agenda.

Rolf Ekéus seized the opportunity offered by the Security Council's anger over the reports that Iraq was indeed developing nuclear weapons to achieve both objectives. The US offered to fly U2 flights (aircraft that were a later version of the U2 plane Gary Powers was flying when he was shot down over Sverdlovsk in the Soviet Union on May Day 1960) to gain systematic aerial photography coverage of Iraq. This had many advantages over using satellites, including the fact that the US had great difficulty in releasing any satellite imagery outside the tightly knit Canukus intelligence community (the intelligence services of Canada, the UK, the US and Australia). While there were still difficulties over releasing U2 photographs, the issue was less sensitive.

Accepting this offer, Rolf Ekéus on the one hand lobbied hard within the non-aligned caucus of the Security Council to get their agreement to a UN-flagged operation (one operating under UN control for purely UN purposes) and, in turn, used the requirements for obtaining the non-aligned countries' consent with the US to ensure that the operation would indeed be a UN-flagged operation. Thus, when the time came to vote on the extraordinary resolution 707 which mandated the flights, even such age-old enemies of the US and victims of US spy-plane overflights as Russia and Cuba voted for the resolution. Iraq's remaining friend in the Middle East, Yemen, also switched from an abstention on the ceasefire resolution to a yes vote for resolution 707.

That should have been the end of the negotiations and the beginning of a fruitful relationship with the U2. However, the briefing following the first overflights was an extreme disappointment to Rolf and his non-American colleagues at UNSCOM. There were very few photographs: they were fuzzy, deliberately degraded to prevent UNSCOM (and others) from accurately judging the quality of images the U2 was capable of generating, and they were delivered to UNSCOM weeks after they had been taken. What is more, although Rolf had told the US authorities what he had wanted the U2 to photograph within the 'window' available for flights, the US briefers had given no indication of where the aircraft had flown between the points represented by the meagre collection of photographs, nor the timing of those flights. This left UNSCOM blindsided when Iraq accused it of coordinating its surveillance flights with Israeli Defence Force incursions into its air space. In fact, UNSCOM had no precise idea of where or when the U2 had flown until it received the Iraqi letters of complaint addressed to the UN Secretary-General, which plotted onto a map its precise flight path as recorded by Iraq's air defence tracking radars. UNSCOM had enough experts in its staff to know that a U2 flight produces literally thousands of photographs of high quality, each individually stamped with not only the time but also the GPS (the very precise reading of latitude and longitude taken from the Global Positioning Satellite system used for navigation by most of the world's shipping and aircraft). Rolf complained.

The second briefing, however, was no better.

Rolf Ekéus called the briefers into his office on the thirty-first floor of the UN building in New York, with its spectacular view of Mid-Town and the Chrysler building. In addition to the intelligence analysts, a few USAF top brass and Thomas Pickering (the US ambassador to the UN) sat in for one of Rolf's bravura performances.

He first reminded them that this was meant to be a UN operation conducted under his authority. He told them that the U2s, so long as they were UN-flagged, were his aircraft. The pilot, while he wore UN insignia, was one of his staff, not a US military person. Despite this, he told them, he did not know where his aircraft had flown until the Iraqis told him. And what did these aircraft produce? Picking up a handful of the precious U2 photographs handed over at the briefing, Rolf answered his own question – a few lousy, fuzzy photographs that were no use to anyone. This, he said with a rhetorical flourish, was what the US and the Security Council had been prepared to go to war over. He demanded to be fully informed of where and when each flight had taken place, and to be given all the photographs taken, or he would end the U2 operation. With that, he threw the U2 photographs into his waste paper basket.

There was a shocked silence in the room, eyes fixed in disbelief on the offending photographs in their new, undignified home. Thomas Pickering was the only American in the room amused by this performance.

But it did produce the desired effects. The third briefing was held soon after the next U2 flight. The photographs were suddenly remarkably sharp and useful, and they were stamped with the time, GPS and name of the facility photographed. The briefing also kicked off with a slide showing the flight path of the aircraft over Iraq. In due course, once UNSCOM had recruited some photographic interpreters of its own, it also received the negatives of the films shot by the U2, providing yet higher resolution and more information. There were to be no more problems for UNSCOM from the US side over the U2.

Meanwhile, in the face of British and American opposition, Rolf Ekéus began to assemble an Information Assessment Unit (IAU) so that UNSCOM could in future independently assess both Iraq's declarations and the various other intelligence reaching the commission. Geoff St John was recruited from Canada to head up this operation, Roger Hill from Australia, Patrice Palanque from France and Scott Ritter from the US. The nationalities of these expert analysts were no accident. Given the sensitivity of the intelligence being received, and its provenance (the vast majority being from either US or British sources at that stage), the decision was made to recruit primarily from the Canukus countries. To do otherwise would have meant that UNSCOM would simply have received much less intelligence, the providers being unwilling to hand over intelligence to countries they did not trust. The exception provided by Patrice was also deliberate. The purpose of the IAU was precisely to avoid charges of bias or susceptibility to outside pressures. If the IAU were entirely Canukus, UNSCOM would be open to criticism that it was merely an Anglo-Saxon tool. Patrice's inclusion thereby served a dual purpose: it undermined such criticism and opened the door to a greater contribution from the French intelligence community.

Recruitment to the IAU started in August, with the first members arriving in New York in September. UNSCOM was now taking on its final shape, and a significant shift in power between the supporting nations and UNSCOM had taken place. At the outset it had had no personnel and no means of gaining information other than from the Iraqi declarations, whereas the intelligence agencies had a large capital of intelligence on Iraq (gathered in the years before the war and from the defectors who left Iraq in the confused aftermath of the war), along with satellites and other information-gathering technology. Now much of that intelligence had been used up on the first inspections, and most of what had not been used was becoming less relevant with age. Conversely, UNSCOM was now conducting extremely intrusive inspections and asking pointed questions of Iraqi officials; it had access to its own aerial photography from which it could draw its own site plans for conducting inspections it would itself instigate, and it had the staff to undertake the analysis and plan the inspections.

Meanwhile, Iraq was refusing to accept the terms of resolution 707, particularly those provisions which dealt with the overflights of its territory by the U2 and by helicopters. Germany had agreed to provide UNSCOM with two large CH-53g helicopters to transport inspection personnel and their equipment around Iraq. This capability would make it much easier for UNSCOM and the IAEA to conduct truly no-notice inspections, swooping down on the target from the sky. The helicopters, from the Bundeswehr, were in Bahrain, ready to fly into Iraq. Saddam was refusing to agree to their use, arguing that, in order to protect the UNSCOM helicopters from his own anti-aircraft batteries, he would have to shut down his air defences each time they flew, thereby leaving the country open to aerial attack from Israel or Iran for the duration of each helicopter flight. This was patent nonsense – any air defence system has to be able to recognise friend from foe. Instead, Iraq suggested that UNSCOM and the IAEA should avail themselves of Iraqi helicopters if they really needed aerial transport.

UNSCOM wisely refused this offer. To have accepted would have meant that inspections were dependent on pilots and helicopters being made available, giving Iraq an ostensibly 'technical' set of excuses for blocking inspection activity. There were other good reasons why the offer should be rejected, as Johan Molander was to find out.

Johan was in Iraq with a small team of chemical experts, which included the British commissioner, Bryan Barrass, and another British chemist, Ron Manley (now with the Technical Secretariat of the Organisation for the Prohibition of Chemical Weapons, in the Hague). Their task was to inspect the Muthanna State Establishment site to ascertain whether and how it could be used to destroy Iraq's stocks of chemical munitions, bulk agents and precursor chemicals. Muthanna lies an uncomfortable two-hour drive to the north-west of Baghdad. It is a huge site, covering some 25 square kilometres. By far the most efficient way to inspect it for the purposes of Johan's mission was by helicopter. But the Iraqi authorities were still refusing to allow UNSCOM to use its own.

Reluctantly, and without relinquishing any of UNSCOM's claims to the right to use its own helicopters, Johan agreed to use an Iraqi helicopter for this one inspection. The flight out to Muthanna was unremarkable. However, two notable things happened on the way back. First, Johan, who was sitting up front next to the pilot, saw from the compass that they were flying in diametrically the opposite direction of Baghdad. He asked the pilot whether he knew that they were supposed to be flying to Baghdad. The pilot acknowledged that he did. Johan pointed out that they were flying in the wrong direction. The pilot disagreed, insisting that he knew the way. Johan pointed out that the compass showed that they were flying westwards, not eastwards. At this point it became clear that the pilot did not know how to navigate by compass and map. He knew the roads, and had merely followed the highway from Baghdad to Muthanna. Now he was doing the same, but had followed the road in the wrong direction.

To rectify his mistake, he performed a sharp U-turn, banking the plane sharply to the right. Johan, who was sitting on the right, held on tightly, which was just as well. As the helicopter reached its steepest incline, the door on Johan's side of the helicopter fell off. The pilot landed the helicopter next to the offending door and the return trip to Baghdad was held up while efforts were made to re-affix it. After half an hour of futile attempts, they flew off leaving the door behind, for a very windy and noisy return flight.

Back in Baghdad, Johan pointed out to the Iraqis that not only were there matters of principle and matters of inspection effectiveness that required UNSCOM to operate its own helicopters, but there were also practical and safety reasons. Iraqi pilots could not navigate, and their helicopters were clearly unsafe.

* * *

The nature of the UN disarmament programme in Iraq had now irrevocably changed; it could have been a rapid and cooperative effort but had now deteriorated into a slow game of cat and mouse. Iraq had chosen the path of concealment and deceit, forcing the UN into ever more intrusive methods of inspection. Naturally, this adversarial relationship (which was no fault of the inspectors, being purely of Iraq's choosing) would necessarily mean that the disarmament effort would take longer. The longer Iraq lied and cheated, the more evidence would be required to convince the outside world that it was telling the truth or that UNSCOM had uncovered the full extent of its weapons programmes. Furthermore, the longer Iraq tried to hide any capability from UNSCOM, the more UNSCOM became convinced that Iraq intended to retain that capability and rebuild the relevant banned weapons programme. Finally, the more vague Iraq's explanations about its plans, intentions and achievements for each of its weapons programmes, the more detail UNSCOM would have to go into to ensure that it had not missed anything in its own accounting.

This vicious spiral was nowhere more apparent than in the case of the biological weapons programme, where it would take analysis into the finest detail of Iraq's activities and imports to crack the case open.

CHAPTER 6

Paper Chases and Parking Lots

'In war, resolution; in defeat, defiance; in victory,
magnanimity; in peace, goodwill.'

WINSTON CHURCHILL

'In a serious struggle, there is no worse cruelty than
to be magnanimous at an inopportune time.'

LEON TROTSKY

By August 1991 Iraq had failed to show resolve in war but was
showing defiance in defeat. The coalition had tried to show
magnanimity in victory by not requiring unconditional surrender.
But there was a shortage of goodwill from the Iraqi side in the
peace.

David Kelly's first biological weapons inspection had not
completed its wish list of inspections. As with the inspections into
other weapons systems, Iraq's additional declarations and its
continuing concealment efforts had changed the course of the
inspection. David now wanted to extend his inspection into a
second week to visit the sites on its original list and to visit the
'warehouse' at al Hakam.

But other teams were also wanting to change and extend their
operations. David Kay was succeeding in wringing astounding
admissions from the Iraqis about their attempts to separate highly
enriched uranium, the fuel for nuclear bombs. He needed to
extend his inspection for a few days to follow up these admissions

and act on intelligence about Iraq's bomb-building capabilities at the al Atheer site, about 60 kilometres to the south of Baghdad. UNSCOM had also had to rush in a missile inspection team in mid-July to act on time-sensitive aerial photographic evidence that Iraq was hiding operational SCUD missiles and launchers at the town-sized military complex at Taji just north of Baghdad. The team had not seen the missiles which, Iraq later admitted, had been removed from the site minutes before the inspection team arrived at the front gates. However, that team did find other undeclared and banned missile items and destroyed them; it also concluded that Iraq had yet to declare all its missiles, charitably ascribing this failure to Iraq's lack of organisation and inability to interpret its obligations, rather than simple cheating.

When I received my briefing from the British Ministry of Defence in January 1992 before going to New York to join UNSCOM, this inspection was still rankling. The British had been outraged at the failure of the UNSCOM team to act quickly on good intelligence, thereby letting the SCUD missiles slip through its fingers. They were even more incensed at the chief inspector's willingness to give the Iraqis the benefit of the doubt. In part due to pressure from Britain and the US following this (as they saw it) disastrous inspection, UNSCOM was forced to push through with another missile inspection.

This third inspection was to investigate Iraq's missile production, repair and maintenance facilities in order to ensure that, if Iraq had hidden SCUD missiles, it would at least be deprived of the means of keeping them operational. It was also acting on aerial photographs that proved that, despite Iraq's denials, it had constructed a supergun and had stocks of components for building four more. These superguns were the brainchild of the Canadian ballistics genius, Gerard Bull, who was murdered in Brussels in 1990 by an unknown assassin (claimed by the Iraqis to have been from Israeli intelligence). His original concept was that these guns should be powerful enough to project satellites into space, offering a cheap alternative to rocket launching. The gun was designed to lob 1-tonne munitions at Iraq's enemies over long distances. This team arrived in Iraq on 8 August 1991.

The dilemma was this: there were three inspection teams in Iraq, each with urgent and high-priority missions to conduct, but there was logistics support – translators, cars, radios, medics, drivers – sufficient for only two teams. One team had to be axed. Given the tensions between UNSCOM and the IAEA at this stage, and given the pressure from the UK and US on missiles issues, the biological team drew the short straw and had to withdraw. With the team went the chance to inspect al Hakam before it was, like Salman Pak and many other sites around Iraq, sanitised of incriminating evidence.

The tension between UNSCOM and the IAEA had several sources. The first, and most obvious one, was the turf battle that became inevitable as soon as the Security Council decided to split the disarmament task between two UN agencies, rather than have it all under one roof; having already created a fertile ground for organisational rivalry, the Council then exacerbated the situation by giving the right to designate undeclared sites, nuclear or non-nuclear, solely to UNSCOM. This meant that the IAEA had to seek UNSCOM's permission to inspect an undeclared site, giving UNSCOM a *droit de regard* over all the nuclear disarmament issues and, in most cases, a first and more extensive look at US intelligence on nuclear matters. Both these issues rankled with the IAEA.

Additionally, there was the personalities issue. The world of disarmament is a small one. Rolf Ekéus, Executive Chairman of UNSCOM, and Hans Blix, Director General of the IAEA, are both Swedes, both lawyers by training and had both joined the Swedish Foreign Ministry in 1962. In virtually every other detail they are dissimilar.

Hans Blix came from an academic background to be the Foreign Ministry's long-serving legal counsel. Hans comes from the liberal side of Swedish politics. He is, based on his liberal and scientific training, a proud atheist. In 1976 Sweden voted in its first liberal government for decades and Hans was elevated to Under-Secretary in the Foreign Ministry, serving in that position from 1976 to 1978. After a brief interlude of socialist government the liberals were re-elected in 1979 and Hans was elevated to the position of Foreign Minister. He was appointed Director General of the IAEA on 1 December 1981 (where his special assistant – private secretary in British parlance – for his first four years of tenure was none other than Johan Molander, who in the summer of 1991 was Rolf Ekéus's special adviser).

Rolf Ekéus, on the other hand, joined the Foreign Ministry as a career diplomat after his military service and apprenticeship at the bar. He comes from the socialist camp and is a devout Catholic. Rolf and Hans had found themselves on opposite sides of policy arguments within the Swedish Foreign Ministry on more than one occasion.

In addition, there was the Richard Kennedy/Bob Gallucci history. Kennedy was still very much on the scene and influential in Vienna. Bob brought with him to UNSCOM his philosophical belief that IAEA Safeguards were not stringent enough to prevent nuclear technology for ostensibly civil purposes being diverted clandestinely into nuclear weapons programmes. This was seen by the Kennedy faction and the IAEA as an unwelcome assault on a fundamental activity of the agency and hence to a key part of its financing. Bob also brought with him a barely concealed conviction that the IAEA had failed appallingly in Iraq prior to the war, failing to spot a full-scale weaponisation programme under its nose.

Niggling differences had kept these tensions to the fore. Hans Blix had initially argued that the IAEA did not have to be covered by the new Status Agreement between Iraq and the UN because the IAEA already had its inspection rights under the Safeguards Agreement with Iraq, whereas Rolf Ekéus had successfully argued that the inspection rights required to disarm Iraq, potentially against its will, would have to be far more extensive and watertight than those negotiated with Iraq as equal partners under the Safeguards Agreement. Rolf had held up the first nuclear inspection team over this issue.

Bigger differences had emerged during the high-level mission to Iraq in June/July. Rolf Ekéus felt that both Hans Blix and Mohammed el Baradei had been too quick and too willing to accept Iraqi protestations that there had never been a nuclear weapons programme and that the inspectors under David Kay must have been mistaken if they thought they had seen calutron components on the trucks leaving Fallujah. While Hans Blix spoke forcefully with the Iraqis in the meetings during the mission, there had apparently been some heated behind-the-scenes exchanges between him and Rolf. And it was Rolf who insisted that Hans sit in on the final meeting with Ahmed Hussein when the conclusions of the mission were read out. The UNSCOM team was convinced that Hans had been reluctant to do this because he did not share those conclusions.

David Kay was also feeling the pressure and was beginning to get caught in the IAEA–UNSCOM cross-fire. He, more than anyone else, was insisting that the items were calutrons and that the readings taken by the team were consistent only with efforts to separate HEU. The Iraqis were arguing with Hans Blix and Mohammed el Baradei that the sampling techniques David claimed to have used were not reliable, whereas David insisted that they were, and yet felt under pressure from both Hans and Mohammed to accept the Iraqi version of events and to question his own findings. On the other hand, he felt his only support was coming from the UNSCOM component of the high-level mission, not his own.

Tensions within the IAEA had spread further. Dimitri Pericos felt that the US intelligence services did not treat all IAEA inspectors equally, reserving the best intelligence, and hence the more attractive inspections, for their own inspectors, David Kay prime amongst them. Having seen Dimitri in an intelligence briefing, I can well understand how he might have come to that conclusion. But I disagree with his implied reasons. Dimitri was so dismissive of the intelligence and so aggressive with the intelligence analysts – a species not used to sunlight and not best armed with the social skills to deal with intimidation – that they completely clammed up. No wonder he did not benefit from the intelligence briefings.

The worst incident to date had occurred during the fourth IAEA inspection, led by David Kay, while David Kelly's biological inspection was still in Iraq. Iraq had declared possession of some 2.5 grams of plutonium in the course of the first inspection, but the IAEA had chosen not to make a big issue of it. During IAEA4, as noted in the previous chapter, David Kay was in touch with New York every three hours to call in the team's location so that UNSCOM could ensure that any US military action against Iraq did not accidentally hit his team. During these conversations David would also give UNSCOM's duty officer sitreps (situation reports – essentially blow-by-blow accounts of what happened during an inspection) on the latest events. During one of these conversations he reported the discussions with the Iraqis on their reprocessing experiments, which had isolated plutonium.

Bob Gallucci, as a committed nuclear disarmer, immediately seized upon the significance of Iraq's efforts to isolate plutonium. There are two principal designs for a nuclear bomb: the implosion bomb or the gun design.

In the implosion bomb, you surround the HEU core with very high-quality explosives and many triggers connected to extremely precise timer switches. The nuclear reaction is started by setting off the explosives so that the uranium is squeezed in on itself until it reaches critical mass and nuclear fission starts. Clearly, to avoid merely squirting the uranium out of one side of the bomb, the explosion – termed the explosive lens – has to be highly accurate, implying highly engineered timers and extremely uniform explosives. British and American customs had intercepted Iraqi attempts to purchase these triggers, which implied that Iraq could not itself build these and had to purchase them elsewhere – a weak link in its supply chain for a nuclear bomb of the implosion type.

The gun design involves shooting a bullet of plutonium into a mass of HEU. The collision of the two elements brings about criticality and the fission reaction that creates the nuclear explosion. This design is not reliant on highly engineered and difficult to make timers or explosives, but upon difficult to make plutonium. If Iraq were capable of making plutonium, it would not be reliant on an external supply of components for bomb-making.

Bob Gallucci, without reference to Hans Blix in Vienna, took this news to the Security Council, fanning the fury that produced resolution 707. David Kay, still in Baghdad, was the immediate target of the ensuing fury from Hans (and everyone else on the IAEA Action Team) at being left out of the loop. David was told to break his direct contact with UNSCOM New York and to submit his sitreps to Vienna, who would then pass them on. He refused to do this, saying that his team's safety would be put in danger from US bombing if he did not call in regularly to report their location, and threatened to resign if the order were not rescinded. Hans saw reason, but it was another wedge driven between David Kay and the IAEA.

Given this situation, UNSCOM could hardly inform the IAEA that its own biological and missiles inspections were both more important than David Kay's nuclear inspection. David Kelly lost out on the bids for logistical support and his first biological weapons inspection team was forced to withdraw.

After IAEA4 another UNSCOM–IAEA sore opened. Both the IAEA and UNSCOM were required under the terms of the ceasefire resolution to draw up plans for monitoring Iraq's industry to ensure that its 'dual-purpose' capabilities were not used to reacquire banned weapons systems. 'Dual-purpose' capabilities are materials, equipment and know-how which have legitimate civil and military uses but could also be used to make the banned weapons of mass destruction or long-range missiles. One example is phosgene. This chemical can be used in the production of foam for furniture, but it is also a 'choking agent' – it will make an unprotected person choke to death. Another example is thiodiglycol, which is used as an additive to the ink used in ballpoint pens to ensure that it flows smoothly and yet does not leak. Thiodiglycol is also a precursor chemical used in the production of mustard agent.

The IAEA had prepared its plan for ongoing monitoring and verification and submitted it to the Security Council without reference to UNSCOM. As soon as they saw it, UNSCOM's experts and Rolf Ekéus realised that there were huge discrepancies between the two plans, reflecting completely different ways of dealing with nuclear and non-nuclear issues. Given the fact that UNSCOM had *droit de regard* over nuclear issues and that some dual-purpose items had nuclear and non-nuclear implications, the two plans clearly had to be harmonised. Rolf insisted that the IAEA plan be withdrawn and experts from the two organisations get together to ensure that the two plans were consistent with each other.

Relations between UNSCOM and the IAEA hit their lowest point at what should have been a moment of crowning glory for both organisations.

The US had been debriefing a number of defectors from the Iraqi nuclear programme. The intelligence analysts were now confident that they could pin down the precise location of key documents about Iraq's nuclear weaponisation programme. It was time to launch an inspection to go after these crown jewels. And this is where all the organisational and personal grievances came to the fore.

By now, Bob Gallucci was opposed to giving the IAEA any responsibility. In his view, the IAEA's failure before the war to spot the nuclear programme, Hans Blix's apparent reluctance to see through Iraq's lies, and the failure of the IAEA to make an issue out of the plutonium experiments meant that it was not fit to conduct the inspection. This was a view shared in the non-Kennedy faction of the US administration (PolMil – the Politico-Military Section – in the State Department, the Pentagon, the CIA and DIA, and, importantly, the US Mission in New York).

As it was, Dimitri Pericos and Hans Blix had been very reluctant to pick up the documents search project when it was first mooted in June: blockading an entire building while inspectors rummaged through all the documentation inside did not sit well with an agency used to conducting consensual Safeguards inspections of respectable States Parties.

Now the US was insisting that the inspection should go ahead, but that it would either be led by David Kay or withdrawn from the IAEA and run as an UNSCOM inspection. Seeing the danger of letting this inspection slip away from the IAEA to the upstart UNSCOM, Hans Blix bit the bullet and reluctantly agreed to let David Kay lead the inspection.

This type of inspection requires a particular mind-set which is different from that needed in the usual scientific and diplomatic discourse. The inspectors' first objective was to reach the target site without alerting the Iraqis to where they were heading. Once there, all the exits from the building had to be blocked immediately so that no one and nothing could leave the site without first being inspected. Then they needed to gain access to all parts of the building – in particular those designated by intelligence as likely locations. This might mean picking locks or breaking down doors if the Iraqis failed to 'find' keys or used other excuses to prevent access to the required rooms. Finally, several Arabic speakers and note-takers were needed to scan the documents and to inventory all the items earmarked for confiscation. This inspection would be the first of its kind.

* * *

David Kay arrived in Iraq for the sixth nuclear inspection on the morning of 22 September 1991. Bob Gallucci was his deputy. The team assembled at 5.30 the next morning in the lobby of the Rasheed Hotel and, with their Iraqi minders, set off for the Nuclear Design Centre, a multistorey building across the road, next to the heavily bombed former Conference Centre. The team knew there was a chance that their activities might be blocked if the Iraqi minders realised what they were after or, more particularly, what they had found. Consequently, the inspectors had agreed on a set of code words that could be used over the Motorola radios to indicate a significant find, without using plain English.

The team secured the building and spread out to inspect each and every floor. According to the intelligence, the key documents were in a basement room in an annex to an L-shaped building. While this proved to be accurate, it was not a lot to go on in view of the size of the building complex.

At ten o'clock David Kay received the code word over his Motorola. He was on the eighth floor. The documents were indeed in the basement. The lifts were not working so, trying to hide his excitement, David trotted down the stairs. There were several trunks of documents there, including a report from the al Atheer site detailing progress made up to May 1990 on an implosion-type nuclear bomb.

David's first priority was to get this evidence out before the Iraqis realised what was going on. Help was at hand. One of the American inspectors was in a bad way with a stomach infection. He was losing so much body fluid that he had become seriously dehydrated. David asked one of the medics – a New Zealander – to evacuate him: a car would take him directly to Habbaniyah air base, where the UNSCOM aircraft was still on the ground preparing to return to Bahrain. David shoved a few key documents, including the al Atheer report, into the jacket of the sick inspector and sent him on his way. The aircraft, with the sick man and the documents, lifted off from Habbaniyah at 2 p.m., landing in Bahrain two and a half hours later. By the end of the working day copies of the report had been faxed to Vienna and New York.

By then, David Kay's worries about the Iraqis' reactions had been vindicated. At around 3.30 p.m., despite the inspectors' best efforts to disguise their find, the Iraqis realised what was going on and what had been found. They were demanding a full inventory of the items that were being confiscated. As a further precaution, the inspectors had been marking each of the relevant documents as they read them, and keeping their own inventory. David now gave orders for the trunks of documents to be loaded onto the UNSCOM vehicles to be taken back to the field office. At this point the Iraqi minders blocked the team's departure.

The time was 3.45. David gave the chief minder until four o'clock to gain authorisation from higher up for the team to leave. A short stand-off ensued. CNN, resident in the Rasheed Hotel across the road, caught wind of the trouble and brought a camera crew down to film the events. The Iraqi minders tried to keep them away, but they were still able to get a limited view of the scene and broadcast it to the world. At 4.30 more Iraqi officials arrived and started inventorying the documents on the UNSCOM trucks. At 6.25 Dr Jaffar Dhia Jaffar – who was, according to the al Atheer report, in charge of the nuclear weapons programme and deputy chairman of the Iraqi Atomic Energy Commission (IAEC) – turned up demanding an inventory of every document. David in return demanded that the team be allowed to leave at 6.30.

At around seven o'clock the Iraqis tired of the stand-off and moved in to confiscate the material from the unarmed inspectors at gunpoint. The team could do no more than photograph this violent infringement of their inspection rights and flagrant breach of the ceasefire terms, and return to their hotel. At two o'clock the next morning the Iraqi minders turned up to return the documents. A quick check against the team's own inventory proved that all the most relevant ones had been removed.

But tomorrow is another day, they say. And so it proved.

* * *

David Kay gathered his team in the hotel lobby at 6 a.m. There were a least three times as many Iraqis present as on the previous morning. The team made a great show of loading up the vehicles as if for a major outing. In fact, they were going less than 100 yards around the corner, to the headquarters of the PC-3 (Petrochemical 3) Project – the code name they had found on the al Atheer report the previous day. From the outside this building looks like any other block of apartments, and that is indeed what it was originally. But at some stage it had been converted into offices and was now the headquarters of Iraq's vast programme to build nuclear weapons. The team arrived at 6.20.

Here they immediately found large quantities of relevant documents. The Iraqi minders were very unhappy from the outset, and Dr Sami was constantly losing his temper and shouting at the inspectors. Given the events of the previous day and the fact that the element of surprise was now gone, David Kay instructed the team to load the relevant documents onto the UNSCOM vehicles as they were discovered. By 10.50 Dr Sami had had enough. He ordered all inspection activity to be halted. Naturally, the team objected and tried to continue. One by one the inspectors were manhandled out of the building. Dr Sami now told David Kay to unload the documents from the vehicles and leave. David replied that they were not leaving without the documents and that they refused to unload them. The Iraqis would have to seize the documents themselves if they wanted to remove them from vehicles protected by the UN flag. Dr Sami stopped short of this, and at 12.30 Dr Jaffar Dhia Jaffar arrived at the site, demanding that the team hand back all the confiscated documents and film. Thus started the four-day parking-lot stand-off.

Meanwhile, the communicator, a New Zealander, had set up the satellite telephone so that David Kay could call Vienna to bring Hans Blix up to date with events and Bob Gallucci could likewise inform Rolf Ekéus in New York. Over the next few days the satellite phone was to prove the inspection team's most powerful weapon.

Rolf Ekéus had quickly recognised the importance of using the media to gain popular support for UNSCOM's mission. Now he immediately saw the potential value of the media to the inspection team – satellite communications meant that every local radio and TV news anchor could chat live to David Kay or Bob Gallucci, who could tell the world that they had proof that Iraq had been trying to build nuclear weapons and show how desperate the Iraqis were to prevent the UN from destroying these weapons.

Rolf rang David and told him that various news organisations had rung UNSCOM in New York asking for live interviews with the inspection team; would David mind doing them? Although he was clearly in favour of this, he left the decision to the man on the ground, for which David was grateful. David accepted. For the next four days the satellite phone rang in a non-stop media frenzy (no doubt to the delight of shareholders of INMARSAT, the operator of the communications satellite – satellite calls at the time were charged at something over $11 per minute). The media attention also meant that, while the CNN and other cameras were rolling on the inspectors night and day, the Iraqis were unlikely to harm them physically.

Dr Sami is, on the face of it, very Westernised. He studied at Ann Arbor and MIT, specialising in nuclear physics. He dresses and talks like an American. He loves American sports. Yet he was a willing participant in Iraq's nuclear programme: it gave him the chance to put into practice his years of study that he would have had nowhere else. He exudes love of his job. But, despite his Americanisms, he seriously missed the measure of David Kay's team. In a show of Arab hospitality he ordered the minders to bring out chairs and put them in the shade of the buildings for the inspectors to sit on. Instead, to a man (and woman) they rounded on him, telling him that they did not want to sit down in the shade, they wanted to get on with the job they had come to do. This rejection genuinely hurt Sami; he said that the sole female inspector was free to return to her hotel if she wished, as the hot sun was no place for a woman. The inspector in question was offended by the offer, and Sami was once more rebuffed.

Meanwhile, New York was the scene of frantic rounds of diplomatic activity to try to resolve the crisis before US patience snapped and the military were asked to go in again. Rolf Ekéus was holding talks with members of the Security Council and the Iraqi ambassador. Iraq was reminded by everyone of the assurances given just two months previously by Saddam Hussein that he would comply and that every official in Iraq had been ordered to cooperate with the inspections. Yet here was Iraq preventing the inspectors from doing their job at gunpoint once again. Iraq, for its part, was organising demonstrations of women, children – anyone who could walk – against the iniquities of the inspection. It accused David Kay of being a CIA spy sent to seize the personnel files of those involved in 'Iraq's peaceful nuclear activities' so that they could be hunted down and assassinated.

Bob Gallucci was also managing to upset people – the IAEA and UNSCOM. At one point the team was urgently trying to contact UNSCOM in New York to pass on some information by fax via the satellite link. For some reason New York was not answering. Bob called the only other number he knew well, the fax in the PolMil Division in the State Department in Washington DC, asking them to forward the information to UNSCOM and the IAEA. This broke a golden rule – that all reporting from inspections should be through either the IAEA or UNSCOM; there should be no direct contact between inspectors and their respective governments.

This rule was laid down for three principal reasons. First, inspectors are UN employees and therefore owe their loyalty to the UN. Secondly, the information they collect in the course of inspections is privileged under diplomatic immunity and cannot be released in an unauthorised manner to outsiders. And thirdly, to protect the inspectors against the accusation that they are spies, thereby also protecting the credibility and independence of the UN. While Bob Gallucci would argue that the extraordinary circumstances of the stand-off and the failure of the link with UNSCOM justified a break with procedure, this action provoked a severe reprimand from Rolf Ekéus and fury from the IAEA in Vienna. UNSCOM–IAEA relations were now at a very low ebb, and David Kay's own position in the IAEA had become untenable. He submitted his resignation upon his return from the inspection.

For the members of the inspection team, it was a long ninety-six hours of hot days and cold nights. In the absence of cloud cover, once the sun sinks over the horizon, the temperature in Baghdad quickly plummets. The support staff in the UNSCOM office would bring the inspectors food and drinks, but they were worried, particularly as the demonstrations against them grew bigger and more vocal, that the Iraqis might do them actual bodily harm.

Privately, David Kay and Bob Gallucci had discussed this possibility. They had concluded that, with the blanket media coverage, nothing was likely to happen in daylight. However, things would be different under cover of night. They arranged to have one third of the team awake at all times to guard against any attack. In the event, David Kay was not really worried until the third night, when many more Iraqi soldiers assembled at the site and moved in closer. At this point he and Bob Gallucci took Dr Sami to one side and told him that, if the Iraqis were intending to use force against the team, they should do so against the two of them, not the others. Some of the other team members had Special Forces backgrounds, and neither David nor Bob wanted to vouch for their reaction to physical aggression. They wanted to ensure that any use of force did not escalate.

In the event, agreement was reached in New York during the

afternoon of 27 September on the release of both the team and the documents. The team would leave with the documents and then both sides would, in UNSCOM's offices, review and inventory the documents and films seized and Iraq would keep a copy of this inventory. Irrelevant documents would be returned to the Iraqis. However, the chief inspector would judge what was relevant and what was not, and his decision would be final.

Baghdad is eight hours ahead of New York, so it was 5.46 a.m. locally on 28 September 1991 when the team and documents were released.

The team spent the whole of that day reviewing the 60,000 or so documents seized. On 29 September UNSCOM's support staff shipped the documents out to the safety of Bahrain while the team searched a further three sites. Not surprisingly, the sites had already been cleaned out. On the third day of the parking-lot stand-off the team had seen smoke from a fire on the top floor of one of the two target buildings – Iraqis busily burning documents.

An amusing and worrying footnote to this episode is that, after the deal was struck and the documents taken to the UNSCOM office, Dr Sami approached David Kay and Bob Gallucci and asked whether their offer of the night before still stood. Neither David nor Bob had a clue what he was talking about. Suddenly the light bulb went on in Bob Gallucci's head. 'Oh, you mean the one where you beat the shit out of us and take the documents back?' Sami's head nodded in agreement. I have it on good authority that Bob's reply was unprintable …

Despite the trials and disappointments and the strained relations between all involved, it was a spectacularly successful inspection and did much to restore the standing of the IAEA with its critics. In its report, the team concluded that it had:

> obtained conclusive evidence that the Government of Iraq had a program for developing an implosion-type nuclear weapon

and it found documents linking this program – code-named 'Petrochemical Three' (PC-3) – to Iraq's Ministry of Industry and Military Industrialisation, the Iraqi Atomic Energy Commission (IAEC) and Iraq's Ministry of Defence. Documents were found showing that the nuclear weapons program was supported by a broad-based international procurement effort. Contrary to Iraq's claims of having only a peaceful nuclear program, the team found documents showing that Iraq had been working on the revision of a nuclear weapon design and one linking the IAEC to work on a surface-to-surface missile project – presumably the intended delivery system for their nuclear weapon.

The documents showed clearly that the al Atheer facility was the centre of the nuclear weapons design work, even though Iraq had claimed that the site had no nuclear connection, civil or military. They also linked Iraq's exploration of gaseous diffusion and centrifuge enrichment techniques for uranium to the weapons programme; work on these had started as early as 1982 and had continued at least until 1988. While the team had seen brochures and correspondence from potential suppliers to Iraq's nuclear weapons programme, the early forcible termination of the inspection had meant that many relevant documents had been kept from the inspectors. Those that had been confiscated or read by the team indicated that Iraq had developed an elaborate web of cover explanations for its purchases of items for the programme. Furthermore, procurement of materials had often been coupled with on-site training of Iraqi personnel at the site of the manufacturer. Finally, the documentation showed that Dr Jaffar Dhia Jaffar, despite his protestations that no nuclear weapons programme existed in Iraq, was in fact a senior administrator for the programme. Indeed, the team came to the conclusion that Jaffar was the director of the nuclear weapon programme.

These conclusions were scary enough. The fact that the Iraqis were trying to retain their documents and know-how about nuclear weapons implied that they had use for them in the future.

And there was more bad news. Along with the other documents was a memorandum, dated two weeks before the inspection had taken place, and one week before the first briefing of the inspection team itself, informing the person responsible for the documents found at the Nuclear Design Centre that an inspection team would be coming shortly, led by David Kay, to search for documents relating to Iraq's nuclear weapons programme. Fortunately, the person in charge had replied that he did not have enough time to move the documents.

Very few people had known about the inspection at the time the memorandum was written: either there was a very high-level leak in Washington, New York or Vienna, or Iraq had somehow managed to penetrate the inspectors' offices or communications. In any case, UNSCOM and the IAEA now knew that Iraq was not just taking centrally organised passive measures to conceal the truth about its weapons programmes but was actively seeking to undermine the effectiveness of the inspection process. They could be in no doubt now how hostile the inspection environment was.

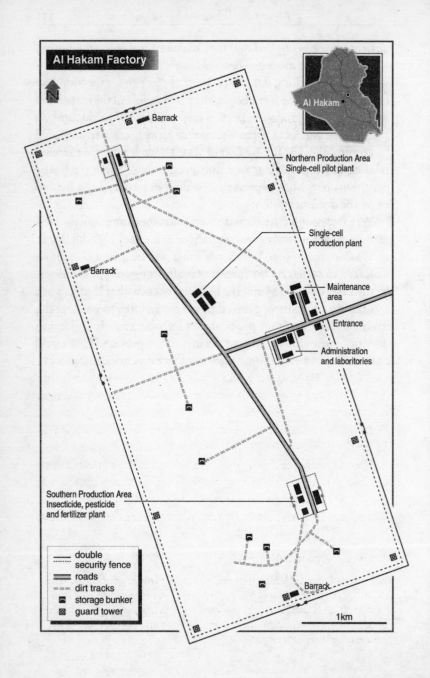

Al Hakam Factory

N

Al Hakam

Barrack

Northern Production Area
Single-cell pilot plant

Single-cell
production plant

Maintenance
area

Entrance

Barrack

Administration
and laboritories

Southern Production Area
Insecticide, pesticide
and fertilizer plant

Barrack

double
security fence
roads
dirt tracks
storage bunker
guard tower

1km

CHAPTER 7

Expensive Cattle Fodder: The Second Biological Inspection

'He would, wouldn't he.'
MANDY RICE-DAVIES (upon hearing that Lord Astor
had denied her allegations of a sexual liaison)

'It is undesirable to believe a proposition when there
is no ground whatsoever for supposing it true.'
BERTRAND RUSSELL

Unaware of the excitement to come, David Kelly and his team assembled in Bahrain for training and briefing in mid-September 1991. Their mission was to inspect ten sites suspected of being involved in Iraq's undeclared biological weapons programme. These included the five sites left over from the first inspection – al Hakam and four others.

They arrived in Baghdad on 20 September, the day before David Kay led his document search team into Iraq. The atmosphere was already tense. Iraq was still refusing to allow UNSCOM to fly its helicopters into and around Iraq. A week earlier, a frustrated

Opposite: Diagram 2: Al Hakam

Iraq claimed that al Hakam was just a civilian plant producing protein for cattle feed from fermentation of bacteria. The large size of the site, the dispersion of buildings, the military-style security arrangements and the presence of air-conditioned storage bunkers all suggested it was in fact a biological weapons factory.

missile inspection team (UNSCOM13/BM4) had terminated its inspection early. They had intended to use UNSCOM helicopters to scour the western Iraqi desert for fixed SCUD missile launchers. These were banned by the ceasefire and Iraq was required to declare them for destruction. It had failed to do so, but it was clear from the U2 photography that there were many such launchers, aimed at Israel. Once again, Iraq was clearly in breach of its obligations.

Even worse, to kill the time while discussions on the helicopters were taking place, the missile team inspected a couple of sites close to Baghdad. At the Khan al Mahawil Barracks, some 60 kilometres south of Baghdad, to their utter disbelief, the team found four of the SCUD missile transporters that the first missile inspection team had dismantled in the first week of July. The Iraqis had recovered the parts of the 'destroyed' transporters and spot-welded them back together again. The team destroyed these repaired transporters again, but withdrew from Iraq on 13 September with no resolution of the helicopter issue in sight. Iraq was in multiple breach of its obligations – failure to allow access with UNSCOM's own aerial transport, failure to declare banned items, reconstituting banned capabilities ...

At the airport in Habbaniyah David Kelly's team met the fifth IAEA inspection team, led by Dimitri Pericos, leaving Iraq with yet more details about Iraq's undeclared efforts at gas centrifuge separation of highly enriched uranium – further evidence that Iraq was trying to build a nuclear bomb.

Despite the tensions and the impending threat of US-led military action to force Iraq to allow the helicopter flights, the inspection had to go ahead. Given the intelligence community's assessment that Iraq did indeed have a programme to develop biological weapons – not just an aimless research programme as Iraq would have UNSCOM believe – the team's primary objective was to try to identify the sites where Iraq might have been making, or planning to make, bulk quantities of the biological warfare agents. In particular, they were looking for the ability to make large quantities of anthrax spores, botulinum toxin and the plague bacterium, Yersinia.

Four of the sites turned out to be of no interest. One, for example, was a bakery. The biological inspectors were faced with unique problems: to build a nuclear bomb you need a lot of very large plant. The electromagnetic isotope separation of highly enriched uranium requires massive amounts of electricity and so you can use aerial photography to identify a plant involved in this type of operation from its power supply. Chemical factories are also large, because chemical weapons require huge quantities of agent in order to be militarily significant. Missile-production facilities also have large 'fingerprints' that enable photographic interpreters to identify them with some degree of confidence.

The same is not true of biological weapons facilities. Every stage of the production process is potentially dual-use. The seed stocks of the fatal bacteria and viruses have legitimate use in medical research and vaccine production. The 'complex growth media' used to grow the bacteria can be used in medical assays when doctors are trying to identify the causal agent of infection. Certain types of complex growth media are also used in biological research and in some civilian industry, such as single-cell protein production – a process whereby you ferment up a lot of bacteria in a broth and, once the bacteria have exhausted their supply of food, harvest the bacteria, which themselves are rich in protein, and process them to make food, mainly for animals such as dairy cattle. The fermentation vessels used for making biological warfare agents are also used in bakeries or breweries. Similar, easily adaptable vessels are also used to tan leather. Driers of various sorts are used in the same industries, just as they are used to harvest biological warfare agents after fermentation is complete. Grinding machines, used to reduce the bacterial product to the right particle size for efficient dispersal over the battlefield, are used in many industrial applications; the grist used in such machines, bentonite, is used in engineering small earth dams and weirs for agricultural purposes. Filling machines are used in most factories making a powdered product, such as flour mills, but could easily be adapted to fill biological bombs with bacterial or viral agents. And agricultural crop-dusting equipment could be used to spray the biological agent over enemy troops. Even the munitions and bombs can be dual-use – a smoke round for an artillery piece can easily be adapted to deliver chemical or biological agents instead of smoke.

And, worse still for anyone trying to hunt down hidden biological weapons, you don't need large quantities of these agents to have a significant capability. That means that you do not need large-scale equipment and you don't need to use the equipment all year round to maintain a military stock – you can make agent for, say, only one month a year and, for the rest of the year, use the self-same equipment to make other innocent biological products, such as vaccines or even beer.

The al Hakam facility stands near al Latifiyah, about 55 kilometres to the south-west of Baghdad in the dusty desert. Like those at Salman Pak, the buildings from the outside are nondescript. The landscape is barren and flat, with broad roads linking the widely separated one- and two-storey buildings. David Kelly's team spent three days at the site. Dr Rihab Taha met the team and now called the plant a 'single-cell protein facility', not the warehouse referred to in the answers to the questionnaire drawn up by David and Nikita Smidovich. The reason for the change in designation was clear as soon as the team entered the buildings – al Hakam was evidently a production plant, not a warehouse.

David and certain others on the team were immediately suspicious. The facility was in the middle of nowhere, far from any water – which, for an industrial process that would require a workforce to operate it and a constant, high-quality and generous water supply, did not make sense. It was massive, beyond what could have been economic – the site was 3 kilometres by 6 kilometres. Its two main buildings were 4 kilometres apart – hardly conducive to efficient worker interaction and far more consistent with working on dangerous items where distance provides safety from cross infection. It was surrounded by security fencing more appropriate to a military facility than to an industrial complex.

Once again, the Iraqis were unhelpful. Their answers on the origin of the plant were evasive and vague. There was evidence that equipment had been moved around there within the previous twenty-four hours. David suspected that the separator had been moved to a different position in the production line to disguise the true purpose of the plant. Furthermore, there was evidence that the operators had tried at some stage to build an air lock between the research and development area and the rest of the facility – another major indication that the facility had been used for, or had been intended for, work with harmful organisms rather than those used in single-cell protein production.

That said, the site as now configured seemed more or less consistent with its cover story. Some of the team members thought it was unlikely to have been used to produce biological weapons because there were no obvious containment measures to protect the operators from infection (apart from the air lock). But these inspectors were 'mirror imaging' – they were assuming that Iraq would have the same regard for health and safety procedures as we do in the West. David Kelly pointed out that, with the fermentation vessels used at al Hakam, a degree of containment could be obtained simply by swathing the fermenter vessel in plastic cling film and heat-sealing it to make the plastic encasement airtight. Others disagreed.

The report on the inspection of this site reflected something of that disagreement:

Although at this point there is absolutely no evidence of participation in a biological weapons programme, the team was concerned that it might feature in the development of such a programme and thus made specific recommendations that the UN monitor designated activities, future building construction and/or modifications of the buildings, and purchases of equipment as well as prohibit use of human and animal pathogens on the site.

In fact, it was later learned that the Iraqis had operated it without containment, having considered the issue and come to the conclusion (correctly) that, if the plant were operated to reasonable professional standards, the chance of contamination was very low indeed.

The story was similar at the other production sites visited. They were all fairly close to Baghdad – the Foot and Mouth Disease Plant at al Dawrah, 5 kilometres to the south-west, the al Kindi Veterinary Vaccine Company, 27 kilometres to the west, and the Serum and Vaccine Institute at Amariyah, 60 kilometres to the south-west – and were adjudged capable of producing sufficient quantities of biological agent to meet weapons requirements, but no proof could be found that they had done so. And each of the sites was being put to its declared, legitimate use.

The team also visited the al Fudhaliyah Agricultural Research Centre; according to intelligence reports dating back to the mid-1980s, businessmen from a European maker of high-quality fermentation vessels had visited the centre on a sales trip, meeting none other than Dr Rihab Taha and Dr Nissar al Hindawi. The site had been badly damaged in the Gulf War and nothing remained of the biological production facilities.

On the face of it, this was not a successful mission – it had not proved that the Iraqis had a biological weapons programme, despite the fact that most of the inspectors were convinced that they did. In fact, the selection of sites for the first two inspections proved, years later, to be extraordinarily accurate. Of the eleven sites inspected then (none of which had been declared by Iraq before the inspections), six were later admitted to be biological weapons production facilities.

This must have come as a nasty shock to the Iraqi authorities. Their ultra-secret biological weapons sites were known to Western intelligence, even if UNSCOM could not prove that they were part of the programme. The team's failure to prove the link testifies to the inherent difficulties in tracking down biological weapons, and to the determination of the Iraqi authorities to keep them secret.

The end of this inspection marked the end of the first chapter of the story of the hunt for Iraq's biological weapons. UNSCOM had used its best intelligence to pinpoint the sites, but its highly professional and competent team had come back suspicious but empty-handed. There was simply no new intelligence on which to base new inspections. And, while repeated visits to the same sites would ensure that they were not converted back to weapons production, such inspections were unlikely to have any greater success than the first two in revealing the truth about their past usage. Indeed, as time passed, further modifications to the plants ensured that what evidence still remained was incrementally removed and that the actual current usage of the plants became quite innocent.

A different approach was needed to uncover the truth: inspections and the collection of physical evidence had proved ineffective, and were replaced by analysis and interrogation.

This change in approach was taking place naturally in each of the different weapons programmes investigations. When UNSCOM was established, it had no personnel and hence no expertise. It had no history, and hence no organisational memory. And it had no assets of its own with which to collect data. As these circumstances changed, so did the nature of UNSCOM's investigations.

The First Stage: Checking Declarations and Assessments

The first inspections in each of the weapons areas necessarily had to be launched with the help of 'supporting governments' – namely those member states of the UN that most wanted Iraq disarmed of its weapons of mass destruction. In the early days this meant the

US, its closest allies, and France and Russia. The intelligence analysts of these countries would come into the UNSCOM offices in New York, give briefings on the sites they thought needed to be inspected and provide overhead photography so that the small UNSCOM operation staff could plan the inspection. On the basis of these briefings, Rolf Ekéus would then decide whether the inspection should proceed and, if so, what the objectives should be and which sites should be visited. The operations officers would have to assess the size of team required to achieve these objectives and the areas of expertise needed, and then ring round the New York diplomatic missions of the supporting governments, begging them to offer personnel with the requisite expertise for the dates of the planned inspections.

Once sufficient experts had been recruited, the team would assemble in the Holiday Inn in Bahrain, site of UNSCOM's field office, for briefing on the mission and each inspector's function, and for safety training. In the early days, before the sites had been cleared of land mines and unexploded bombs from the war, inspectors had to be taught to recognise munitions and what to do if they identified one missed by the explosives disposals experts. Similarly, in the early days many of the nuclear and chemical sites were contaminated as a result of the bombing. Teams had to learn how to operate equipment for detecting contamination (such as the Chemical Agent Monitor invented by Bryan Barrass), and how to don their noddy suits (the nuclear, chemical and biological protective suits) and gas masks quickly in the event of exposure to contamination or entry into an area known to be contaminated, such as the chemical weapons storage bunkers.

These teams concentrated on checking the inventory of Iraq's physical assets both against the Iraqi declarations and against intelligence assessments. Their principal aim was quickly to get their hands on as much of Iraq's banned weapons and weapons manufacturing equipment as possible and to ensure that these assets were destroyed.

* * *

The Second Stage: No-Notice Inspections

After the first round of inspections the emphasis changed and teams tried to obtain a full account of the capabilities Iraq had developed so that a plan for the destruction of those capabilities could be drawn up.

If the first stage had been relatively straightforward because the inspectors were merely checking what the Iraqis were willing to admit to, this second stage inevitably became confrontational, given Iraq's decision to withhold all information about the weapons systems it wished to retain or revitalise. Iraq had expected the inspection process to be a typical UN operation: desk-jockey bureaucrats would come along, gratefully accept the obsolete and dangerous weapons stocks handed over to them by the Iraqis and believe what they were told about the extent of the past weapons programmes. After the second nuclear inspection it became clear that this was not going to be the case. Indeed, during the high-level mission in June Tariq Aziz stated that Iraq recognised that the inspectors were professional and could not be fooled with obvious lies. Iraq's response, though, was not to tell the truth but to be more inventive with its lies and to plan countermeasures – systematic operations to pre-empt the inspections.

The balance between UNSCOM and the supporting governments now shifted a little. UNSCOM had its own staff, had recruited analysts and was beginning to get its own information from the on-site inspections conducted by the teams. After August 1991 it also began to receive its own aerial photography via the US-operated U2. This, coupled with the steady flow of new intelligence from supporting governments, allowed UNSCOM to be more effective and less reliant on the supporting governments' intelligence services.

UNSCOM could now identify additional sites for inspection. Human intelligence would describe verbally the buildings and location of a site at which banned items were kept or banned activities undertaken. These descriptions would then be matched, where possible, to the aerial photography and plotted onto a map. From this, an inspection could be launched. However, more often than not, the description was inaccurate: it matched neither the photographic record nor the physical features of the purported location. This is where the art of the analyst comes to the fore – in trying to find the best real match to the overall picture described by the informant.

Alternatively, UNSCOM analysts could analyse the raw aerial photography, with no reference to other intelligence reports, and look for 'fingerprints' – the tell-tale signs that a site was a high-security military facility capable of being used for banned weapons purposes. This was a useful, but limited exercise. Plant for the production of both nuclear and chemical weapons is large and relatively easily identified. Facilities for missile production are less easily recognised, and those for biological weapons production have virtually no unique 'fingerprint'. Consequently, for biological sites one has to rely on proxy signatures, such as evidence of high security, high-capacity air conditioning (associated with maintaining buildings with high containment measures), or indeed the type and volume of traffic that comes in and out of the site.

The Iraqis' countermeasures at this stage were fairly heavy-handed. Their first priority was to identify as soon as possible the discipline of the incoming inspection team. IAEA teams were clearly on nuclear inspections, but it was less obvious whether an UNSCOM team would be chemical, biological or missiles, so they maintained a log of all inspectors who had served in Iraq, marking their area of expertise against their names. They kept a close watch on the comings and goings at the Holiday Inn in Bahrain so that, as soon as they recognised a member of the incoming inspection team, they could refer to the log and assess what his or her expertise was. If it were missiles, then they would be given notice to clean up their missiles facilities before the team arrived. Likewise, if it were chemical, the chemical weapons sites would be cleaned up. It was even suspected that Iraq had tapped into the airline booking computers used at the UN. Airline tickets were booked in the names of the inspectors on David Kay's team even before its planning was finalised, which might explain how the Iraqis received prior notice of the visit. To counter this, UNSCOM made sure that it left purchasing tickets as late as possible.

Once Iraq had identified the discipline of the inspection team, key items of equipment and key documentation were loaded on trucks and simply driven around the country until the inspection was over. Thus, even if the intelligence was good and the inspectors went to the correct sites, their chances of finding truly incriminating evidence was minimal. This explains why, after October 1991, inspections rarely caught the Iraqis red-handed; they usually found only peripheral equipment or documents, rather than key items.

The last stage of Iraqi countermeasures in all inspections was to block access, at gunpoint if necessary, to a site if entry would have enabled the inspectors to catch them red-handed. An Iraqi refusal to allow access to a site became the surest sign that an inspection was close to a banned item.

The Third Stage: Interrogation

Once UNSCOM had acted upon all the highest-grade intelligence available to the original supporting governments' intelligence services, the balance of power between UNSCOM and government shifted further in UNSCOM's favour. UNSCOM was opening up relations with a broader spectrum of governments, becoming less dependent on any one source. The emphasis of its internal processes also changed from an analysis of intelligence to an analysis of Iraq's overall weapons-making capacity.

The first stage in an analysis of a country's weapons-making capacity is to enumerate each and every step in the production of the weapons system in question and the materials, equipment and technology required to perform those steps. The second stage is to identify which of those materials, equipment and technology are in the country. From this, the analysts can gain an idea of which capabilities are definitely available, which capabilities are probably available, and which the country does not have. From this, they could determine what Iraq needed to import for its weapons programme.

If, for instance, Iraq declared that it had no VX programme, but UNSCOM could prove that Iraq possessed all the raw materials for making VX, the equipment for making it and the know-how for making it, then in all probability there had been a programme to make VX and questions should be asked about it. In short, inspections should look for evidence of VX production. If UNSCOM was aware that Iraq had all but one item required for making VX, then it was a good bet that it had a VX programme, and UNSCOM should try to prove that it had stocks of the undeclared item. Finally, if UNSCOM could ascertain that Iraq definitely did not have the capability for completing a key step in a production process – say it could not produce gyroscopes for the guidance and control systems of a missile – but did possess all the other capabilities and materials for making missiles, then UNSCOM would start checking its imports. In all likelihood, there would be a programme and Iraq would have supplemented its indigenous capabilities with imports to fill its technology gaps.

This process of checking Iraq's declared or known capabilities against the capabilities required to make weapons systems provided invaluable pointers for inspection planners and for interrogators of Iraqi officials about their past activities. UNSCOM was allowed to interrogate any Iraqi official about the weapons programmes and Iraq was obliged to permit this, but insisted on having a 'minder' – one of those who accompanied the inspection teams to all the sites – sitting in on such interviews. The inspectors spoke in English. If the official did not speak good English, the question was translated into Arabic by one of the Iraqi interpreters. The official would then reply in Arabic and UNSCOM's interpreters would translate the answer back into English. Thus both sides could check the faithfulness of the interpretation.

This process eventually helped UNSCOM to understand the full extent of Iraq's indigenous capabilities for producing ballistic missiles, and to force Iraq to admit that, contrary to its denials for four years, it had in fact produced large quantities of VX and biological weapons.

To pursue this process effectively, UNSCOM needed good information on the weapons-making equipment supplied to Iraq. There were two main ways of obtaining this information, given that the Iraqi government had clearly taken a high-level decision to protect its supplier network and had ordered its officials to refuse to answer questions on suppliers. First, the inspectors could look for evidence of the origin of equipment they found during inspections, either from the operating manuals, purchasing invoices, sales brochures or serial number plates. Likewise, by looking at the labels on containers of raw materials, such as chemicals, they could identify the exporter of those items. Or they could approach the home government of the known suppliers, requesting information on precisely what those companies had sold to whom, via where and whom, when, in what quantities, and with which payment method.

By tracking down both the goods and the payments, UNSCOM could get an idea not only of the overall capabilities acquired by Iraq, but also of the administrative structure of the organisations and the names of the people involved in the weapons programmes. This helped it to identify new sites to inspect (sites belonging to the organisations involved in the purchasing process) and people to interrogate.

The added advantage of this process is that UNSCOM analysts were able to delve ever deeper into the production and organisational aspects of the programmes. While this obviously slowed things down, it made it very much more difficult for Iraq to stick to its cover stories. It is very easy to maintain a simple lie. Arguments about whether you did do something or did not

inevitably boil down into childish exchanges of 'Did!', 'Didn't!'
Once an interrogation reaches this point, there is nowhere to go
until new evidence comes in – as the biological analysts had found
after the second inspection.

However, if you are able to pose more open-ended questions
that require the interlocutor to describe actions or explain
evidence in detail, the interviewee has one of three options:

- To lie in detail, which is extremely difficult to do consistently:
  the more a person says, the more material the interrogator has
  on which to question him, and the lie ends up being too
  complicated to remember
- To keep the lie simple by making the answers vague. However,
  while this will make it difficult for the interrogator to get to the
  truth, systematic loss of memory and vague replies are a clear
  giveaway that a person is lying
- To tell the truth.

UNSCOM now systematically engaged the Iraqis in detailed
discussions on all aspects of their declared activities, forcing
officials to describe not only what had been achieved, but precisely
how it had been achieved, by whom, under whose orders, paid for
by whom, for which end-user, and for what military reason or
purpose. They were asked to describe safety procedures adopted
at the plants and to present for questioning the doctors
responsible. Over time, Iraq was manoeuvred away from simple
lies into more complex ones, which developed into such comical
farces that, bit by bit, it was forced to admit the truth.

However, in the meantime, the Iraqis responsible for countermeasures were not taking things lying down. They often refused to
make available those individuals whom UNSCOM wanted to
interview, or claimed that they were no longer contactable or had
died or left the country. When witnesses were brought forward,
they had all been coached, and showed a remarkably uniform
amnesia about all relevant details of what had been their bread and

butter only a few years previously. And the Iraqi authorities never allowed one-on-one interrogations, insisting that an Iraqi official sit in on all interviews, thereby inhibiting anyone who might have wanted to tell the truth.

At sites, Iraq also removed all identifying labels from containers and all tags from equipment. Documents which indicated the original manufacturer of equipment were systematically removed, leaving the operators without operating manuals. And when they were nearly caught red-handed, they would destroy such documentation as the inspection team rolled up. On several occasions inspectors noticed piles of burning documents as they drove up to a site.

The Fourth Stage: Technology

This stage overlapped with and complemented the interrogation stage. UNSCOM offered itself up as a field laboratory to test all the latest means of detecting hidden weapons capabilities, and encouraged national science laboratories in numerous countries to try out their latest sensors.

Five different ground-penetrating sensor technologies were evaluated for use in inspections looking for buried items: ground-penetrating radar, gravitometry, magnetic variance, electromagnetic induction and ground sonar. Ground-penetrating radar was fixed to helicopters for use in a 'SCUD hunt' – UNSCOM's largest inspection of all time, launched in response to reports that SCUDs had been buried in the sand at various locations around Iraq.

Sensors for detecting gamma radiation and specific sonic signatures were fixed to other helicopters to conduct a survey of radioactive elements of the principal nuclear sites. Identification of different ions helps in identifying precisely what types of activities were undertaken at the contaminated site. The degree of magnetisation of a crane at the Tuwaitha site was measured and found to be so high that it was taken as clear proof that the crane had been close to an extremely strong magnetic field – the type of field that could only be created by a facility constructed for electromagnetic isotope separation of uranium.

Infrared satellite imagery was used to identify hot spots in Iraq. Emissions of heat and of warm water could be indicators of the hidden nuclear reactor that many reports insisted was there. Samples were taken from the various rivers in Iraq to check for levels of radioactivity in the water and silt – a nuclear reactor upstream would inevitably leak out some radioactive isotopes into the water courses. An aircraft set up for multispectral analysis – surveying a region using a variety of wavelengths in the electromagnetic spectrum – was evaluated, as was a lidar system of using a ground-based laser beam to analyse the contents of smoke effluent from factories.

Chemical sniffers were developed to sample the air downwind of Iraq's chemical facilities. The samples taken from these could be analysed in a field mass spectrometer, capable of detecting parts per billion of banned chemicals. Other samples of water, air, soil and accumulated dust or grease on equipment or in air filters could be analysed in laboratories for evidence of banned nuclear, chemical, biological or missiles activities or materials. Munitions and missile warheads were analysed to assess what had been put in them previously. Even raw materials, such as uranium ore and maraging steel, could be analysed and its molecular makeup used to identify the supplier.

Paper and ink on documents offered by the Iraqis as proof of their accounting for banned items could be analysed in police forensic laboratories to check whether the document was authentic or not.

The irrefutable evidence gleaned by these technologies, along with the knowledge gained from Iraq's former suppliers, gave the inspectors the information necessary to conduct interrogations at such a detailed level that they broke down the Iraqi cover stories.

There was little Iraq could do in the face of such technological expertise except to try to modify its cover stories to explain the results. Certainly, it was eager to learn the technical limitations of the technology so that it could plan its countermeasures around it. For example, the Iraqis claim proudly that, during the Gulf War, they knew exactly when the US military satellites would be overhead looking for the mobile SCUD launchers; just before the overpass they called a halt to all activity to cover up the launchers. Had they been able to discover the capabilities of UNSCOM's new sensoring technologies, they would undoubtedly have planned their illegal and deception activities around them.

The net result of this process was that UNSCOM analysts became more expert than their counterparts in national intelligence services. At UNSCOM they had access to more raw information because the commission was at the centre of a spider's web of data exchanges. They also had a better understanding of the technologies used by Iraq in its weapons programmes. The result was that UNSCOM was now better placed to assess the relevance of any individual scrap of information than the national agencies. Thus, over time, the nature of the information given to UNSCOM changed. At first, governments had provided only assessments, not raw data, expecting UNSCOM to act on their assessments. Once UNSCOM's own assessment capability was in place, however, Rolf Ekéus was less willing to take such assessments at face value and demanded the underlying information on which they were based. UNSCOM then received sanitised data that had already been screened for quality and declassified by governments. Finally, once UNSCOM's ability to assess the reliability of intelligence and to place it in context had been fully established, it started to receive raw, unscreened information. UNSCOM was no longer a beggar, but a fount of knowledge.

The Fifth Stage: Monitoring

The fifth stage was to be monitoring – that is, the tagging of key items of equipment and the video monitoring of their usage so that

UNSCOM inspectors could be certain that no dual-use item in Iraq was used for rebuilding banned weapons.

The ceasefire resolution had explicitly required Iraq to accept monitoring of its dual-purpose capabilities. UNSCOM and the IAEA had spent the summer of 1991 drawing up details of how this should be done. On 11 October 1991 the Security Council adopted the plans for monitoring Iraq. The plans were effective immediately and Iraq was required to provide comprehensive declarations of all its dual-purpose capabilities in each of the four weapons categories within thirty days.

The date of 10 November 1991 came and went without any such declarations. The Security Council demanded to know Iraq's reasons for failing to comply.

CHAPTER 8

A 'Dangerous Precedent':
The Plans for Monitoring

'The greater the power, the more dangerous the abuse.'
EDMUND BURKE

'A desperate disease requires a dangerous remedy.'
GUY FAWKES

The ceasefire resolution called upon UNSCOM to draw up a plan for the future ongoing monitoring and verification of Iraq's compliance with its undertaking not to use, develop, construct or acquire any of the items associated with the acquisition, manufacture, maintenance, testing or repair of nuclear, chemical or biological weapons or long-range ballistic missiles.

Originally, before UNSCOM had even been created and hence before it could submit its plans, the UN had intended such targeted and specific monitoring and verification of Iraq to be short-lived. Once it was reintegrated into the international community, the special measures created for Iraq would give way to the existing international agreements covering these weapons systems: the Safeguards Agreement operated by the IAEA under the Non-Proliferation Treaty; the Chemical Weapons Convention, overseen by the Technical Secretariat of the soon-to-be-formed Organisation for the Prohibition of Chemical Weapons; and the new verification provisions of the Biological Weapons Convention that were being considered at the time the ceasefire resolution was adopted. It appears that no one considered who might monitor

Iraq's missile activities in the future: no international body with that responsibility existed and there were no plans to create one.

The events of the summer of 1991 had changed virtually everyone's view on this. *Pro forma* monitoring was no longer on the agenda. People – not least the Kuwaitis and Iranians, who had both recently suffered from Iraqi adventurism – were seriously concerned that Iraq intended to rebuild its missiles and chemical weapons, even its nuclear weapons, as soon as it could get rid of or fool the inspectors. The 'ongoing monitoring and verification' regime, therefore, had to be more stringent than any of the international verification regimes – those were agreements between civilised countries that had voluntarily waived the option to acquire the banned weapons and hence could be assumed to be acting in good faith and seeking to prove that good faith to the world. Iraq was a most unwilling and deceitful partner in the disarmament effort and its response to monitoring could be assumed to be equally questionable.

The IAEA, drafting the plan in Vienna, insulated from the strength of feeling in New York, had produced something that reflected the original intent rather than the new reality. UNSCOM's plan, in stark contrast, was an extraordinary document, giving the Special Commission powers that no UN agency had ever before enjoyed. It was impossible to allow these two plans to proceed together. The IAEA's plan was modified to bring it more into line with UNSCOM's.

I still have my original copy of UNSCOM's plan. The margins are dotted with the comments I made as I read it for the first time. I had thought that I knew about the new-style, ultra-intrusive arms control verification regimes. During my two years in Geneva with the Conference on Disarmament I had sat in the British seat in the negotiations to ban chemical weapons. I had introduced the concept of a special protocol to be attached to the convention on how 'challenge inspections' – the convention's no-notice inspections – should be conducted. I had written the conference paper submitted by the UK which contained the full text of such a protocol as the UK would like to see it. This was the first paper submitted at the conference proposing language for the protocol. At the time I thought that the provisions detailed in that paper were very intrusive. And I had considered myself to be in the vanguard of those who sought to introduce the most demanding verification regimes.

At one point my comments in the margins of UNSCOM's plan are reduced to a very large exclamation mark, followed by the single word – 'WOW'. What had prompted this amazement was the realisation that the plan called for Iraq to:

> Provide to the Special Commission full, complete, correct and timely information on any additional activities, sites, facilities, material or other items that the Commission may designate for provision of information on a regular basis ...
>
> Provide to the Special Commission, fully, completely, and promptly, any additional information or clarification that the Commission may request and respond fully, completely and promptly to any questions or requests from the Special Commission.

Next to this last phrase, 'any questions or requests', I had written 'with no justification?' My thought at the time was not that UNSCOM should justify its questions to Iraq – Iraq would simply abuse any right to justifications to avoid providing information. Rather, my thinking was that UNSCOM should, if called to account by the Security Council, be able and required to justify the questions asked in relation to its mandate. There appeared to be no linkage in the plan between the questions that Iraq was required to answer and the mandate of the Special Commission.

My amazement at the extraordinary powers given to the Special Commission by the Security Council was clearly matched by the disbelief and anger felt by Iraqi officials when they read the same passages. The next document I saw was Iraq's response to the adoption of the plans for monitoring and verification, contained in a letter from the Iraqi Foreign Minister, Ahmed Hussein, to the President of the Security Council.

In the letter Hussein presents his 'observations ... on the resolution and on the Secretary-General's plan'. He starts off brazenly, stating that 'Iraq has met all of its obligations under [the ceasefire] resolution'. He notes that 'with the exception of the two teams led by the United States intelligence agent David Kay, all the inspection teams issued statements and reports that called attention to the fact that the Iraqi authorities had cooperated with them'. He then goes on to say that, 'Given the cooperation shown by my country ... it might be supposed that the Security Council would take the anticipated step of lifting the unjust economic embargo and discontinuing the other arbitrary measures taken against Iraq.'

He then lays into the plan:

The Plan entrusts the task of monitoring these activities to standing bodies that enjoy absolute powers, thereby placing Iraq, in practice, under the permanent tutelage of the Special Commission ... and leaves ... Iraq a permanent hostage in the hands of one or two influential States in the Security Council ... [there are] examples of unlawful features and of arbitrariness in the ... Plan ...

The Plan accords the Special Commission absolute powers to designate for inspection any site, facility, activity, material or other item ... and demands that Iraq shall accept unconditionally the inspection of any site, facility, activity, material or other item ... We ask ourselves whether it is possible for the powers of the Special Commission and its inspection teams to have such a degree of generality and such an absolute character. Why is there no reference to whatever it is that brings the rights accorded to the Special Commission into congruence with its mandate? ...

If it is the intention that the Plan should be imposed by force under threat of Chapter VII, then why does it demand co-operation of Iraq? ... when will the implementation of the Plan, with all its arbitrary demands, be completed? ... the Plan ... requires surveillance ... on a continuous basis for an unspecified period of time ... with unlimited powers.

The crux of Iraq's objections are to be found on the sixth page of this seven-page diatribe:

it becomes clear to us that the Plan was drawn up in this way deliberately and intentionally so as to enable anyone what-soever to direct accusations against Iraq of non-cooperation with the United Nations and failure to fulfil its international obligations and, consequently, permit the continued imposi-tions of the economic embargo against the people of Iraq and use it to threaten armed aggression at any moment.

While this interpretation is incorrect in ascribing any such intentions to the drafters, it is not so far from the truth in regard to their effect. Iraq had been found in repeated breach of its obligations and had been threatened repeatedly with military action. But the fault lay with Iraq for its refusal to give up its banned weapons, not with the Council's 'wilful and abusive misinterpretation of Iraq's obligations'. Perhaps this letter was in fact a statement of Iraq's intention not to comply with the ceasefire's terms?

The tail of the letter contains the sting – the outright rejection of the plan as 'a gross intervention in [Iraq's] internal affairs ... incompatible with the letter and the spirit of the United Nations Charter, the norms of international law and international and humanitarian pacts and covenants ...' The letter concludes that the plan 'constitutes a dangerous precedent, causing the gravest damage to the credibility of the United Nations in its funda-mental role in the protection of the independence and territorial sovereignty of Member States.'

This last comment is perhaps the most revealing. The first sub-paragraph of the First Article of the United Nations Charter, entitled 'Purposes and Principles', states the aim of the United Nations 'to maintain international peace and security and, to that end: take effective collective measures for the prevention and removal of threats to the peace and for the suppression of acts of aggression or other breaches of the peace ...'

This difference of interpretation of the UN Charter shows to what extent Iraq was a pariah in November 1991. It chose to interpret the Charter as a means of protecting itself from the consequences of its own aggression against Kuwait. All fifteen members of the Security Council, including Iraq's erstwhile friend Yemen, chose to interpret the Charter as a means of prevention and removal of threats to the peace – represented by Iraq's possession of weapons of mass destruction and long-range missiles – and to act unanimously and collectively against Iraq to that end, acting under Chapter VII of the Charter, which authorises the use of force to maintain or restore international peace and security.

That said, the concept behind the plan was not extraordinary. In fact, it was firmly based on the new directions being adopted in voluntary arms control agreements around the world. Many of its provisions were adaptations of the draft Chemical Weapons Convention, which itself had borrowed heavily from the Russo-American bilateral treaties (such as INF and START) and from NATO–Warsaw Pact arrangements (such as the CFE inspections which dealt with limitations on conventional armed forces in the European theatre).

The principles were simple. Certain materials and equipment can be used either to make banned weapons (be it nuclear bombs, biological agents or missile guidance and control systems) or to make perfectly legitimate civil or military items (such as fuel rods for nuclear power reactors, vaccines against nasty diseases, navigational systems for battle tanks). These items are called dual-use or dual-purpose items in arms control speak. To assure themselves of the good intentions of the other parties to arms control agreements, states want to be sure that all dual-use items, whether imported or made locally, are used only for legitimate means and are not diverted for illegal weapons programmes.

The measures used to provide these assurances are many. Accounts are kept of inventories and consumption of key materials. If legitimate use accounts for every last gram of a material, then you can be assured that none has been diverted for illegal use. This is the principle behind the IAEA Safeguards – the agency tries to account for all the uranium and plutonium generated for peaceful purposes, thereby assuring states that none of it is being diverted for clandestine nuclear bomb-making. In fact, accounting systems are never able to account for 100 per cent of a material, so this approach is less useful for materials that are used in massive quantities for legitimate purposes. In such cases, a 1 per cent accounting error could mean that thousands of tonnes of the material are 'missing' – unaccounted for – and so no meaningful level of assurance is achieved. Thus accounting methods need to be supplemented by other means.

Tamper-proof tags and seals are used to label or seal key items of equipment. Tags are useful for two reasons. First, if inspectors find an untagged item of dual-use equipment, the host state has to explain why a controlled item was not declared. Second, if a tagged item turns up at a different place, the inspectors will want to know why. Particularly, they will want to know to what new use the equipment is being put.

Seals are designed so that, once they are broken, like Humpty Dumpty, they cannot be put back together again. They also have several other uses. The aim is to place the seal in such a position that any unauthorised action with the equipment will break it. Thus, correctly placed, seals can be used to detect movement of the equipment from one location to another, reconfiguration of the equipment (for example, by switching pipe connections in a chemical reaction vessel so that different chemicals are fed in to make different end products), or even access to control panels for resetting the parameters, such as pressure or temperature, under which reactions take place.

For production plants using gases or liquids, flow meters (appropriately sealed so that any tampering with the meter will be detected) can be installed to record the quantities of each chemical that flows through the meter; these record information that will tell inspectors what was produced, when and in what quantities.

Closed-circuit television, time-lapse video cameras, or even twenty-four-hour video cameras can be installed in key production areas to monitor visually the use to which equipment is put. These cameras can be linked to motion or other sensors so that they only operate when something is happening. Such sensors can vastly reduce the manpower required to review the recorded tapes. Cameras can be remote-controlled or even linked by telephone line or satellite link to a remote monitoring centre. Video cameras can provide both real-time monitoring and a time-series record of what has happened at a facility in the past.

Various sensors can be installed to monitor continuously for the presence of certain chemicals or radioactive substances. These can even be wired to trigger an alarm at a remote monitoring centre, or to start the monitoring cameras rolling. They can be set up at any stage in the production process, from the loading bay and warehouses in which raw materials are stored, through to the warehouses from which the end product is dispatched. Sensors can also be used to monitor effluent and waste products from the production process – waste products can often be used to confirm what has actually been produced.

Samples can also be taken of the air, water, soil, dust, grease, filters, raw materials, intermediary materials, effluents and end-products for off-site analysis, again to confirm that only declared items are being produced. These samples can be taken either on site or remotely.

Finally, and most importantly, well-trained inspectors can see very quickly what a factory is being used to produce and what it could be adapted to produce. By visiting monitored sites regularly and taking the readings from the various sensors, by talking to the managers and personnel of the factory and getting them to answer highly specific questions and, where necessary, support their answers with production records, the inspectors can gain hard evidence about what the factory has actually produced.

None of these measures on its own is sufficient to ensure that a factory has only been used for legitimate production. Some would argue that you can never be sure of that. But taken together, they do provide adequate assurance in normal circumstances.

What these measures cannot ensure is that the state being inspected is not conducting illegal activities elsewhere in undeclared sites, with undeclared equipment and materials. Therefore, if it is to provide any level of assurance that the country as a whole – rather than a set of declared sites – is not conducting illegal activities, a monitoring system has to be backed up by no-notice inspections of undeclared sites. If a country knows that any of its buildings can be inspected, it will generally be keen to make full declarations about its dual-purpose capabilities. It also means that inspectors can ensure that the monitoring system is comprehensive; they are able to identify factories and equipment that have not been declared but should be monitored.

Without no-notice inspections, a state determined to build banned weapons could cynically join the treaty banning such weapons (both to give other nations a false sense of security and to encourage its enemies to give up the weapons), declare its legitimate activities, welcome the inspectors with smiles and hugs, go through the motions of facilitating thorough inspections of the declared factories, when, in fact, it is all the while quietly building bombs in its secret factories. This would give the cheat a greater advantage over its enemies than if there were no treaty.

No-notice inspections are key to any monitoring or verification activities. Without them, the system is a dangerous sham, creating a false sense of security and allowing the determined cheats to gain an advantage over those who act in good faith.

Iraq's rejection of the plans for ongoing monitoring and verification put UNSCOM in a bind. It needed to start monitoring activities for a number of reasons.

UNSCOM was very concerned that Iraq had dispersed much of the equipment and materials from its banned weapons programmes amongst industrial facilities to hide them from the inspectors. The longer these items remained undetected by UNSCOM, the more effectively Iraq could incorporate them into genuinely legitimate activities, keeping them intact and available for possible later restitution. If Iraq accepted the plan, it would have to declare all its dual-use factories and equipment, giving UNSCOM the locations of tens, possibly hundreds, of new sites to inspect. These inspections would mean that UNSCOM could assess Iraq's full production capabilities and implement measures to ensure that Iraq was unable to use any of the monitored facilities, even if they retained contraband material and equipment, for reactivating the banned weapons programmes. Finally, a full-blown monitoring regime would provide a good deal of new information – such as the names of suppliers – that would almost certainly help UNSCOM to understand more about Iraq's past weapons programmes.

Some members of the Security Council were urging UNSCOM to push on with monitoring activities despite Iraq's objections. Rolf Ekéus and John Scott immediately saw the danger in this approach. Certainly, the longer UNSCOM delayed, the more information might be lost because of Iraq's countermeasures. But to act swiftly might be to mortgage the future for short-term gain. Rolf was concerned that if monitoring were started without Iraq's explicit and formal acceptance and acknowledgement of the terms of the plan, Iraq could at any stage start questioning what could and should be monitored. After all, Iraq's official position was that it accepted the concept of monitoring its compliance with its obligations, as stated in the ceasefire resolution, but that it did not accept the interpretation of that concept as expanded in the plan for ongoing monitoring and verification.

John Scott had two more legalistic, but equally pertinent and practical objections. If Iraq did not acknowledge its obligations under the plan, then it could argue that it was not bound to respect the diplomatic immunities of the inspectors if and when they were operating under the plan, rather than under the ceasefire resolution. If UNSCOM pushed ahead with monitoring activities regardless, Iraq might claim the right to decide whether any UNSCOM activity were ceasefire- or plan-mandated; it would therefore be able to pick and choose which activities could proceed and which questions could be answered – to the detriment of all UNSCOM activities, whether they were related to monitoring or to tracking down the existing weapons capabilities.

John's other concern was that, if UNSCOM pushed ahead without Iraq's acknowledgement, and Iraq initially complied to the extent that the sanctions against it were lifted, Iraq could then at any point put an end to monitoring activities on the grounds that it had never accepted the obligations, that it had voluntarily suffered them as a sign of goodwill, and that it now no longer wished to do so.

Both Rolf Ekéus and John Scott wanted the monitoring activities, once they were started, to be on an absolutely firm legal basis, with no room for doubt over UNSCOM's mandate, powers or immunities, or their duration.

The question was, how could they corner Iraq into acknowledging its obligations?

This was the dilemma that faced UNSCOM when I joined it in January 1992.

CHAPTER 9

New Faces, New Lies: Full, Final and Complete Fairy Tales

'A truth that's told with bad intent
Beats all the lies you can invent.'
WILLIAM BLAKE

'... fables and endless genealogies ...'
1 TIMOTHY:4

16 January 1992. My arrival in New York was not auspicious. The skies were an overcast grey and, although the city was experiencing a mild winter, it felt cold. The taxi driver dropped me off outside 2 Tudor City, part of the gothic-looking apartment complex immediately across First Avenue from the UN headquarters building. I had rented an apartment here from a Jamaican friend, Trevor Edwards. From the moment he laid eyes on me, the cab driver saw a pasty-faced Englishman and dollar signs. He had brought me to Manhattan the long way, along Shore Parkway and Leif Ericson Drive, rather than taking the Mid-Town Tunnel. The meter showed $55 instead of the more normal $35. I cursed my ineptitude in allowing myself to be ripped off, but gave him two bills – a $50 and a $20 – asking for ten back. The cabby palmed the $50, replacing it with a $5, and demanded more money. Fortunately, I had already taken my luggage out of the boot and there was a policeman across the road, sitting in his patrol car sipping a cup of coffee. The suggestion that we talk the matter over with the policemen seemed to convince the cabby that the $5 was

in fact $50. In any case, he left quickly with no further money exchanging hands.

While theft was rarely an issue in the UN weapons inspectors' relations with Iraq, the cabby's sleight of hand was good training for my new job.

The welcome at the UN was warmer. Many of my old friends and colleagues from my days at the Geneva Conference on Disarmament were there. UNSCOM was holding a meeting of intelligence analysts from the US, UK, France, Germany and Russia to help it to review Iraq's declarations about its banned weapons and its dual-purpose capabilities. While I did not know any of these analysts, I did know most of those drafted by UNSCOM: Bryan Barrass from the UK, Jack Ooms from the Netherlands, Marjatta Rautio from Finland and Johan Santesson from Sweden were all in town. In addition, UNSCOM had a few old faces – among them, Nikita Smidovich and Dave Dorn (now one of UNSCOM's nuclear analysts) – from various disarmament delegations in Geneva, as well as Agnes Marcaillou from the UN Secretariat there. Others, like John Gee and Peter von Butler, whom I did not know, knew many of my friends from Geneva. Much as I had tried to escape chemical weapons diplomacy when I left the Foreign Office, intending to go into management consultancy, it was fun to be back with a crowd I knew.

Johan Molander had recruited me to take over his position as Rolf Ekéus's special adviser – essentially his political and strategy adviser. In the interim between my first conversation with Johan and my arrival in New York, Johan had already left and Rolf had temporarily filled this position with a counsellor from the Swedish Mission to the UN, Stefan Noréen. Consequently, my position was now to be 'conceptual thinker' (Rolf's phrase) and press relations officer.

The 'conceptual thinker' component was really to devise a strategy to get Iraq to accept the plans for ongoing monitoring and verification. The press relations bit rapidly expanded to cover all external relations – with the Security Council, governments, the media, academia and the public. When Stefan left, I inherited his tasks too, and so attended all Rolf's strategy meetings.

Because of this central position, I was, over the next four years, co-opted into several *ad hoc* tasks, such as chairing meetings on chemical or biological issues, becoming chief aerial inspector or devising security procedures.

Rolf Ekéus is the master strategist. He had soon recognised that it was essential for UNSCOM to develop an independent analytical capability to protect it against accusations that it was merely a tool of those providing the intelligence. He had seen the importance of publicising what Iraq was doing and had followed a policy of openness with the media, and gave regular briefings to all members of the Security Council, not just its privileged and powerful permanent members. But equally, he needed to be seen by the Iraqis as a credible interlocutor – an unbiased if strict implementer of the mandate. Presentationally, it was necessary to down-play the US influence within UNSCOM and make it clear that all UNSCOM decisions were his, as Executive Chairman of the Special Commission.

He also knew how to operate the machinery of the UN. Manipulation is too strong a word for the way in which he dealt with the Security Council. But Council members were briefed in such a way that they were either wittingly or unwittingly expertly manoeuvred into one course of action – that planned by Rolf Ekéus. What enabled him to get away with this was his obvious dedication to the mandate, the mandate and nothing but the mandate. Equally, nothing less than the full mandate.

With the Iraqis, he had seen the importance of not negotiating. The first sign of compromise, quite apart from destroying the commission's credibility with the US and the UK, would have been exploited relentlessly by the Iraqi authorities to roll back the inspection rights until nothing but a sham was left. Rolf had latched on to the fact that as the Security Council had set the mandate, only the Security Council had the power or competence to amend it. UNSCOM's role was merely to implement this mandate and so it was in no position to enter into any negotiations with Iraq on its scope. His insistence on full compliance was, he told the Iraqis, in their own best interest. If UNSCOM lost its credibility with the US and the UK, both of whom held the power of veto over the lifting of the economic embargo imposed on Iraq, then no favourable report from the commission would be taken seriously by them. Only by maintaining its credibility with the US and the UK, by fulfilling its mandate, could UNSCOM be of any assistance to Iraq. 'Negotiate' and 'compromise' were banned from the inspectors' vocabulary.

Seeing Rolf in operation, I learnt another strategic tool – the use of status or appearance. I am not talking about using status to stroke feeble egos, but rather as a means of power positioning in meetings with Iraq over its non-compliance.

If the Iraqis were to treat him and what he said seriously, he had to be seen as someone they had to deal with, rather than circumventing him each time he said something they did not like. One means of achieving this was to make himself the sole interlocutor in the UN–Iraqi dialogue on disarmament issues. He therefore avoided being drawn into detailed technical issues, leaving that to UNSCOM's true weapons experts; nor did he enter into disputes at the beginning, preferring to send in other colleagues until matters had escalated to a stage where the Security Council had to get involved and support UNSCOM. And, where possible, he liked to be able to speak to the Iraqis not just as Executive Chairman of the Special Commission but also with the full backing and authority of the Security Council.

Things had not reached that stage with the looming crisis over Iraq's rejection of the plan for ongoing monitoring and verification. While Iraq had described the plan as incompatible with the UN Charter, and while the declarations it had made in response to its monitoring obligations were totally inadequate, it had not said that it would not implement the plan. Rolf needed to engineer a sufficiently clear rejection of the plan so that he could take it to the Council. But he did not want to get involved just yet.

The strategy was to put together a 'special mission', led by two members of the Special Commission (two of the officials representing the twenty-one nations at the bi-annual meetings of the commission – UNSCOM's equivalent of a board of governors) to lend it seniority and authority, to seek Iraq's acknowledgement of its obligations under resolutions 707 and 715, both of which it had lambasted (the full disclosures of its past activities to acquire banned weapons required by resolution 707, and the initial declarations of its dual-purpose capabilities required under resolution 715). Despite the successes of the inspections in 1991, UNSCOM and the IAEA were convinced that they still did not know the full story of Iraq's weapons programmes and that Iraq was still systematically hiding evidence and information from them.

This mission was to be led jointly by John Gee, the Australian member of the commission and coordinator of its Chemical and Biological Weapons Group, and Peter von Butler, the German member and coordinator of the Future Compliance Monitoring Group. Also on the team were Nikita Smidovich, to engage the Iraqis on biological weapons issues, Johan Santesson, the chemical weapons expert from Sweden, and Patrice Palanque, a ballistic missiles expert from France. The special mission's objectives were:

> To emphasise to Iraq that its failure to provide the information requested under Security Council resolution 715 (1991) constituted a serious obstacle to the implementation of the monitoring and verification of Iraq's compliance with its obligations under resolutions 687 and 715 (1991) ... to request Iraq to make full, final and complete disclosure of all aspects of its programmes to develop weapons of mass destruction and

Right: *Hans Blix, Director General of the International Atomic Energy Agency (centre), Rolf Ekéus, the first Executive Chairman of UNSCOM (second from right), and Johan Molander, special adviser to Rolf Ekéus (far right), giving a press conference in UN headquarters in New York in 1991* (UN Photo)

Right: *Rolf Ekéus (right) and David Kelly, frequent chief inspector on biological weapons inspections, giving a press conference in UN headquarters in New York in 1991* (UN Photo)

Left: *The author, Tim Trevan, giving a press conference in UN headquarters in New York in 1992* (UN Photo)

Above: *Richard Butler (left) introduces Kofi Annan (UN Secretary-General, centre) to Scott Ritter (veteran UNSCOM inspector) in 1998* (UN Photo)

Below: *Kofi Annan and Iraqi deputy prime minister Tariq Aziz in February 1998* (Popperfoto/Reuters)

Above: *UNSCOM's Baghdad Monitoring and Verification Centre, housed on the top floor* (UN Photo: H. Arvidsson)

Left: *The CH53g transport helicopter, operated on UNSCOM's behalf by the German Bundeswehr in 1991–6* (UN Photo: H. Arvidsson)

Right: *The C-160 transport aircraft operated by the German Luftwaffe to transport UNSCOM's personnel and equipment from its field office in Bahrain into Iraq* (UN Photo)

Above: *UNSCOM's U2 high-altitude surveillance aircraft, operated under UNSCOM's command by the US Air Force* (UN Photo)

Below: *An UNSCOM Bell helicopter armed with ground-penetrating radar during a hunt for buried SCUD missiles in 1993* (UN Photo: H. Arvidsson)

Above: *A SCUD-type missile about to be destroyed after being disarmed* (UN Photo: H. Arvidsson)

Below: *Inspectors examining a chemical warhead for a SCUD-type missile* (UN Photo: H. Arvidsson)

Left: *Dredging a canal for missile components as part of the verification process for items unilaterally destroyed by Iraq* (UN Photo: H. Arvidsson)

Below: *The supergun prior to destruction by UNSCOM in 1991* (UN Photo: H. Arvidsson)

Above: *Part of a destroyed calutron, eventually shown to David Kay's nuclear inspection team in August 1991. Calutrons are used in the electromagnetic isotope separation process for producing weapons-grade uranium for a nuclear bomb* (UN Photo)

Below: *Unfilled chemical bombs awaiting destruction* (UN Photo: H. Arvidsson)

Left: *Unfilled chemical bombs after being cut and crushed* (UN Photo: H. Arvidsson)

Below: *The Chemical Destruction Group at Khamissiyah in southern Iraq, preparing 122mm sarin-filled rockets for destruction. Sarin is a nerve agent that blocks the body's vital functions* (UN Photo: H. Arvidsson)

Left: *The pit in which Iraq's 122mm sarin-filled rockets were destroyed in spring 1992* (UN Photo: H. Arvidsson)

ballistic missiles with a range greater than 150 kilometres, as required under Security Council resolution 707 (1991).

In preparation for this special mission intelligence assessment meetings were held in New York on 22 and 23 January 1992. Each of the five countries briefing at these meetings had very different assessments of Iraq's biological weapons programme: some believed that the Iraqi programme was small, had not progressed far, had essentially been destroyed in the Gulf War and had not been renewed; others believed that disclosures to date had barely scratched the surface of an extensive weapons production programme that might well have succeeded in producing and deploying biological weapons.

However, there was consensus on one thing – that Iraq's history of deceit made it unlikely that it had come clean on the full extent of the biological programme. Particular concerns related to:

- **The overall organisation of the programme.** It was claimed to have been operated under the umbrella of the Technical Research Centre (TRC), whose director-general, Dr Ahmed Murtada, was also the director of the Badr Scientific Establishment, a munitions design and production factory. This linkage implied an intention to weaponise the biological warfare agents that were researched and/or made at the Salman Pak site. The analysts wanted much more information on the original orders given to set up the biological programme, feasibility studies undertaken, planning documents, progress reports, budgets, organisational charts, lines of commands, and relationships to other factories and institutes such as al Hakam.
- **The activities declared to have been conducted at Salman Pak.** Iraq stated that this was simply basic research conducted with no particular end-purpose in mind. The analysts worried that, on the contrary, the few documents handed over by Iraq indicated an advanced programme. The papers on temperature

stabilisation and aerosolisation of biological agents, the choice of agents and the organisational links to Hussein Kamal Hassan at the Ministry of Industry and Military Industrialisation (MIMI), a known weapons-producer, all indicated a clear intent to weaponise. Analysts wanted full site plans of the Salman Pak site as it had been before Iraq destroyed some of the buildings there and explanations of why those buildings were destroyed and what activities had taken place in them. They wanted details of the past activities at Salman Pak and its links with al Hakam, the Technical and Scientific Materials Import Division (TSMID), the Serum and Vaccine Institute and the Iraqi Ministry of Defence. They wanted to know why there were primate cages at Salman Pak and what they had been used for. And they wanted Iraq to account for its research into bacteria that it had imported but had yet to declare, including the current location of the undeclared bacteria.

- **The true purpose of the al Hakam site.** The analysts believed that the security measures and military defences around the site were inconsistent with Iraq's story that the site was and always had been a civilian single-cell protein production factory. They suspected that the high speed with which it was constructed, without planning permission, and the fact that the Iraqi Council of Ministers were kept informed about its operations indicated that it was in fact a high-priority Iraqi military project. The analysts wanted documentation on this site, including original architect's plans, planning approvals, progress reports and the like. They wanted a clear explanation of its links with other sites, such as Taji, a large military camp which had transferred equipment to al Hakam in 1990.

- **The personalities involved.** The analysts were not convinced that Dr Rihab Taha was the most senior official involved. Dr Nissar al Hindawi, the director of al Hakam, was considered a more likely technical leader of the programme. The link to Hussein Kamal Hassan, cousin and son-in-law of Saddam Hussein who had since been promoted to Minister of Defence, indicated that he was the political and military authority behind the project. If that were the case, it was further indication that the programme was much more than a basic let's-find-out-what-we-can research project.

While they were up in New York for the seminar, the US analysts took the opportunity to brief Rolf Ekéus and the UNSCOM experts on photographs showing that Iraq still had SCUD missiles. These photographs had been taken in the summer of 1991, but after the UNSCOM inspections to destroy Iraq's remaining stocks of SCUDs. They proved that Iraq had been lying when it made a declaration of only fifty-two SCUD missiles in May 1991, and was still lying in maintaining that story. This knowledge bolstered UNSCOM's missiles experts in the upcoming discussions with the Iraqis: they now had something solid against which to judge the Iraqi statements. They were proof positive that Iraq had sought to preserve a major part of its SCUD missile force. The significance of these SCUDs went far beyond their ability to deliver quantities of high explosive inaccurately over a long range. They could deliver, or merely threaten to deliver, any chemical or biological weapons that Iraq had withheld from the UN. Given UNSCOM's suspicions that Iraq had an entire biological weapons programme that it had not declared, a missing missile force and an undeclared biological weapons programme was a combination that could not be ignored.

The special mission was not a success, in the sense that it did not obtain the acknowledgements from Iraq that Rolf Ekéus wanted; nor did it get the 'full, final and complete disclosures'. It did, however, give Rolf the ammunition with which to go to the Security Council.

It arrived in Baghdad on Monday 27 January 1992. That evening the mission had a meeting with the Minister of State at the

Iraqi Foreign Ministry, Mohammed al Sahaf. In response to the request for an acknowledgement by Iraq of its obligations under resolutions 707 and 715, Sahaf stated that Iraq's views on resolution 715 were as set out in his Foreign Minister's letter to the President of the Security Council – the diatribe of 19 November 1991. He added that Iraq had nothing to add to that letter and, furthermore, had disclosed all the information required of it under the ceasefire resolution and so, by definition, as required under resolutions 715 and 707. He magnanimously offered to have experts answer specific questions that the inspectors might have, and technical meetings were arranged for the following two days.

General Amer Rasheed al Ubeidi headed up the technical talks on the Iraqi side. He had recently been promoted to head up the Military Industrialisation Corporation (MIC), the successor to the MIMI that had been responsible under Hussein Kamal Hassan for Iraq's chemical, biological and missile programmes. General Amer and Hussein Kamal Hassan had a close relationship. Amer had been an Under-Secretary at MIMI when Hussein married Saddam Hussein's daughter and so catapulted himself into senior public life. He had shown Hussein the ropes only to see him promoted over him as head of MIMI.

General Amer Rasheed opened the discussions by stating that Iraq was prepared to answer all questions except two: questions on operational issues, such as the deployment of weapons or their past use, and questions on foreign suppliers for its past weapons programmes would not be answered.

This was a bad start. In order to be sure that all Iraq's banned capabilities had been destroyed, UNSCOM would have to know what Iraq had produced or imported, and then how it had all been disposed of, whether through operational use or through the destruction activities of UNSCOM and Iraq after the Gulf War. For example, UNSCOM knew that Iraq had imported 819 SCUD missiles from the Soviet Union. How could it account for all these and assure the Security Council that they had all been destroyed if it did not know how many of them Iraq had used in its war with

Iran or in the Gulf? Similarly, Iraq was known to have used large quantities of chemical weapons in 1983, 1984 and 1987 against Iran, and in 1988 against the Kurds. How could the chemical inspectors conduct a 'material balance' for Iraq's import, production and disposal of relevant chemicals if it was not able to ascertain what quantity of chemicals had been used in war?

Similarly, the news on suppliers was bad. First, in the absence of any honest declarations from Iraq about its past programmes, suppliers were the obvious route to obtain information about Iraq's imports, providing at least some baseline of knowledge from which to conduct a material balance. Secondly, the withholding of supplier names indicated a desire to protect the supplier network and so raised deep concerns that Iraq intended to reactivate those networks as soon as it could.

The special mission made these points forcefully, but General Amer Rasheed replied that operational information would be used against Iraq to assist its enemies. Moreover, Iraq had to maintain its credibility with its suppliers, and therefore had to protect them. However, he was aware that UNSCOM had gained some information on suppliers from other sources and would answer specific questions arising from this information. But Iraq would not volunteer supplier information, nor would it provide information on the identity or nationality of a supplier.

Given Iraq's refusal to discuss operational issues, little progress was made on chemical weapons. Some progress was made on missiles: Iraq admitted that it had unilaterally destroyed ancillary equipment for its ballistic missiles force in the summer of 1991 and buried the scrap in order to hide it from inspectors. According to Amer, Iraq now realised that this action had been a mistake; UNSCOM could now dig up the scrap to verify that the equipment had indeed been destroyed.

The discussions on biological weapons issues did nothing to address the concerns of the analysts. General Amer Rasheed went further than in previous statements about the limited scope of the programme, denying that Iraq had ever said that the results of the 'biological research' (Amer refused to let it be called a 'pro-gramme') could have been used for either offensive or defensive warfare purposes. He insisted that the research had only ever been for defensive purposes and that no Iraqi had ever stated otherwise (despite the record of Dr Murtada's comments). He insisted that inspectors had already received all relevant documentation and that there was nothing more to give or to hide. He insisted that Iraq had not been required to declare its purely defensive research activities, even though the special mission pointed out that the ceasefire resolution explicitly demanded such declarations. And he claimed that the Salman Pak activities had no link with any military organisation – or any other organisation for that matter.

In diplomatic language, the special mission told General Amer Rasheed that they did not believe him.

The upshot of all this was that Iraq refused to acknowledge its obligations under the monitoring plan and the mission informed Iraq that, in the circumstances, it could not allow the re-deployment of any dual-purpose equipment used in the past weapons programmes ('tainted' equipment) for legitimate uses. If UNSCOM could not monitor the equipment to ensure that it was not being used to reinstate Iraq's banned weapons programmes, it would have to be destroyed.

The special mission left Baghdad at 2.30 on the afternoon of Thursday 30 January 1992. That evening, from the UNSCOM field office in the Holiday Inn in Bahrain, it submitted its report to Rolf Ekéus in New York. In terms of generating a stir, the report could not have been better timed.

There is a nine-hour time difference between Bahrain and New York, so the report was on Rolf's desk first thing on Thursday morning. That left the whole day to brief the members of the Security Council.

As part of George Bush's 'New World Order', a summit meeting
of the Security Council at head of state and government level had
long since been arranged for Friday 31 January 1992. That
morning and afternoon Manhattan was traffic chaos. Policemen
lined many of the streets and avenues, blocking some off to traffic.
Sharp shooters took up positions on all the tall buildings around
the UN headquarters. From my office on the thirty-first floor I
could see men in dark blue fatigues clearing the roof terraces of the
Tudor City apartment blocks and other neighbouring buildings.
Mid-Town had come to a halt as long cavalcades – Bush's was, of
course, the longest – converged one after the other on the UN
building.

This was the first time a meeting of this kind had ever been held.
All but two of the fifteen members of the Security Council were
represented by a monarch (the King of Morocco was there), a
president, or a prime minister.* Their principal reason for being in
New York was to discuss how, post-Cold War, the organs of the
UN could best be used to manage the world's problems. In
particular, the US – sponsor of the whole event – was keen to thaw
relations with Russia to ensure that the Security Council was able
to meet the challenges to peace thrown down by tyrants such as
Saddam Hussein.

How, then, could this august assembly fail to react to Iraq's
latest challenge to the authority of Security Council resolutions?

---

* The fifteen were: John Major, Prime Minister of the UK as President of the
Council; Dr Franz Vranitzky, Federal Chancellor of Austria; Wilfried Martens,
Prime Minister of Belgium; Dr Carlos Alberto Wahnon de Carvalho Veiga, Prime
Minister of Cape Verde; Li Peng, Premier of the State Council of China; Dr Rodrigo
Borja-Cevallos, Constitutional President of Ecuador; François Mitterrand,
President of France; Dr Geza Jeszensky, Minister of Foreign Affairs and personal
emissary of the Prime Minister of Hungary; P. V. Narashima Rao, Prime Minister
of India; Kiichi Miyazawa, Prime Minister of Japan; King Hassan II of Morocco;
Boris Yeltsin, President of the Russian Federation; George Bush, President of the
USA; Dr Carlos Andres Perez, President of Venezuela; and Dr Nathan
Shamuyarira, Minister of Foreign Affairs and personal emissary of the President of
Zimbabwe.

Particularly those adopted under Chapter VII of the Charter – those dealing precisely with the issue of maintaining and restoring international peace and security that was the reason for their coming together.

These fifteen leaders condemned Iraq's non-compliance and refusal to acknowledge its obligations and demanded that it should comply forthwith. Perhaps in large part due to the Iraqi situation they also released a statement affirming that 'the proliferation of all weapons of mass destruction constitutes a threat to international peace and security'. They also underlined the need to 'prevent the proliferation in all its aspects of all weapons of mass destruction'. Although India withheld its approval of this part of the statement, it was nevertheless ground-breaking. Translated into layman's terms, it meant that the Council would be justified in authorising military action in reaction to the new acquisition of nuclear, chemical or biological weapons by a state that had not previously possessed such weapons, with the aim of removing the 'threat' – i.e. the weapons in question.

It was time to increase the pressure on Iraq. On 14 February Rolf Ekéus sent a letter to Wissam al Zahawi, adviser to the Iraqi Foreign Minister on UNSCOM issues, informing him that a further ballistic missiles inspection team would be arriving in Baghdad on 21 February to destroy Iraq's ballistic missiles repair and production facilities. But there was a twist.

In an enclosure with the letter, al Zahawi was told that the items to be destroyed fell into two categories: those that had to be destroyed come what may (listed in Annex A of the letter), and those items that might possibly be released for reuse (listed in Annex B). Rolf knew that Iraq wanted to save all the items, but the enclosure went on to state that:

> The Special Commission may authorise such a release only in exceptional cases provided of course that the reuse of the item

will not prejudice in any way the destruction of the missile
capabilities prohibited by resolution 687 (1991). Such a release
could be made only in response to clearly identified civilian
needs of Iraq and will require special arrangements for the reuse
of the item, including appropriate monitoring arrangements
under the plan for future ongoing monitoring and verification
of Iraq's compliance with relevant parts of section C of
resolution 687 (1991) (S/22871/Rev. 1) approved by the
Security Council in its resolution 715 (1991).

Translated: Iraq could only save its beloved missile production and
repair equipment and factories if, and only if, it would accept the
monitoring plan on the UN's terms, not its own.

However, a single-pronged attack would be too simple. At the
same time Rolf Ekéus submitted a written report to the Security
Council on the special mission's failure to obtain Iraqi
acknowledgement of its obligations under the monitoring plan or
to get the 'full, final and complete disclosures' of its past
programmes. The standard procedure was that such reports had
to be submitted through the office of the Secretary-General. They
also had to be translated into the other five official languages of the
UN (French, Spanish, Russian, Chinese and Arabic). The report
was made available on 18 February 1992.

On 19 February the President of the Security Council, who
for the month of February was Ambassador Thomas Pickering
of the US – UNSCOM's greatest supporter – called a closed-
door meeting of the Council to consider this report. The
meeting had been orchestrated ahead of time. Rolf Ekéus had a
packed suit-carrier in his office, as did his legal adviser (John
Scott), his special adviser (Stefan Noréen), his secretary (Olivia
Platon) and I.

The meeting ended with agreement on a statement, drafted the
previous day, that Pickering should make on behalf of the

members of the Council. The essence of it was that, as planned by Rolf Ekéus all along:

> the Council supports the decision of the Secretary-General to dispatch a special mission headed by the Executive Chairman of the Special Commission to visit Iraq immediately to meet and discuss with the highest levels of the Iraqi Government for the purpose of securing the unconditional agreement by Iraq to implement all its relevant obligations under resolutions 687 (1991), 707 (1991) and 715 (1991). The mission should stress the serious consequences if such agreement to implement is not forthcoming.

Rolf Ekéus would now be going to Iraq with the full weight of the Security Council behind him and with the Council asking him to deliver an implicit threat (of 'serious consequences') should Iraq not tell him what he wanted to hear.

The mission arrived in Bahrain in the evening of 20 February, having flown non-stop since the Council's meeting. There, we met up with Christopher Holland's team of ballistic missiles experts who were coming to Iraq to destroy the list of production and repair facilities listed in the letter of 14 February to Wissam al Zahawi.

Upon arrival in Baghdad the next day, a preparatory meeting was set up for the first evening, Friday 21 February, in the Ministry of Foreign Affairs, just around the corner from our hotel. When the time came, we were whisked into a gaggle of government hospitality cars, accompanied by out-riders, and driven at high speed the two hundred or so yards between the hotel and the Ministry, rushing through the red lights at the junction of the two roads. The guards on the Ministry gate had to lower the dragons' teeth set across the entrance to shred the tyres of unwelcome visitors. The cars pulled up under an arch by the main door and we all poured out into the lobby – a high-ceilinged, white marble room. The lifts were slow to come, and too small to accommodate us all comfortably. Being squashed in a lift is not the best way to prepare for a high stakes meeting.

Bursting out of the lift when it arrived at the second floor, we were guided down a narrow corridor to an oblong corner room with a large table which seated forty. The Iraqi delegation was lined up to meet us: the Minister of State, Mohammed al Sahaf, headed up the Iraqi side, flanked by General Amer Rasheed al Ubeidi and Dr Human Abdul Khaliq (director of the IAEC). Wissam al Zahawi was also there. Mohammed al Sahaf was in his dark green battle fatigues and army beret – a signal, I was later to learn, for a more confrontational meeting; civilian suits indicated that a more civil meeting lay ahead.

Rolf Ekéus opened the meeting by conveying the essence of the message from the Council: it recognised that some progress had been made, but much remained to be done; it expressed grave concern at Iraq's rejection of the monitoring plan, which the Council viewed as a continuing material breach of Iraq's obligations; and it urged Iraq to make 'full, final and complete disclosures' of its past programmes. It stressed the fact that the monitoring plan was an integral part of the ceasefire and that Iraq's unconditional agreement to implement all its obligations was a *sine qua non* for the lifting of sanctions against it; that the mission's purpose was to obtain Iraq's unconditional acceptance of all its obligations; that there would be serious consequences if Iraq did not, which included the destruction of more of Iraq's dual-use production facilities than might otherwise be the case; and that the mission was required to report the results of its visit to the Council immediately upon its return.

Mohammed al Sahaf's response was that Iraq had nothing further to declare. He denied that Iraq had rejected resolution 715 (and so the monitoring plan): it had problems with its general provisions and could not accept all of them. It had explained its position on this. Iraq would look at practical ways of implementing the monitoring of its compliance with the obligation in the ceasefire resolution not to reacquire banned weapons. Sahaf was trying to have it both ways: he said that he did not reject the plan, but then talked about an alternative way of monitoring compliance, implying that this should be negotiated with Iraq to obtain its approval.

General Amer Rasheed admitted that Iraq might not have presented its declarations in the most coherent manner, and offered to resubmit them, if that would help. Rolf Ekéus noted that further clarification of Iraq's past activities would be welcome; however, that was not the purpose of this trip, which was to gain Iraq's acceptance of the monitoring plan and its other obligations.

The next day a second meeting was set up with Iraq's Deputy Prime Minister, Tariq Aziz. Aziz reiterated the position set out by Mohammed al Sahaf the night before – Iraq had not rejected its monitoring obligations under the ceasefire resolution, but merely stated its position on resolution 715. There should be linkage, he said, between Iraqi cooperation and the lifting of sanctions. He even suggested that the lifting of sanctions should be linked only with the destruction of weapons, not with the monitoring of Iraq's industry. He also questioned the objective behind UNSCOM's decision to destroy dual-use items, asking whether it was aiming to 'return Iraq to the pre-industrial age', as James Baker had threatened to do during his meeting with Aziz just before the air war. Rolf Ekéus explained that monitoring, by its very nature, would be non-destructive but that, if Iraq refused to acknowledge and implement the monitoring plan, then more items would have to be destroyed.

The meeting ended with both sides agreeing to exchange position papers listing their concerns, in the hope that a common way forward might be found.

The meeting resumed at 7 p.m. that same day in the Ministry of Foreign Affairs, with Mohammed al Sahaf leading the Iraqi side. By now, Wissam Zahawi had dropped out of the discussions and his place was taken by Dr Riyadh al Qaysi, a former legal counsel to the Iraqi Foreign Ministry and now the director of its Department of International Organisations.

We had spent the afternoon preparing our position paper. It laid out the assurances required if UNSCOM were to continue with its work. Come the evening meeting, it transpired that the Iraqi side had not done its homework and had no position paper to hand over.

Mohammed al Sahaf, upon reading our paper, pointed out that Iraq's priorities were different. There should be assurances that compliance would lead to the lifting of sanctions and there should be a final list of the equipment to be destroyed (with the implication that nothing new could be added to this, regardless of subsequent inspection findings). General Amer Rasheed picked up on this idea of drawing a line under the investigation into Iraq's past activities. He suggested a seminar in New York or Baghdad to deal 'once and for all' with past issues. If issues still remained outstanding, they should be appended to the seminar's report. But that would be it – there would be no revisiting of these issues.

Rolf Ekéus replied that sanctions would be lifted once Iraq was in full compliance. Monitoring was an ongoing exercise: it did not have to be completed; the arrangements for it merely had to be 'up and running'. He pointed out that no list of outstanding issues could be 'once and for all', because if new information came to light, it would have to be addressed.

Another meeting was to be held once the Iraqi position paper was ready – first thing in the morning, we were told. We hung around in the hotel all day waiting for it to be delivered. It finally arrived at 3.30, and a meeting was set for 6.30.

In this final meeting Mohammed al Sahaf let it be known that Tariq Aziz intended to visit New York in March to present the Iraqi case to the Security Council. It soon became apparent that, in view of this, no concessions were going to be offered to Rolf Ekéus: the meeting would go nowhere. Sahaf suggested drafting a joint statement; Rolf rejected this on the grounds that, without Iraqi acknowledgement of the monitoring plan and its other obligations, such a statement would be meaningless. If Iraq's

intention was to use Tariq Aziz's visit to announce its acknowledgement of these obligations, its interests would be better served
by doing so during the present meeting. Sahaf ignored this.
Instead, it was agreed that both the UNSCOM and the Iraqi
position papers would be included in the mission's report to the
Security Council.

The mission left Baghdad the next day, 24 February. That evening
in Bahrain we wrote up our report to the Security Council. The
next two days were spent in meetings with Bahraini ministers and
officials and the team boarded the plane home shortly after
midnight on the 26th, arriving in New York at about 2 p.m. By
four o'clock Rolf Ekéus was with the Security Council.

He had bad news to report, not only on Iraq's failure to respond
to the Council's demands, but also on its refusal to proceed with
the destruction of ballistic missile repair and production facilities.
Christopher Holland's team had been prevented from going ahead
with their destruction plans.

Iraq compounded the matter by ill-advisedly sending a letter to
Rolf Ekéus about the destruction issue. This letter stated that:

it is not ... clear and neither can it be justified that a particular
machine or piece of equipment should be destroyed when it can
be modified and altered in such a way as to become permanently incapable of producing any weapons or any prohibited items and will remain useful for non-prohibited
activities.

It suggested that:

the matter should be considered within the general picture of
the totality of the substantive matters which the high-level Iraqi
delegation will present to the Security Council and to you
during the month of March for the purposes of ... preserving

Iraq's industrial capabilities for civilian and non-prohibited purposes.

It was a clumsy attempt to drive a wedge between the Council and its own subsidiary, UNSCOM, which the Council had set up specifically to implement the disarmament provisions of the ceasefire. It sought to make the Council the arbiter in technical decisions where Iraq disliked UNSCOM's stance. The letter also served further to highlight Iraq's non-compliance, saving Rolf Ekéus from having to make the case.

The Council reacted angrily. It issued another statement on 28 February, agreeing with Rolf Ekéus's assessment that Iraq was refusing to give its unconditional agreement to implement all its obligations. It deplored Iraq's failure to provide 'full, final and complete disclosures' and its failure to comply with the monitoring plan. It concluded that Iraq continued to be in material breach of its obligations. It further condemned Iraq's failure, within the specified period, to start destruction of its ballistic missile repair and production factories. It described Iraq's plea to save these factories, contained in Sahaf's letter to Rolf Ekéus, as unacceptable and a further material breach of the ceasefire. The Council demanded that Iraq immediately convey both its acknowledgement of its obligations and its willingness to comply with UNSCOM's decisions on what should be destroyed. It invited the Iraqi government to explain itself in a Council meeting in early March.

Meanwhile, the IAEA were drawing up their plans for the destruction of the al Atheer complex.

In preparation for the Council meeting with Aziz, Rolf Ekéus had obtained US approval to show the satellite pictures of the undeclared SCUD missiles to Council members should it prove necessary. In the event, it did not.

Tariq Aziz's trip to New York was a disaster for Iraq. He arrived on 8 March and spent the first few days ignoring UNSCOM, in an attempt to undermine its authority and circumvent its decisions on destruction. His efforts focused on the non-aligned members of the Council. His failure to win over friends there must have come as a rude shock. They had been carefully briefed by Rolf Ekéus before Aziz's arrival, and instead of meekly accepting his diatribes against UNSCOM and the US, they subjected him to searching questions about Iraq's behaviour.

In the Council meetings on 11 and 12 March Aziz infuriated Council members by lecturing them on the Council's obligations to Iraq and by brushing aside questions posed to him. He gave the Council none of the assurances it sought and refused to agree to the destruction of the missile factories. His performance left most Council members convinced that Iraq intended to rebuild its banned weapons programmes and left them more determined than ever that it should be stopped. In its concluding statement, the Council strengthened the position of UNSCOM, reaffirming its status as a subsidiary organ of the Council and confirming that UNSCOM's decisions on technical matters, including what should be destroyed, were final and not subject to appeal in the Council.

When Tariq Aziz and Rolf Ekéus finally met privately, Rolf confronted Aziz with the fact that UNSCOM had incontrovertible evidence that the Iraqis had had more operational SCUD missiles after the Gulf War than they had yet admitted, indicating that the evidence was photographic. Aziz wanted to see the photographs and, when Rolf refused, asked how many missiles were in them. Again Rolf demurred, mindful that if he told Aziz how many were in the picture, only that number of additional SCUDs would be declared. Aziz promised to look into it.

* * *

On Friday 13 March 1992 Rolf Ekéus and General Amer Rasheed were leading their respective sides in technical discussions, trying to resolve some of the outstanding issues about Iraq's weapons programmes. I had been sitting in the meetings most of the day in the windowless conference room on the thirty-first floor of the UN building, then part of the Centre for Disarmament Affairs. After hours of talks the room was hot, smelly and airless. When Olivia Platon came in and gave me a note saying that I had hundreds of calls from the press to answer, I gratefully left the room. It soon became apparent that most journalists simply wanted to know if the talks would continue into Saturday – whether they could plan pleasant weekends or whether they would have to hang around waiting for our talks to finish.

One of the journalists happened to mention to me that a second US carrier fleet was sailing up the Gulf. He thought it was a routine relief of one fleet by another, but asked me if there was anything more significant behind it. I pointed him in the direction of the Pentagon spokesman, Peter Williams, if he wanted that question answered.

Innocently, at about 4.30 p.m. I wandered back into the conference room to ask Rolf whether the meetings were scheduled to end that evening or not. Discussions were still going on. Rolf Ekéus hated being talked to in the middle of discussions, so I wrote him a note and told him about the US fleet movements. I stood there waiting for a reply.

General Amer Rasheed stopped talking and asked me what I wanted to know. I looked at Rolf, but he kept quiet. After deliberating for a moment, I said that the press wanted to know whether the talks would continue past the evening, given current developments. Amer demanded to know what developments. Still Rolf did not intervene, so I told Amer about the extra US aircraft carriers sailing up the Gulf.

The effect was extraordinary. Amer got into a huddle with his team. Rolf told me he would get back to me, so I left the room. Within five minutes the entire UNSCOM team had started to return to their offices. The meeting had broken up with Amer claiming he could no longer concentrate. I had my answer, and the journalists had their weekend.

CHAPTER 10

X Marks the Spot

'PEACE, n. In international affairs, a period of
cheating between two periods of fighting.'
AMBROSE BIERCE, THE DEVIL'S DICTIONARY

Definition of a compromise: 'An agreement
between two men to do what both agree is wrong.'
LORD EDWARD CECIL

The warships were to remain in the area for some time. Despite
General Amer Rasheed's shocked reaction to the news of another
fleet arriving within striking distance of Baghdad, even now Iraq
did not meekly bow to the diktats of the Council. Instead, it gave
with one hand whilst taking away with the other.

Tariq Aziz and General Amer had recognised the mood of the
Council on the matter of the missing SCUD missiles. Faced with
unknown incontrovertible evidence that they had lied about the
missiles, they had to come up with a story that the Council would
believe, whether it was true or not. While in New York, General
Amer Rasheed had also tried to find out from UNSCOM how
many missiles it knew about but, like Rolf Ekéus, the experts did
not fall for that. In fact, UNSCOM had proof of only three SCUDs.
But General Amer, still ignorant of this, opted to reveal that they
had indeed hidden eighty-nine SCUDs and three training rounds
from the first inspections. However, he claimed Iraq had destroyed
these missiles in August 1991 and buried them, and various other

missile components, near the large military encampment at Taji. Yet more key missile components, including the all-important gyroscopes needed for the guidance and control systems that Iraq was unable to make, were dumped in a canal.

Ironically, the U2 overflights that Iraq so strongly objected to came to its defence here. The international community was highly sceptical about this new story and wondered whether Iraq had only recently destroyed these items. In fact, the photographic record from the U2 flights showed that the earth at the burial sites was disturbed in the period specified, providing strong collaboration for the Iraqis.

They now tried to use their 'honesty' in revealing this new information as leverage in the discussions. They argued that a new chapter of openness and trust should be established between the UN and Iraq, under which most of the missile production machinery should be converted to civilian use and therefore spared. More amazingly, they told the IAEA that the al Atheer facility – which the documents seized during the parking-lot stand-off proved had been built solely for the engineering of nuclear bombs – was in fact a civilian site and should be left intact. However, they were still refusing to allow monitoring to go ahead as planned by the UN.

Iraq was warned by senior members of the Security Council that, one way or another, the facilities and equipment would be destroyed. The standing joke amongst the frustrated inspectors sent to oversee the destruction was that, if the Iraqis continued to refuse to allow them to get on with their work, at least they could paint large Xs on each of the roofs of the buildings containing banned equipment.

However, UNSCOM agreed to review each and every missile item with a view to avoiding destruction where possible. But it also insisted that, in the absence of an Iraqi agreement to monitoring under the required terms, this would apply only to those items that could be irreversibly converted to civilian use. UNSCOM could not risk allowing Iraq to reconvert items to missile production if it did not have the means to assure itself, on an ongoing basis, of the purely legitimate use of that equipment.

However, the same generous approach could not be applied to the al Atheer facility. The IAEA delivered its final verdict on 25 March 1992: everything at al Atheer had to be destroyed. The eleventh IAEA inspection team performed the task in April 1992. And, in the event, Iraq was unable to come up with convincing plans for the irreversible conversion of its missile production equipment. Consequently, most of this was also destroyed during the course of three inspections between March and May 1992. The first of these teams was also able to dig up the items Iraq claimed to have destroyed unilaterally in August 1991 and corroborate its account.

Two important principles had been established in this crisis which would help UNSCOM in the future. First, the Security Council had decided that UNSCOM was the sole arbiter of all technical interpretations of what needed to be done in order to rid Iraq of its weapons of mass destruction. Second, and more significantly in terms of precedent, it had decided that no distinction should be made between the Council and UNSCOM – UNSCOM was merely a subsidiary part of the Council, to which a specific mandate had been given. Iraq would not be allowed to drive a wedge between the Council and UNSCOM by asking the Council to arbitrate between UNSCOM's decisions and Iraq's objections. UNSCOM was to be the sole interlocutor with Iraq on technical aspects of its disarmament. In practice, by continuing to send Rolf Ekéus to Iraq with messages from the Council, UNSCOM was also made the *de facto* sole interlocutor with Iraq on the political aspects until crises reached the stage where enforcement action was needed from the Council. Loss of this privileged position, in October 1997, was to spell the beginning of the end of UNSCOM as an effective disarmament body.

* * *

Iraq now went onto the diplomatic offensive. UNSCOM started to dispose of Iraq's ageing chemical weapons at the Khamissiyah Ammunition Depot in February 1992, destroying some 463 122mm rockets there. These sarin-filled rockets were too dangerous to move to the main destruction facility being built at Muthanna. Destruction of the large remaining stocks at Muthanna, which included bulk quantities of mustard agent, sarin and tabun and precursor chemicals, started in June 1992. With all its major nuclear and missile facilities now dismantled, with the destruction of its (declared) chemical weapons and stocks of chemical warfare agents well under way, Iraq started to argue that it was in full compliance with the ceasefire resolution and that sanctions should be lifted.

While this was not the first time it had claimed full compliance, it could now do so with more conviction. It could now point to the fact that its declared weapons capabilities in each area had been destroyed or, in the case of the chemical weapons, were being destroyed with its full cooperation. While the US, the UK, France and Russia all shared UNSCOM's concerns that Iraq had not yet made full declarations about its past weapons programmes, and all agreed that sanctions could not be lifted until Iraq accepted monitoring under the UN's terms, UNSCOM was on the PR defensive for the first time.

Everyone could understand why Iraq's weapons had to be destroyed. With some persuading, most could understand the need to destroy Iraq's weapons production facilities. It became harder to convince non-aligned nations of the need to maintain sanctions against Iraq because Iraq was refusing to allow the UN to monitor its legitimate defence and civil industries. And the issue of whether Iraq was lying or not, in the absence of hard proof to the contrary, became a matter of Iraq's word against UNSCOM's. Incontrovertible proof of deceit was now hard to come by – the easy evidence had already been gathered. And while UNSCOM's credibility was higher than Iraq's, the longer inspections failed to produce proof of cheating, the more sympathy Iraq could attract for its disingenuous contention that 'UNSCOM has conducted x number of inspections, has been allowed to go anywhere, and has found nothing, therefore nothing remains to be found.'

UNSCOM needed to find a way to uncover Iraq's deceit, particularly in relation to the biological weapons programme – the area of gravest concern and the area where UNSCOM had the least to go on. Three new avenues of investigation might provide evidence: tracking down Iraq's suppliers; searching for biological weapons; and searching for documents reporting the progress of the biological weapons programme, similar to the ones found about the nuclear programme.

Suppliers

Iraq was not only refusing to provide UNSCOM with the names of its suppliers, it was actively trying to block UNSCOM's own efforts to find them. UNSCOM inspectors had, from the outset, noted the details of suppliers from the serial number plates on pieces of equipment and from labels on containers of materials such as feedstock and chemicals. Noting this, the Iraqis then systematically removed all identifying marks from the equipment and all labels from containers. UNSCOM had been able to track down the suppliers of bacterial cell cultures and of several items of equipment, including fermenters, aerosol generators and milling machines. Inspectors had photographed these items, along with containers of complex growth media which clearly showed the names of the suppliers. These items had all been supplied to Iraq by the same organisations that handled imports for Iraq's chemical weapons programme, providing strong circumstantial evidence that they were intended for a biological weapons programme.

However, this did not prove that Iraq was lying about its biological weapons production. UNSCOM further knew that, if it could start monitoring Iraq's dual-purpose biotech industry and research centres, it would find the names of more suppliers, some of which might have sold items to Iraq's biological weapons programme. But Iraq was blocking efforts to start the monitoring. Reluctantly, UNSCOM's biological weapons analysts had to conclude that this avenue of investigation was unlikely to provide any breakthroughs until Iraq accepted full monitoring. In response, UNSCOM's strategists were thinking up ways to precipitate a crisis which might force Iraqi acceptance of monitoring.

Biological Munitions

Meanwhile, efforts continued on the second track – looking for biological munitions. The first chemical weapons inspection had inventoried all the declared chemical munitions. UNSCOM had demanded declarations on the markings used on munitions to distinguish chemical and biological munitions from conventional ones. In May 1991, before the first inspection, Iraq had informed UNSCOM that there were four types of unconventional weapons fills with four concomitant markings – 'yellow, black, red and white' being markings for 'mustard, sarin, tabun and CS' respectively. All these are chemical weapons. Mustard is a blister agent, sarin and tabun are nerve agents, CS is tear gas. The first inspection team did indeed find munitions with each of these markings, but none of the black ones found by inspectors had ever been filled. This was not a total surprise. Tabun was the first nerve agent produced by Iraq, but quality control had been a problem and the munitions filled with tabun had a very short shelf-life. To get around this problem, Iraq had in the 1980s resorted to producing sarin and tabun for immediate use, not for storage. In addition, the suspicion was that Iraq had abandoned its sarin and tabun programmes because of these problems and had decided to concentrate instead on its newer VX nerve agent programme.

Thus the Iraqi account of the munitions markings was accepted. With hindsight, perhaps it should not have been, and perhaps UNSCOM should have insisted on seeing 'black' munitions which had previously been filled, even if they had since been decommissioned, so that it could analyse the shells for traces of the agent used as the fill. If such a shell had been provided in the summer of 1991, it would almost certainly have uncovered the Iraqi lie. 'Black', it was learnt in 1995, was in fact the marking for anthrax-filled munitions.

Having failed to find biological munitions amongst the declared Iraqi stocks, UNSCOM went about looking for undeclared stocks. During the latter half of 1991 it had used its U2 aircraft to identify undeclared munitions storage bunkers throughout Iraq that might have been used to store either chemical or biological weapons. There are several distinguishing characteristics of bunkers designed specifically for such weapons. Generally, given the special protective measures that those looking after such munitions are required to take, they are stored separately from conventional high-explosive munitions. Also, special air-conditioning and cooling arrangements are required to store biological weapons optimally – high temperatures will kill living bacteria and break down toxins. Also, one would expect such bunkers to have additional security features.

On the basis of its aerial photographs, UNSCOM identified several sites with the above 'fingerprint'. A joint chemical and biological inspection was launched in November 1991. Two sites that had 'twelve-frame' bunkers were visited – Salman Pak, the declared site of Iraq's 'military biological research', and Karbala. The team noted that the isolation and air conditioning of the bunkers at Salman Pak, in addition to their proximity to known biological research, made them highly suspicious, but no direct evidence of biological weapons was found; nor was there any evidence that these bunkers had been used for biological weapons storage in the past. The story was similar at Karbala, where the team also noted the especially high security around the bunkers. Iraq admitted that these bunkers had been used in the mid-1980s for storing mustard agent, proving their suitability for storing biological and chemical weapons, but again, no direct evidence of biological weapons was found there.

S-shaped bunkers were found at military airfields at Mosul, Kirkuk and K-2 (in the middle of nowhere, some 185 kilometres due west of Baghdad). The design of these bunkers was unusual for high explosives. They were also found singly, rather than grouped together, and isolated from all other structures at the airfields, strengthening the conviction that they were designed and built for chemical or biological munitions. However, there was again no evidence that either chemical or biological weapons had been stored there.

The same inspection team had visited the Mosul sugar factory which, Iraq had admitted to the first chemical inspection team, had been used to store chemical bomb-making equipment. The team found equipment for making 250- and 500-gauge bombs – both known to have been used for delivering chemical weapons. They did not find any equipment for making other munitions Iraq had declared as being for chemical weapons – the DB-2 and R-400 bombs, and the 122mm rockets used for delivering sarin nerve gas tactically. The team also found some undeclared SCUD carriers. The team marked all the equipment it found, told the missile inspectors about the SCUD carriers, and demanded that Iraq bring all the bomb-making equipment together for destruction, including that equipment not found at the Mosul sugar factory.

Archives

For UNSCOM, Iraq's archives were the crown jewels. Iraq denied having any, categorically stating that all relevant documentation about its past programmes had been destroyed on the express instructions of Saddam Hussein. UNSCOM had been cajoling Iraq to hand it over to speed up the inspection process and hence the lifting of sanctions. Indeed, during one meeting in Baghdad in

1992, when Rolf Ekéus was pressing General Amer Rasheed on this point, Amer responded by stating that he had disseminated the President's order to destroy all relevant items in 1991. He dramatically dictated to me a full account of the action he claimed to have taken and then signed it, as one would an affidavit.

The argument was this. Iraq had already lied and cheated so much that UNSCOM could no longer take any assurances about past programmes at face value – each statement had to be supported by corroborating evidence. Furthermore, proving a negative – that Iraq had no banned weapons – was scientifically impossible. Therefore, the problem had to be turned on its head. UNSCOM had to prove a positive – that it had accounted for all Iraq's past banned capabilities.

However, UNSCOM had no means of knowing the full extent of Iraq's past programmes and, in the absence of such knowledge, it was difficult even to start a process of accounting for the programmes – without knowing what needed to be accounted for, how could UNSCOM do a balanced account, a material balance? If Iraq handed over the archives, UNSCOM could quickly ascertain, through cross-referencing and forensic analysis of paper and ink, whether the archives were full and authentic. By archives, UNSCOM meant the full set of orders to start each of the programmes, feasibility reports, progress reports, laboratory notebooks and logs, production logs, delivery journals, inventory books, organisational charts showing lines of command and reporting, and all the other scraps of paper that accumulate during such large-scale projects. Having established the comprehensiveness and authenticity of the archives, UNSCOM would be able to determine, with a very high degree of confidence, the full extent of each of the programmes. From this baseline, proper accounting could start.

Catch 22. If Iraq admitted to having such archives, it would be the strongest proof yet that it intended to rebuild its banned programmes. Why else retain, at the cost of $25 million lost oil revenues a day, documents that were otherwise useless? Hence

Iraq's cover story that it had destroyed every last scrap of documentary evidence relevant to the past programmes. However, UNSCOM was convinced that the archives existed – in large part because it seemed likely that Iraq did indeed intend to resume its banned weapons programmes at the earliest possible date – as soon as UNSCOM was off its case, or sooner if Iraq could find a way to cheat without being caught red-handed. This conviction was reinforced as, each time Iraq needed to corroborate its latest account of its past actions, it was able to produce the relevant document (despite the party line that all documents had been destroyed).

Iraq explained this apparent anomaly by claiming either that just a few scraps had survived the general purge, or that the individual official responsible for that part of the project had been so distraught at the prospect of his life's work being destroyed that he had spirited away key logs and documents for safe-keeping in his own home. Naturally, UNSCOM did not buy this, labelling it yet another of Iraq's 'full, final and complete fairy tales'. If there were only scraps of the original documentation left, statistically they would not cover all the incidents for which Iraq had to find supporting documentary evidence. And if the officials involved had so blatantly disobeyed Saddam Hussein's express orders on a matter of vital national interest, one would not expect to see those same officials surviving the admission of guilt, let alone staying on in key positions.

In June 1992 UNSCOM was working on three separate approaches to try to break the impasse. First, it decided to follow up on the investigation of Iraq's munitions. Second, it sought to increase the pressure on Iraq by using its helicopters not just for transport but also for aerial monitoring of declared sites. And thirdly, it was planning another document search. On the basis of intelligence from two different supporting governments, it had identified a building in which the archives of Iraq's past weapons programmes, including the denied biological weapons programme, might be stored.

On 26 June 1992 the second joint chemical and biological weapons inspection team arrived in Baghdad to destroy all the bomb-making equipment and to look for new bunkers that might be storing biological or chemical weapons. Its mission was simple and uncontroversial enough. But all that was to change in the next few days. A subsequent addition to its planned activities would result in the lives of its inspectors being threatened, and bring the UN and Iraq back to the brink of another war.

CHAPTER 11

Palaces and Death Threats

'The world must be made safe for democracy ...
The right is more precious than peace.'

WOODROW WILSON,
from his speech to Congress of 2 April 1917

Bastille Day. On the afternoon of 14 July 1992 I found myself in an anomalous situation. I was at the Thirty-Eighth Street heli-pad in Mid-Town Manhattan, waiting to catch the helicopter to JFK Airport – the first leg in my trip to Baghdad. I was going there to become chief aerial inspector, in charge of the team conducting aerial monitoring of Iraqi sites from UNSCOM's helicopters based at the al Rasheed airfield on the outskirts of Baghdad. Yet this short trip from Manhattan to JFK was my first ever helicopter flight.

I was somewhat nervous – not about the impending hop to JFK, but about dealing with the Iraqis. It is one thing to be an adviser in high-stakes negotiations. It is quite another when the buck stops with you as the leader of an inspection.

There were only eight of us in the waiting room. One, a short, good-looking man, was talking animatedly into a mobile phone in Belgian-accented French. I recognised the accent, as Alice Hecht, UNSCOM's administrator, was a francophone Belgian. The man looked so good in his denim jeans and shirt that I took him for a male model. But the face looked familiar. It was only at JFK, as the mini-bus carrying us to our various terminals pulled up outside

British Airways, that I realised who he was. He told me in his unmistakable Belgian-accented English to 'Take it easy, guy' as I tugged rather too energetically at my luggage to free it from under the pile. Jean-Claude Van Damme.

It struck me that my life with UNSCOM would be very much easier if I was in one of his films, where all that is needed for good to prevail is a heart of gold and skill at kick-boxing.

By May 1992 everyone in UNSCOM was becoming worried that Iraq's charm offensive might lead to the lifting of sanctions before the ongoing monitoring and verification regime was put in place. If this were to happen, Iraq would surely never agree to monitoring of any kind. Everyone was convinced that, without such monitoring of Iraq's imports and indigenous dual-purpose industry, it could easily rebuild its banned weapons programmes. Iraq would be able to hide the illegal imports of materials and machines for these programmes in amongst the very large volumes of items required to repair its war damage. Iraq had to be pressured into accepting the plans for monitoring. There was a sense of urgency.

Nikita Smidovich came up with a clever plan for applying such pressure and, in doing so, providing a useful way of monitoring Iraq's most dual-purpose sites without formally prejudicing UNSCOM's position that monitoring could only be implemented with Iraq's formal acceptance of the plan. He proposed using the UNSCOM helicopters operated by the German Bundeswehr to make regular flights over the sites UNSCOM knew would have to be monitored, such as Salman Pak, and photograph them from low altitude.

Such a photographic record would enable the UNSCOM analysts in New York to identify any changes to the sites over time that might indicate that Iraq was rebuilding or reconfiguring them for weapons-building purposes. As an 'aerial inspection' could encompass several sites per sortie at no notice, this was a time- and cost-effective way of monitoring the sites of most concern. It would also deter Iraq from converting such sites; it would have to build entirely new facilities if it wanted to restore banned programmes – building activity that should be picked up by the regular U2 aerial surveillance. Finally, UNSCOM knew that this activity would annoy the Iraqis. They hated any high-profile UN presence. It implied that they were under UN tutelage, which undermined the standing of the regime in the eyes of its subjects. The sight of helicopters flying at low altitudes over Iraq with their UN insignia clearly visible was bound to create a stir.

Rolf Ekéus had learnt from earlier crises with Iraq that the Security Council found it easier to threaten enforcement actions against it if there were a tangible obstruction of UNSCOM's activities, such as blocking access or refusing to allow items to be destroyed. Its refusal to acknowledge its monitoring obligations in accordance with the UN's plan was somewhat too abstract a concept to go to war over. However, if Iraq refused to allow the helicopters to fly on 'aerial inspection' missions, there would be a tangible issue for the Council to address. A serious confrontation might force Iraq to accept the monitoring plan.

This point was not lost on the permanent members of the Security Council when Rolf Ekéus informed them of his plans to start aerial inspections. Any proposed UNSCOM activity that might result in Iraqi defiance was put before Council members, particularly those upon whom military action would fall; they could then decide how best to support UNSCOM. The US was keen for UNSCOM to go ahead with this plan. George Bush was seeking re-election and was sensitive to allegations that, while he might have won the war with Iraq, he had lost the peace. Thus any activity to hold Iraq to the terms of the ceasefire was welcome.

The UK and France, however, were against the idea. Immediately after the war was over, the Council, sensitive to criticisms that sanctions were hurting the innocent in Iraq, not the regime, had put together an aid programme to distribute food, medicines and other essentials. Saddam Hussein hated this, as it implied that his regime could not look after its own people, and because he saw the UN's insistence that UN personnel distribute the aid directly to the Iraqi people as an affront to his authority. Worse still, he feared his own subjects would also spot this affront and see him as weak. Furthermore, with the UN distributing food fairly within Iraq, he was denied the opportunity of punishing those who opposed him (by withholding deliveries) and rewarding his supporters.

The Memorandum of Understanding (MoU) between the UN and Iraq, under which this aid was distributed, had come up for renewal, but Saddam was refusing to sign an extension. The UK and France, in early June 1992, did not want Rolf Ekéus to initiate helicopter inspections until this other difficulty was resolved. They thought that Iraq would take it as a provocation, which would scupper the chances of renewing the MoU. Rolf Ekéus pushed ahead with his plans, setting aside the British and French objections.

In the event, Iraq did not kick up a stink. In early June 1992 Nikita Smidovich led a team to Iraq to explain the concept to General Amer Rasheed and to agree procedures for the aerial inspections. Flights started in the latter half of June. This demonstrates how second-guessing can lead to missed opportunities. The MoU was never renewed. Had Rolf heeded the Anglo-French advice, UNSCOM would never have flown its helicopters in inspection mode and would have been denied a key monitoring tool – all just in case the action upset Iraq.

Of course, part of the purpose of the aerial inspections had been to upset Iraq. That was why I was sent to Baghdad in early July – not because of my non-existent expertise in aerial inspections or helicopter-flying, but to be a calm political head to deal immediately and firmly with expected Iraqi objections to the manner in which the inspections were conducted. The plan was to rotate in experienced staff from UNSCOM New York on three-week stints as chief aerial inspector until all the teething problems expected from the Iraqis over these aerial inspections were resolved. Each of us had a full-time job to do in New York and so could not afford to be away too long. I was to be the second chief aerial inspector (the first was the head of the IAU, Geoff St John) and there would be three more after me before it was decided that the aerial inspections had become accepted by the Iraqis as part of the routine.

In this regard, UNSCOM had been right to expect an Iraqi reaction. The Iraqi minders started out by demanding to be told the night before the aerial inspection the location of the site to be inspected. That would, of course, have made the inspections pointless, based as they were on the concept of 'no notice'. Iraq insisted that it needed to know where the helicopter would be so that it could ensure that its air defence batteries did not shoot it down.

This was an entirely spurious argument. Each UNSCOM helicopter flight was accompanied by at least one, usually two, Iraqi Army helicopters. An air defence system that cannot distinguish between friend and foe is an entirely useless one – it would keep the defender's own air force grounded whenever enemy aircraft invaded.

Before he left Baghdad, Nikita Smidovich had proposed a solution and General Amer Rasheed agreed. UNSCOM would inform the Iraqi minders the night before that there would be an aerial inspection, but would not say where it would be. A network of air corridors was plotted out on a map of Iraq, which would be used by the helicopters for coming and going. Upon arrival at the al Rasheed airfield on the morning of the inspection – that is, within thirty minutes of take-off – the chief aerial inspector would inform the Iraqi minders which of the air corridors would be used. Thus Iraq could, if it really wanted to, shut down various components of its air defence system (I seriously doubt it ever did). The Iraqi minders and the escorting Iraqi helicopters were not informed of the final destination until the aircraft were less than five minutes' flying time away. This was too little notice for Iraq to shut down any banned activities or hide any banned items before the team's arrival. And any frantic activity would be seen and photographed from the air.

This half-hour notice did not give away much about where the inspection was headed as there were only four major corridors and hundreds of potential target sites per corridor. Of course, the Iraqi minders could have phoned any clandestine weapons factory near the selected corridor, instructing the site manager to clean up the factory before the helicopter got there, but Iraq would have to have closed down one quarter of all its factories each day. Thus, at the very least, the aerial inspections would be a massive disruption to any clandestine Iraqi attempt to rebuild a weapons building capacity.

However, there were still plenty of problems for me to deal with once I arrived. The Iraqi minders on board the UNSCOM helicopter tried to determine which sites were relevant to the ceasefire resolution, and hence stop us from photographing others. At the end of one inspection the chief minder tried to confiscate the film. I, and the other inspectors, had to remind him that UNSCOM, not Iraq, was the arbiter of what was relevant and what was not, and that we had the right to photograph anything we thought necessary. The minders also constantly tried – in vain – to get the inspectors and the helicopter pilots to give them more than the five minutes' notice, and to limit the time spent over the site.

In short, while the aerial inspections turned out to be a very useful interim monitoring measure until full-blown implementation of the plan was accepted by Iraq, and while they certainly irritated the Iraqis, they failed to precipitate the crisis that might force them to agree to the plan.

Crises with Iraq, however, were not in short supply that summer. Arriving in Baghdad on 16 July to take up my position, I walked straight into what was to become one of UNSCOM's biggest crises. As I stepped off the C-160 at Habbaniyah air base, I was greeted by Rachel Davies, a member of Karen Jansen's inspection team and shortly to succeed Geoff St John as head of the IAU. The team had been denied access to a building in search of Iraq's weapons archives. Rachel, and other members of her team, were being rotated out of Iraq as new inspectors, now led by Mark Silver, came in to continue the vigil outside the Ministry of Agriculture.

Karen's team had been put together in April and May to continue the search for chemical and biological munitions and to destroy bomb-making equipment found during her previous mission in December 1991. It had been carrying out this task since 26 June 1992 without incident.

Meanwhile, UNSCOM had received time-sensitive information from two European countries indicating that a building in central Baghdad, not far from the UNSCOM offices in the Sheraton Hotel, was being used to store Iraq's archives from its past weapons programmes. A team was hastily put together to exploit this information. On Friday 3 July 1992 Rolf Ekéus's signature was sought on two items: a letter to the Iraqi ambassador to the UN, informing him of an impending inspection and the fact that Mark Silver would be chief inspector; and a NIS – notification of inspection – giving the precise map coordinates of the site to be inspected, for Mark Silver to take with him to Iraq and give to the Iraqi minders only upon arrival at the inspection site, in line with standard procedure for conducting no-notice inspections.

That Friday, like all Fridays, was hectic. Olivia Platon frequently complained that the Operations officers always left getting letters typed up for Rolf's signature either until the day he was due to leave the office on a trip or until Friday afternoon. Sure enough, there was a large bundle of letters for typing and signature. There was also a farewell party for a departing UNSCOM colleague. Olivia Platon herself was on holiday in the Philippines, attending the wedding of one of her daughters: her stand-in was under pressure. The letter to the Iraqi ambassador was sent out that Friday afternoon, but when Mark Silver, who was leaving for Bahrain the next morning, came up to Rolf's office at around 6.30 to get his NIS, he found that it too had been sent to the Iraqi ambassador.

Mark Silver and Agnes Marcaillou tried to retrieve the letter, but it was too late. The no-notice inspection had been blown. All that could be done was to make sure that the Iraqis had very little time to prepare. Mark changed the flights so that his team would reach Iraq on 5 July. The team members assembled in Bahrain on the evening of Saturday 4 July. They flew into Iraq the next morning, leaving Bahrain at 4.30 a.m. They went straight from Habbaniyah air base to the inspection site, meeting up with Karen Jansen's team. In the meantime, Karen had been sent an urgent and confidential message: she and her team were to inspect the Ministry of Agriculture on 5 July; a twenty-four-hour duty roster had been drawn up in UNSCOM's New York office.

Karen's team arrived outside the building at 9.30 a.m. on Sunday 5 July 1992. Mark Silver presented the NIS and moved towards the door, but the chief Iraqi minder stopped him, informing him that the building was the Ministry of Agriculture and Irrigation and that the inspection would not be allowed. Karen informed him that there were no exceptions to their right to access. If the team were prevented from gaining access Iraq would be in breach of its obligations and she would have to inform Rolf Ekéus in New York. The Iraqi minder remained adamant.

Karen used the satellite telephone to call New York and inform them of the situation: it was 1.30 a.m. there. Within the hour she was told to maintain a watch on all the exits from the building, until such time as access was permitted or the team was placed in danger, and to prevent the Iraqis from removing any items. By noon Baghdad time the Iraqi propaganda machine was farcically alleging that UNSCOM had taken hostage 250 employees of the Ministry of Agriculture. UNSCOM had not prevented anyone from entering or leaving the building, only from taking documents away. It was six o'clock in New York that Sunday morning (2 p.m.

in Baghdad) when Rolf Ekéus called the President of the Security
Council to inform him of the stand-off and a crisis team was called
together in Rolf's office.

By four o'clock Baghdad time the local TV was there to capture
the 'release' of the elderly and pregnant hostages that the Iraqi
minders claimed to have negotiated. No such negotiations had
taken place, because no one had ever been prevented from leaving
the building. The Iraqis made a show of taking meals in to the
remaining 200 'hostages'.

By 6 p.m. the staging of the protests had become absurd. A truck
arrived at the rear of the building and the Iraqi minders helped to
unload its cargo of eggs, fruit and vegetables. At 6.15 a number of
buses with government registration plates turned up. The govern-
ment-supplied women who stepped out began a 'spontaneous'
angry demonstration against UNSCOM, throwing the govern-
ment-supplied eggs, fruit and vegetables at the worried-looking
government officials, who made ostentatious shows of protecting
the UNSCOM inspectors. Then the press cameras stopped rolling,
the shouting and screaming stopped, the minders relaxed and
started laughing and joking with the crowd which had, moments
previously, been 'hostile'.

At a quarter past midnight on the morning of Monday 6 July the
Iraqis got bored and gave up pretending to be hostages. The
remaining employees in the Ministry went home. By roughly this
time (five o'clock on Sunday afternoon in New York), all the five
permanent members of the Security Council had been informed, as
had the director of the Secretary-General's office.

On the morning of Monday 6 July Rolf Ekéus held meetings
with the President of the Security Council, the ambassador of Cape
Verde, who went by the hopeful name of Jesus. Out of this meeting
came a strong draft presidential statement condemning Iraq's
material breach of its obligations – obligations that were 'a
condition precedent to the establishment of a formal ceasefire
between Iraq and Kuwait and the member states cooperating with
Kuwait'. It warned that 'continuation of such a material breach

will give rise to serious consequences' – code for military enforcement action. The Council met in open session that afternoon to consider the situation and to adopt the draft statement. To everyone's astonishment, there, in front of the world, US Ambassador Perkins demanded the deletion of the words 'serious consequences' from the resolution, signalling that the US was not prepared to take military action to back up UNSCOM. Perkins had clearly not told his British counterpart, Sir David Hannay, who was sitting next to him, about his intentions. Someone who had attended the meeting later told me that Sir David very nearly fell off his seat.

The weakened statement still referred to a material breach, and still demanded that Iraq should give UNSCOM access, but it did not threaten any action if Iraq failed to comply. The significance of this was lost neither on Rolf Ekéus, who was furious with the Americans, nor on the Iraqis. It was clear that Iraq saw this as a big chance, with no threat of retaliation, to establish some ground rules that would limit UNSCOM's activities and access. There was a spring in the step of all the Iraqis we dealt with.

On the face of it, nothing much happened in the remainder of that week. The inspectors had organised themselves into shifts so that at all times there were at least three inspectors in each of the three UNSCOM vehicles outside the exits to the Ministry. Each day small, half-hearted demonstrations were organised against the inspectors, but these were short-lived. Behind the scenes, Rolf Ekéus was lobbying hard with the members of the Security Council, especially the US, to shore up support for UNSCOM and reverse the immense damage caused by Perkins's actions.

The following weekend things started to hot up in Baghdad. On Saturday 11 July there was a staged show of self-immolation. A young Iraqi poured petrol over himself while his friend stood by with a blanket, ready to douse the flames. Things did not go according to plan. There were so many journalists crowding round the flaming man that the blanket-holder could not get through the crush quickly enough and his friend was burnt more severely than he had intended. The next day the demonstrations started to get larger and longer. The Iraqi minders and security personnel 'protecting' the inspectors allowed those demonstrators who would provide good photo opportunities through to harass the inspectors.

Back at the UNSCOM offices, there were sudden systematic attacks on UNSCOM property. UNSCOM vehicles had their wheels slashed, aerials ripped off, and windows smashed. Graffiti was sprayed all over them. This vandalism continued throughout the week, to the point where UNSCOM no longer had sufficient vehicles with four good tyres to mount inspections. The field office in Bahrain had to send for new stocks of tyres and windscreens.

On Thursday 16 July, the day I arrived in Baghdad, tensions really rocketed. A UN guard accompanying those distributing UN aid within Iraq was killed in the northern Iraqi town of Dohuk. That night, at 3.30 a.m., all UNSCOM personnel, in bed in their hotels, received death-threat telephone calls. Mine threatened to fire-bomb my room. The next day the team outside the Ministry was informed by letter that it should leave by six that evening or offensive actions would be taken. Meanwhile, things back at the UNSCOM office and the hotel were no better. I bumped into a visibly shaken Roger Hill, one of the most level-headed and calm inspectors, and an UNSCOM veteran of almost a year. Someone had just tried to run him over as he crossed from the Sheraton Hotel, which housed the UNSCOM office, to the Palestine Hotel, where both he and I were staying. The demonstrations outside both the Ministry and the two hotels were now almost permanent. All UNSCOM personnel seeking to cross the road between the two were pelted with fruit and stones. Even inside the hotels there was no respite, with threats made and one person even trying to spray-paint one of the inspectors.

That afternoon Rolf Ekéus arrived in Baghdad to try to resolve the situation. He did not have what he wanted from the Council – a strongly worded threat of serious consequences if Iraq did not comply – and the Iraqis knew it. The absence of a threat afforded them a rare opportunity to show outright defiance.

The first meeting was held at nine the next morning with the Iraqi Minister of State for Foreign Affairs, Mohammed al Sahaf. Dr Human Abdul Khaliq, General Amer Rasheed al Ubeidi and Nizar Hamdoon (then Under-Secretary at the Iraqi Foreign Ministry, later to replace al Anbari as Iraqi ambassador to the UN in New York) also attended. Rolf was accompanied by me, Doug Englund (UNSCOM chief of Operations) and Alice Hecht. The Iraqi side were hostile, and Sahaf walked out at 10.45. The meeting continued until noon but made no progress. A second meeting was held at nine that evening, with the same participants. Sahaf remained uncompromising. The essence of the Iraqi argument was that resolutions adopted under Chapter VII of the UN Charter (i.e. all those relating to UNSCOM's mandate and Iraq's obligations to disarm) could not be invoked to impose against the will of a member state conditions that infringed upon its national sovereignty. Consequently, Iraq did not accept that the ceasefire resolution gave UNSCOM the right to go anywhere in Iraq, only to those places which were relevant to the weapons programmes – implying that Iraq should nominate the sites. Sahaf claimed that the Ministry of Agriculture contained nothing of relevance; to allow access would set a dangerous precedent on access to all central ministry buildings and other politically sensitive sites (code for presidential residences), which would be unacceptable infringements of Iraq's sovereignty.

Rolf Ekéus responded that Iraq's legal reasoning was false – Chapter VII resolutions could impose obligations that infringed national sovereignty. The terms of the ceasefire were therefore fully binding on Iraq, whether they were imposed against its will or not. UNSCOM had wide-ranging rights, but used them with the greatest of circumspection and only for the purposes of fulfilling its mandate to disarm Iraq. Where possible, UNSCOM would respect Iraq's legitimate concerns over sovereignty and national security. But UNSCOM had good information that the building in question did contain items of relevance to banned weapons and so, whether that information proved to be accurate or not, it had to inspect the building.

After the meeting we returned to the Rasheed Hotel, where Rolf was staying. There was more bad news. Off-duty air crew who had been using the swimming pool that day had very nearly been seriously injured by glass bottles thrown by Iraqis from floors overlooking the pool. The other incidents of vandalism and intimidation were continuing, and the demonstrations were getting larger and more aggressive.

The next day two more meetings were held. At 9.30 a.m. the same UNSCOM team met the Iraqi Foreign Minister, Ahmed Hussein, with Nizar Hamdoon in attendance. The minister launched into an extraordinary diatribe against Rolf Ekéus, accusing him of being personally responsible for the malnutrition of Iraqi children and their deaths through lack of medication. He even went so far as to say that Iraqi mothers, when they wanted to get their children to stop misbehaving, would threaten them with Rolf Ekéus, the Bogey Man.

Fortunately, this was a short meeting, ending at eleven o'clock. At 11.30 we met Tariq Aziz, the Deputy Prime Minister. Now, at last, UNSCOM heard Iraq's terms. He suggested that the Ministry could be inspected by a team of experts made up entirely of nationals of the neutral and non-aligned countries in the Security Council, provided that it operated entirely independently of UNSCOM. This inspection, he insisted, should not be conducted under the auspices of the various UN resolutions. In addition, the team should not report to UNSCOM but independently and directly to the Security Council.

Rolf Ekéus immediately told him that this was unacceptable to UNSCOM and was bound to be unacceptable to the Security Council. After all, Aziz had only recently tried the same ploy in his visit to the Council in March, when his idea of engaging a third operational party to replace UNSCOM or of the Council itself taking over UNSCOM's mandate had been flatly rejected. He advised Aziz against even proposing the idea to the Council. Instead, Rolf suggested that an experienced and trusted UNSCOM inspector should conduct a pre-inspection survey of the building to assess whether a full-blown inspection was required or not. Only if that survey indicated the need for an inspection would it proceed, but operating under normal inspection procedures as laid down in the Status Agreement (which describes the UN's inspection rights and Iraq's obligations in great detail). Tariq Aziz rejected this out of hand.

Under further pressure from Tariq Aziz to present the Iraqi proposal to the Council, Rolf Ekéus suggested that the idea might be considered provided that the inspection was conducted under and in accordance with the UN resolutions, and provided that the experts chosen were approved as competent by UNSCOM and were trained and briefed by UNSCOM. Tariq Aziz rejected this proposal and the meeting ended without agreement on substance. Rolf agreed to relay the Aziz proposal faithfully to the Council, but again warned that he thought it was ill-advised.

Rolf Ekéus had also raised the issue of the death threats on UNSCOM personnel and the actual attacks on both personnel and property. He demanded that the Iraqi authorities take action to stop the attacks and protect UNSCOM personnel. Tariq Aziz, in one of the more chilling moments of my time at UNSCOM, denied that the Iraqi government had played any part in the attacks and threats, claiming instead that they were an expression of the people's frustration with the UN because of sanctions. While security arrangements would be redoubled, Aziz stated darkly that he could not, given the strength of feeling in the populace at large, guarantee that Iraqi officials would be able to ensure the safety of UNSCOM personnel at all times. Indeed, he implicitly suggested that the problems were of UNSCOM's making: its reporting of the situation in Iraq had been 'unbalanced' and it used too many Americans in the inspection teams.

The hostility of the Iraqi statements and the aggressiveness of its negotiating position during this round of meetings convinced me of what we had feared on 6 July when Ambassador Perkins withdrew the threat of military action: Iraq would only comply so long as this threat was imminent and credible. And Rolf Ekéus would only be able to talk the Iraqis into allowing access if he were bearing a tough message on behalf of the whole UN Security Council.

It was during this visit of Rolf's that I was, for the one and only time in my tenure with UNSCOM, genuinely frightened for my life. Excluding my time as chief aerial inspector, I visited Baghdad only as part of a delegation led by Rolf Ekéus. The Iraqis were hardly likely to harm anyone in these delegations – the US and its allies would have been furious. If they were to harm any UNSCOM staff, it would be the inspectors or, more probably, the lower-profile permanent support staff in Baghdad – the communicators, medics, interpreters and logistics staff supplied by the UN, the New Zealand Army and the German Army. However, on this trip, perhaps to underline the argument that there was genuine popular hatred of UNSCOM, at the end of a long meeting the Iraqi hospitality cars took Rolf Ekéus's entire delegation right into a massive anti-UNSCOM demonstration. Between the two bridges on either side of the river Baghdad had come to a standstill. Some demonstrators pressed their faces to the windows shouting abuse; others rocked the car and beat on the roof. While I was convinced that the Iraqis intended only to intimidate us, I was well aware that no amount of policing or state terror can control a crowd that size once it gets excited. I was extremely relieved when the cars finally pulled clear of the crowds and sped off to the Sheraton.

Rolf Ekéus went back to New York that afternoon, Sunday 19 July. After thirty hours of almost non-stop travel, he arrived back at JFK at around 2.30 p.m. the next day. At three he was back in his office and went straight into a meeting with the US ambassador, Perkins, the British ambassador, Sir David Hannay, and the French ambassador, Jean-Claude Mérimée. Forty-five minutes later he met the President of the Security Council and at four o'clock the Council met to receive Rolf's oral and written reports first hand.

Incredibly, the Council again failed to react decisively and made no statement formally rejecting Aziz's proposal. This was taken by Iraq as a further sign that its policy of confrontation was working.

Meanwhile, in Baghdad, tensions were still mounting. On Tuesday 21 July the Iraqi authorities mobilised the largest demonstration to date, which comprised some several thousand people. I watched from my vantage point on the fifteenth floor of the hotel, estimating numbers by counting the people in one area and multiplying this figure to cover the whole area of the demonstration – between two and three thousand, I guessed. On the ground, the inspection team were giving New York figures of over ten thousand. It probably felt like it on the front line – there was a lot of surging forward, and burning of US flags and effigies of George Bush.

I also watched as a film crew corralled together a bunch of no more than fifty demonstrators into a small area, so that they were closely pressed together. The cheerleader was then encouraged to inflame the group's indignation and up the chant volume. The desired effect achieved, the crew filmed from a low angle to make the angry mob look even bigger. Later I saw this piece of stage-managed journalism on television. It certainly gave a convincing impression of a mass demonstration, but it left me fuming.

Not all the events that day were so phoney. UNSCOM personnel were physically attacked as they tried to go to a supermarket. The pickets outside the two hotels were now spitting on all UNSCOM staff as they came and went; occasionally, items were also thrown. Two of the UN guards were attacked in their vehicles with bricks and iron bars and had to pull out their small arms to disperse the attackers. Iraqi actions against the UN seemed set to change from severe intimidation to outright physical attacks.

Back in New York, the pressure was at last mounting on Iraq. After a further Security Council meeting on the morning of Tuesday 21 July the President summoned the Iraqi ambassador, Abdul Amir al Anbari, and informed him that Aziz's proposal was unacceptable. The Russian ambassador also spoke with al Anbari, telling him that Iraq should stop its games. And at last the US was beginning to make bellicose noises.

At 6.30 a.m. on Wednesday 22 July my hotel telephone rang. Expecting yet another death threat, I picked it up. The caller was Mark Silver. He informed me that at 5.30 a.m. a lone Iraqi, after talking with the Iraqi security personnel supposedly guarding the UNSCOM inspectors outside the Ministry of Agriculture, had approached one of the UNSCOM vehicles. The Iraqi security officials made no attempt to stop him as he calmly attempted to stab one of the inspectors in the car. Fortunately, both the inspectors had seen the man and were alert to his movements. The inspector was able to evade the stabbing, and he and his colleague were able to restrain the man until the officials finally intervened. As soon as the UNSCOM inspectors let him go, so did the Iraqi guards, and the man was able to flee the scene without hindrance.

Mark Silver felt that he should withdraw the team, but he wanted my opinion before calling Rolf Ekéus. Without hesitation, I agreed with him. I did so for two reasons. First, given all the other acts of intimidation and the evident complicity of the Iraqi security personnel in this attack, this seemed as clear a signal as we were likely to get from the Iraqis, short of an inspector being seriously hurt, that unless the team withdrew they now intended to resort to physical attacks. Mark's instructions were clear – to maintain the watch on the Ministry building either until access were obtained or until the team's continued presence there would place them in physical danger. Second, after seventeen days of stand-off, I was convinced that nothing incriminating was left in the building. That being the case, it was in UNSCOM's interest to have a period without surveillance before access was obtained. If an inspection team then gained access and found nothing, UNSCOM could easily claim that things could have been removed in the intervening period; this would protect the credibility of the intelligence on which the inspection was based. It would be harder to explain how everything had been spirited away from under the noses of the inspectors watching the three exits if access were obtained without any such gap.

Alice Hecht, who was still in Baghdad, was also consulted, as the most senior full-time UN staff member in UNSCOM and as UNSCOM's administrator and personnel manager. She agreed with Mark and me. It was unanimous – the team should be withdrawn.

Mark Silver rang Rolf Ekéus just before eight on Wednesday morning Baghdad time – just before midnight Tuesday, New York time. Rolf was clearly unhappy with the decision. He felt he was near to a deal with the Iraqi ambassador, Abdul Amir al Anbari, to gain access. He wanted the team to hold out for another couple of days and spoke to all three of us individually. We all gave the same advice – we felt that the team was now under imminent threat of actual physical harm and that the only safe course of action was to withdraw. To Rolf's considerable credit, despite of the fact that he doubted whether the Iraqis were prepared to actually harm our staff, and wanted the team to hold out until his negotiations were successfully completed, he accepted the advice from the field.

The team withdrew at 8.30 a.m. Baghdad time (half past midnight New York time) on Wednesday 22 July.

•

I still think the decision to withdraw was the right one. It took another four days of intense dialogue in New York before Iraq finally agreed to an inspection of the Ministry.

On the Wednesday Rolf Ekéus informed the President of the

Security Council that the team had been forced to withdraw following threats to their safety. That afternoon he met Abdul Amir al Anbari and told him that, because the team had been forced to withdraw, all previous bets on special procedures for conducting the inspection were off. Nothing short of a full inspection would be acceptable. Al Anbari wanted Iraq to be involved in the choosing of the inspectors for the team. This request was refused.

The next day, Thursday 23 July, al Anbari repeated the Tariq Aziz offer of an inspection by officials from non-coalition states chosen jointly by Iraq and UNSCOM and acting under special written instructions. Rolf Ekéus again rejected this, saying that he, as Executive Chairman of UNSCOM, would choose the team and that it would inspect using standard operating procedures. Al Anbari promised to report back to Baghdad. Friday was spent waiting for the Iraqi response.

By now the noises from the US war machine were becoming louder, and the teams in Baghdad were discussing evacuation plans – both to avoid being the victims of US military action, and to escape any potential Iraqi backlash against UN personnel in the aftermath of such actions. At last the Iraqis seemed to be taking the threat, and hence their dialogue with UNSCOM, seriously. Each day I arrived at the al Rasheed air base with my colleagues in the aerial inspection team, there were fewer and fewer aircraft visible. Military assets were being removed from military camps and dispersed throughout the Iraqi countryside. Fields were dotted with aircraft, or radar trucks, or aviation fuel tankers. Any valuable military asset was being moved out of harm's way and anti-aircraft batteries were beehives of activity.

Abdul Amir al Anbari called Rolf Ekéus on Saturday 25 July to discuss the composition of the inspection team. He reported the results of that meeting back to Baghdad. In Baghdad, CNN was reporting the news of Ross Perot's extraordinary rise in the opinion polls as an independent candidate for the US presidency, and George Bush's concomitant decline. The Iraqis were hanging on every word of the political talking head shows, wondering whether Bush was manipulating the situation in Iraq: by bombing Iraq, perhaps he hoped to reverse the trend in the opinion polls and see off the joint threats of Perot and Clinton. We knew that all the Iraqi ministries watched CNN.

This time I was somewhat happier with the television reporting. By airing such views, however erroneous, it was planting the seed of fear in the minds of the Iraqi decision-makers, thereby strengthening UNSCOM's negotiating position.

On Sunday 26 July, at just after midday in New York, Abdul Amir al Anbari informed Rolf Ekéus that Iraq agreed to an inspection of the Ministry of Agriculture by a team chosen by him on terms laid down by UNSCOM. Rolf immediately left for Baghdad with the inspection team.

They arrived shortly before 10.30 a.m. on Tuesday 28 July. At 11.30 Rolf Ekéus, Doug Englund (chief inspector), Achim Biermann (deputy chief inspector) and I met Mohammed al Sahaf, with his usual coterie. The details of the inspection procedures were explained and a time set for the inspection – 3.30 that afternoon. It concluded the next day at half past midday and the team left Baghdad at 3.30 p.m. By 3 p.m. the following day, Thursday, Rolf Ekéus was back in New York, reporting the successful outcome of the inspection to the President of the Security Council, but also warning that the Council would have to react faster and more firmly to any future Iraqi obstructionism if similar crises were to be avoided.

The results of the inspection were an entirely predictable anti-climax. No archives were found. However, the team found ample evidence that the building had been 'sanitised' before their arrival. Dirt lines on the wall and indentations on the floor indicated that furniture had recently been shifted and shelving removed. Later intelligence reports and (much later) Iraqi admissions confirmed that documents had been stored at the Ministry of Agriculture.

When I returned to New York I realised how ironic the documents' location was: congressional hearings were under way to investigate how US agricultural credits, given to Iraq in the 1980s, had been diverted to Iraq's weapons programmes.

The excitement was not yet over for the summer of 1992. The very evening that Rolf Ekéus left Baghdad after the successful inspection of the Ministry of Agriculture, which established UNSCOM's right to inspect anywhere within Iraq, I received a phone call from the German helicopter aircrew: the Iraqis were blocking the next day's aerial inspection. They claimed that the zone we intended to inspect included Baghdad and that flights over Baghdad were forbidden. In meetings the next day it was quickly, if tacitly, ascertained that the Iraqis were worried that we might try to inspect Saddam Hussein's principal residential palace, sited on the edge of Baghdad International Airport, on its own artificial lake, on the western outskirts of Baghdad. The site we intended to inspect was some 8 kilometres from the palace and so, just for that inspection, we agreed not to fly over certain areas that were described as Baghdad, and to conduct the actual inspection at low altitude so that we could not overlook the palace.

In the event, that proved unworkable. The Iraqis had insisted that we fly at a mere sixty feet. As we hovered over the site, not only did the helicopter start fanning up a cloud of dust so that we could no longer see – let alone photograph – the buildings; the down draught of the large CH53g's engines was so great that it started to blow them over. We immediately climbed up to our usual 300 feet, and finished the inspection following normal procedures.

Back in New York, the US had now acquired the zealous indignation of the newly converted. Having been in large part responsible for the protracted nature of the Ministry of Agriculture crisis, the US was now urging Rolf Ekéus and

UNSCOM to re-establish their right to inspect any building in Iraq, including ministries and palaces, by launching another document search inspection based around such high-profile sites. UNSCOM had long been planning inspections of this sort. Nikita Smidovich and Scott Ritter put together a team based around a shopping list of sites. Once in the country, they would be told which sites from this list should be inspected. Two of the sites were high profile: the Ministry of Defence and MIC's headquarters – General Amer Rasheed's own offices.

The team arrived in Baghdad on 7 August. I met them at Habbaniyah air base on my way out, having completed my three-week stint as chief aerial inspector. I cannot say I was sad to leave. Those remaining in Baghdad were glad to have survived the last crisis without being on the receiving end of a flurry of Tomahawks. They fully expected this incoming team's mission to result in another crisis, and most were convinced that this time the bombs would fall.

Iraq had somehow caught wind of the nature of the coming inspection. The US had been building up the rhetoric about the consequences if Iraq again blocked UNSCOM's right to access, be it to ministries or anywhere else. Iraq was making it plain that any attempt to inspect certain key ministries, such as the Ministry of Defence, or a presidential palace, would be resisted. The US seized on this to press Rolf Ekéus to go ahead with an inspection of both a palace and the Ministry of Defence – just to establish the precedent and prove the right, even if there were no intelligence to link them specifically to banned weapons capabilities.

Rolf Ekéus resisted this pressure, arguing that UNSCOM had inspected two ministries already – the Ministry of Agriculture just inspected, and the Ministry of Industry and Minerals, inspected without any fuss or ado earlier in the year by a team led by Doug Englund looking for computer records relating to both the nuclear and missile programmes. In addition, a missile team under Nikita Smidovich had already inspected a palace, and so both the rights and the precedents had been firmly established.

So in the event, MIC was inspected, but the Ministry of Defence was not. Another military confrontation was averted. And the cynics marvelled that George Bush failed to get his August surprise to help reverse his re-election fortunes. But that was not UNSCOM's problem – at least, not yet.

The Ministry of Agriculture crisis had been useful in underlining UNSCOM's inspection rights and in hardening support within the Council for UNSCOM's mandate. But it had not succeeded in furthering UNSCOM's knowledge of Iraq's undeclared biological weapons programme, as we had hoped it might when we received the intelligence about the archives.

CHAPTER 12

Expulsion

'War is too serious a thing to be left to the military.'
GEORGES CLEMENCEAU

'A week is a long time in politics.'
HAROLD WILSON

The telephone was ringing incessantly. I strained my head up from
the pillow and looked at the radio alarm – 8 a.m. Saturday 16
January 1993. It had been a hard week and I needed a lie-in. I let
the phone ring. It stopped only to start again. Reluctantly, I picked
up the receiver. Raghida Dirham, the UN correspondent of the
London-based Arabic daily, *al Hayyat*, was on the other end. I was
immediately wary. Raghida and UNSCOM had a love-hate
relationship. We called her the Druze Missile after her aggressive
questions in press briefings. That said, there was mutual respect.
Enough to put my sleep-bleary mind on alert.

'Tim, have you received the letter yet?'

'What letter?'

'The letter from the Iraqis agreeing to let your aircraft fly
again?'

'No.'

'Well, you'd better get into the office. It's coming.'

'How do you know?'

'Someone who should know told me.'

'Someone' had to be Nizar Hamdoon, the newly arrived Iraqi

ambassador to the UN, a savvy operator who knew how to deal with the press – and most diplomats and politicians for that matter. It was almost certainly true that a letter was coming. This was urgent news. The Iraqis had for the past week prevented UNSCOM from flying its aircraft into their airspace, threatening to shoot them down if they did. US, UK and French military assets were in place for a strike against Iraq to force it to remove the threat to UNSCOM aircraft. This letter might stop an imminent missile strike on Iraq.

I jumped out of bed, without pausing to shower or shave, threw on some jeans and a brightly coloured Peruvian sweater and ran across the road. I was still living in Tudor City. My joke at the time was that my vertical commute was longer than my horizontal one: I had to descend from the seventh floor, cross First Avenue, and ascend to the thirty-first floor.

I arrived in my office just after 8.20. No letter. I rang Raghida to question her source. She assured me that a letter, if not already within the UN building, was on its way and advised me to stay in the office. I rang the UNSCOM duty officer and the Deputy Executive Chairman, then Pierce Corden. The letter arrived at around 10 a.m., but it was not what UNSCOM wanted, nor what the Security Council would accept. Ahead lay a busy day of coordinating with Rolf Ekéus, who was in Vienna with the Swedish delegation to the CSCE (the Conference on Security and Cooperation in Europe), and the members of the Security Council to draft a response to this letter. Rolf, in turn, was in contact throughout the day with the outgoing US National Security Adviser, Brent Scowcroft, who was in touch with President George Bush, President François Mitterrand and Prime Minister John Major.

Throughout the day the office phones rang incessantly, with journalists wanting to know if it was war or not. With so few of us in the office, we decided to implement a press black-out until the response had been sent to Iraq. At 6 p.m., exhausted, I arrived in the lobby of the UN building on my way home, having forgotten about the media. As I stepped out of the lift, the TV camera lights went on, the microphones were pushed into my face, and the barrage of questions started. It lasted for thirty minutes. This was my first taste of media attention – unwashed and unshaved, stressed and tired. For all the gravity of the situation, the friends who saw me on television could talk only of my Peruvian sweater.

The origins of this crisis had little to do with UNSCOM. The Safwan Agreement, dictated to the Iraqis by General Schwarzkopf on 1 March 1991 in a dusty tent in southern Iraq, imposed a ban on Iraqi aircraft flying anywhere in Iraq. This was part of the terms for an end to hostilities and was formalised in Security Council resolution 686 (1991), adopted on 2 March 1991, which demanded that Iraq 'cease ... flights of combat aircraft'. For some reason the US interpreted this as a ban only on fixed-wing aircraft flights. This enabled Saddam Hussein's regime to suppress the uprising in the south of Iraq in the spring of 1991 using its helicopter gunships.

This resolution was never rescinded. For a year Iraq continued to observe the no-fly injunction on all its fixed-wing aircraft. But when Iranian aircraft invaded Iraqi airspace in March 1992 in order to attack an encampment of Iranian opposition forces to the east of Baghdad, the Iraqi Air Force took to the air. To the astonishment of close observers, the US did not object to this breach of the ban. Indeed, US diplomats went further, indicating that that ban was no longer in force. Thereafter, Iraqi Air Force flights became increasingly frequent.

By August 1992, however, these flights were becoming an embarrassment to the Western members of the coalition. Led by the US, these members had in April 1991 pushed through a resolution – in addition to the ceasefire resolution – aimed at guaranteeing basic human rights in Iraq: resolution 688 (1991). This demanded that Iraq end the repression of its civilian populations and allow immediate access by aid organisations to all parts of the country to address the needs of the oppressed. It was Iraq's rejection of this resolution that led to the creation of the Kurdish 'safe haven' in the north.

In the summer of 1992 Iraq set about quelling all forms of opposition in the marshland areas to the south, between the two great rivers, the Euphrates and the Tigris. It was using its newly airborne aircraft in these attacks. The tame acquiescence shown by the US following the resumption of Iraqi military flights in March was coming back to haunt it. But, rather than reimposing the complete ban on fixed-wing flights, the US, UK and France agreed to put in place a no-fly zone south of the thirty-second parallel and started aerial patrols to enforce it.

The Iraqis immediately objected to this new ban. They also sought to use it. On 2 September they informed UNSCOM that, as they could not guarantee the safety of its flights over Iraqi airspace south of the thirty-second parallel, UNSCOM henceforth would not be permitted to fly through the no-fly zone but would have to fly into Iraq via Jordan.

This was a specious argument. UNSCOM did not need Iraqi protection from US, British or French aircraft. All it needed was a guarantee that Iraq would not attack its aircraft. Furthermore, the proposed air route through Jordan was totally unworkable. Worse, it was a breach of UNSCOM's right to fly anywhere in Iraq. If Iraq were allowed to start dictating where UNSCOM could fly, it would be the beginning of the slippery slope. Soon Iraq would be banning UNSCOM from flying anywhere, and laying down the law on other aspects of how inspections should be conducted.

So, for reasons of both practicality and principle, UNSCOM rejected Iraq's demand. On 4 September Kevin St Louis, the head of UNSCOM's field office in Baghdad, informed his Iraqi counterpart, Brigadier Tahseen, that an UNSCOM flight would be entering Iraqi airspace on 5 September from Bahrain, via Kuwaiti airspace, as usual. That is, the aircraft would fly through the no-fly zone. However, by the morning of 5 September Tahseen had still not acknowledged this flight plan to provide assurance that the Iraqis would not attack the aircraft, and could not give Kevin the required assurance. Kevin called the director of UNSCOM's field office in Bahrain, Alistair Livingstone, and the flight was cancelled. Pierce Corden, the Deputy Executive Chairman, was informed of the situation and wrote to the President of the Security Council, informing him of a new impending crisis with Iraq, and warning him that yet further enforcement action might be necessary. Pierce then informed the Iraqi deputy ambassador in New York, Dr Samir al Nima, of his actions and asked him to intercede with Baghdad to reverse its decision.

Kevin St Louis, upon orders from Pierce Corden, resubmitted the flight plan for 6 September. To everyone's relief, Tahseen called him that evening to acknowledge the flight, giving the assurance that Iraq would guarantee its safety. The flight proceeded as planned.

Soon after his election in November 1992 to the US Presidency, Bill Clinton was asked what he thought of Saddam Hussein. He made some remarks that were immediately criticised by several leading US newspapers as politically naïve, and greeted with groans of dismay in UNSCOM. In particular, Clinton said that, as a southern Baptist, he believed in deathbed conversions: he hoped he could reason with Saddam Hussein. Those of us with first-hand experience of Saddam's regime knew that this would be misinterpreted. It would not be taken as the philosophical musings of a new President wishing to be loved by everyone, but rather as a sign of weakness to be exploited. And so it proved.

Iraq had not given up on the flights issue. This soon became intertwined with another long-standing Iraqi complaint. Once it had become clear in the summer of 1991 that Iraq was trying to hide weapons and production equipment from UNSCOM and the IAEA, the Security Council gave both organisations greater and more intrusive powers. One of these was the explicit right for UNSCOM to fly its helicopters and aircraft anywhere in Iraq for any purpose connected with the inspections. Iraq simply never accepted this.

Nevertheless, UNSCOM started high-altitude surveillance flights over Iraq almost immediately. Iraq objected to these flights, and still objects to the UN Secretary-General in writing each month.

After a tense few weeks spanning August and September 1991, Iraq acquiesced to the helicopter flights. It did so during Rolf Ekéus's visit to Baghdad in late September 1991 to discuss the aftermath of the parking-lot crisis. Rolf used the pressure of the occasion to force Tariq Aziz to accept UNSCOM's use of helicopters to speed up and improve the inspection process. Aziz acquiesced, but made clear Iraq's objections to the flights.

Rolf Ekéus was keen to seal agreement on the use of helicopters for the urgent task of finding and destroying Iraq's fixed missile launch pads, dotted throughout the Western Desert. He also wanted to transport inspectors quickly to sites for genuine no-notice inspections. In order to secure these important objectives, he agreed that, as a standard practice, UNSCOM would not fly the helicopters over heavily populated areas.

Iraq interpreted this to its advantage – that helicopters would never be permitted to fly over Baghdad and other large cities. Thus when, on 2 December 1992, UNSCOM's aerial inspectors sought to fly over two engineering factories that had supplied components for Iraq's nuclear weapons programme, Iraq blocked the flight on the grounds that the factories were in Baghdad. In fact, they lay in the distant south-eastern outskirts of the city, at Rabiyah and Zaafaraniyah. Rolf Ekéus sent an 'aide mémoire', a formal diplomatic communication, to Dr Samir al Nima the same day, reminding him that UNSCOM had the right to fly anywhere over Iraq for surveillance purposes and demanding that Iraq comply with its obligations.

Nothing happened for a week, but on 10 December he received

a letter from Mohammed al Sahaf, now promoted to Foreign Minister, again refusing to allow the aerial inspection over the two sites. Rolf immediately wrote back, again insisting that the flights must go ahead or the issue would be reported to the Security Council as a serious instance of Iraqi non-compliance. On the same day Pierce Corden wrote to the President of the Security Council informing him of the developing situation.

Iraq's response came on 14 December 1992 in the form of a letter from Nizar Hamdoon to the President of the Security Council. This was a wide-ranging liturgy of Iraqi complaints against UNSCOM and sanctions, but it also contained an assertion that there was an agreement that UNSCOM helicopters would not overfly Baghdad. On 17 December Pierce Corden asked the President of the Security Council to bring both the UNSCOM and Iraqi letters to the attention of all Council members.

At this stage the holiday season intervened. After the tough year UNSCOM personnel had been through, it was decided to shut down operations in Baghdad for a two-week period, leaving only a skeleton staff behind to look after the offices and the helicopters. The bulk of UNSCOM's Baghdad staff – some fifty people – flew out of Baghdad on 23 December, planning to return on 5 January 1993.

I arrived back in New York on 5 January, having attended a conference on biological and chemical weapons disarmament in Geneva and then spent Christmas and New Year with my family in England. The issue of aerial inspection and landing rights was high on the priority list. The problem was how to elevate Iraq's refusal to countenance flights over sites on the outskirts of Baghdad and to permit UNSCOM's transport aircraft to land at other airports than Habbaniyah into an issue that was grave enough for the Council to consider enforcement actions.

Iraq and serendipity provided the answer. On 5 January the C-160 Transall transport aircraft was ready to take off from Bahrain, loaded with equipment and supplies. As the inspectors and helicopter crews were preparing to board, the aircraft developed an engine fault. The inspectors and crews were sent back to their hotels, and the Luftwaffe engineers who maintained the aircraft got to work repairing the engines.

At this stage there was no sign that Iraq would intervene. True, on 4 January the Secretary-General had received two letters, dated 31 December 1992, from Mohammed al Sahaf, complaining bitterly at the decision of the Sanctions Committee not to allow Iraqi Airways to resume commercial operations within and outside Iraq. Such operations had been banned by the UN in August 1990 as part of the sanctions imposed on Iraq following its invasion of Kuwait.

On Thursday 7 January, in response to the new flight plan for the return of UNSCOM personnel, lodged with Brigadier Tahseen on 6 January, UNSCOM's Baghdad office received an official note from the Iraqi Foreign Ministry stating that henceforth no UN aircraft would be allowed to use the Habbaniyah air base. On the same day the UN operation monitoring the border with Kuwait (UNIKOM) received a similar notice.

Effectively, UNSCOM was out of business.

The machinery of crisis management once again cranked into action. Within fifteen minutes of receipt of the note in Baghdad, the President of the Security Council in New York was informed of the situation by Pierce Corden. This was followed up the next morning with a letter explaining the situation in greater detail and the Council met that Friday evening to consider what action to take. At 9.30 p.m. it issued a statement: Iraq's actions, it said, had put it in material breach of its obligations and 'serious consequences' would follow if it did not rescind its decision.

Meanwhile, Rolf Ekéus (who was still in Vienna but with whom we were in hourly contact), Pierce Corden and I knew that Iraq would paint UNSCOM as the guilty party by trying to show that our insistence on the right to fly according to our flight plans, without reference to Iraq, was unfair. Consequently, we were eager not to yield any moral ground on any issue. We decided to ensure that we replied to any Iraqi communiqué on this issue on the same day, and always to offer the Iraqis a way out of their position – that is, not to paint them into a corner of defiance.

So, the next morning, Saturday 9 January, a letter was sent under Rolf Ekéus's signature to the Iraqi Foreign Minister, informing him of the Council's demand that flights resume and of its warning. Kevin St Louis was also instructed to deliver the same message in person to the Iraqi Foreign Ministry, together with another flight plan taking the aircraft into Iraq through the no-fly zone. When he turned up at the Ministry, he was informed that a letter had been sent that day from Mohammed al Sahaf to the President of the Security Council, linking the resumption of UN flights with the resumption of Iraqi Airways flights. Iraq was setting terms for the Council, rather than the other way around.

The next day we received a letter from Nizar Hamdoon to Rolf Ekéus with the same message. We also received a note from the Iraqi Foreign Ministry dated 9 January, stating that, under the circumstances, any foreign flights in Iraqi airspace were fraught with danger; by 'circumstances' they meant the enforcement of the no-fly zone in the south. On-board sensors on US, British and French aircraft patrolling the no-fly zone had detected that they were being 'painted' by Iraqi air defence radars – that is, the radars had been targeting the aircraft for their air defence ground-to-air missiles. In response, the coalition aircraft had fired at several Iraqi radar vehicles. Sunday morning was spent ringing round the members of the Security Council to inform them of this new Iraqi letter.

Meanwhile, Iraq was doing its best to compound its problems. That same day Iraqi forces crossed the Kuwaiti border to seize equipment, including four HY-2G anti-ship missiles which the UN had set aside for destruction. On Monday they again crossed the border to retrieve materials from their former naval base at Umm Qasr.

First thing on Monday morning the President of the Security Council summoned Nizar Hamdoon to tell him that the arguments that Iraq had used to justify the blocking of UN flights were unacceptable. Hamdoon, however, did not tell the President what the Council wanted to hear – that flights could resume safely. The President called a meeting of the Council that afternoon. After a discussion behind closed doors, the Council resumed in formal open session at 9.30 p.m. – an unusual step, meant as a message to Iraq that this was the unanimous position of the Council. Iraq was again told to behave or face the consequences.

Never one to let a good crisis subside, Saddam Hussein upped the ante. On Monday evening the acting Iraqi Foreign Minister (the Foreign Minister was out of the country) sent a letter to the UN Secretary-General, pointing out that the previous U2 flight had concentrated its surveillance on the Iraq-Kuwait border area. It claimed, incorrectly, that this was clear evidence that the plane was being used for military planning purposes not related to UNSCOM's mandate – for spying. Iraq demanded that the U2 flights be stopped.

As if that were not enough, the next morning Mohammed al Sahaf sent a letter to the UN Secretary-General objecting to the statement made by the Council the previous day. He requested a dialogue to negotiate a mutually acceptable solution. The President of the Council immediately summoned Hamdoon to tell him that the Council's warning and demand stood, and to reject the idea of a dialogue as Iraq had proffered no solution.

An answer from Sahaf came the next day, Wednesday 13 January. Iraq would allow UNSCOM flights on a case-by-case basis but could bear no responsibility for the safety of UNSCOM's aircraft. This was clearly unacceptable – Iraq was saying that it, not UNSCOM, would dictate the pattern and path of flights and even then the aircraft would fly at their own peril. That evening in Baghdad, vandalism of UNSCOM vehicles resumed – for the first time since the Ministry of Agriculture crisis in July. We took that to mean that Iraq was moving into an even more belligerent mode, where attacks on UNSCOM aircraft would be a distinct possibility.

However, we could not give up our right to fly our own aircraft when and where we needed to for inspection purposes. On Thursday 14 January Pierce Corden again instructed Kevin St Louis in Baghdad to resubmit flight plans for each day from 15 to 18 January for the entry of the C-160 into Iraq and to seek Iraqi acknowledgement in writing of the flights (implying assurance of their safety) in good time for them to proceed. We knew this was the end game. If Iraq refused to permit these flights, action would move from UNSCOM to the coalition forces massed in the Gulf – from diplomacy to military force.

By the next morning no acknowledgement of these flights had been received, and the first flight had to be cancelled. A last-ditch effort was made. Rolf Ekéus called Nizar Hamdoon from Vienna on Friday morning telling him that acknowledgement of the flight plan for Saturday 16 January was required by four o'clock that afternoon, New York time. I called the Secretary-General's office to put them on alert that there might be a major development over the weekend. At 2 p.m. Dr Samir al Nima from the Iraqi Mission in New York rang me and read out the text of a letter it was sending. Iraq now dropped the demand for a case-by-case approval of UNSCOM flights but still insisted that they flew at UNSCOM's peril. I told him that this was still unacceptable – Iraq had to guarantee the safety of the flights.

At 4 p.m., the deadline for acknowledging the flight plans, the Iraqi Mission contacted us again, but not to acquiesce. A letter from Nizar Hamdoon addressed to Rolf Ekéus stated that under the current circumstances Iraq could not guarantee the safety of the U2 flights and requested that they be postponed. A further telephone conference with Rolf Ekéus resolved our strategy. To avert military action, UNSCOM would continue to provide Iraq with a way out of its position. We wrote a letter to the President of the Security Council, telling him that Iraq's letter about the flights still constituted a refusal to allow the aircraft to fly in accordance with the ceasefire resolution because it was refusing to say that it would not endanger the safety of the aircraft and the people on board. This letter was faxed to the Iraqi Mission in New York at 10 p.m. with a new set of flight plans. Both the letter and the flight plans for 19 and 20 January were presented by Kevin St Louis to the Iraqi Foreign Ministry in Baghdad the next morning, Saturday 16 January. The time in New York was 3.40 a.m.

8 a.m. Saturday 16 January, Raghida calls. The Iraqi note, when it arrived, said that UNSCOM could operate its own aircraft and that Iraq would guarantee their safety if, and only if, all UNSCOM aircraft entered Iraq from Jordanian airspace.

For us, this was a dangerous suggestion. It sounded reasonable, because that way UNSCOM aircraft would not need to pass through the disputed no-fly zone. But it was bad for reasons of principle, for reasons of practicality, and for reasons of motivation. If UNSCOM accepted the plan, it would be acknowledging that Iraq could decide that there were areas of Iraqi airspace in which UNSCOM aircraft could not fly. That would be the thin end of the wedge: soon we would not be able to fly anywhere. Also, it would mean relocating UNSCOM's Bahrain field office from the friendly and secure military air base in Bahrain to the Iraqi intelligence-infested streets of Amman. If operations were conducted out of Amman, it would be impossible to maintain secrecy; hence no-notice inspections would be a thing of the past. But equally it would be impractical to keep operations in Bahrain while flying the 'long route' – it would add several hours to the current two-and-a-half-hour flight, and the C-160 Transalls would need to refuel before returning, which jeopardised our evacuation contingency plans. The only option would be to move the Bahrain office to the British sovereign base areas in Cyprus – either Larnaca or Akrotiri. But there were well-rehearsed political problems with such a move.

The ingenious Iraqi proposal had to be rejected without making

UNSCOM look unreasonable. We needed to throw the ball back into their court. The main priority was to deflate the idea that Iraq could not guarantee the safety of our aircraft whilst flying through the no-fly zone. In our consultations throughout that Saturday, we checked again that, even if other hostilities were taking place, the coalition forces would be able to recognise the UNSCOM aircraft. The answer, as we knew, was yes. We also checked with air defence experts that the Iraqi air defence equipment could distinguish between the UNSCOM C-160 Transall (whose flight path Iraq would know) and other aircraft flying with hostile intentions in the no-fly zone at the same time. The answer, as we knew, was again yes. Thus Iraq's claim that UNSCOM flights through the no-fly zone would force it to switch off its air defence system in order to guarantee that the UNSCOM aircraft were not shot down was entirely specious.

Our response to Iraq, delivered in another note to the Iraqi Foreign Ministry, was to reject the 'long route' on practical grounds but to free Iraq from any obligation to guarantee the safety of our aircraft from attack by coalition fighters. In other words, we would undertake to ensure our own safety *vis-à-vis* the coalition, but the Iraqis would still be responsible for not shooting at us themselves. An Iraqi refusal to such a commitment would be unreasonable. The onus of appearing reasonable had shifted from us to them.

That was the message I delivered to the press outside the lift on Saturday evening. I was nervous about the briefing – I wondered whether the message was too subtle and too clever. I was most relieved when the majority of the assembled press both understood and accepted the reasoning.

At 8 a.m. the next day, Sunday 17 January 1993, the telephone rang. It was Raghida Dirham again. Another Iraqi letter was on its way. This time I did not rush. I showered and shaved, then put on my jeans and a different Peruvian sweater. After the experiences of the previous day, I was sanguine that the Iraqi letter would not be there immediately. And Rolf Ekéus had approved of the jeans and sweater look – it illustrated quite clearly to television audiences that this was a crisis. Officials wearing weekend clothes, not weekday suits. Crisis, not routine.

In the office I again called Rolf Ekéus (who was still in Vienna) and Pierce Corden. Iraq's response came at 10.30: it now offered to allow UNSCOM to fly through the no-fly zone and to guarantee the safety of its aircraft provided UNSCOM could guarantee that, while UNSCOM aircraft were in the no-fly zone, no coalition aircraft would enter Iraqi airspace. This was clearly not a guarantee that UNSCOM could make. Nevertheless, we were determined not to allow UNSCOM inaction to be blamed for any military action that might take place. Rolf Ekéus rang Brent Scowcroft to tell him of the news. Scowcroft immediately said that it was not for Iraq to set terms for how the coalition policed the no-fly zone.

What Brent Scowcroft did not say was that the letter was too late anyway. This was George Bush's last day in office as President of the US. Clinton's inauguration ceremony was set for that afternoon. Bush's presidency literally ended with a bang – forty-three to be precise: forty-three Tomahawk missiles were on their way from US ships and submarines in the Persian Gulf and the Red Sea to the two factories Iraq had refused to let us inspect from the air – Rabiyah and Zaafaraniyah. By the end of the day neither of the plants was operational, having been heavily bombed. Unfortunately, a few Tomahawks landed in residential areas around the plants, resulting in civilian casualties.

One of the cruise missiles was damaged by Iraqi anti-aircraft fire and was knocked off course. It landed just outside the reception area of the Rasheed Hotel – the hotel where we, along with all the foreign correspondents, stayed while in Baghdad. Unfortunately, there were several deaths and injuries as a result. In protest, the hotel staff made a mosaic of Bush at the entrance, with the label CRIMINAL, so that all visitors would have to walk over his face.

Unaware of these events (it took some of the missiles two hours to reach their targets), we sent a further note to the Iraqi Foreign Ministry, telling Iraq that UNSCOM was in no position to make such deals. We sent copies of the latest round of correspondence to the President of the Security Council. It was just as well – these letters were useful proof that UNSCOM was not a party to the enforcement action taken on our behalf by the US. This kept the important distinction between UNSCOM as a technical implementation agency with the Council and the members responsible for enforcement actions.

Two days later, on Tuesday 19 January, the Iraqi Revolutionary Command Council met under the chairmanship of Saddam Hussein. They issued a statement offering to stop shooting at coalition aircraft at midnight on 20 January, to give the new Clinton administration time to reassess its policy on the no-fly zones. At 1 p.m. we received by telephone assurances that our aircraft could fly in accordance with established procedures. That is, when we decided and by which routes we decided.

Iraq had backed down fully. A few days later our aerial inspection team flew over the Rabiyah and Zaafaraniyah site. UNSCOM's interpretation of the September 1991 understanding had been upheld and the Iraqi interpretation quashed. UNSCOM would not as a rule fly over heavily populated areas, but where there was an operational need to do so, it would.

This was Iraq's first attempt to bring an end to UNSCOM's activities. It came before UNSCOM had had the chance to break down any of Iraq's lies about the biological weapons programme. The biological analysts in UNSCOM feared that this was only the first such effort to throw off the shackles of UNSCOM inspections and that other attempts might prove successful before progress was made on tracking down the biological weapons.

It was a time of great frustration for the biologists. But the crisis that would open up the biological weapons investigation was now brewing.

CHAPTER 13

Salami Tactics and Missile Tests

'*Die Politik ist keine exakte Wissenschaft.*'
(Politics is not an exact science.)
PRINCE BISMARCK

'Men should be either treated generously or
destroyed, because they take revenge for slight
injuries – for heavy ones they cannot.'
NICCOLÒ MACHIAVELLI

In December 1992 a joint biological and chemical weapons team
was sent to Iraq to try to break the log jam in listing all Iraq's
chemical weapons and elicit a credible account of the biological
weapons programme. It was led by the Swedish chemical and
biological weapons expert, Johan Santesson.

This inspection mixed all kinds of disciplines and methods. The
thirty-five team members included munitions experts, chemists,
microbiologists, pharmacologists, experienced weapons inspectors and doctors. The hope was that, by including people with
complementary areas of expertise and getting them to operate
together, there would be a cross fertilization of ideas, with the team
making linkages about Iraq's activities that might otherwise be
overlooked. In particular, the team was to examine whether some
of Iraq's chemical munitions might have been adapted for biological weapons use. The answer was that technically they could
be adapted, but there was no proof that they had been.

The team's methods included interrogation of Iraqi officials involved in the weapons programmes, visits to ammunition depots, inspections of chemical and pharmaceutical factories and former ministries and other possible hiding places for the archives of the past weapons programmes. These documentation inspections, like the successful inspection led by David Kay in September 1991 and the Karen Jansen inspection of the Ministry of Agriculture, were based on persistent defector reports that Iraq was still hiding its weapons archives.

Johan's daily inspection reports, the sitreps, made at once amusing and worrying reading. He has an accent that brings to mind the Swedish chef on *The Muppet Show*. He is also blessed with a dry and sardonic sense of humour, which was evident in each sitrep: I could not read these reports without hearing the voice of the Swedish chef.

But while the presentation was humorous, the substance was not. On 6 December the team inspected the building that had seen David Kay's unplanned four-day encampment – the former headquarters of Iraq's nuclear weapons programme (the PC-3 building) just around the corner from the Sheraton Hotel. This inspection was conducted jointly with an IAEA team led by Professor Maurizio Zifferero, the Italian leader of the IAEA action team for Iraq. When the two teams arrived at the building, the Iraqi minders stopped them from entering. While they were trying to resolve this problem, team members observed some Iraqi officials leaving with documents and others throwing documents out of the windows to people standing below. When Zifferero tried to intercept the officials leaving with documents they boarded a bus. The Iraqi minders ignored Zifferero when he asked them to stop the bus and so the documents were whisked away.

Even when access to the building was obtained, the problems were not over. One inspector saw plans for a pharmaceutical building and wanted them copied so that one of the pharmacologists could see if they were relevant to the production of biological weapons. The Iraqi official refused to hand them over, claiming that the inspectors had to prove the plans' relevance to weapons manufacture before they could be copied or removed. This was the same old story that David Kay had heard fifteen months previously. As then, the inspectors inventoried the documents and marked them so that they could be re-examined once the pharmacologist arrived and so that they could be sure that they were examining the same documents and not substitutes.

During the interrogation sessions the biological and chemical sessions were separated out from the nuclear ones. Here, the story was, if anything, bleaker. The Iraqis being interrogated about biological and chemical issues were obviously uncomfortable with the incisive questioning led by Johan. The same was happening with Maurizio Zifferero's talks. The Iraqi officials must have reported the situation to their seniors. The results had all the hallmarks of a coordinated strategy.

Maurizio Zifferero was told on 7 December by Human Abdul Khaliq (chairman of the IAEC and now also Minister for Higher Education and Scientific Research) that it was pointless discussing monitoring activities until Rolf Ekéus had given Iraq cast-iron guarantees that sanctions would be lifted once it complied with the disarmament provisions of the ceasefire and that no additional conditions would be imposed. Until such time, Iraq would not consider progressing into monitoring activities: first the past programmes files should be closed, then the sanctions lifted, and only then would Iraq consider permitting monitoring.

On 8 December Johan Santesson heard an even tougher message. General Amer Rasheed al Ubeidi, Iraq's top weapons official, called him to his headquarters at 9 p.m. Amer was flanked by the chief Iraqi minder – Brigadier Hossam Amin – and the two people presented as the heads of the chemical and biological programmes, respectively Dr Ghazi Faisal (Dr Gas) and Dr Rihab Taha (Dr Germ). Johan presented three problem areas in the talks: the need to gain the names of suppliers for both the chemical and the biological programmes; the need to account for Iraq's use of chemical weapons in the period between 1983 and 1988 (an euphemism for the Iran–Iraq War); and the need for Iraq to provide supporting documentary evidence to justify its declarations. He said that the technical issues could be resolved; the political obstructions were more difficult.

General Amer Rasheed then launched into a tirade lasting nearly two hours. He strongly criticised Rolf Ekéus's November report to the Security Council, accusing him of not reporting to the Council objectively and failing to give the Council members a true picture of Iraq's cooperation with UNSCOM. He said that the inspections were just a political game with predetermined objectives that went beyond the ceasefire resolution; it was a game controlled by Iraq's enemies – namely, the US, the UK and France. These countries were using UNSCOM inspections to achieve their ulterior, extraneous objectives. It was clear, Amer asserted, from Ekéus's actions that nothing would ever change. That being the case, the inspectors would 'get nothing more, nothing. It is finished. You can bomb us or occupy us, it doesn't matter.' Amer turned to Dr Ghazi Faisal and Dr Rihab Taha, then said to Johan, 'If my subordinates provide you with anything beyond technical answers I will break their backs.'

Amer is a great actor in the melodramatic style of Arabic television. Iraq, he said (knowing full well that he was lying to UNSCOM about Iraq's biological weapons programme), had trusted UNSCOM but had been deceived: he himself had argued for cooperation with UNSCOM, but he now saw that this had been a mistake – that phase was over. The aerial inspections were nothing more than an intelligence-gathering exercise for Iraq's enemies and an attempt to humiliate the Iraqi regime. He would never allow the helicopters to fly one metre inside Baghdad air space. The Iraqi people, he said, hated UNSCOM more than they hated the US Air Force and would like to drink the inspectors' blood. He ended the tirade by repeating that he would break the necks of any Iraqi who provided inspectors with the names of his suppliers or of other persons involved in Iraq's past weapons of mass destruction programmes.

On 13 December Johan Santesson had another meeting. General Amer Rasheed had instructed Brigadier Hossam Amin to make some points clear. Iraq would not answer trivial questions, questions that had already been asked, or questions that were not relevant to the ceasefire resolution.

This approach assumed that it was up to Iraq to define what was trivial and what was irrelevant. Left unchallenged, this position would lead to a situation where Iraq refused to answer any embarrassing questions. And the ban on questions previously asked conveniently ignored the fact that the answers already given were patent lies or were deemed incredible. Few answers, even the honest ones, had been complete.

Reading these two reports, and bearing in mind the fact that Iraq was currently blocking the aerial inspection of the Rabiyah and Zaafaraniyah sites, I became worried that Iraq was launching a new campaign to challenge each of UNSCOM's inspections at a level just below the threshold that would justify a military response from the Council. My worry was that, if this became a systematic policy, it would gradually undermine the entire inspection regime until it was rendered ineffective. At that point we could all give up and go home. The danger was that, if Iraq attacked the inspection rights in small enough chunks, it might achieve its objectives unchallenged – what the British Foreign Office call 'salami tactics'. I immediately started a file labelled 'Breaches and Violations' to assemble together all Iraq's minor infractions. The first three papers in it were Maurizio Zifferero's report of the delayed access to PC-3 headquarters, and Johan Santesson's reports on his meetings with General Amer Rasheed and Brigadier Hossam Amin. At the front of this file I kept a log of all the incidents, by date and by type of challenge.

In the course of the next nine months, at the end of which Iraq finally agreed to the monitoring of its industry in accordance with the UN's monitoring plans, rather than its own dictates, I logged some 200 such 'salami tactic' incidents – about one every working day. These incidents covered the whole gamut: threats to the safety and security of our personnel, equipment and property; attempts to limit the scope of inspections, declaring areas or inspection activities off limits; denial, delay or restriction of access to buildings, equipment and Iraqi officials wanted for questioning; refusals to yield documents for inspections; attempts to interfere with the aerial inspections (Iraq's pet hate and the subject of the largest number of incidents); attempts to dictate the composition of inspection teams (i.e. to block experienced inspectors or those with pertinent expertise who might prove successful); moving key dual-purpose equipment and materials around within Iraq without first gaining the permission of UNSCOM; proven instances where Iraqi officials lied to inspectors to hide key facts both about past and about continuing, ostensibly short-range missile programmes; and attempts to stop the inspectors from taking photographs or samples.

My hunch was right. We took the precaution of keeping the Council informed of these behaviour patterns, through our regular series of six-monthly reports. In the end the Iraqi tactics did not work. As ever, Rolf Ekéus was also alive to the threat and, with Nikita Smidovich and Scott Ritter, devised a plan to create another crisis around Iraq's refusal to accept the monitoring plans. Again, as with the introduction of the aerial inspections in June 1992, the intention was to precipitate a crisis which would be on UNSCOM's terms, not Iraq's, and which would provide the grounds for an effective Security Council intervention to force Iraqi acceptance of monitoring.

This time the strategy worked.

Both Nikita Smidovich and Scott Ritter were worried about the whole issue of how to monitor Iraq's obligation not to reacquire long-range missiles. The language of the ceasefire resolution had created a technical nightmare. It did not ban all missiles, only long-range ones. Therefore Iraq was permitted to keep, produce and develop short-range missiles.

The ceasefire defined long-range missiles as those with a range of 150 kilometres, ground-to-ground, but it made no mention of the payload that such missiles should carry. Consequently, a missile that could be adapted to fly that distance ground-to-ground without any payload would be banned in a literal reading. This would include air defence missiles which normally delivered small payloads at vertical – that is, ground-to-air – distances of tens of kilometres. Launched in a flatter trajectory, they might cover the 150 kilometres.

A more technically sound cut-off definition would have been based either on the thrust of the rocket motors or on the payload to be delivered that distance. The untechnical language of the ceasefire meant that either (a) Iraq could own and develop missiles that could be adapted at a moment's notice to cover the 150 kilometres, or (b) the ban on its missile developments had to be redefined in stricter terms. Either way, UNSCOM would have to monitor almost all Iraq's missile research and development programmes and production facilities, regardless of stated range of the missiles being worked on, as the technologies and production equipment developed for shorter-range missiles could be readily adapted to missiles of banned range.

UNSCOM knew that Iraq was working on a variety of new missiles at several research and development sites. The main concern was the Ibn al Haitham Centre, where rocket motors were being developed. Both Nikita Smidovich and Scott Ritter were concerned that the longer UNSCOM failed to initiate monitoring of these sites, the more the equipment and personnel from these sites might be spirited away to other, as yet undeclared sites, out of view of UNSCOM. They wanted to start intensive and protracted inspections of this and other missile sites as a way of keeping an eye on them.

Thus was born the concept of interim monitoring teams. These teams would conduct no-notice inspections of the sites to be monitored, not just once, but regularly over a protracted period. The same site would be subjected to repeated inspections. This way UNSCOM would get a much deeper and realistic understanding of what work was taking place, who were the real researchers and managers, how they worked and what they were really achieving and planning. It was also hoped that, as the Iraqi personnel became used to these frequent visits, they would drop their guard and perhaps give away information about undeclared links between their work place and other relevant centres; UNSCOM might then discover the names of other experts to interview. Interim monitoring would also enable UNSCOM to spot changes to the work patterns and layouts of the sites, thereby deterring illegal activities.

The first such inspection, named IMT1a, was led by a Russian missile expert, jovial veteran of the Ministry of Agriculture crisis, Azad Vekilov. It started its work at the Ibn al Haitham Centre on 25 January 1993 and continued there until 23 March. Iraq quickly cottoned on to the nature of this inspection. On 31 January the adviser to the Iraqi Foreign Minister, Wissam al Zahawi, wrote to Rolf Ekéus noting that the team's work programme 'differs from the working procedures of the teams that preceded it'. Iraq, he said, was providing the team with the necessary assistance; but it considered 'the new arrangement by the inspection team in question for the Ibn al Haitham Centre to be based on the provisions of resolution 687'. In plain language, this was not, in Iraq's view, monitoring under the UN's monitoring plans, but inspection activity under the ceasefire resolution.

For once, UNSCOM and Iraq were in agreement. Rolf Ekéus and John Scott had no intention of letting Iraq claim these *ad hoc* arrangements as full satisfaction of its obligation to accept monitoring of its missile capabilities. They still wanted Iraq to accept the monitoring plans in full.

The wisdom of this approach soon became apparent. Virtually every day Azad Vekilov's team came across new Iraqi obstacles to their work – refusals to allow the team to look at missile blueprints (on the grounds that the missile in question was short-range and hence of no interest to the inspectors, regardless of the fact that its technology could readily be adapted to missiles of banned range).

On 13 February Iraq's position was clarified further. A missile inspection led by the French missile expert resident in UNSCOM's New York headquarters, Patrice Palanque, was visiting various missile-related sites. The team's objective was to record the names of suppliers of equipment and materials for Iraq's missile programmes, to establish what missile components Iraq had been able to manufacture indigenously, to assess its rocket motor testing capabilities and to search for undeclared SCUD missiles that the US was convinced still existed. The team collected valuable information on suppliers from machine plates and labels on containers. It concluded that Iraq had produced moulds and dyes for making components of rocket motors, and that it had imported quantities of maraging steel – a high-quality steel required for the manufacture of gyroscopes.

General Amer Rasheed asked to meet the team. He told Patrice Palanque that he expected UNSCOM to tell the Council that Iraq had fulfilled the conditions for the lifting of the sanctions. If there were any outstanding questions, UNSCOM should list them all and Iraq would answer. This was reminiscent of his 'once-and-for-all' statements made in February 1992, during the crisis over the destruction of missile production equipment. He accused UNSCOM of passing on information about the Rabiyah and Zaafaraniyah sites to the US for its Tomahawk raid and said that henceforth inspectors would not be able to take GPS (Global Positioning Satellite) readings to record the location of sites inspected. (Given the many different names of Iraqi factories and sites, the many different ways in which Westerners transliterate Arabic words into Roman script, and the huge size of many of the sites, UNSCOM needed these accurate GPS readings in order to track which buildings it had been to and instruct new teams precisely where to go. Of course, the US had no need of UNSCOM GPS readings to know where to send its cruise missiles.)

Amer then addressed the issue of monitoring. Iraq, he said, was sensitive to the activities of Azad Vekilov's team. They were staying at the Ibn al Haitham Centre too long. He hoped it would not be the target of the next US attack. He regretted ever trusting UNSCOM; Iraq would not give information on its suppliers until 'there was a change in the political situation' – meaning agreement to lift the sanctions. On monitoring, he stated outright that, in his opinion, Iraq would never sign resolution 715 (which adopted the UN's plans for monitoring Iraq's industry). No government, he asserted, would ever accept the colonialist general provisions of the plans. Iraq could accept implementation of the technical annexes to the plans, but only if such monitoring were conducted under the ceasefire resolution, not 715.

At around the same time an IAEA inspection team was having its own problems with Iraq. There had been persistent rumours of an underground Iraqi nuclear reactor to which access could only be gained from below water. Intelligence analysts had problems tracking down an exact location on a map to inspect. They plumped for the dam at Badush, 380 kilometres north-north-west of Baghdad. A team of crack French frogmen joined the team to search the river banks for signs of a hidden entrance below the water line – to no avail.

But the team did have other startling successes which had serious implications for monitoring. At the al Hatheen establishment in al Mussayib, about 60 kilometres south of Baghdad, the team found 242 high-precision CNC machines which could have been used in the engineering of the nuclear programme. Iraq hastened to state that it had 'forgotten to declare' these items. At the very least, these machines would have to be monitored continuously by the IAEA. If they had been used in the nuclear programme, they should have been destroyed.

At the wrap-up meeting following the inspection, the Iraqis refused to answer the team's questions on the grounds that they were too vague. The chief Iraqi official, Abdul Halim Ibrahim al Hajjaj, said that they would give serious consideration to answering questions of a specific nature. He complained that the inspection had been very aggressive; the IAEA, he said, 'had probably submitted to pressure from New York' – a reference to the fact that Iraq found UNSCOM's inspections more intrusive than the IAEA's.

Pressure was obviously building up again. Even IAEA inspectors were now the targets of abusive or threatening late-night phone calls. Up in the Kurdish provinces in northern Iraq, life was becoming really dangerous for the UN guards. Car bombs and hand grenades were going off on an almost daily basis. The UN was being targeted.

In March 1993 the third biological weapons inspection team flew to Iraq. The failure to find evidence of biological munitions or weapons production facilities meant that efforts to uncover the truth had to be focused elsewhere. The team had two aims: to look at munitions-filling machinery to assess whether it was or could have been used to fill biological munitions; and to track down Iraqi scientists who might have been involved in the programme but had not been named by Iraq. This team was led by David Franz, perhaps the world's leading biological weapons expert outside Iraq and Russia – the only two countries known to have produced biological weapons since President Nixon unilaterally halted US production in 1968. At the time he was working for the US Army Medical Research Institute for Infectious Diseases at Fort Detrick – the US Defense Department's biological defence research centre.

Despite its clear and uncontroversial objectives, this team ran into the same obstructions encountered by the nuclear and missile teams. On 13 March 1993 David Franz and his team arrived by helicopter at the large Muthanna chemical weapons site to pick up a munitions expert from the Chemical Destruction Group to supervise the destruction of Iraq's vast chemical weapons arsenal.

He wanted the expert to look at munitions-filling equipment at the Sa'ad 13 plant, some 140 kilometres north-west of Baghdad. Out of the blue, the Iraqi minder, Dr Ghazi Faisal, refused to allow the munitions expert to join the team on the entirely spurious grounds that he was part of the Chemical Destruction Group and therefore could not be a biological weapons inspector. David firmly told Ghazi that it was for UNSCOM and UNSCOM alone to decide who should be on which inspection team and that any delay to the inspection would be reported to New York as a violation of Iraq's obligations. After thinking the matter over, Dr Ghazi Faisal backed down.

But the next day he was at it again. The team turned up at the Baghdad University Veterinary School to assess how its known biological research capabilities might have contributed to a biological weapons programme and how it should be monitored in the future. Ghazi refused to allow them onto the campus, stating that an inspection would 'violate the sanctity of an educational institution and would hurt the students' feelings'. This was probably the weakest excuse ever given to an UNSCOM inspector.

After nearly four hours, with David Franz threatening to report a violation to New York unless he was given access with adequate numbers of inspectors and his own interpreter, and Ghazi trying to set more restrictive terms for the inspection to proceed, David lost patience and told Ghazi that they were returning to the UNSCOM office to report the situation. As the team gathered to board the bus back to their hotel, Dr Ghazi Faisal caved in and allowed them in. In the event, they concluded that the equipment could have been adapted to fill biological weapons, but had probably not been.

In neither case was Iraq trying to hide a banned activity. These obstructions were just further indications that it was building up to another confrontation. This time it was not aimed specifically at UNSCOM – indeed, the UN guards appeared to be getting the worst of it. Rather, it was a general challenge to the authority of the Council. Things were serious enough for the heads of the various UN agencies to start dusting off their emergency evacuation plans.

Jaakko Ylitalo, Kevin St Louis's Finnish replacement as head of the UNSCOM Baghdad office, started to keep a daily security log of incidents against UNSCOM personnel and property.

At the end of March Azad Vekilov's IMT1a missile interim monitoring team was replaced by IMT1b. In a joint meeting with a missile inspection team led by Nikita Smidovich and the incoming interim monitoring team, Brigadier Hossam Amin complained that the interim monitoring was going on too long. It was affecting the normal operation of the Ibn al Haitham Centre. UNSCOM, he said, had started monitoring without first engaging the Iraqis in dialogue. Iraq would prefer monitoring to be undertaken by surprise inspections at irregular intervals, rather than by quasi-permanent teams.

In the event Iraq did not interfere with the activities of IMT1b, which broadened the scope of the interim monitoring to investigate Iraq's ability to produce solid rocket propellant for missiles. Regular visits were now being conducted not only at Ibn al Haitham, but also at the al Rasheed factory and the al Qaa'qaa State Establishment about 40 kilometres south of Baghdad. Thus, while extremely useful work was being done by the team, the strategy of prompting a crisis over monitoring was not yet working.

Meanwhile, a reprise of an old crisis was brewing. On 6 April 1993 one of my Russian counterparts in the Geneva chemical weapons negotiations, a colleague of Nikita Smidovich's, led a chemical weapons inspection team into Iraq. Igor Mitrokhin is a military officer with a great deal of experience in chemical and biological weapons. One of my closest friends and colleagues in Geneva, Terry Taylor (who was later to become a prominent biological weapons inspector), knew Igor well – not just as a chemical weapons negotiator, but also as one of the key interlocutors in the trilateral biological weapons inspections instigated after Yeltsin's admission in 1992 that the Soviet Union had for years been in breach of the Biological Weapons Convention by running a clandestine biological weapons programme. It had fallen to Igor to shepherd the joint US–UK team around the Russian institutions and scientists who had been involved in the programme. He was thus an ideal inspector – he knew the weapons systems, knew how to hide them from prying eyes, and knew what to look for.

Igor Mitrokhin's task was to take an inventory of the chemical weapons production equipment in Iraq with a view to destroying it and the remaining precursor chemicals once the Chemical Destruction Group wound down its destruction of Iraq's chemical weapons, planned for the end of June. On 15 April Igor handed the Iraqis a letter telling them to move most of the production equipment at the al Fallujah plants 80 kilometres west of Baghdad to the Muthanna site by 31 May, in preparation for destruction. All these items had been acquired by Iraq specifically for the production of chemical weapons and had been used only for this. There was no way in which they could irreversibly be converted exclusively for other uses. In short, they met UNSCOM's criteria, established the previous February during the crisis over the destruction of missile-production equipment, for items that must be destroyed.

On 29 April General Amer Rasheed responded with a letter to Rolf Ekéus saying that Iraq wanted to redeploy this equipment for the production of pesticides (similar in chemistry to chemical nerve agents). On 14 May Rolf responded, stating that because of the criteria, these items of equipment had to be destroyed. Riyadh al Qaysi, the chief of the International Organisations and Conferences Department at the Iraqi Ministry for Foreign Affairs and former legal adviser, responded on 27 May, accusing UNSCOM, the Sanctions Committee and the Security Council of an orchestrated policy of revenge against the Iraqi people. In particular, he alleged that UNSCOM had overstepped its mandate in refusing to countenance the redeployment of the equipment. He

Map 5: July 1993 Crisis Centres

Two crises arose in the summer of 1993 when Iraq refused to move chemicals and equipment from the chemical factories at al Fallujah to the Muthanna State Establishment for destruction under UNSCOM supervision, and when it refused to allow UNSCOM to place monitoring cameras at the rocket motor test stands at al Rabiyah and al Rafah.

asked Rolf Ekéus to reconsider. In a letter to Riyadh al Qaysi dated 4 June, Rolf stood by the decision to destroy the equipment, explaining that it 'could not be rendered harmless as the equipment was intrinsically capable of being used for prohibited purposes and could quickly be reconverted for such'. He gave Iraq until 10 June to move the equipment to Muthanna as ordered, or the Council would be informed. In fact, the Council already knew, and military preparations were under way. Iraq was alert to this and started dispersing many of its assets, including materials that were ordered to Muthanna for destruction.

Iraq failed to meet the deadline, but on 11 June Rolf received another letter from Riyadh al Qaysi, by now promoted to Deputy Foreign Minister, stating that 'Iraq remained prepared to give the Special Commission, through bilateral technical consultations, practical guarantees to ensure the peaceful use of this equipment in the long term.' Rolf rejected this proposal and submitted a formal report on the situation to the Security Council on 16 June.

Meanwhile, the monitoring crisis had come to fruition. Patrice Palanque led the third interim monitoring team, IMT1c, into Baghdad on 5 June 1993. The aim was to get a tighter grip on Iraq's missile-making capabilities. The team was to target high-precision machine tools and rocket motor test facilities. High-precision machine tools, similar to those the IAEA had found in al Hatheen, are required in the production of metal components for missiles. In particular, a sub-team, led by Mark Silver (chief inspector of the Ministry of Agriculture inspection team), aimed to up the monitoring ante by installing permanent monitoring cameras at two rocket motor test stands located at Yawm al Azim (meaning the Great Day – a missile facility located at al Musayyib, 60 kilometres south of Baghdad) and at the Shahiyat Liquid Engine Research, Development, Testing and Evaluation Centre (located at al Rafah, a further 5 kilometres away). Nikita Smidovich accompanied the team into Iraq in case there were any problems.

When Mark and Nikita separately informed the Iraqis on 5 June of the planned monitoring cameras, they were asked for technical literature on the cameras, the better 'to be able to persuade their superiors to support the idea'. The answer came the next day – no cameras were to be installed. Iraq viewed this as 715 (the UN monitoring plans rejected by Iraq) through the back door. This was formally confirmed in a letter from Riyadh al Qaysi to Pierce Corden on 8 June, in which he claimed that the installation of the camera systems did not fall within the framework of the provisions of the ceasefire resolution but 'rather comes within the framework of matters and questions that are still the subject of dialogue between the Iraqi authorities ... and the Special Commission'.

The arguments were batted back and forth over the next ten days. On 18 June the Security Council made a statement on both the camera and chemical equipment issues. It found Iraq to be in material breach of its obligations, reminded it of the similar statements made in January (just prior to the bombing of the Zaafaraniyah facility) and warned of similar serious consequences if it did not agree to UNSCOM's demands.

'Matters and questions' was an Iraqi euphemism for monitoring in accordance with the UN plans – resolution 715, which was such anathema to Iraq that it would not even refer to it in official communications with the UN. The dialogue was an Iraqi idea, put forward as a means of killing two birds with one stone: setting up a seminar to resolve 'once and for all' the outstanding questions relating to Iraq's past activities – a long-standing Iraqi objective – and side-lining UNSCOM by having this review conducted by experts from the P5 – the five permanent members of the Council (China, France, Russia, the UK and the US) – rather than by UNSCOM staff.

Iraq had been pushing the 'once-and-for-all' concept since my arrival at UNSCOM. While it seemed attractive, the intention was not to resolve all outstanding issues, but rather to draw a line under UNSCOM's prying investigations into its past activities, and hence into what it had not declared.

The idea of the Council arbitrating between Iraq and UNSCOM had already been rejected in March 1992 when Tariq Aziz had proposed it to the Security Council. But the Iraqi Foreign Minister, Mohammed al Sahaf, had revived the idea in a letter dated 30 May 1993, addressed to the Russian ambassador to the UN, Yuriy Vorontsov, in his capacity as President of the Security Council that month. He left it open to Vorontsov whether the review of Iraq's compliance, and hence of the lifting of the sanctions, should be undertaken by Iraq and the P5, or by Iraq and the Security Council as a whole.

Rolf Ekéus, ever aware of the danger of losing his status as sole interlocutor with Iraq on weapons issues, was ahead of the game. The remarks made to the various inspection teams, hinting that Iraq would not address certain issues until other political matters were resolved as part of an end game, suggested that it was about to attempt to go over UNSCOM's head, appealing directly to the Security Council to 'resolve' – that is, renegotiate – those issues that Iraq did not like about monitoring and the conditions for easing the sanctions. Rolf had alerted the P5 to this possibility and it was agreed that the Council should throw the idea back at Iraq, suggesting instead that high-level talks be held between UNSCOM and Iraq to address all outstanding issues. And two weeks before Sahaf's letter arrived on Vorontsov's desk, Rolf had written to Riyadh al Qaysi stating that 'once-and-for-all' technical talks between UNSCOM and Iraqi experts were no more likely to succeed than the numerous technical discussions that had taken place within the various inspections throughout the two previous years – unless they were part of higher-level technical contacts about the whole range of compliance issues, including the ongoing monitoring and verification plans and the full disclosure of all aspects of Iraq's past weapons programmes. Rolf indicated that he intended, upon his return to New York in June, to hold talks with

Nizar Hamdoon on preparations for these high-level meetings.

On 20 May Iraq declined Rolf's invitation to high-level talks in New York, countering with a proposal to hold talks in Baghdad. We were reluctant to accept the Baghdad venue for two prime reasons. With military tensions increasing, we did not want to have any more of our personnel in Baghdad than was absolutely necessary. But, more importantly, if the aim of the talks was to resolve as many of the technical issues as possible, in addition to the political ones, then our experts would need access to their files in New York. Given Iraq's already proven aggressive counter-measures against UNSCOM (by this stage theft from the UNSCOM office in Baghdad had become commonplace and so nothing of any confidentiality was left in it), we simply did not want to expose our information and assessments to the risk of compromise.

On 9 June Rolf Ekéus told Nizar Hamdoon that he would agree to high-level talks in Baghdad on the bigger issues, provided that preparatory technical discussions first took place in New York and provided that Iraq agreed to both the installation of the monitoring cameras and the destruction of the chemical production equipment. A tentative date of 12 July was set for the technical discussions, to allow both sides adequate time to prepare in detail.

Meanwhile, Tomahawk targeteers were eyeing up the rocket motor test stands at Yawm al Azim and al Rafah and the chemical assets at al Fallujah and Muthanna.

In fact, the missiles did not land on Baghdad in support of UNSCOM. On 27 June 1993 the US retaliated following the botched Iraqi attempt on President George Bush's life during a farewell trip to Kuwait in March 1993. Evidence given during the trial of the would-be assassins implicated Iraqi intelligence. Various Iraqis had been found guilty, on forensic evidence jointly gathered and analysed by Kuwait and the US, of crossing into Kuwait in order to set off a car bomb along the route of one of Bush's trips there. The plot had failed, and the new US President, Bill Clinton, had vowed to take revenge on those responsible once they were identified. With the Kuwaiti courts having convicted the men and exposed their links with an Iraqi intelligence operation, Clinton was now bound to respond. Twenty-three Tomahawks landed on the Iraqi intelligence headquarters in downtown Baghdad during the early hours of the 27th. The timing of the raid – night in Baghdad – was intended to make civilian casualties unlikely. Severe damage was done to the building, and the Iraqis realised that Clinton, like Bush, was willing to exercise force. Mohammed al Sahaf, in a letter to the President of the Security Council, condemned the attack as a cowardly act of aggression and alleged that the mere fact of UNSCOM's regular U2 flight over Baghdad a few days previously was irrefutable evidence that it had carried out the reconnaissance for the attack.

On 28 June Mohammed al Sahaf wrote again to the President of the Security Council informing him that Iraq would comply with the demand to move the chemical production equipment to Muthanna, but continued to hope that it could be modified. On the installation of cameras, Sahaf urged that the issue be deferred until the review of Iraq's compliance he had requested in his letter of 30 May had been completed.

By 29 June Iraq had transferred all the chemical production equipment and most of the chemicals from the al Fallujah plants to Muthanna. Hossam Amin informed Nikita Smidovich that the decision to do so had been taken to 'deprive Iraq's enemies of all pretext for hostile actions' but declined to state whether that meant that the cameras could also be installed. Later that afternoon the Iraqis informed the head of the Chemical Destruction Group that the final batch of chemicals would be moved to Muthanna later that evening. The chemical crisis was effectively over.

But the monitoring crisis still had some way to go. Time was up for IMT1c and the camera installation sub-team. Partly because the team members had other things to do, and partly to increase the pressure on Iraq to allow the camera installation to proceed, the team was ordered to withdraw on 5 July. Before it left, Hossam Amin informed Nikita Smidovich that Iraq had complied on the big issue – the destruction of chemical production equipment. The camera-installation issue was 'too small' to hold up the dialogue between UNSCOM and Iraq. Even so, Iraq was anticipating a military attack on the rocket motor test stands at Yawm al Azim and al Rafah and had dismantled them, dispersing the equipment. He insisted that, as the stands had been dismantled, no rocket tests could take place; the monitoring cameras were therefore unnecessary.

CHAPTER 14

Mission Accomplished: Monitoring Begins

'If you open that Pandora's box you never
know what Trojan 'orses will jump out.'

ERNEST BEVIN

'Words are also actions.'

RALPH WALDO EMERSON

Iraq's dispersal of equipment from the rocket motor test stands
without UNSCOM's prior approval put Iraq further in breach of
its obligations. But it provided a new tactic to force the issue of
monitoring. Between them, the missile team of Nikita Smidovich,
Mark Silver and Scott Ritter came up with the idea of sending
another team into Iraq to inventory and tag each of the items Iraq
had removed from the test stands.

On the morning of 7 July Rolf Ekéus tried this idea out on the
P4 – the US, the UK, France and Russia. These were, at the time,
UNSCOM's strongest supporters in the Council and it was upon
the first three that enforcement action would fall if Iraq continued
to object to monitoring. Keeping these four nations informed of
decisions that could result in military action was of paramount
importance. As it was, the French ambassador had already complained in June when his Mission could not be contacted before a
letter was sent by Rolf Ekéus to Mohammed al Sahaf. France had
called the meeting to 'compare notes' on the situation.

Sensitive to the French criticism (mainly directed against Pierce

Corden and myself), Rolf Ekéus flattered them, thanking them for the opportunity to seek their wise counsel. He reported the progress on the chemical equipment issue, and then told them about the dismantling of the rocket motor test stands. He also reported that the aerial inspection team had flown over and landed at both sites, in the face of Iraqi protests, to take photographs. Those photographs would be in New York shortly to show to the Council. However, Rolf did show them earlier photographs showing the sites before they were dismantled and pointed out where each of the main components now lay. He also refuted statements attributed to Nizar Hamdoon in the *New York Times* that the camera issue was a trivial technical one – Iraq had in fact sought to make it a political issue based around its rejection of resolution 715. He also denied Hossam Amin's assertion to Nikita Smidovich that, with the test stands dismantled, monitoring cameras were no longer required. The test stands could be reassembled and made operational within forty-eight hours: they had to ensure that they were not used for rocket tests while unobserved.

He noted that the test stands were too small for testing SCUD missiles and that was why they had not been destroyed. Indeed, if UNSCOM wanted to destroy these test stands it might legally require a new Security Council resolution broadening its mandate. However, activities conducted on them could be relevant to the development of banned, long-range missiles. Thus their use had to be monitored. The least intrusive way of achieving this was, of course, the option that Iraq had rejected – the installation of non-interfering monitoring cameras. If cameras were not installed, the two options remaining were to tag and seal the equipment in such a way that it could not be used until monitoring was initiated, or to pass a new resolution (something Rolf knew the Council would wish to avoid) mandating their destruction.

The British ambassador, Sir David Hannay, was rightly concerned that an attempt to broaden UNSCOM's already extraordinary mandate would weaken, rather than strengthen, its support. Would monitoring of the sites through regular aerial and ground inspections to confirm that the equipment remained dismantled be a sufficient interim solution? Rolf Ekéus replied that UNSCOM did not have the resources for that. Failing the destruction of the equipment, camera monitoring was the only viable long-term strategy. Feigning reluctance, Rolf conceded that sealing the equipment might prove a viable interim solution but wondered what would happen if Iraq blocked such a move.

The French deputy ambassador, Hervé Ladsous, commented that, as the equipment was dual-purpose, Iraq would probably object. The Russian ambassador, Yuriy Vorontsov, noted that that would help to create a defensible logic for destruction – if Iraq would accept neither non-interfering monitoring nor non-destructive sealing of the equipment, it would be clear to all that it was forcing the Council's hand. Ladsous suggested a phased approach – first seal, then install monitoring cameras. Hannay, too, liked this idea. As Iraq wanted to use the test stands, it would eventually see that cameras were in its own interests.

Having got the P4 to adopt precisely the strategy he had sought, Rolf Ekéus now proceeded to the big issue – gaining Iraqi acquiescence on the full monitoring plans and acknowledgement of resolution 715. Hannay noted that this was a much more complex problem, covering hundreds of sites, rather than just two. That said, sanctions could not be lifted until monitoring was in place.

Rolf Ekéus agreed, pointing out that Iraq was systematically blocking the use of sensors, not just cameras, in a large number of sites. Even if the test stand equipment were destroyed, UNSCOM would still have to address difficult issues, such as monitoring the use of petrochemical facilities. These were a bigger problem than rocket test stands – Iraq's economy could not afford to see them destroyed or moth-balled under seal. The next stage would therefore probably be a major chemical interim monitoring inspection at one of Iraq's principal petrochemical facilities. Hannay wondered why such an inspection had to be conducted under resolution 715, which Iraq rejected outright, rather than under the ceasefire resolution, which it reluctantly accepted. That might avoid a conflict.

John Scott, careful not to admit that bringing the 715 situation to a head was precisely the aim of UNSCOM's entire strategy, noted that launching the petrochemical inspection as a ceasefire inspection would not be credible, as the sole purpose would be to prepare for the installation of long-term monitoring devices. Hannay immediately picked up on this, seeing that if UNSCOM launched a 715 inspection and Iraq blocked it, it would be one more entry in the record of non-compliance and so strengthen the Council's hand in taking corrective action.

Rolf Ekéus then reminded the P4 that UNSCOM and the IAEA were planning other actions that would support this strategy. French gamma ray detection equipment was being installed on UNSCOM's Bundeswehr-operated helicopters in Baghdad to conduct a baseline radiological survey of key nuclear facilities. The result of this survey was a radiation contour map for the site showing existing hot spots. Regular surveys would show up any new nuclear activity as changes to this radiation contour map, and might also provide useful new information about what nuclear activities Iraq had got up to in the past. The helicopters would also be fitted with new German technology to detect the operation of high-speed centrifuges – indicative of gas centrifuge separation of weapons-grade uranium for a nuclear bomb. The surveys would probably take place in August.

Turning to the proposed dialogue with the Iraqis, Rolf Ekéus noted that he was prepared to proceed provided Iraq accepted the sealing of the test stand equipment. He was told rather brusquely by Hannay that the terms of Security Council resolutions were not negotiable, but how UNSCOM chose to go about securing their full implementation was its own business. The Council would not intercede on the terms for the dialogue.

Thus Rolf Ekéus came away from the meeting with precisely what he wanted. He was instructed to write to the Iraqis telling them of an impending mission to seal the rocket motor test stand equipment as an interim solution, and was authorised immediately to threaten its destruction should they refuse. He should proceed with the other plans to increase the pressure on Iraq to accept full-blown monitoring under resolution 715, and report in writing to the Council both on the current situation and on any further developments. The Council would meet in full the next morning to ratify the approach outlined by the P4.

Rolf Ekéus sent a letter to Riyadh al Qaysi that afternoon. It appointed Mark Silver, kicking his heels in the UNSCOM office in Bahrain and now dubbed 'Mr Crisis' by the Iraqis in recognition of his role at the head of both the Ministry of Agriculture team and the camera installation sub-team, as chief inspector of the test stand equipment sealing team. The letter specifically told Iraq that items at the two test sites would be inventoried and placed under seal to prevent them from being used until such time as monitoring cameras could be installed. Until then, Iraq was not to move any of the sealed items without prior notification and consent of UNSCOM.

Mark Silver's inspection became one of the shortest on record. He arrived on 10 July with his team. That evening he and Scott Ritter met General Amer Rasheed, Brigadier Hossam Amin and Mohammed Kamal – the chief Iraqi minder for missile teams – to inform them of their plans for sealing the equipment.

General Amer Rasheed said that he had understood UNSCOM's objective to be to prove that no illegal activities were taking place at the test stands. Mark agreed, but noted that Iraq had prevented UNSCOM from doing this by blocking the installation of monitoring cameras. Amer said that Iraq was not against cameras *per se,* but against resolution 715, which would be discussed in the upcoming technical talks in New York. Because Iraq feared that it would be subject to aggression, it had dis- mantled industrial equipment from a number of sites and moved it away from likely targets of air strikes. Given that situation, UNSCOM could ensure that no illegal activities were taking place through its helicopter and U2 surveillance. There was no longer anything at the sites to monitor or even to fix the cameras to.

Mark Silver responded brilliantly. He pointed out that this was the first that UNSCOM had heard about Iraq removing all the equipment from the test sites. It should have been informed first. Just as Iraq could, in the absence of monitoring cameras, move equipment away from the sites without UNSCOM's knowledge, so it could move it back and start using it. Amer had anticipated this response, and suggested that UNSCOM could inspect the equipment at its dispersal points to ensure it was not moved. Mark countered by saying that that was not a practical solution, as inspections would have to take place every two or three days, whereas the camera or seals options would require only intermittent inspection.

General Amer Rasheed now asked why, given that the equipment was not prohibited, it should be sealed. Mark answered that tests had to be stopped at the sites because of Iraq's blocking of the non-intrusive method of monitoring–cameras. Amer then said the magic words. Placement of seals on equipment was a sensitive issue for Iraq. It took UNSCOM operations beyond actions under the ceasefire resolution and into the domain of resolution 715, which Iraq rejected. When the crisis was over, Iraq would conduct missile tests as it was allowed to do, and without monitoring cameras.

Mark Silver, seeking a clear position to report to New York, asked whether General Amer Rasheed was saying no to the seals. Amer said that he was not saying no, he was saying they were unnecessary. Mark told him that he interpreted what Amer was saying as a no.

At this stage General Amer Rasheed again offered to allow the team to inspect the equipment at the dispersal site. He even offered, because of the looming military crisis, to collect all the equipment in one site, such as Baghdad or Muthanna. He did not

want to give the US a pretext for bombing Iraq again. Mark Silver
pointed out that, by blocking the inspection, Iraq was giving the
Council precisely that – justification for enforcement action. Amer
repeated that he was not stopping the team from carrying out its
duties.

Scott Ritter interceded to remind Amer of the logic of
monitoring. A missile inspection in 1992 had found documents
recording Iraqi studies on how to extend the range of the Ababil
100 missile from 100 kilometres (permissible under the terms of
the ceasefire) to more than the 150-kilometre limit. Clearly, in
order to assure the world that Iraq was not developing missiles of
prohibited range, UNSCOM would have to monitor Iraq's
shorter-range missile research and development plans as these
could rapidly and easily be converted to longer-range. Amer
rejected this, stating that the same logic could involve UNSCOM
in controlling all Iraqi students' higher studies. Did UNSCOM
intend to ensure that Iraq did not develop its infrastructure but
rather, like Kuwait and Saudi Arabia, squandered its oil wealth on
decadent pursuits?

Mark Silver refused to be drawn down that path, again
demanding to know whether this was a denial. General Amer
Rasheed said that if UNSCOM stuck to implementing resolution
687, it was not a denial. If UNSCOM were merely following the
dictates of Warren Christopher (the US Secretary of State) to
obtain an Iraqi refusal to set up the destruction of the missile
testing facilities, then UNSCOM's credibility would be eroded.
Mark asked Amer if he were aware of the seriousness of the
consequences, and Amer assured him that he was. The meeting
closed with Mark saying that he would relay Amer's comments to
Rolf Ekéus, but personally saw the discussion as being a denial of
UNSCOM's right to carry out its mandate.

The meeting ended at 7.45 p.m. Baghdad time on 10 July (11.45
a.m. in New York). As soon as Mark got back to the UNSCOM
office, he called Rolf Ekéus and was told to stand by. At 11 p.m.
Baghdad time he was ordered to visit the rocket test stands the

next day, photograph them and attempt to place the seals. Mark rang Hossam Amin and informed him of his decision to inspect the missile test stands the next morning, leaving the Sheraton Hotel at 8 a.m.

The team, accompanied by Hossam Amin and a host of Iraqi minders, arrived at the al Rafah test site at around 9.45 a.m. on 11 July. Henry Arvidsson, the Swedish chief aerial inspector, took still photographs of the scene. He then switched to video to record the scenes that followed. Henry is truly a mountain of a man – not someone to be argued with. My first glimpse of him was on film. Victoria Schulz from the UN's Information Department had made a film about the first year of inspections in Iraq, which I had seen in February 1992 in UNSCOM's meeting room – the bunker – at its New York headquarters, along with several other UNSCOM staff. Henry had been on the inspection team involved in the parking-lot stand-off. When David Kay arrived in the Nuclear Design Centre basement, he was caught on film saying, 'Right, I need someone to man the door. Henry!' Henry's huge frame had all but blocked out the entire doorway. All those watching the film had burst out laughing.

On the test stand Mark Silver took out one of the seals and informed Hossam Amin that he intended to place it on the stand. Amin became very animated, referring to the previous night's discussion and Iraq's position on the issue of seals. He asked Mark to remove the seal. Mark asked Amin if he was denying the team the right to install a seal. Amin knew he was trapped. He noted Henry's video recording and objected to the staging of the denial. He claimed it was a clear act of provocation. In response to Mark's repeated question, Amin finally admitted that he was blocking the placement of the seal on the test stand.

At that point Mark picked up the satellite telephone and called Rolf Ekéus. He was told to proceed directly with his team to Habbaniyah airfield and withdraw to Bahrain. At the same time Mohammed Kamal had contacted General Amer Rasheed, who supported Amin's blocking actions. Amin bitterly acknowledged a well-choreographed UNSCOM provocation and congratulated Mark on a performance worthy of an Egyptian soap.

By 2.30 p.m. on 11 July Mark's team was back in Bahrain. He had been in Iraq less than twenty-four hours.*

By now, Iraq was fully expecting to be bombed again. Its military aircraft were yet again being removed from airfields and parked in fields and near civilian buildings to protect them from air strikes.

As soon as Mark Silver's team had departed, Mohammed al Sahaf wrote to the President of the Security Council listing the reasons for Iraq's refusal to let Mark place the seals on the test stands. He argued that UNSCOM had:

> begun to implement the provisions of resolution 715 (1991) without having committed itself to informing the Security Council that Iraq's compliance with section C of resolution 687 (1991) makes it incumbent upon the Council to begin considering in earnest the lifting of the economic sanctions imposed in Iraq. This is the main issue.

Rolf Ekéus responded to this in a briefing note which the Council considered the next day, 12 July. In the note, Rolf observed that Sahaf's letter:

> unequivocally raised the issue from a specific issue of moni-

---

* An ironic footnote to the incident which eventually succeeded in forcing Iraq to accept resolution 715: Scott Ritter insists that the crisis revolved around the wrong incident. He claims that Mark Silver misunderstood his instructions: he was to collect the dispersed equipment at one site and seal it in a crate. Instead, he visited the empty test stand and attempted to seal it. Whatever the truth of the matter, it achieved the desired result.

toring two missile-engine test sites to the level of the principle of Iraq's acceptance of ongoing monitoring and verification under resolution 715 (1991). While an interim solution preventing use of missile test sites might be possible, the permanent solution, through the installation of monitoring cameras, would not be found until Iraq could be convinced that it must accept and implement resolution 715 (1991).

Rolf went on to say that UNSCOM 'had always understood Security Council resolutions 687 (1991), 707 (1991) and 715 (1991) to constitute an indissoluble whole' and 'could not therefore consider reporting to the Security Council [that the conditions for lifting sanctions had been fulfilled] until it deemed Iraq to be in compliance not only with [resolution 687 (1991)], but also with resolution 707 (1991) and, in particular, resolution 715 (1991)'. He ended by coyly suggesting that 'in the present circumstances, there might be some utility in conveying this message, with the full support of the Council, to the highest levels of the Iraqi Government'.

Of course, Rolf's intention was that he should be the purveyor of the message. He got his way. The confrontation was now entirely focused on Iraq's full acceptance of the terms of resolution 715, and Rolf was sent by the Council to make this clear. The strategy to raise resolution 715 to the forefront was half complete – the Security Council was on board.

The next day, 13 July, the usual suspects left New York for Baghdad: Rolf Ekéus, John Scott, Olivia Platon and me. We arrived on 15 July and, in the course of the next four days, held over thirteen hours of discussions with the Iraqis. The usual suspects, too, were present on their side: Tariq Aziz, Mohammed al Sahaf, General Amer Rasheed, Human Abdul Khaliq, Riyadh al Qaysi and Hossam Amin, with various others.

The outcome was anything but the usual.* At the fourth

meeting, on 18 July, the Iraqi side handed over a position paper on all the issues of concern to Iraq. Stating their desire to see the economic embargo lifted, the first paragraph gave us a pleasant shock. It stated that 'Iraq is ready to comply with the provisions of the plans for ongoing monitoring and verification as contained in resolution 715 (1991).' It appeared that the second part of the strategy had also come good.

Of course, there were hitches. Iraq laid down eight conditions for its acceptance of 715. It wanted:

1. The UN to respect its sovereignty, internal security and dignity.
2. The UN to guarantee Iraq's right to industrial, scientific and technological progress.
3. UNSCOM to replace its own aerial reconnaissance assets (the Bundeswehr-operated helicopters and the US-operated U2) with Iraqi aircraft.
4. A guarantee that monitoring would be carried out in accordance with the rules and methods of relevant international agreements currently in force.
5. A guarantee that sanctions would be lifted without additional conditions.
6. A guarantee that the Council would lift the arms embargo on Iraq.
7. A pledge on the part of the Council and UNSCOM to work earnestly to secure a zone free of all weapons of mass destruction in the Middle East.

---

* Upon my return to New York, Nizir Hamdoon could not contain himself. He invited me to lunch to find out what on earth could have happened in the discussions in Baghdad to have brought about this change in the Iraqi position. I could do little more than surmise that it was the consistency with which we had been delivering the message that, if Iraq complied with all the provisions of the ceasefire, including the plan for monitoring, UNSCOM would indeed report to the Council that the conditions for lifting sanctions had been met.

8. An end to the no-fly zones north of the thirty-sixth parallel and south of the thirty-second.

With suitable caveats, the first two could easily be accommodated. The replacement of UNSCOM's aerial reconnaissance assets had long been an Iraqi priority of which we were extremely suspicious. But the issue was finessed by saying that, depending on the level of confidence between UNSCOM and Iraq, the matter could be considered. We pointed out that conditions five to eight were outside the competence of UNSCOM but undertook to report Iraq's concerns faithfully to the Council. In addition, Rolf Ekéus confirmed that UNSCOM would, as soon as it believed Iraq to be in compliance and without additional conditions, report to the Council with a view to lifting the economic sanctions. But he pointed out that it was the Council that would take the decision, not UNSCOM.

The fourth condition was tricky. International disarmament agreements set up the rules for inspecting states that have willingly and in good faith forgone the right to possess certain weapons. Their verification and monitoring provisions would probably not be adequate to spot a determined cheat like Iraq. Acceptance of this condition would eviscerate the monitoring regime – indeed, it was effectively saying that we, Iraq, accept monitoring under resolution 715 provided that you do not monitor as provided under resolution 715. I suggested some weasel words to avoid this pitfall, changing the end of the condition to read 'carried out in the same spirit as relevant international agreements in the field of international arms control and disarmament' – meaning that the degree of intrusiveness of the monitoring regime would reflect the degree of confidence in Iraq's compliance with its obligations.

Iraq bought it – at least to the extent that it agreed to the installation of the cameras at the two missile test stands as an interim measure to permit the high-level technical talks to proceed in New York. The compromise was that they would not be switched on until progress was made in these talks. The key item on the agenda was to be the nature and implementation of ongoing monitoring and verification. The talks would also address all other outstanding issues (i.e. Iraq's failure to account adequately for its past programmes) with a view to resolving them. This was an acknowledgement of General Amer Rasheed's desire for a seminar to resolve issues 'once and for all', but it did not commit UNSCOM to end its investigations should the talks not resolve issues to its satisfaction.

The crisis was on hold, but now with the prospect that the issue of long-term monitoring might be resolved.

The remainder of July and August 1993 was a hectic time, spent preparing for these talks and monitoring the situation at the test stands. By the end of July the monitoring cameras were installed, but not operational, and a *modus operandi* had been reached on notification and observation of Iraq's missile tests. Iraq would give advance warning of its intention to test a missile, and UNSCOM would send a team of missile experts to the test stand to observe it. The interim arrangements were working well on the ground.

We were at one and the same time optimistic that we might achieve what we had been striving for – the implementation of the monitoring plans – and fearful that Iraq might so surround its acceptance of the plans with conditions that it rendered the regime ineffective – in a manner that made it difficult for UNSCOM and the Council to reject the conditions. We also hoped against hope that the discussions of outstanding issues might at last result in full disclosure of Iraq's past programmes, including the still undeclared biological weapons programme.

The talks took place in New York between 31 August and 9 September.

I chaired the discussion of the biological issues. It was an extremely frustrating experience. Dr Taha was still being presented by the Iraqis as the sole mover and shaker behind the biological research programme, a claim we simply did not believe.

Taha merely repeated the tired Iraqi party line to each of our questions. She demanded specific questions, rather than general ones, but as soon as our questions became specific, her answers grew vague and evasive. She refused to answer questions on the whereabouts of aerosol generators and inhalation chambers that we knew had been imported by Iraq's weapons programme purchasing body, the Technical and Scientific Materials Import Division (TSMID), claiming that in order to do so she needed the precise details of the equipment and suppliers. We were reluctant to let on precisely what we knew because, in the past, as soon as we did that, Iraq had amended its story to incorporate what we had just announced, but no more. If we left some doubt in the Iraqi's minds about what we knew, in order to satisfy us they would have to declare more than just the individual items for which we had information.

In addition, we were demanding a full list of suppliers and users of toxins, pathogenic micro-organisms and complex growth media (the stuff on or in which bacteria are grown, such as agar in a Petri dish). Our conclusion was that we had gained no new information. We remained convinced that Dr Rihab Taha was not telling the whole truth, but were unable to break down her stone-walling lies. And we remained concerned that Iraq might have conducted biological weapons production at as yet undeclared sites and with undeclared personnel.

Talks in the other weapons areas were similarly frustrating, although some progress was made. The major result of these meetings was that Iraq, having heard in great detail how UNSCOM would implement and run the monitoring system, now accepted the use of tags, seals and sensors for dual-purpose items under the monitoring plans. General Amer Rasheed pushed Rolf Ekéus to set a finite period after which monitoring and verification would be in place and the recommendation to lift sanctions could be made. Rolf wisely declined to do so, but said that, in the best of all circumstances, the first baseline inspection could take place in December 1993 and the monitoring system might be in place six months afterwards. Amer also wanted regular joint reviews by UNSCOM and Iraq to monitor implementation of the monitoring plans. We happily acquiesced.

The long and short of it was that this meeting identified the key outstanding issues, but did not resolve any of them satisfactorily. Follow-up technical talks were planned to address the outstanding issues before Rolf Ekéus arrived in Baghdad for high-level political discussions. But the monitoring cameras at the missile test stands were still not switched on. Rolf told Mohammed al Sahaf that the follow-up talks would be off unless they were running. Sahaf acquiesced on 23 September, and at last the cameras rolled.

I returned to Baghdad on 27 September, a few days ahead of Rolf Ekéus, with a small team of experts – the German Horst Reeps, Roger Hill and Igor Mitrokhin – all with knowledge of both biological and chemical weapons. Our discussions (conducted in English, as the Iraqi scientists involved were all British-educated) mainly revolved around getting Iraq to admit that it had produced far more chemical weapons than previously admitted. Iraq had denied using chemical weapons against Iran, but their use was well documented. Consequently, declarations about past production left out huge quantities of chemical weapons made for the Iran–Iraq War. We could not report having a complete 'material balance' for Iraq's chemical weapons programme until this matter was resolved. Huge amounts of imported precursor chemicals remained unaccounted for.

After several fraught days Dr Ghazi Faisal was finally authorised to admit to the production and 'disposal' of large quantities of mustard agent and the nerve agents sarin and tabun in addition to what he had previously declared. However, the Iraqis still denied working successfully with a more potent nerve agent, VX. They claimed that their investigations into VX were merely conducted at laboratory level and that production was too dangerous and difficult for them. This did not tie in with a document found amongst those seized two years earlier during David Kay's parking-lot inspection.

This was a letter written by General Faiz al Shahine, who at the time was director-general of Muthanna and also of the Samarra Drug Company. He was now Deputy Minister of Oil. The letter discussed the list of chemicals to be controlled under the Chemical Weapons Convention being negotiated in Geneva. It was startling, because it used the Geneva list as a shopping list for the Iraqi chemical weapons programme. General Faiz al Shahine was responding to a question asking whether Iraq could produce all the chemicals on the list and, if not, whether it could import them. Worse still, the Geneva schedule had clearly alerted Iraq to chemicals it was unaware of. The letter asked how certain of the chemicals on the list could be used for chemical weapons production – in other words the Geneva disarmament list was being used by Iraq to reverse-engineer chemical weapons. Amongst these chemical agents was VX.

The interview with General Faiz al Shahine was depressing. While he admitted that the letter was genuine, he denied everything, saying we had simply misunderstood it. In fact, it was very clear and there was nothing in it to misunderstand.

Meetings on the biological issues with Dr Rihab Taha fared no better. Taha failed to produce either the aerosol generators or the inhalation chambers, and she continued to give vague responses to our questions.

Nikita Smidovich's missile team, which included Mark Silver, Patrice Palanque and Scott Ritter, did obtain some additional information about Iraq's indigenous missile production programmes, but they, too, remained unsatisfied.

When Rolf Ekéus arrived in Baghdad on 2 October 1993, I joined his team of John Scott and Olivia Platon for the political talks.

UNSCOM's French nuclear weapons expert, Lydie Gérard, also attended because these meetings had been expanded to include the IAEA, represented by Professor Maurizio Zifferero and Robert Kelley.

Rolf came under immediate and considerable pressure from Tariq Aziz, General Amer Rasheed and Mohammed al Sahaf to declare that UNSCOM now had full accounts of Iraq's past programmes and that all banned weapons capabilities had been eliminated. This was the price that Iraq was seeking in return for finally accepting the monitoring plan.

In the end a report was prepared and signed by General Amer (on behalf of Iraq), Rolf Ekéus (on behalf of UNSCOM) and Maurizio Zifferero (on behalf of the IAEA). It restated Iraq's position on its compliance, and the positions of UNSCOM and the IAEA. Iraq considered that it was now in full compliance with all its obligations; it was prepared to announce its formal acceptance of the monitoring plans under resolution 715 if it obtained guarantees that the Council would lift sanctions without additional conditions. Moreover, it would allow intrusive inspections to continue alongside monitoring, provided the Council lifted the sanctions.

Still, Iraq wanted a written assurance from UNSCOM that the outstanding issues had all been resolved. Clearly, given the state of the VX and biological weapons investigations, we could do no such thing. The discussions with Tariq Aziz became heated, and dragged on until late. We broke at 10.30 p.m. to have dinner in the Ministry of Foreign Affairs – a groaning table of Iraqi dishes that belied the food shortages Aziz constantly complained about. By 2 a.m. John Scott and I had come up with the weasel words which allowed Iraq to believe that it had got what it wanted, but which fully safeguarded our position. The report as signed stated that:

> With the provision by Iraq of the necessary information on critical foreign suppliers as defined in annex I to document S/26451 ... and upon its verification as necessary, the

Commission can conclude as follows:

(a) In the light of the totality of the information available to the Commission in the ballistic and biological areas, Iraq has fully discharged its obligations to provide information in relation to its past activities in these areas ...

(b) ... The Commission hopes ... in the chemical area, to make the same determination as it has done above in relation to the ballistic and biological areas.

Iraq read this as 'The Commission can conclude ...', without realising the importance of the qualifying rider. Indeed, it interpreted the deliberately ambiguous phrase 'With the provision by Iraq ...' to mean that the provision had already taken place. Its intention, of course, was that once, and only once, the provision took place in the future, then the Commission could reach the stated conclusion. This use of constructive ambiguity was my greatest achievement in nearly four years with UNSCOM. It turned a bad-tempered meeting into the temporary love-in between UNSCOM and Iraq that resulted in Mohammed al Sahaf, on behalf of Iraq, formally accepting resolution 715 and the monitoring plans a month later, in a letter to the President of the Security Council dated 26 November 1993.

It also led to new sources of information that would breathe new life into the very investigations that Iraq thought had been closed.

CHAPTER 15

Yoghurt and Beer: Monitoring Inspections

'*Fere libenter homines id quod volunt credunt.*'
(Men willingly believe what they wish.)

JULIUS CAESAR

'I cannot forecast to you the action of Russia. It is a riddle wrapped in a mystery inside an enigma.'

WINSTON CHURCHILL

UNSCOM was in better shape than it ever had been. The Security Council was much relieved that Rolf Ekéus's strategy for gaining Iraq's acceptance of resolution 715 and the monitoring plans had worked; it no longer needed to take any action to enforce Iraq's compliance. As a result of this, and Rolf's earlier work, his personal standing with Council members was at an all-time high.

On the ground, UNSCOM was also in good shape. Most of Iraq's banned weapons and production capacity had been destroyed. Monitoring, with all the rights and technologies UNSCOM wanted, was rapidly being put in place and Iraq would now no longer be able to manufacture or develop banned weapons without running the risk of being caught red-handed.

But there were still doubts. The biological story was not believed. The suspicion was that Iraq had declared only its defunct chemical weapons; were it to resume chemical weapons production, it would surely concentrate on the one agent it had yet to admit to – VX. While Nikita Smidovich was relatively confident that all bar one or two of the SCUD missiles imported by Iraq from the former Soviet Union were now accounted for, there was growing concern that Iraqi efforts to build long-range missiles were further advanced than had been supposed. Iraq could have declared only those missiles UNSCOM could find out about from the suppliers, keeping hidden an unknowable quantity of home-made missiles. And UNSCOM's French commissioner, Michel St Mleux, did not believe that Iraq had yet declared its full achievements in nuclear weapons research and development. There was a deep suspicion that Iraq was continuing its nuclear research, even if this were limited to computer modelling of nuclear explosions.

UNSCOM's moral standing would only deteriorate from this point. Several factors were at play. First and foremost, UNSCOM was to become a victim of its own success. With the majority of weapons – and machines to make them – destroyed, and with the monitoring system now being put in place, the threat posed by Saddam Hussein's regime was perceived to be much diminished. This led to a more relaxed view about Iraq's future challenges to UNSCOM. UNSCOM's finds of significant undeclared weapons-related items also slowed down, which led to increased sympathy for Iraq's specious claim that UNSCOM's failure to prove that Iraq was not telling the truth meant that it was telling the truth.

UNSCOM's funding was a mess too. Under the ceasefire resolution, Iraq was responsible for funding all UN operations in Iraq that were a direct result of its invasion of Kuwait. This included UNSCOM. Consequently, there was no UN budget for UNSCOM. Iraq had paid nothing, and so UNSCOM relied on donations from supporting governments – either money or equipment and personnel – and on Iraqi assets that had been seized abroad. After the invasion most Western countries had 'frozen' Iraqi bank accounts in their territories. The US alone had frozen some $750 millions, and had been using these both to fund UN operations in Iraq, like UNSCOM, and to settle legitimate claims made against the Iraqi government by commercial entities. These frozen assets were now running out – and, with them, UNSCOM's funding. On several occasions in the coming years, UNSCOM would be technically bankrupt.

Realpolitik was also coming into play. Russia and France were massive creditors of Iraq and were looking forward to the day when Iraqi oil flowed to provide funds to pay back Iraq's debts. French and Russian oil companies had also pencilled lucrative contracts to exploit major oil fields in Iraq once the sanctions were lifted. Russia's entire stance towards the West and the US would also change in mid-1994. It would no longer automatically fall into line with the US position, seeking rather to re-establish its independent place at the top table. At times it seemed that Russia was opposing the US just for the sake of it.

Weariness with sanctions, coupled with genuine concern for the suffering they were causing because of Saddam Hussein's refusal to accept the Council's oil-for-food offer, weakened support for them. The Council had from the outset tried to minimise the suffering inflicted on ordinary Iraqi citizens by exempting foods, medicines and basic essentials from the sanctions regime. It had also offered to allow Iraq to sell a certain quantity of its oil, under UN supervision, in order to finance purchases of food and medicines and to pay for the UN operations. Saddam saw the food-for-oil deal as a threat to his overall strategy of using this suffering to get sanctions lifted without having to comply on the elimination of his weapons of mass destruction. If the deal went through, there would be no suffering, and no clamour to lift the sanctions on humanitarian grounds. If sanctions were lifted before Iraq came clean, the carrot element of the carrot-and-stick strategy for encouraging Iraqi compliance would be gone, leaving only the increasingly weak goad of military action to force Iraq in the right direction.

While we could not predict these changes, we understood that our window of opportunity – the period during which we could rely on the full support of the Council – was probably limited. Quite apart from that, we wanted to be able to say we had done our job fully, and report that the conditions for lifting sanctions had been met. That would be a major feather in the cap of all those involved in UNSCOM.

We all threw ourselves into the task of setting up the monitoring regime. The concept for monitoring was borrowed from the Chemical Weapons Convention, and further developed. Iraq was to make declarations about all its dual-purpose capabilities (materials, equipment and technologies) and activities, giving the location of where they took place. It was also to make declarations about its imports of dual-purpose materials for a period just prior to the starting of monitoring. UNSCOM would then analyse these declarations and draw up a list of sites to inspect in order to assess whether they needed to be monitored or not and, if so, how and with what frequency.

This would be followed by a series of 'baseline inspections' of the sites designated for monitoring. These inspections would inventory and tag all key dual-purpose equipment so that the monitoring inspectors could keep track of their location and usage. These teams would also, for each site, write a 'site protocol' describing the activities undertaken at the site, the key items to be monitored, the key personnel at the site, and prescribing how the site should be monitored.

Next, technical teams would install the monitoring and sensing devices recommended in the site protocols. At the same time a Baghdad Monitoring and Verification Centre would be set up, complete with analysis laboratories, television screens linked into the monitoring cameras at each of the sites so that UNSCOM personnel could watch the monitored activities in real time, and all the logistical support required for monitoring, including resident teams of experts in each of the weapons areas. The permanent presence of weapons inspectors in Baghdad would also enable UNSCOM to launch more effective no-notice inspections, as there would be no assembly of teams in Bahrain for Iraq to observe ahead of time.

Finally, the monitoring system would be launched and tested for a period to gain confidence in its effectiveness. At that stage, provided Iraq had come clean about its past programmes, Rolf Ekéus would report to the Council that the conditions for lifting the sanctions had been met.

A final element – an export/import monitoring regime –would have to be put in place; this was less dependent on Iraq than on the other members of the UN. It would be a double accounting system. Iraq was to report to UNSCOM ahead of time its intention to import a dual-purpose item. The exporting country would then report the conclusion of a contract to supply the item to Iraq. A further notification was required by the exporting country to inform UNSCOM of the shipping details (quantity, value, port of origin, port of arrival, dates, etc.). Iraq was then to notify UNSCOM of the receipt of the item at its final destination. A monitoring team could then visit the site and assess what action needed to be taken to monitor the item, such as tagging or the installation of additional cameras. Lastly, Iraq was to notify UNSCOM of the export of any dual-purpose item.

Thus UNSCOM could maintain a 'material balance' of all dual-purpose items: Items imported + items produced in Iraq = Items under monitoring + items consumed + items exported.

If the two sides of the equation did not balance, or if Iraq's declarations of its imports did not tally with the exporting nations' notifications, there would be a problem. It would mean that there were dual-purpose items in Iraq not being monitored. The base assumption was that any such unmonitored items were part of a clandestine and illicit weapons production programme and hence subject to automatic destruction, unless Iraq could come up with compelling explanations to the contrary.

The methods and technologies for monitoring Iraq's biological activities were more limited than in other areas. Essentially, key items could be tagged with tamper-proof unique labels, key control panels or valves could be fitted with tamper-proof seals, and equipment and activities could be recorded on time-lapse video or watched in real time by monitors in Baghdad (linked to the cameras on site via land line or radio link) or New York (via satellite link). On-site camera surveillance could be supplemented with aerial surveillance to observe general changes to the site that might indicate a change in function, or changes in traffic levels into and out of the site, which might indicate increased or changed production.

However, nothing could replace the knowledge of people – of the Iraqi experts or of the UNSCOM inspectors. Knowing where Iraqi experts were and what they were working on would be a key element of monitoring. For obvious reasons, tagging of Iraqi scientists could not be considered. So it would be down to the inspectors to keep track of where they were, and to be alert to significant numbers with complementary areas of expertise disappearing from view – a firm indicator of clandestine activities somewhere unless Iraq could prove otherwise.

Similarly, no amount of tags, seals and cameras could replace regular visits by knowledgeable inspectors. In addition to taking air, water, soil, raw materials, end product and other samples for analysis in the Baghdad Monitoring and Verification Centre, inspectors could quickly assess what was probably going on in a factory just by walking around and observing the layout of the equipment, the activity levels of the personnel and any changes that had taken place. This could be supplemented with checks of the fermenter or reactor vessel production logs and the factories' accounts or store ledgers, and by chatting with the manager about the factory's recent activities. The more people are drawn into giving details of their actions, the harder it is for them to lie consistently.

The whole system of monitoring was to be buttressed by further no-notice inspections so that UNSCOM could be sure that no illicit activities were taking place in undeclared sites not subject to monitoring.

* * *

The first item on the agenda was to obtain and analyse Iraq's initial declarations. In November 1993 UNSCOM's reinforced biological weapons team spent long hours with the Iraqi delegation led by Dr Rihab Taha discussing how the declarations should be presented and what information they should contain. A French lawyer recruited from the UN's Legal Department, Annick Paul-Henriot, was put in charge of coordinating UNSCOM's biological monitoring effort.

Iraq's first biological declarations were received in December 1993 and were pitifully inadequate. Whole issues, such as previous imports of dual-purpose items, were omitted. Few sites were declared – in fact only those already mentioned in Iraq's revised biological declaration of 1991 or subsequently inspected by UNSCOM teams. It took time and effort to explain to Dr Rihab Taha and her associates just what was required of them before even baseline inspections could start. It also became clear that the annexes to the monitoring plan, as originally written in 1991, needed to be expanded in order to give the Iraqi experts a better idea of what was required under monitoring.

Annick Paul-Henriot coordinated the preparation of new forms for Iraq to use for its revised declarations. UNSCOM insisted on the answers being made to a standard format – entering the information into the database would otherwise have been a nightmare. These new reporting forms were sent to Dr Rihab Taha in mid-January 1994. Shortly afterwards she sent revised declarations covering thirty-five sites. UNSCOM then called a meeting of international experts in biological weapons and biotech industries to assist in the evaluation of the declarations. The conclusion was that the declarations were still hopelessly inadequate. Annick led a team of experts in talks with Dr Taha to explain once again how to complete the forms and what information to provide.

A meeting of international experts on biological arms control and export controls was held in New York in March 1994 to review the list of controlled biological items. They compiled a much more detailed and explicit list of items to be declared, and made further refinements to the declaration forms. These new lists and reporting forms were given to Dr Rihab Taha in a further round of talks in mid-March.

UNSCOM's early biological monitoring efforts did not cover themselves with glory either. The first such inspection, BW4, was launched on 8 April 1994. Its original objectives were threefold: to follow up on outstanding biological issues from the past programmes, to conduct baseline inspections of the thirty-five sites declared by Iraq, and to visit two undeclared sites to assess whether they should be monitored. The sites included: university, medical diagnostics, veterinary and food control laboratories; breweries; industrial alcohol production factories; and production facilities for vaccines, single-cell proteins, fertilisers, castor oil and pesticides. The conclusions reached by this inspection were little short of disastrous.

The chief inspector, a German expert who had been involved in several earlier inspections and analysis seminars hosted by UNSCOM in New York, proved a major disappointment. He declared at the end of the inspection that UNSCOM now knew all there was to know about Iraq's biological activities and that future new data would involve only technical omissions and oversights. He also concluded that the al Dawrah Foot and Mouth Disease Vaccine Institute, the al Kindi Veterinary Vaccine Production Plant and the Serum and Vaccine Institute at Amariyah were not capable of producing biological weapons. Fortunately, he did recommend that they should be monitored. The final insult was the conclusion that the al Hakam site could not be used for biological weapons production because it did not have the proper containment facilities.

This report infuriated some of the inspectors on the team and UNSCOM's own biological weapons analysts. Each of the named institutes had been on David Kelly's first list of probable biological weapons production sites. And David had believed that, given the low health and safety standards in force in Iraq, skilled operators could use the al Hakam plant relatively safely if they wrapped the fermenter in cling film.

Partly as a result of this, but partly because Dr Rihab Taha consistently failed to report in full all the sites and items that needed to be reported, the baseline inspections of Iraq's biological capabilities became a complete muddle. The second baseline team, BW5, led by the UNSCOM veteran Johan Santesson and including two of UNSCOM's new permanent recruits – Dick Spertzel and Amelia Jones – went back in May to thirty-one of the sites inspected in April by BW4 to tag and inventory the equipment for the site protocol, only to find many items that had not been reported by the previous team or by Iraq. It also disagreed with the findings of the earlier team on both the capabilities of the sites inspected and the levels of monitoring required. Its work, though, was more thorough. It tagged, photographed and described in detail some 330 pieces of equipment. It also chided Taha for moving equipment around between BW4 and BW5 without informing UNSCOM and detailed the process of notification that Iraq should follow if it wanted to move, or use differently, a tagged item of dual-purpose equipment which was being monitored.

A further inspection, BW7, was sent in June to resolve the discrepancies between the various sets of information: Iraq's by now numerous different sets of initial declarations, the first team's findings and the second team's findings. Dr Rihab Taha questioned the need to visit university laboratories, breweries, tanneries and yoghurt factories. UNSCOM pointed out that they, and any other production factory whose fermenters could be used for biological weapons production, needed to be monitored because the equipment used in them could be reconfigured rapidly for biological weapons production or transferred to a biological weapons factory. Factories producing fermenters and importers of fermenters should also be visited. Taha was concerned that UNSCOM would end up monitoring everything and anything to do with biology or biotech. UNSCOM assured her that the aim of the visits was, in the first instance, only to assess whether the sites should be monitored. In any case, the monitoring of dual-purpose equipment put to permitted uses was designed to make the process as non-intrusive and non-disruptive as possible. As a result of these discussions, Taha was asked to provide initial declarations for a further twenty-four sites.

Dick Spertzel's second inspection, in June 1994, was another baseline team, BW6, led by Jeff Mohr, a Canadian who had been on several of the earlier biological weapons inspections. This team visited thirty-five sites. Some of these were repeat visits whilst others were to undeclared sites to see whether they should have been declared. It came to the conclusion that eight of the undeclared sites should be monitored and hence should have been declared by Taha. More ominously, at several of the higher education institutes there were inexplicable anomalies. At one site the staff were altogether too well briefed on the UNSCOM personnel in the team. Their level of expertise, the amount of equipment available to them and the department's budget all appeared excessive for a regional university. The expertise in anaerobic microbiology was worrying (anthrax and clostridium are grown anaerobically). At another, undeclared dual-purpose equipment, bearing markings indicating that it had been stolen from Kuwait, was found. Again, there was an excessive amount of equipment related to anaerobic microbiology. At a third site, the well-qualified staff had simply ignored large quantities of equipment for anaerobic microbiology, which lay unused in storage. The overall impression was that there was a centrally organised campaign to disperse equipment for researching and producing anaerobic bacteria in seemingly innocent locations in order to hide them from the prying eyes of UNSCOM inspectors.

Dr Rihab Taha's repeated and persistent failure to make adequate initial declarations was raised by Rolf Ekéus in the technical talks held in Baghdad in July. General Amer Rasheed promised that renewed efforts would be made to get it right.

Yet another biological inspection, BW8, started in July and stayed until September. Its task was to visit each of the fifty-five sites already selected for monitoring to write site protocols for them. It planned to draw up general guidelines for conducting biological monitoring, site-specific questionnaires for Iraq to complete on a regular basis, and detailed site-specific monitoring instructions. This team was clearly frustrated by the inconsistencies between Iraq's declarations, the reports of the previous inspections, and what it was finding on the ground. Iraq had clearly been moving items around between the inspections. Consequently, this team spent a lot of time requesting accurate and current information that should have already been made available to it. However, this eventually turned out to be very useful. Amongst the vast amount of information collected were organisational charts showing the management structure of the various institutions visited.

In August BW9 was sent to assess whether remote monitoring sensors might be installed at five key sites. This team clearly disagreed with the findings of BW4. It recommended the installation of monitoring cameras at al Hakam, the Foot and Mouth Disease Vaccine Production facility at al Dawrah, and the al Kindi Veterinary Vaccine Production Facility.

At the end of August Dick Spertzel led yet another team, BW10, to carry on the unfinished work of BW8, writing site protocols for an additional seven facilities and installing monitoring cameras. But UNSCOM was still finding it hard to get the Iraqis to make accurate and consistent declarations: each time they submitted a new declaration to rectify the faults of a previous one, new inconsistencies and errors crept in. In short, UNSCOM was failing to establish a baseline from which to launch monitoring because the sands seemed to be shifting under its feet. This issue was again raised with General Amer Rasheed during another round of high-level meetings in New York in September 1994. Amer suggested that a team should visit Baghdad again later in September to set out for Dr Taha what additional information was required.

By now Dick Spertzel had so many air miles that he was treated like royalty by British Airways, the airline UNSCOM used to get from New York to Bahrain and back. He returned to Iraq with BW12 at the end of September 1994 in response to General Amer

Rasheed's suggestion. Dick tried to explain to Dr Rihab Taha and her colleagues the link between full accounting for Iraq's past activities, full declarations of current dual-purpose items, and comprehensive monitoring. Without knowing what dual-purpose assets Iraq had possessed in the past and what had been consumed or destroyed, UNSCOM could not know what should be left to monitor. Without knowing what dual-purpose equipment and materials were currently in the country, it could not establish a material balance between known past imports, what had been consumed or destroyed in the past and what was being currently monitored. In other words, it all had to hang together or it would not hang at all. Taha expressed a willingness to provide whatever information was required as soon as she had a comprehensive list of specific questions ... Back to square one.

Finally, even General Amer Rasheed lost patience with Dr Rihab Taha, to whom he was now reportedly married. Dr Sami, from the IAEC, was put in charge of preparing a new set of complete 'initial' declarations for the biological sites to be monitored.

As the farce of baseline inspections proceeded, another bizarre sequence of events was unfolding. Rolf Ekéus was back in Vienna for CSCE meetings in April 1994, and here he met an old contact who was now an adviser to Yevgeni Primakov, head of Russia's Foreign Intelligence Service (FIS) – the successor of the overseas operations of the KGB. Primakov was an old Arab hand, and friend of Iraq's. It was he whom Gorbachev had dispatched to Baghdad in late 1990 to talk to Saddam Hussein in an attempt to avert the Gulf War.

This contact intriguingly implied that the FIS had solid evidence that Iraq had indeed had a full-blown biological weapons programme. He invited Rolf Ekéus to visit Yevgeni Primakov in Moscow to discuss the matter. To those of us who knew about the Soviet Union's own clandestine biological weapons programme, this had a ring of logic to it. If any country had helped Iraq to build biological weapons in secret, it would have been the Soviet Union – whose own biological warfare programme was so secret that its own government did not know about it. Russia might very well have true inside knowledge about Iraq's real biological warfare programmes, be it offensive or defensive.

When Rolf returned to New York, we set about arranging this visit. A date was set in June 1994. Unfortunately, by the time we arrived in Moscow, the political winds had changed. Russia's love affair with the US was over and Primakov denied that Russia had ever imagined that Iraq had a biological weapons programme. Indeed, he claimed that the Iraqi declarations were accurate. It is tempting to think that the change in Russia's foreign policy and the change in the FIS's story on Iraqi biological weaponry were not unrelated.

But what fortune takes with one hand, it gives with another. In December 1993 I received a phone call from another old colleague from Geneva days, Jenny Pickford, now with the Arms Control and Disarmament Agency in Washington DC. She was involved in the track two events surrounding the Middle East Peace Process. 'Track two' is the term given to informal contacts between influential individuals from both sides of the negotiating table aimed at increasing mutual understanding and hence improving the chances of success at the peace talks.

Jenny told me that the University of San Diego was organising a track two event in the Greek town of Delphi, home of the Oracle, in early January 1994. It was being run in parallel with the ACRS (Arms Control and Regional Security) component of the Oslo talks between the Israelis and the Palestinians. The idea was to invite the negotiators, experts and other useful people, with their spouses, to a retreat, away from other distractions, to allow a relaxed, personal and informal discussion of the issues surrounding the peace talks, and to allow the various proponents and their

spouses to get to know each other. Increased mutual understanding, touchy feely. She asked me whether anyone from
UNSCOM would be able to attend to toss the UNSCOM experience into the mix. I told her that I would be the only one available
for the dates of the meeting – Rolf Ekéus was with his family in
Sweden, from whence he would travel to Vienna. Pierce Corden
was in Washington. John Scott was on a cruise in the Seychelles.
She was stuck with me.

I found the meeting extremely interesting. It was eight years
since I had professionally followed Arab–Israeli issues. At that
time I was in Yemen. The Palestine Liberation Army had been
thrown out of Lebanon following the massacres in Sabra and
Shatila, and the bulk had found refuge in Yemen. As the most
junior member of the British embassy's political staff, I was given
the task of getting to know the large Palestinian community in
Sana'a and of liaising with the PLA leadership.

Much had changed since 1985. The prospects of the Oslo
process were exhilarating for anyone who loves the region. One
thing that had not changed was the mutual lack of trust about the
other's military intentions and the total mismatch of threat
perceptions. In one of the discussions about threat perceptions, the
old chestnut of the injustice of Israel's nuclear bomb came up. A
crusty Israeli official stood up and said that Israel would not
confirm or deny its capabilities; it needed to maintain the
ambiguity in order to deter the likes of Saddam from launching
chemical weapons at Israel. An Egyptian stood up and reminded
the Israeli that UNSCOM had destroyed Iraq's chemical weapons
and SCUD missiles. The Israeli contemptuously dismissed the
idea, effectively saying that the UN (read UNSCOM) could not
organise a piss-up in a brewery, that according to Israel's
information Iraq was still hiding a lot from UNSCOM, and that
Israel could never afford to leave its security in the hands of others.

The attack on UNSCOM was a little too rich for me. I stood up
and said that UNSCOM had acted extremely effectively on all the
quality intelligence it had received about what Iraq was hiding. As

a result, UNSCOM had destroyed vastly more of Iraq's weapons of mass destruction and missiles capabilities than the entire Desert Storm operation. Even George Bush had admitted this. UNSCOM itself doubted whether it had found all Iraq's weapons, but it had run out of good sources. If Israel had good intelligence information on what Iraq was hiding where, it should tell UNSCOM. Indeed, it was obliged to. If Israel chose not to, it had no right to criticise UNSCOM. It was put up or shut up.

Needless to say, this message did not go down too well. However, at the end of that debating session another Israeli approached me and said that I should not get too upset – Israel was just not used to the UN acting in its favour or being treated by the UN as a full member. He thought the crusty old gent and I should get together to discuss the matter further.

Indeed, he did organise a meeting, which the crusty old gent clearly found distasteful. But as a result of this short discussion he told his colleague, a brigadier in Israeli Military Intelligence, to talk to me. This brigadier was much more *simpatico*. He asked whether a meeting with Rolf Ekéus could be arranged to discuss an exchange of information about Iraq's weapons capabilities. I replied that I could not speak for Rolf, but would put the idea to him. However, while it did have regular contacts with a number of intelligence organisations, UNSCOM did not go in for exchanges of information: it would give information only to those agencies who were in a position to help UNSCOM, and then only information which would facilitate that help. The brigadier accepted this point and gave me the name of a friend of his in the Israeli Mission to the UN in New York.

Back in New York I received a phone call from the Israeli mission. A meeting was set up for April 1994. It was held in great secrecy in the basement meeting room of a New York hotel and attended by Rolf Ekéus, Charles Duelfer – the new Deputy Executive Chairman who had replaced Pierce Corden – John Scott, Nikita Smidovich and me. The brigadier had brought a couple of his analysts with him.

The first meeting did little more than explore the ways in which the two sides could cooperate. But it did result in setting up another meeting in New York for UNSCOM's analysts to give the Israelis a full assessment of Iraq's known past programmes, and a detailed listing of what UNSCOM believed was still unaccounted for.

The Israelis were clearly deeply impressed by the briefings organised by Nikita Smidovich. Further meetings were set up to talk about each of the weapons areas in detail; these became a regular fixture, with Israel providing a stream of high-quality and actionable intelligence, particularly about Iraq's imports of dual-use items.

The combination of Iraq's new declarations organised by Dr Sami, Israel's data about Iraqi imports, and the detailed questioning of Iraqi personnel managing the monitored biological sites was to provide the information that would undermine the foundations of Dr Taha's stone-walling and force Iraq to admit that it had made biological weapons.

CHAPTER 16

Breakthrough: Broth and Air Filters

'*La diligencia es madre de la buena ventura.*'
(Diligence is the mother of good fortune.)
MIGUEL DE CERVANTES

'*Le hasard ne favorise que les ésprits préparés.*'
(Chance only favours the prepared mind.)
LOUIS PASTEUR

That year, 1994, saw a significant increase in the number of biological experts at UNSCOM. We had been planning for monitoring for two years before Iraq accepted the proposals in November 1993. In the course of their inspections, teams had been compiling lists of sites that might need to be monitored as they became aware of them. From these lists, we had gained an idea of the numbers of inspectors required to monitor effectively all Iraq's dual-purpose biological capabilities, and of the types of expertise needed. In addition, we had always known that the way to discover the truth about Iraq's past biological weapons programme was by analysing the facts. The problem until now had been insufficient facts to analyse, to prove what we feared – that Iraq had indeed made biological weapons.

The plan was to increase the staff in two ways: to have inspectors permanently stationed in Baghdad to do the actual monitoring of the sites; and to have analytical staff in New York to cope with the avalanche of Iraqi declarations and monitoring reports that would now be generated. A second round of recruitment would be needed once the export/import monitoring system was in operation to handle all the declarations about trade in dual-purpose goods.

We hoped that the three different activities – investigating the past programmes, monitoring dual-purpose sites, and monitoring trade in dual-purpose goods – would be complementary. A full understanding of Iraq's past programmes, the assets it had and what had been used or destroyed, was essential if we were to know what we should be monitoring. Iraq's declarations about its legitimate dual-purpose activities, both current and in the recent past, might provide clues to undeclared aspects of the past programme. In particular, they might give hints about companies whom we could approach about their supplies over and above the legitimate items declared by Iraq. And the monitoring of new, permitted trade might reactivate old supplier contacts that Iraq had until now kept quiet about. We wanted to observe which individual, or organisation, was responsible for legitimate imports, so that we could see if they had commissioned imports in the past. This analysis, we hoped, would clearly indicate which past imports had been for legitimate purposes and which for military programmes.

Annick Paul-Henriot joined the team in the autumn of 1993 to coordinate monitoring activities. To her fell the task of identifying the few suppliers named in Iraq's initial declarations and writing to them to seek confirmation of the items sold to Iraq – when, in what quantities, for how much, via which ports/vessels, and to which organisation. We also sought the names of the Iraqi individuals involved in the purchasing decisions and payments. She sent out the first batch of letters in December 1993.

These letters were sent to the governments of the countries in which the exporting companies were located. This was a cumbersome procedure. A letter went via the country's mission in

New York, which forwarded it to the Foreign Ministry back home, which forwarded it to the ministry responsible for export licences, which sent it on to the company. The replies returned via the same route in reverse. This was because UNSCOM was mandated to inspect only Iraq, not the supplier countries or the supplier companies. The provision of supplier information was therefore a voluntary matter, both for the government concerned and for the company. Most of the goods in question had perfectly legitimate civilian uses – medical, biotech, brewing, dairy, agricultural, baking, tanning – and were not subject to export controls. Indeed, there were no export controls of any type on biological production equipment until the late 1980s – after the Iraqis had bought the equipment and materials for their biological programme.

It was some months before the first replies started to come in. Even though we knew that we had only written to a small percentage of Iraq's suppliers, the replies were useful, if frustrating. They gave us more details about Iraq's imports of fermenters, aerosol generators and inhalation chambers – all items that would be needed for making biological weapons, but could also be explained away by the Iraqi cover story (that its general research programme into biological warfare had no specific aim of making biological weapons). Thus the responses fuelled our conviction that Iraq was lying, but provided insufficient evidence to prove the case against it.

Another change in the biological team came with the departure at the end of 1993 of the Australian veteran inspector and analyst Roger Hill, recalled to duty with the Australian armed forces. He was replaced by his compatriot, Rod Barton. Rod is a very intelligent but self-effacing character. He was to prove to be an exception in UNSCOM – someone who was happy to spend most of his time being a backroom analyst, rather than seeking out the high-profile role of inspector. His calm and reserved character was also a perfect foil to some of the more volatile characters recruited by UNSCOM. Rod threw himself into the task of analysing Iraq's declarations.

Another of Annick Paul-Henriot's tasks was to write to various governments asking them to put forward names of experts whom they were prepared to lend to UNSCOM for protracted periods, either as monitoring inspectors in Baghdad or on the analytical team in New York.

The British provided a young microbiologist, Amelia Jones, from its Chemical and Biological Defence Establishment at Porton Down. Another recruit, in March 1993, was Ray Zalinskas, a professor in Microbiology at Maryland University who worked part time in the US government's Arms Control and Disarmament Agency (ACDA). Here US inter-agency politics came into play. ACDA had been established under Jimmy Carter's Democratic administration to give the disarmament community within the US government a stronger and more unified voice. Other parts of the administration still viewed the organisation as a group of peaceniks. Upon hearing of Ray's appointment, the Pentagon was piqued. If there were to be an ACDA implant in UNSCOM, then there should be a Pentagon one too.

Lisa Bronson, another veteran of the Geneva chemical weapons negotiations, was now the big fish in the Pentagon on biological weapons issues. She rang round to see whether someone from the US armed forces could provide a useful counterbalance to Ray. The obvious place to call was Fort Detrick – the US biological warfare defence facility and former home of its biological weapons programme. Its director, David Franz, had been chief inspector of UNSCOM's third biological weapons inspection in March 1993. Obviously, David could not spare the time himself; nor did he want to lose any of his full-time staff to what promised to be a prolonged detachment to UNSCOM. So he recommended a retired ex-Fort Detrick man, Dick Spertzel. Dick had been in the US Army for twenty-eight years, retiring in 1987. He was now an independent consultant, specialising in biotechnology issues. However, twenty-two of his years in the army had been spent either directly or indirectly on biological warfare – much of that time at Fort Detrick. He had a veterinary degree and both a Masters and a PhD in Microbiology, after which he had specialised in virology. His particular expertise was in defensive equipment to protect against biological weapons, although he had worked indirectly on the US biological weapons programme before it was wound up in 1969. Indeed, he still had luncheon every Thursday with a group of old Fort Detrick hands, all of whom had worked on the programme in some capacity. He therefore brought an invaluable range of expertise with him – an insight into making biological weapons, extensive knowledge of defensive systems, and up-to-the-minute knowledge of the biotech industry. Lisa Bronson called Dick on 23 March 1994 and asked him to start work on 1 April.

While his previous work had meant that he had incidentally read intelligence reports on the Iraqi biological weapons programme, at the time he joined UNSCOM Dick knew little more than he had read in the newspapers. Just about the only privileged information he had seen were intelligence reports referring to buildings E and H at a Project 324; these buildings were reported to be fitted with HEPA filters* and negative air pressure – both indicators of high containment, implying work on dangerous pathogens. No one knew where Project 324 was.

This was, with the continuity knowledge of two veteran British inspectors – David Kelly and Hamish Killip – and a German inspector, Gabriele Kraatz-Wadsack, the core of the team that was to crack the case open.

The only problem was that they were receiving information faster than they could handle it. BW8 had gathered vast amounts of information about the fifty-five sites for which it wrote site

---

* High efficiency particulate air filters.

protocols. Among these were blueprints for the buildings and plans for the layout of equipment, lists of the equipment and materials at each site, and names of the managers. The biological team was particularly interested in the personnel issues – several of those who had apparently worked on the 'military biological programme' were now managing purportedly civilian operations at precisely those sites that David Kelly's team back in 1991 had suspected of being the production facilities for the biological weapons programme – the Foot and Mouth Disease Vaccine Institute at al Dawrah, the Veterinary Vaccine Production Plant at al Kindi and the Serum and Vaccine Institute at Amariyah. The link seemed more than fortuitous. Another scrap of information, though, lay unnoticed in the files under this mound of paper – an architect's blueprint handed over at one of the monitoring sites, clearly indicating buildings E and H.

At the same time replies were coming in from Iraq's former suppliers. And the Israeli connection was now also providing actionable information on biological issues. Of particular note was an Israeli assertion, made in June 1994, that Iraq had in the late 1980s imported very large quantities of complex growth media. This is the broth in or on which bacteria are grown, both in laboratories for assay purposes, and in factories for large-scale production (such as vaccine production, single-cell protein production, or biological weapons production).

Amongst all this monitoring activity it was clearly now time to take stock of the new information available to UNSCOM and analyse it in relation to what was known about Iraq's past programmes.

Analysis was done on two levels:

1. A detailed assessment of what was inconsistent, incomplete, vague or illogical in the Iraqi statement about its past programme.

2. A detailed comparison of what was known from other sources
with what Iraq had declared.

The first analysis – of the completeness and credibility of the Iraqi
declarations – was damning. Even if it were an accurate declaration,
it was far from complete and open. Many of the questions were
answered in the vaguest of terms or simply evaded – not what one
would expect from a country that had chosen to come clean and
wanted to put the issue behind it so that economic sanctions could
be lifted. And some of the answers were contradictory.

Iraq gave no information on the thinking behind the setting up
of the biological programme, on the decision-making and review
process, on the bureaucracies involved or on the stated goals. All
Dr Rihab Taha would say is that it was her baby from the start, that
she had no particular objective, and that she reported through Dr
Ahmed Murtada, then head of the TRC, to Hussein Kamal
Hassan, then in charge of MIMI. The military had at no stage been
involved or consulted in this 'military biological programme'.
UNSCOM believed that there must have been a longer gestation
period, with military involvement, feasibility studies and high-
level discussions. In other words, many more people and organisations must have been involved. The conclusion was that they
were being hidden from UNSCOM so that the truth would not
come out.

The declared results of the 'four years of work' by a team of ten
people were paltry: even if UNSCOM accepted Iraq's cover story
('Well, we were only dumb Iraqis – what more could you expect?'),
it did not believe this was a full account of the research conducted.

Iraq's declarations simply avoided many of the questions. There
were non-answers to such questions as 'What was the
programme's doctrine?', 'What parameters were examined?',
'What unsuccessful lines of research did you pursue?', 'How was
the programme assessed for military purposes if there was no
contact with the military?' Likewise, there was no proper
explanation of why Dr Rihab Taha had sought to preserve the

cultures of micro-organisms, including anthrax and botulinum, after the Gulf War.

Dr Taha also refused to give the names of the other ten people who had allegedly worked on the programme; details of their areas of expertise and scientific experience and where they were currently working were also withheld. On the other hand, one of the ten researchers was acknowledged to be a soldier, even though Taha disclaimed any link between the programme and the military. Of the two others named as participants in the 'military biological programme', one was now apparently working at the al Razi Institute, a monitored site whose declaration nevertheless stated that there were no military personnel there. No explanation was given of why these people were recruited to the programme, nor, ostensibly, was any job description ever agreed for any of the ten. According to the Iraqi declarations, none was set work objectives. The inspectors were asked to believe that Iraq simply did not work like that – again the 'dumb Iraqi' story.

The Iraqis stated that none of the ten had been trained abroad, yet Taha herself admitted – and university records showed – that she had received her PhD from the University of East Anglia in the UK. No foreign consultant had ever been involved in the programme, they stated, which did not accord with an earlier statement, made in November 1992, that 'we cannot remember his name'.

Dr Rihab Taha could give no considered scientific reason why the programme had worked on the chosen bacteriological agents. Nor did she say what she had understood by the term 'significant quantity' when answering the question, 'Did Iraq ever produce significant quantities of these agents?'

In response to a question about the equipment used in the programme – the equipment type, the manufacturers' names, the model name, serial and model numbers, date of purchase and name of importing and purchasing companies, Dr Taha merely referred back to the declaration Iraq had made at Salman Pak back in August 1991 – an answer known to be incomplete as it included very little of the equipment needed to undertake even the small amounts of work it admitted. And that declaration had not included any of the required information on suppliers, or purchasing agencies, or dates of acquisition.

Dr Taha denied any link between the programme at Salman Pak and any other organisation (except a reporting one through MIMI). And yet she now worked at al Hakam and equipment from Salman Pak had been moved to al Hakam as early as May 1991 when, in response to Nikita Smidovich's questionnaire, Iraq first declared its stocks of dual-purpose equipment capable of making biological weapons. That first response had stated that 'Iraq does not have a central [biological] military research laboratory' – a statement recanted on the first day of David Kelly's August 1991 inspection. It went on to say that the al Hakam plant was 'at a preparatory stage, and one where maintenance and repair operations are being carried out on old imported production systems', some of which David Kelly was told had come from Salman Pak immediately after the Gulf War. It seemed most unlikely that there was no connection between these two sites. And Taha, while claiming that Salman Pak's equipment had been distributed to various sites after the Gulf War, would not give names or details of these sites other than al Hakam.

Furthermore, why would Dr Rihab Taha store the cultures of micro-organisms salvaged from Salman Pak at the Serum and Vaccine Institute in Amariyah if there were no link between the two organisations? Again, her declarations had no answer.

Dr Rihab Taha not only denied that she or Dr Nissar al Hindawi had ever been connected to a Project 85; she now even denied the existence of the project. Yet in November 1993 she had given a description of 'TECO project 85' as being related to the biopesticide project. To cover this, she admitted there was a project at TECO, but insisted she could not say what equipment had been involved.

The situation was the same with her responses to questions about other organisations and institutions whose involvement in the programme was suspected by UNSCOM but denied by Taha. Answers to such questions were either not forthcoming or extremely vague, giving no details that might be hard to back up. There was insufficient information on the Scientific Research Council – thought to be behind the original decisions to proceed with the programme – the Technical and Scientific Materials Import Division (TSMID) and the Agricultural Supplies Company – both likely front organisations for the purchase of equipment for the programme. No documents recording TSMID's import activities could be found, even though ostensibly it was a civilian operation: its staff should not have been subject to the general injunction to destroy all documents relating to Iraq's past weapons of mass destruction programmes.

In fact, Dr Rihab Taha had come up with none of the documentation that UNSCOM had requested. We had asked for import documents, letters of credit, contracts, bank records of transfers of funds, shipping and warehousing records, budget proposals, accounts, funding requests, building permits, personnel records, administrative records, records of meetings concerning any aspect of the programme, research documents and lab notes or logs – anything that in any way, directly or indirectly, could substantiate her account of the programme. Nothing, she claimed, was available, even from the organisations with even the most peripheral relationship with Salman Pak.

Perhaps it was the fact that Taha could not come up with a single piece of corroborating evidence to support her minimalist account of what her project did, and that she failed to remember the sort of details that make a true story credible, that convinced the UNSCOM team that the Iraqi declarations were neither complete nor accurate.

The other analysis – of what UNSCOM knew from other sources about the capabilities imported by Iraq – was coming to the same conclusion. Israel was reporting that Iraq had imported large

amounts of complex growth media – amounts consistent with the
production of large amounts of biological warfare agent.
UNSCOM already knew from Iraq's declarations that Dr Rihab
Taha had cultures of the biological warfare agents anthrax and
botulinum and fermenters large enough to grow militarily
significant quantities of biological warfare agents. Put these three
together and Taha had the means to make them.

It was also known that Dr Nissar al Hindawi and Dr Taha had
tried to purchase a turn-key, industrial-scale fermentation facility
from a company that had supplied Iraq with a good deal of
equipment suitable for biological research and production. Most
significant amongst this was a freeze-drier and a filling and
stoppering machine. With these, Iraq could take the liquid brew
containing the biological warfare agent from the fermenters, dry it
and put it into munitions. Another freeze-drier was known to have
been sent from the suspect Serum and Vaccine Institute at
Amariyah to a central stores depot at al Dabash for repair.

Finally, BW8 had inspected a couple of airfields for biology-
related items. At both Mosul and K2 it had found military aircraft
equipped with sprayers. Dr Rihab Taha explained that these
sprayers were for 'cloud seeding' (dropping chemicals into clouds
in order to induce rain). However, agricultural sprayers would be
an effective way to deliver biological warfare agent over a target
without having to 'weaponise' it – that is, without having to fill the
agent into a bomb, rocket, missile or artillery shell. The aircraft,
provided it was not shot down itself, could deliver an even and fine
spray of warfare agent over the battlefield at just the right height
and with aerosol droplets of just the right size to cause maximum
damage.

This was significant: it is difficult to disperse biological agents
over a battlefield effectively without destroying the agent. Heat
and shear forces generated in the explosion of a warhead tend to
kill it. Using explosive munitions does not result in even distri-
bution of the agent over a wide area; it produces small areas of high
concentration dotted around the battlefield. And there is no way

of controlling the aerosol droplet size or the height at which the agent is released.

Finally, it was known that Dr Rihab Taha's programme had imported inhalation chambers and aerosol generators – items that indicated experimentation on how best to deliver biological warfare agents, rather than on how to protect against them. During discussions in New York in November 1994, in response to questions about aerosol generators put to her a year earlier, Taha had finally given us some answers. She claimed that Iraq had many aerosol generators for many different purposes, including fumigation, crop-spraying and smoke-generation to protect sensitive military facilities. She named four companies that had supplied them, but when I asked her how many there were of each kind she told me that that information was not available. However, she had forgotten that I read Arabic. Her notes were on the table and I could clearly see three columns: one with the name of the company, one with the number supplied, and another with the number of units still in working order. Taking pains not to appear to be reading her notes, I was able to jot down the names and supplied quantities before she covered them up. Iraq had imported some 150 aerosol generators.

It was clear that Iraq had the capabilities to conduct a biological warfare programme. The evasiveness of Dr Rihab Taha's answers and declarations made us believe that she was hiding much about her programme from us. In fact, it led us to believe the worst.

It was time to go back to the Iraqis with all this new information and try to get to the bottom of the past programme.

Rolf Ekéus called me into his office on 9 November 1994. He wanted me to go on the next biological inspection – the first interrogation inspection. I knew immediately from the way in which he broached the subject that there was to be a sting in the tail. My relations with the UNSCOM New York biological team were at a low. With the exception of Rod Barton, they all wanted to spend their time in Iraq doing inspections rather than staying in New York to analyse the information coming in. I felt there was probably a lot of pertinent information in Iraq's declarations and in the site protocols prepared by BW8 throughout the summer of 1994. I knew that much of this information was sitting unopened in boxes in the offices on the thirtieth floor. I was convinced that it would be more productive to analyse this data than to repeat the fruitless interrogation sessions with Dr Rihab Taha that had been going on since 1991. I had not been backward in coming forward with this view -- to the anger of Annick Paul-Henriot and Dick Spertzel.

What I did not know was the extent of the information that had come in from Israel and other governments leading to the above analysis. Access to this information was limited to a few on a need-to-know basis.

Rolf asked me to go on the inspection to keep an eye on the inspectors. Dick Spertzel was known to be excitable and prone to angry outbursts. David Kelly, although he never lost his own temper, had on several previous occasions provoked Dr Rihab Taha. And there was to be an unknown factor for UNSCOM in this inspection – the British Criminal Investigations Division (CID) had provided a criminal psychologist to interpret the body language of the Iraqi officials as they were being interrogated.

On the other hand, Rolf Ekéus knew that Dick Spertzel would not accept me as chief inspector over him. He was putting me in the invidious position of going as his representative on a mission in which I did not believe, without any real power to affect the outcome, and with people with whom I was already in disagreement and who would see me as nothing more than a spy in their ranks. I tried to wriggle out of it, but Rolf insisted.

In the event, I think I lost my patience with Dr Rihab Taha more than Dick did, and certainly did more to upset her than David did.

Pressure was building for UNSCOM to declare that its monitoring system was in place and that it had accounted for all Iraq's past weapons programmes. A year had passed since Iraq had accepted resolution 715, and General Amer Rasheed kept on reminding Rolf Ekéus that he had said that implementing monitoring might take only six months. (Rolf had at the time qualified that by saying 'in the best of all circumstances' – a caveat that Amer chose to forget.) The biological monitoring system was still not properly in place, essentially because Iraq had failed to make adequate initial declarations. Both General Amer and Rolf Ekéus believed that this issue should be resolved quickly.

Thus Charles Duelfer, Rolf's deputy at UNSCOM, accompanied Dick's team (BW15) and me into Baghdad for separate talks with General Amer Rasheed. He was to stay in Baghdad to be available if the new initial declarations prepared under the supervision of Dr Sami turned out to be inadequate, which would mean further intervention with General Amer to knock heads together.

(Charles also wanted to see the newly completed Baghdad Monitoring and Verification Centre, with its real-time monitoring through the remote-controlled video cameras in factories throughout Iraq. Our reactions to the operations room were diametrically opposite – Charles was disappointed not to see a vast bank of television monitors covering one of the walls; I was impressed with the miniaturisation, with the fact that the split-screen software allowed you to look at sixteen factories of your choice simultaneously.)

In fact, Charles did not have to hang around. Dr Sami had done a creditable job. The declarations from the academic institutions were almost complete and, while there were still many gaps in the responses, the new declarations were generally good enough to serve as the basis for monitoring.

This led to a major dispute between myself and Dick Spertzel. The interrogations were going badly. Hossam Amin and Dr Rihab Taha sat in on them, although we insisted that the officials interviewed should not be interrupted or corrected. But it was clear that every interviewee had been thoroughly coached beforehand.

Worse, there was the most extraordinary case of collective amnesia
I have ever witnessed.

The doctor at Muthanna, who had been responsible for the
health and safety of the biological programme while it was briefly
housed there in 1985, could not remember what his office looked
like, what equipment it had, or who his patients were – that is, who
worked on the programme. The guy brought forward as the
handyman at Salman Pak could not describe the buildings there.
The two other scientists who worked on the programme in
addition to Taha claimed to be totally unaware of each other's
work and hers. All claimed that Salman Pak had no link with any
other organisation, and that there was no objective to their work
other than to investigate in general the issue of biological warfare.

In short, I felt that the interrogations were going nowhere. I did
not need the criminal psychologist to tell me that the Iraqis were
hiding things, not telling the whole story and, from time to time,
lying. On the other hand, I was the only one in the team who had
taken a careful look at the new initial declarations handed over at
the start of the inspection. I suggested that we should take a break
from the interrogations to look at them, as they might contain new
information with which to confront Dr Rihab Taha. But Dick
Spertzel was having none of it and insisted on sticking to the
interrogation.

Of course, in retrospect, Dick was right. We needed to document
for future reference Iraq's story as it stood in November 1994, the
apogee of Iraq's 'cooperation' with UNSCOM. Later, we would
need to be able to show that the Iraqis had been lying – in order to
counter French and Russian assertions either that they were in full
compliance or that any outstanding issues were trivial. With the
verbatim record of these talks captured on tape, and with the
evidence of Iraq's imports from other sources, we would be in a
strong position in the coming spring not only to counter such
pressure, but to convince the French and Russian governments that
we could prove that Iraq was lying in such a systematic and
singleminded way that it could only be to cover up something major.

But I also knew that I was right. In one of the first new initial declarations that I had opened, I was interested to see the addresses of several supplier companies. Quickly flicking through the other declarations, I noticed that there was indeed quite a lot of new information on suppliers. While these were named in the context of declared imports, in all likelihood some of them had also supplied Iraq's military programme. We needed to write to all the named companies to find out what they had supplied, in what quantity, to whom, on what date, via which organisation and for what stated purpose. And, given the growing political pressure for us to say that our work was concluded, we needed to do it quickly – hence my impatience with Dick's position.

One of the names in these declarations was Oxoid, a company based in Basingstoke in the UK, and a supplier of complex growth media.

CHAPTER 17

High Farce: Stories of Stupidity, Rebellions and Spontaneous Combustion

'El original es infiel a la traducion.' (The original is unfaithful to the translation.)

JORGE LUIS BORGES

'"It's a poor sort of memory that only works backwards",' the Queen remarked.'

LEWIS CARROLL

When I got back to New York, I told Rolf Ekéus of my concerns about Dick Spertzel's approach and my view that we should concentrate on the suppliers named in the new declarations. He agreed. But I then got sucked back into my normal work, attending a hectic round of meetings with Rolf and diplomats or politicians, followed by press briefings as part of UNSCOM's never-ending efforts to retain political and public support, and left it to the biological team to do the follow-up.

Dick and the team worked to their own agenda. He arrived back in New York in the last week in November. There were days of audio tape from the interrogation mission to transcribe and analyse. The team had squeezed new information out of the officials they had interviewed and, by eliciting details that the Iraqis alleged to be trivial, had clearly demonstrated how farcical the Iraqi cover story was. In short, they were not able to elaborate on their alibis, and when they tried to improvise, they ended up contradicting either themselves or their colleagues.

There was plenty else going on too. While the November initial declarations were better than any previously supplied, it soon became clear that they were far from accurate and complete. UNSCOM had abandoned all hope of getting proper declarations from Iraq and, in December, no less than three biological inspections went in to conduct intrusive inspections of each of the key sites in order to collect the data that should have been declared. These included inspections of organisations known to have imported biological production and research equipment, or items for its repair and maintenance. As we tetchily reported to the Council:

> By pursuing interim monitoring as a means of obtaining the baseline data required for monitoring, the Commission was relying less on Iraq's openness and more on inspection findings than originally intended. This approach required a greater outlay of resources and so could only be applied to a few sites. The interim monitoring process did not obviate the need for Iraq to report accurately all its biological activities which required declaration ...

On 28 December 1994 a team (IBG1) arrived to test out the monitoring procedures. It started to do monitoring inspections based on the site protocols prepared following the baseline inspections.

In early January 1995 there was a further round of talks on the past programme in New York. Bizarrely, while the Iraqis were talking to our experts in one room, meetings with Israeli contacts were taking place down the corridor. And this time the Israelis were really coming through with the goods. They provided a table showing a large number of contracts arranged by TSMID for purchases of complex growth media between 1987 and 1990. Oxoid featured prominently as a supplier, but there were others too. The quantities involved were mind-boggling – in 1988 alone some 39 tonnes. Such amounts could only be associated with large-scale biological production. They went well beyond what was required for vaccine production, and were way in excess of what was required by all Iraq's medical, research and educational establishments combined. Indeed, according to Iraq's own declarations, received in November 1994, its total hospital consumption of complex growth media averaged only 200kg per annum between 1987 and 1994. Thus the 1988 imports amounted to some 200 years' worth of hospital supplies.

Eureka! Here, at last, was some tangible evidence that Iraq would find it difficult to explain away without admitting to a biological weapons programme.

Dick Spertzel rapidly organised another interrogation mission to return to Baghdad to exploit this data. The interviews could now be extended to all those institutions involved in importing the items detailed by the Israelis. In the kick-off meeting held on the first evening, Dick alluded to the fact that large quantities of complex growth media had been imported. He told Dr Rihab Taha the reference numbers of two of the many letters of credit that Israel had supplied. Taha, realising that UNSCOM obviously knew in detail about Iraq's imports of complex growth media, suddenly started to open doors. At nine o'clock the next morning Dick entered the interview room to find General Nizar Attar, the director of TSMID, and a representative of the State Company for Drugs and Medical Appliances Marketing (SCDMAM) already waiting. A new story emerged – TSMID had made the purchase on behalf of SCDMAM – hence their representative. SCDMAM, Taha said, was the purchasing arm of the Ministry of Health. A new declaration would be provided soon. Dick pointed out that this did not explain why such large quantities had been imported, nor why it involved multiple purchases.

The new story in March 1995 (Rod Barton, UNSCOM113) was that the media had been imported by TSMID for SCDMAM, that some of it had been distributed to hospitals in seven provinces, and that the remainder was either still in the SCDMAM stores or had since been distributed to other centres. To support this story, Dr Taha was suddenly able to find documentation about these imports. Letters of credit, invoices, inventory cards and the like were provided by SCDMAM. These included:

- Three store receipt vouchers (carbon copies on pink slips) from SCDMAM indicating the receipt in 1989 by Store 6 of a total of about 40 tonnes of complex growth media from Oxoid (in two orders), and one from another European company (in one delivery)
- Eleven sales vouchers (carbon copies on blue slips) from SCDMAM covering sales between August 1989 and November 1989 of some 20 tonnes of media from Store 6 to six public health districts
- Eight store cards for 1989 indicating the receipt of media, its sale and the balance in the store (the name and location of which was not identified). These cards corresponded to the sales vouchers.

Dick asked to see the originals of these documents: documents were provided, but they were not the originals because, it was explained, they had been destroyed in a fire. These were documents reconstructed in 1992–3 to maintain the integrity of the records. He also asked for a list of hospitals to which the media had been distributed. Instead, he was given the names of the districts to which Taha claimed it had been sent.

Dick was immediately suspicious. It appeared that complex media had been requested by and supplied to only those parts of Iraq that had seen rebellions after the Gulf War – the Shia south and the Kurdish north. None of the other hospitals, which between them provided medical coverage for over 70 per cent of Iraq's population, had needed this media ...

The next thing to do was to account for all the imported complex growth media. If it had not been used, we needed to find it and verify its location, type and quantity so that we could ensure that all known imports were accounted for and could be monitored from now on. If Iraq could not produce the media, it had to give us credible accounts of how it had been used, supported by credible evidence. 11 tonnes had already been found at the al Adile store and 8 tonnes at al Hakam. That still left some 20 tonnes unaccounted for.

Dick Spertzel asked whether the hospitals to which the 17 tonnes of media had allegedly been sent retained any records of the media, or indeed any remaining stocks. Not surprisingly, he was told that none of the hospitals any longer had records of the media being requested or received. When asked why, Dr Rihab Taha, with the timing and the inevitability of a bad comedian, said that rioters had destroyed all the records during the uprisings. Asked to show the remaining stocks of the media (remember, the orders were large enough to last for decades), Taha said that the media, too, had been destroyed. Yet other supplies were not. UNSCOM knew from its earlier inspections that these hospitals had not been entirely trashed or burnt to the ground – they remained functional. Strangely, none of them had ordered replacement stocks. So the team was being asked to believe that a crowd of rioters had burst into the hospital, sought out those records that related to purchases of complex growth media, destroyed them in a mad frenzy, and then, fired by their daring display of defiance, specifically sought out the media itself and destroyed it, ignoring other equipment and supplies.

Meanwhile, Dick Spertzel was making progress in other areas. General Attar gave his personal account of the setting up and dissolution of the al Hazen Institute, which the US and UK had long suspected of founding the biological programme in the 1970s. He claimed that it had been set up at al Rashad in 1975 and that an electronics division had opened at Salman Pak in 1976. While the institute was dissolved in 1978, the facilities at Salman Pak continued to operate and, following General Faiz Shahine's arrival there from the chemical weapons production plant at Muthanna, a chemical analysis and a forensic laboratory were

Above: *Destruction of a batch of eight 122mm sarin-filled rockets in spring 1992* (UN Photo: H. Arvidsson)

Below: *The pilot sarin production plant at Muthanna, which was converted by UNSCOM for the hydrolytic destruction of Iraq's sarin and tabun nerve agent stocks. Once destruction was complete, this building and the equipment in it were also destroyed* (UN Photo: P. Sudhakaran)

Muthanna State Establishment, C
1-12: Precursor/agent production area, sarin plant
6/14/91; 09:2137-12A

Above: *Munitions storage bunkers at Muthanna, Iraq's chemical production plant, which was badly damaged during the Gulf War* (UN Photo)

Below: *The former administration building at Muthanna, illustrative of the scale of the damage incurred by coalition bombing in the Gulf War* (UN Photo)

Above: *Visiting the chemical destruction plant in 1993. Right to left: Rolf Ekéus, Johan Santesson (behind Rolf), Kees Wolterbeek (chief inspector of the Chemical Destruction Group), Olivia Platon (Rolf's secretary), the author, Jaakko Ylitalo (director of the UNSCOM Baghdad field office), John Scott (UNSCOM legal adviser)* (UN Photo: H. Arvidsson)

Below: *External view of Iraq's principal biological weapons production plant at al Hakam. To the untrained eye, nothing distinguishes these buildings from countless other industrial buildings in Iraq* (UN Photo: H. Arvidsson)

Above: *Overview of the fermenters at al Hakam used by Iraq to brew up anthrax and botulinum in 1990* (UN Photo: H. Arvidsson)

Below: *Entrance to the cold storage bunker at al Hakam. The photograph shows David Kelly's first biological weapons inspection entering the bunker with the Iraqi minders. On the left is the power supply for the air conditioning, crucial to ensure that biological weapons do not degrade in the heat* (UN Photo: H. Arvidsson)

Hakam Single Cell Protein Facility,
26: Cold storage, exterior
9/24/91; 06:3373-32

Above: *External view of the Agricultural and Water Resources Research Centre at Fudhaliyah, another nondescript building. This factory was used for the production of aflatoxin, a biological agent that causes nausea in the short term and stomach cancer in the long term* (UN Photo: A. Hicks)

Below: *The laboratory at the Agricultural and Water Resources Research Centre at Fudhaliyah. Little distinguishes this laboratory from those found in schools, hospitals or universities, but it was used in Iraq's biological weapons programme* (UN Photo: H. Arvidsson)

Above: *Inhalation chambers at the Agricultural and Water Resources Research Centre at Fudhaliyah. These were used to test the effectiveness of biological warfare agents on live animals* (UN Photo: A. Hicks)

Below: *External view of the al Dawrah Foot and Mouth Disease Vaccine Production Plant. This facility was acquired by Iraq's biological weapons programme in July 1990 to work on viral weapons and genetic engineering. Iraq claims that little progress was made in this area and no production of viral agents took place. However, this shows how quickly civilian industry can be adapted for making biological weapons* (UN Photo: H. Arvidsson)

Right: *A fermenter at the al Dawrah Foot and Mouth Disease Vaccine Production Plant. This fermenter was first bought and used for making veterinary vaccines, but was subsequently made part of the biological weapons programme* (UN Photo: A. Hicks)

Dawrah Foot and Mouth D.V.P.F., 46: Fermentor 1425 Liter, serial No #8468.03, Tag No #0092, 12/11/95, S 41746/14

Below: *External view of the al Kindi Veterinary Vaccine Production Plant, which was badly damaged in the Gulf War. This site was suspected of being part of the biological weapons programme and so was bombed by the coalition in 1991. Iraq claims it was not, but that fermenters from here were transferred to al Hakam for making biological weapons* (UN Photo: H. Arvidsson)

شركة الكندي

AL-KINDI Co.
FOR PRODUCTION AND MARKETING
OF VACCINES, SERA & BIOLOGICAL PRODUCTS.

Left: *An unexploded bomb at the al Kindi Veterinary Vaccine Production Plant. Several of the sites inspected by UNSCOM teams were littered with unexploded munitions or dangerous buildings* (UN Photo: H. Arvidsson)

Below: *Media preparation room of the Serum and Vaccine Institute at Amariyah. Complex growth media is mixed specifically for the type of bacteria that needs to be grown. UNSCOM long suspected Amariyah as being part of the biological programme – the facility is capable of making biological weapons. Iraq still insists it was not.* (UN Photo: H. Arvidsson)

founded. An animal testing facility for toxicology studies was added in 1984 (becoming the Chemical Forensic Laboratory); Dr Rihab Taha's biology laboratory had soon followed. As far as Attar could remember, the inhalation chamber was installed some time before 1984. This account contradicted the American and British information, which indicated that the biological activities had started during the al Hazen Institute's brief life, i.e. between 1975 and 1978.

Dick also asked to see the past and present directors of the al Kindi Veterinary Vaccine Production Plant and, in the course of these interviews, established that the fermenters in operation there had been transferred to al Hakam, thus proving a link between al Kindi and al Hakam.

He also asked to see the managers of the factories that had made the DB-0 and DB-2 bombs, destroyed by the chemical destruction group. They explained the bombs' origins. The DB-0 was, purportedly, merely an experimental prototype that was never deployed as an operational weapon. The DB-2 was solely a chemical munition, and was not, they claimed, suitable for biological agents.

But Dick's major success on this inspection came about when he asked to see the plans for the al Hakam buildings and the architects responsible for them. Architectural drawings for the animal house were provided, which included rather high-specification air conditioning – too high for a mere animal house. He asked to see the draughtsman who had prepared them. A representative of the University of Technology Consulting Bureau was produced. He was an air-conditioning design engineer. He acknowledged that the plans were for al Hakam but claimed he had never visited the site and did not know much about it. He referred to it as Project 900. All he knew was that it was for protein production; the building for which he designed the air conditioning was a chicken house. This and other answers indicated that he had been primed, but he was forced to admit that his design was somewhat sophisticated for a normal chicken house. He became nervous at this point, and refused to be drawn on how the customer's design spec had been conveyed to him, and how and with whom he had liaised in drawing up his designs.

The team were surprised to find that the drainage and sewerage for al Hakam were designed by a different organisation, the al Faw Consultative Bureau, a subsidiary of MIC (now headed by General Amer Rasheed). The lady who had designed the sanitation for al Hakam was produced. She was more open about the project specification process, saying that for green-field sites it was normal not to visit the location. Dick Spertzel asked her for the project number for al Hakam, expecting to hear 900 – the number used by the air-conditioning consultant – but she referred to it as the al Faw Project 324. She also claimed she had never been there.

The extraordinary degree of secrecy surrounding al Hakam's origin, the fact that different parts of its design had been given to different design bureaux, and that none of the designers had actually been to the site, all indicated that al Hakam was a top secret project, not the innocent single-cell protein production plant that Dr Rihab Taha would have us believe. But the clincher was the sanitation designer's reference to Project 324 – the name directly linked by US intelligence to the production of biological weapons.

That evening Dick told Dr Rihab Taha that there had been mention of two different project numbers. Were projects 900 and 324 the same thing, or did they refer to different buildings? Taha, unaware that Dick had intelligence about 324, admitted that it was the project name for the entire al Hakam programme.

In New York a quick check of the plans gathered for al Hakam during the site protocol inspection revealed that Iraq had handed over a site diagram clearly showing buildings E and H, corresponding to the negative air pressure laboratory and the animal house. There was now a perfect fit between al Hakam and the intelligence report about the biological weapons production factory.

Al Hakam was the site. The biological team knew that they were closing in on the programme.

* * *

Following the successes of this mission, Rod Barton wrote to all the suppliers named in both the Israeli information and in Iraq's initial declarations, handed over in November 1994. This time, given the urgency of the situation, he broke with protocol and wrote directly to the companies.

Since 1991, when the IAEA had released the names of many of the companies that had supplied the Iraqi nuclear programme, we had been under immense pressure from the press and the US and German governments to release information about Iraq's suppliers for the chemical, biological and missile programmes. We had resisted this pressure on the grounds that we had already informed the host governments of the trade. It was up to them to decide whether any laws had been broken and to take appropriate legal action. We were not in the business of naming and shaming: we had to rely on these same companies to provide us with the evidence that Iraq was trying to deny or hide.

This policy proved to be very wise. When a small team of UNSCOM experts went to Basingstoke, they found the Oxoid staff shocked and dismayed to discover what Iraq had intended to do with their products. They were more than willing to cooperate, provided that their name did not find its way into the press and provided criminal proceedings did not start.* Otherwise their lawyers had instructed them to clam up. A policy of naming and shaming would have denied UNSCOM vital evidence that eventually led to the uncovering of Iraq's biological weapons.

January 1995 saw both tragedy and another new recruit for UNSCOM's biological weapons team. In early January Annick Paul-Henriot died of heart failure at her New York home, while packing up to move to a new house with her husband and daughter. She had been so dedicated to UNSCOM and had so

---

* The story of Oxoid's exports to Iraq had, nevertheless, found its way into the British press by the end of 1995.

enjoyed her work there that she had told no one of her condition. She feared that, had she done so, she would have been barred from going on inspections to Iraq.

On the positive side, UNSCOM recruited a German scientist, Gabriele Kraatz-Wadsack. In the summer of 1994, when UNSCOM was desperately looking for good biologists to conduct the baseline inspections, Gabriele was working at the German Ministry of Defence's biological defence laboratory. Her expertise was the real-time detection of biological warfare agents using monoclonal antibodies. She received a telephone call from the Ministry of Defence asking her whether she would like to spend three months in Baghdad on inspections. Gabriele said she could not get away from her work for a few months, but that in principle she was interested. In the end, one of her colleagues went on the baseline inspection, but Gabriele was called to join UNSCOM in late January 1995. All she knew about UNSCOM came from her colleague's account of the baseline and tagging inspection in the summer of 1994. Even the official who had recruited her had no idea what she would be doing.

She left Germany for Bahrain, where she spent one night and was told only that she was to be the new chief inspector of the second interim biological group, which would be testing out the biological monitoring procedures. The next day she was in Baghdad taking over from the leader of the first group, Ken Johnson, who gave her a copy of resolution 715 and the plan for ongoing monitoring and verification.

Gabriele Kraatz-Wadsack quickly read herself in and was soon out inspecting. The first two inspections were of al Hakam and the Foot and Mouth Vaccine Production Plant at al Dawrah. Her immediate impression was that they were both perfect for biological weapons production. Her team-mates thought she was paranoid.

Everywhere Gabriele went, she found dual-purpose equipment that should have been declared and submitted to monitoring. At the Tuwaitha Agricultural and Biological Research Centre, for instance, there was an untagged gas-chromatograph, an untagged cooled incubator shaker, an untagged orbital shaker and an untagged controlled environmental shaker – all items that one finds in well-equipped biological labs but could also have been part of Iraq's biological weapons programme. Her thoroughness and clear reporting gained approval in New York.

In the high-level talks taking place in Baghdad in parallel with these inspections in March 1995, Rolf Ekéus asked Tariq Aziz why the Ministry of Health had ordered so much media when it only needed 200kg per year. He was told that the Ministry of Health had decided to increase efficiency by collating orders for all hospital laboratories into one. The officials involved had done a good job. A five-year purchase would require around 1 tonne of media. This had been submitted to the head of imports, who was stupid, and who, in order to play safe, doubled the order to 2 tonnes. His immediate supervisor, also stupid, also decided to play it safe and doubled the order again to 4 tonnes. His boss doubled it to 10 tonnes and put the proposal to the minister. The minister, who was extremely stupid, said, 'Let's make it 20 tonnes; no, 40.' Aziz said that this was just one of those 'one-off' mistakes. The minister had been fired.

Tariq Aziz had no explanation why it was imported in 25kg drums, not the 100g or 1kg sachets that are normal for laboratory use – except that everyone in the Ministry of Health was stupid. He also failed to explain why there had been more than one large media purchase, belying his one-off mistake theory. And he could not say why, when these purchases were ostensibly being made on behalf of the Ministry of Health as a consolidation of several years' imports for the entire country, the normal importing agencies at the Ministry of Health had continued to import media in normal quantities separately from this new procedure.

The Iraqi story leaked water from every pore.

Meanwhile, Charles Duelfer, Nikita Smidovich and I were off on an interesting adventure. In January 1995 the head of Iraq's

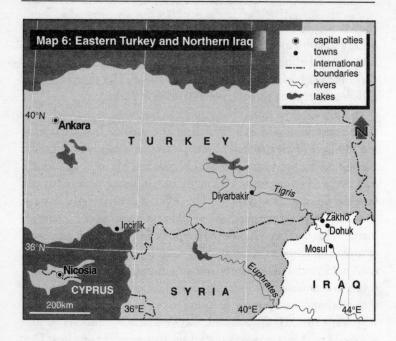

Map 6: Eastern Turkey and Northern Iraq

Meeting the defector, General Wafiq al Samarra'i, involved flying to Ankara, getting a domestic flight to Diyarbakir, flying by military helicopter from the US military base at Incirlik to Zakho, and driving to Dohuk.

Military Intelligence, General Wafiq al Samarra'i, defected to the Kurdish safe haven. Charles, through his contacts in the US government, arranged for us to fly into northern Iraq from the US air base in Incirlik, near Diyarbakir in eastern Turkey – Turkey's equivalent of the Wild West. Getting to Diyarbakir was in itself an experience. We finally arrived on 9 February. Climbing aboard the Apache helicopter, wearing a bullet-proof vest and helmet, was an adrenalin high. The Turkish authorities insisted that we should fly high, presumably to avoid encountering restive Kurds. But once we crossed the border, the helicopter dropped to near ground level. I could almost hear 'The Ride of the Valkyries'. The overall effect was far more exciting than the best of fairground rides. I could understand why the analysts invariably spent too much time getting themselves onto inspections and too little time at their computers doing the analysis.

We were expecting to meet the general at the UN guards building in Zakho. When we got there, we found the building heavily barricaded, with razor-wire on the walls and a steel door firmly bolted shut. There was no sign of anyone. Everything indicated that the streets were not safe, and yet we had nowhere to go. After a while some UN guards arrived, having just returned from Dohuk. They had no idea that Wafiq al Samarra'i was supposed to be at their office. They called up their colleagues in Dohuk, who confirmed that Samarra'i was still there – an hour and a half away, over a mountain pass and across the plain. The UN guards kindly agreed to drive us there, but warned us that the road was dangerous and we should wear our bullet-proof vests. We went in two vehicles – the UN guards riding shotgun in the first, us in the second trailing.

In fact, the journey was uneventful. Convoys of small flatbed trucks passed us going towards Turkey. They all had hand-made containers welded to the platform. They were smuggling out Iraqi petrol in what must be one of the more bizarre examples of pragmatic trade. Iraq sold oil at about one quarter the world price ($5 per barrel) to its sworn enemies, the Kurds, who then transshipped it to no man's land, where it was sold for $10 per barrel to Turks, who then paid another $5 per barrel bribe to smuggle it into Turkey, where they sold it at close to the world price. Everyone made a profit, and was glad of the trade. Iraq had no other outlet for its oil and needed the hard currency; the Kurds needed to fund their internecine wars and made a nice packet as the middlemen; and the Turkish economy in the eastern provinces was in dire straits as a result of the ban on trade with Iraq, and needed the money. The roads from Iraq, through the Kurdish provinces to

Turkey were not only paved with gold; they were covered with oil leaking from these trucks.

Dohuk is a charming town, creeping up the sides of three mountains where they meet in a narrow valley. It has clearly seen better days, but the roads are all properly paved, with drains and kerbed sidewalks. The villas and bungalows have a Mediterranean feel, and the garden walls overflow with grapes and bougainvillaea. The general was renting a pleasant villa halfway up one of the mountains. Its veranda afforded a splendid view of all three mountains and the approaches to Dohuk, and inside, there were ornate Italian furnishings, Iraqi and Iranian carpets, and beautiful tiled floors.

He was not there. He had heard that we were waiting for him in Zakho and had gone there. We must have crossed on the road. We sat down and waited for him to come back. Having arrived at Zakho before 10 a.m., we did not meet the general until 2.30 p.m. Our plans for a one-day trip were out of the window.

Wafiq al Samarra'i was affable and expansive. He was a stocky, dapper man in his late forties or early fifties. A round, jovial face was adorned with the usual Iraqi moustache. For all his military background with the Iraqi regime, his was a face used to laughing.

He made a wide-ranging opening statement. Firstly, he made it clear that he was not responsible for weapons manufacture, although he knew Iraq had programmes for making biological, chemical and nuclear weapons, along with conventional weapons including long-range missiles. Most interesting was that in May 1991 – the dark days for Saddam – he was asked to make an inventory of all the weapons systems available. He talked at length about the operational SCUDs concealed by Iraq and about how documents had been hidden from UNSCOM, but he did not know much about biological weapons. However, two things he said were of interest. He claimed that the 'manager of the chemical weapons programme' included, in his contribution to the May 1991 weapons status report, a statement that there were 'germ bombs'. Samarra'i knew that '500' was somehow related to these bombs, but he could not remember whether it was 500kg or 500lb. He also stated that the Samarra Drug Company was used for hiding documents about the weapons programmes.

I asked him about the extent of Iraq's biological weapons programme, and was told that in 1991 it had had 200 bombs. There was apparently only one report covering both chemical and biological weapons, which implied that both were dealt with by the same people. Samarra'i did not know where the biological weapons programme was located, but stated that it was not co-located with the chemical weapons production. He said that Hamid Yusif al Hamadi, by 1995 Minister for Culture, would know as he had been Saddam's secretary in 1991 and was 'managing the issue'. He thought that it was perhaps in the Zaafaraniyah area south of Baghdad. Nikita Smidovich asked him if he was aware of the activities undertaken at Salman Pak. He immediately said yes, that was the biological weapons area, south of the nuclear project. He volunteered that the Mukhabarat (Internal Intelligence) was initially responsible for the programme. I asked him when the programme had started and who had initiated it and why. He said he was not sure, but that it was under way by 1982, when Barzan al Tikriti (Saddam's half-brother and now banker to the regime in Geneva) was Chief of Intelligence.

I asked him whether Military Intelligence had done a biological threat analysis for Iran or Syria, and whether such an analysis had triggered Iraq's programme. He replied that no such analysis had been done and that Iraq's biological programme was not a reaction to an outside threat. After the superpowers and Israel, Iraq considered itself to be the biggest holder of chemical and biological weapons in the world.

Charles Duelfer told Wafiq al Samarra'i about the Iraqi cover story that all relevant documentation had been destroyed. He laughed and said that it would be easier for Saddam to commit suicide than to destroy the documents. He added that UNSCOM had been denied access to the Ministry of Agriculture because Iraq needed time to remove the documents. He described in some detail the countermeasures that Iraq used to prepare for UNSCOM inspections.

His views on Saddam were enlightening.

You know Saddam, but I know him better. Saddam relies on weapons. His theory is war. He cannot survive without war. I have been with him twenty years in Military Intelligence and eight years in the Military Council ...

Saddam did not use chemical weapons against Israel or the coalition as he was afraid of the response ...

I know him very well. Saddam can never give up these weapons. My village is very close to Saddam's. I have known him for nearly forty years. He told me that it was true that we have left Kuwait now, but the day will come when we will return. He also told Talabani* that he could not forget the idea of greater Iraq. He also said war was glory. It is a side of his character. If I were an inspector, I would never sign that Saddam has no further weapons, as I would be sure that he would be lying.

When Charles Duelfer asked why, if getting the oil embargo lifted was so important, Saddam Hussein held on to these weapons that were only getting older and less useful by the day, Samarra'i again laughed.

First, you cannot measure Saddam according to your own standards. You should measure him against the standards of the region. Iraq is the second weapons of mass destruction power in the region after Israel. According to Saddam, without weapons, he will lose political status outside Iraq and his regime

* One of the two factious Kurdish leaders, variously in bed with Saddam or fighting him, depending on the exigencies of the internecine struggle with the other Kurdish leader, Barzani.

will fall. Money is not an issue with the regime either. In Samarra, there are still over 100 goldsmiths. Saddam is now selling petrol via Turkey, Iran and Jordan to the sum of 150,000 barrels per day. This gives his regime enough to survive. But he cannot cancel the weapons programmes.

I asked him who normally would have been responsible for reviewing progress in the weapons programmes. He replied without any hesitation that it was Hussein Kamal Hassan and our old friend General Amer Rasheed al Ubeidi.

Entertaining though this performance was, it was unfortunately not very useful. It was out-dated information, vague and unsupported with evidence that could upset the Iraqi cover story. There were all the usual problems with human intelligence, too: was the general telling the truth? Or was he an *agent provocateur* doing Saddam's work to try and discredit us? Or was he merely a refugee trying to find favour by telling us what he thought we wanted to hear? Or was he an ambitious politician cynically using us to further his own game plan? There was no way of knowing. Some of the details he had mentioned checked out with what we knew, lending credence to his story. I was eager to tell the biological team about his reference to the 200 germ bombs. I wanted to know whether the DB-0 and DB-2 bombs were 500lb or 500kg bombs. If they were, then the general might have given us something useful.

In February 1995 Nikita Smidovich led a small team of UNSCOM's experts to Baghdad for discussions to resolve the persistent difficulties in each of the three areas: missile, chemical and biological. Following his contacts with Iraq's suppliers of precursor chemicals, Horst Reeps was increasingly concerned that Iraq had not yet told the full truth about its VX nerve agent activities. Iraq was claiming that it had conducted only laboratory-level research into production of this agent, and yet the returns from suppliers indicated that it had purchased hundreds of tonnes of precursors. Igor Mitrokhin had been following up on the Iraqi import of empty munitions, and also questioned whether Iraq had declared all its holdings of bombs and artillery shells that could be adapted to deliver chemical and biological weapons. Finally, Nikita and Scott Ritter had problems in the missile area. In addition to worries about a missile monitoring radar imported by Iraq from China, there were indications that Iraq had tried to import a parachute braking system for its SCUD-related missiles. Such systems could have been adapted to improve the efficiency with which biological and chemical weapons could be delivered by SCUD missiles.

In these meetings Dick Spertzel told Dr Rihab Taha that the numerous letters of credit from the suppliers of complex growth media were not all accounted for by the twenty-two reconstructed documents that she had handed over in January. He also questioned the authenticity of these documents and the alleged reasons for which the media was imported. Dr Taha floated the idea that some of it might have been imported for the biological department of the forensic laboratory at Salman Pak, but this suggestion was dismissed by Dick because it was the wrong type of media, in the wrong quantities and in the wrong size packaging. She withdrew the suggestion and ignored questions about why TSMID had also imported fermenters.

Dick Spertzel then started to question her about the import in 1985 of biological equipment for research and production purposes by the Muthanna State Establishment, Iraq's huge chemical weapons production plant that went under the code name of SEPP (the State Establishment for Pesticide Production) in all its import operations. At that time, before the establishment of the Salman Pak operation, which she joined full-time in 1986, Dr Taha was working part-time at Muthanna and part-time at Baghdad University. Sheepishly, she claimed that she had misused SEPP funds to buy equipment and supplies for her university. Dick's team did not accept that she, a young biologist looking for her first full-time job, would do this. But some of the equipment had ended up at Baghdad University, suggesting that there was a link between the university and the biological programme. Certainly, there seemed now to be a strong link between Iraq's biological and chemical weapons programmes. This was only what the inspectors had expected from the outset. Indeed, it is normal for biological and chemical programmes, be they defensive or offensive, to be run by the same organisation.

Finally, Dick tackled Dr Taha on the real purpose for which al Hakam was built. She stuck to the cover story that it was conceived and built to make single-cell protein. Dick pointed out that:

(a) The facility had been built in secrecy, with no outside agency ever seeing the entire plans
(b) The design was too sophisticated for the stated purpose
(c) The fermenter room was too small for industrial-scale single-cell protein production.

Taha tried out various explanations of why UNSCOM's analysis was wrong. All were negated with evidence put forward by the team. Angrily, Taha said that, no matter what information UNSCOM had, al Hakam was a single-cell protein production plant.

In March 1995 Terry Taylor was recruited to lead the next inspection, BW23. Rod Barton, the biologist from UNSCOM New York, was on the team. Terry was a close friend and colleague of mine. We had been working together in some guise or other almost continuously since October 1985, when I was in the British Foreign and Commonwealth Office's UN Department (responsible for various humanitarian issues including the Red Cross's Rules of War), and he was in the Ministry of Defence's Disarmament and Arms Control Unit dealing with the same issue. Later, we worked together in Geneva on the Chemical Weapons

Convention. By 1995 he was the British-nominated member of the commission, but had left the MoD for a year's fellowship at Stanford University.

Terry's mission was to follow up on the documents handed to Dick Spertzel at the end of his January 1995 inspection; these purported to tell the story of the imports of the vast quantities of complex growth media. Dr Rihab Taha had admitted that these documents were copies, not originals. Terry wanted to speak to the people who had signed the documents and to find out why there were no originals available. He was joined in this mission by Gabriele Kraatz-Wadsack's monitoring team. The inspection began on 12 March.

Rather than immediately asking to see the people who had signed the documents, or forcing a discussion about the documents themselves, Terry asked to be taken to the headquarters of SCDMAM, on whose behalf TSMID was supposed to have imported the complex growth media.

Personnel there were asked about normal purchasing procedures for complex growth media. Terry was told that the head of the Import Division would set the levels based on advice from the head of the Laboratory Materials Section. Both received computer printouts from the Computer Division showing the amounts shipped in the previous year and the amount remaining in stock. The Computer Division received its information from the storeman, who provided it with copies of the store receipt voucher and the sales voucher. The top copy of the store receipt voucher was sent to the Finance Department for payment, and the second copy to Accounting. The storeman retained a copy. All the vouchers were kept in ring-binder files with holes punched in the papers.

The documents handed over to Dick Spertzel's team did not look like the documents that Terry Taylor's team was seeing at SCDMAM. And there were no holes punched in them, indicating that the copies had not been part of SCDMAM's files. The office staff there could not provide any information about the media documents because they had both been recruited after the imports in question had arrived.

Next the financial manager was questioned. Terry Taylor asked him how SCDMAM would go about making purchases through another company, such as TSMID. He replied that he had been with SCDMAM since 1990 and had never heard of TSMID. It was not the practice for one state company to make purchases on behalf of another. He very much doubted that the media could have been purchased for SCDMAM. He pointed out that he had previously worked as the head of the Audit Division at the Ministry of Health, and so should know the procedures.

The fact that no documents relating to the TSMID contracts were found in any of these various departments that were purportedly involved was explained by the fact that all such documents were destroyed after five years, unless payment was outstanding or there was some other contractual reason for keeping them. However, why the TSMID documents had survived the five-year rule remained a mystery.

The team then went to the al Adile store (known as Store 1), which the Iraqis claimed was the only central government store for complex growth media. Terry's team had already visited this site and found 11 tonnes of media, mostly labelled as being for TSMID. In fact, a chemical inspection team had visited this store some time before and failed to notice the media as they were looking for chemical weapons-related materials. They had even caught it on video, without realising what it was or how significant a find it would be for the biologists.

The team searched the whole store, looking for any records of imports of dual-purpose items, including complex growth media. There was no sign of the specific contracts covered by the reconstructed documents. What Terry's team did find, however, was an inventory of items kept in the stores in 1991/92. These Laboratory Materials Audits were recorded in ten books for 1991 and twelve for 1992 – they looked thorough and comprehensive. Each book was numbered and there were no gaps, indicating a complete set. There was no mention of the complex growth media there, but Terry did not draw this fact to the Iraqi minders' attention.

Next, the storeman, Abdul al Razzaq, was questioned at length. He had been storeman since 1981, starting out with the company when the store was at al Dabash (Store 13), and moving with the store in 1990 when it was transferred to al Adile; he should certainly have known about the TSMID contracts. During the three days of his questioning, his story shifted regularly, and he evaded many questions entirely. He was asked to explain the usual procedure for receiving, storing and shipping imports. He described how the store receipt vouchers (recording deliveries) and the sales vouchers (recording shipments) were kept in the central office files, and the store cards (showing current inventory levels) kept in the stores near the actual inventory stocks. He was asked who normally would sign documents, particularly of big orders, and answered truthfully that he would. Terry asked him whether anyone else signed these records, and was told no.

He was asked why, contrary to normal practice, he had not signed the various vouchers and cards for the TSMID contracts. He claimed that, because the purchase was so big, the media had been stored at Store 6 at al Misbah and so the store receipt voucher had been made up by his colleague there but kept at al Dabash for ease of administration. The store card was also kept at al Dabash.

Razzaq was then asked what had happened to the originals. He said that, because he was short of space in his office, he had put all the store receipt vouchers relating to the TSMID contracts in a metal cabinet which was stored in the X-ray repair shop at al Dabash. In September 1989 there was an electrical fault in this store: a cable had fallen onto the cabinet and set the papers on fire. When asked how this could happen, he answered that the drawer containing the TSMID files was open, and only these papers had been destroyed. The documents had been reconstructed from his own hand-written notepads, and from a hard inventory count of remaining stocks. It had been delayed so long because he had been preoccupied with the move from al Dabash to al Adile.

Initially, Razzaq claimed that the sales vouchers and store cards were original but he changed his story the next day. He then claimed that the sales vouchers had been lost in the move from al Dabash to al Adile and had been reconstructed from correspondence from the hospitals that had made the purchases. When asked to produce that correspondence, he claimed that all the letters had since been destroyed.

By now, Terry Taylor's team had become frustrated. Every request for documents to authenticate the reconstructed documents elicited yet another bizarre explanation of why those documents, and only those, were not available in the original, or at all. Requests to talk to the people who had signed the documents were parried with claims that they had either retired and were unavailable, or that they had died. Razzaq was unable to explain why he had not signed the reconstructed documents, as was normal practice, even though he said they were made up on his instructions and from his own notes. The team joked that the next story would be that the notes had fallen off the back of a truck.

Sure enough, the next morning, Abdul al Razzaq changed his story yet again. Now he insisted that even the store cards were not original. They, too, must have been lost in the move of the stores – perhaps, he mused, they had fallen off the back of the truck ...

Terry Taylor now asked why the TSMID documents had survived the five-year destruction rule – there was no sign of other pre-1990 documents at the Adile store. Abdul al Razzaq had no answer, shrugging it off as good luck. But when he was questioned on who had called him in January 1995 asking him to find the documents, he could not remember. Nor could he remember what he had been told to look for.

The team's assessment was caustic:

Whereas individually any of the above circumstances may be believable, their combination casts serious doubts on the authenticity of the Media Documents.

We are asked to believe that an unprecedented purchase of media was made by SCDMAM through TSMID against usual practice of company purchases; that through a selective fire, and loss during a move, the original documents were destroyed or lost, that they were all reconstructed by the authorisation of a storeman but that, unusually, he did not sign any of the forms; that the storeman happened to have records in the form of hand-written notes that gave him details to reconstruct the documents; that by good chance these documents almost uniquely survived the five year destruction rule and that finally no other supporting documentation exists.

It seems likely the documents are therefore fabricated to provide 'evidence' of an import by SCDMAM through TSMID. It also seems likely that the storeman, Mr Razzaq, was not himself involved with the fabrication but that he is covering for some other organisation.

CHAPTER 18

Iraqi Plea Bargaining: An End to Inspections in Return for Admission of Guilt

'The long arm of coincidence.'
HADDON CHAMBERS

'The truth is rarely pure, and never simple.'
OSCAR WILDE

Gabriele Kraatz-Wadsack's monitoring team set out to look for the media. On 28 March 1995 she visited the al Kindi Veterinary Vaccine Production Plant and found eleven 25kg containers of bacteriological peptone, part of the Oxoid contracts. As part of Iraq's cover-up, all except two of the labels identifying the media and the supplier company had been removed. The director of al Kindi, Dr Ahmed Kadoori Amer, explained that the media was currently being used for vaccines against anthrax, gas gangrene and a couple of other anaerobic bacteria. However, there were no working fermenters at the site in which to manufacture the vaccines. Of the two fermenters previously inventoried, one was under repair and the other was being used to store distilled water, its stirrers and controls having been removed.

Then on 30 March the team went to the al Razi Research Centre, where the director was Dr Hazem Mohammed Ali – one of the ten people who were claimed to have been part of the Salman Pak 'military biological research programme' – another link between al Kindi and Salman Pak. In the storeroom were twenty-three 25kg drums of a variety of complex growth media, all bearing TSMID labels. Dr Hazem claimed that these had been sent to the al Razi Research Centre in 1993 by SCDMAM. From the letters of credit available to Gabriele, the drums could be tracked back to either Oxoid or the other European company's shipments. All told, these three sites had accounted for 3 tonnes of media; this meant that, with the 19 tonnes at al Hakam and al Adile, Gabriele Kraatz-Wadsack's team had accounted for 22 tonnes of complex growth media.

However, some 17 tonnes remained unaccounted for. Dr Rihab Taha was sticking to the ludicrous story that it had been distributed to hospitals in the six provinces.

The Iraqis were growing impatient with UNSCOM. In November 1993, when they had finally agreed to accept the monitoring provisions under resolution 715, they had urged UNSCOM to set a firm timetable for the conclusion of its work – a matter of months, they hoped. Tariq Aziz and General Amer Rasheed both expressed displeasure when Rolf Ekéus told them that he could not report to the Council that conditions for lifting the sanctions had been met until the monitoring system was 'up and running'. They were even more dismayed when he said that that would take at least six months. They tried to get him to commit to a shorter time-scale, but Rolf refused. Already the experts, led by Dick Spertzel, felt that six months was perilously short. While there was no mutiny, some of the technical experts were really worried that Rolf, for political reasons, would sign up to something that was not technically sound.

Next General Amer Rasheed tried to get Rolf to agree to make the six months a set period. Again Rolf refused, on the grounds that Iraq's own past behaviour had caused the delays so far. A period of trust-building was required. UNSCOM had no assurance that Iraq would fulfil its part of the bargain within the six-month period. Besides, the ceasefire resolution was very clear – sanctions could only be lifted when all Iraq's banned weapons capabilities had been destroyed and the monitoring was in place. It was not a question of time; it was a question of achieving the necessary elimination of weapons, etc. ... If Iraq did not do its part, then it would take longer than six months. All that Rolf could guarantee was that UNSCOM would not itself be the cause of delay.

In February 1995, when Horst Reeps and Igor Mitrokhin started to hit the Iraqis with the need to come clean on the VX programme, fifteen months had already passed and there was no sign of UNSCOM being ready to close any of the files. General Amer Rasheed had tried to get the files closed individually. Rolf resisted this, even intervening with the IAEA to prevent them from unilaterally declaring the nuclear file closed, on the grounds that the lifting of sanctions was an 'all-or-nothing' affair under the terms of the ceasefire resolution. The declaration that 'Iraq had completed all the actions contemplated' (to eliminate its banned weapons capabilities and to accede to monitoring) could not be made piecemeal.

Both the IAEA and UNSCOM had come as close as Rolf Ekéus would countenance to saying that the nuclear and missile files were closed. The chemical file remained open because of the VX problem. Council members knew about this problem and understood it – it was easy to see why the concealment of enough chemicals to make hundreds of tonnes of VX needed to be addressed. The monitoring system could not yet be declared up and running because of the problems encountered throughout 1994 and into 1995 in the biological area – namely Dr Rihab Taha's failure to provide a consistent and complete set of declarations about the dual-purpose sites and materials that needed to be monitored. But no one outside UNSCOM yet knew that the biological file was a potential show-stopper. Rolf was coming under increasing pressure from the French and Russian ambassadors to assure Tariq Aziz and General Amer Rasheed that, once the VX file was closed, he would report that UNSCOM's work was done.

Tariq Aziz, sensing that the tide of opinion was shifting in Iraq's favour, visited New York in March 1995. For the first week of his visit he pointedly avoided meeting Rolf, or the ambassadors of the US and the UK. Instead, he held bilateral meetings with the remaining thirteen ambassadors of the Security Council member nations. His message was simple, if old and well worn. Iraq had fully complied with its obligations; UNSCOM was operating solely under the influence of the US and the UK; it was not reporting honestly that all the files were now closed but making mountains out of molehills on a series of trivial issues just to enable the US and the UK to maintain the unjust sanctions against Iraq.

Aziz's intention had been clear – to split the Council and to achieve the lifting of sanctions without fulfilling the ceasefire terms.

Rolf Ekéus had once again taken care to brief the Council members in small groups before Aziz's visit. In particular, he had targeted the Non-Aligned Group in the Council, and the Non-non-group (states, such as Brazil, that were not a part of the Non-Aligned Group, or of the Western Group, and were not permanent members). Consequently, Aziz was shocked to find these ambassadors well briefed on the issues and not susceptible to his transparent tactics. In fact, one after the other, the ambassadors lectured Aziz on the need to come clean on the VX issue and to stop messing around on the oil-for-food talks which would allow Iraq to sell oil to fund imports of food and medicine for its people.

Under this pressure, on 25 March 1995 Iraq provided UNSCOM with a new account of its VX programme. This admitted to the production of VX at pilot-plant scales, some 250kg. It denied weaponisation of VX, and it did not account for all the imported precursor chemicals. However, it might be deemed enough for Iraq's allies on the Security Council to argue that Iraq had now closed the chemical file. We knew in UNSCOM that the political pressure to close all the files would only increase once we announced that the monitoring system was up and running, as we intended to in our next written report, due on 10 April.

* * *

Meanwhile, UNSCOM was preparing the Council for the biological weapons issue. In late March 1995 UNSCOM called together a meeting of biological experts from the governments of key countries to review Iraq's unbelievable account of its past biological activities. The invitation stated that the aim of the meeting was to show them the evidence that was available to UNSCOM, and ask for their assessment and advice on how to proceed. The real aim was to gain support for the UNSCOM assessment and thereby undercut any political pressure exerted on their governments to turn a blind eye to the evidence or question UNSCOM's technical evaluation of the issue. Gabriele Kraatz-Wadsack, now at the end of her three months with the interim monitoring team in Baghdad, flew in too.

In addition to the evidence on the complex growth media imports and Iraq's intelligence-insulting explanations about its purpose and fate, these experts were presented with the following about the al Hakam site. Dick Spertzel could not use the sensitive intelligence about Project 324, so he had to rely on other evidence to prove that al Hakam was the biological weapons production facility:

- TSMID was the purchasing arm of the Technical Research Council. There were only two known facilities under the TRC's command – Salman Pak, the declared site of military research into biological warfare, and al Hakam, implying a link between al Hakam and biological warfare. The link with unconventional warfare was strengthened in that the director of the TRC was none other than Dr Ahmed Murtada, one-time director of the chemical production plant at Muthanna. TSMID made all al Hakam's purchases.
- Even if one accepted the Iraqi story that al Hakam was a single-cell protein production facility, according to Iraq's own declarations, there was only one 450-litre fermentation vessel operational there. To have used 17 tonnes of media in such a small fermenter would have taken over twenty years. There

must be a very much larger fermentation capacity somewhere in Iraq, as yet undeclared, to account for such vast imports of complex growth media.

- Neither of the above declared activities at al Hakam involved toxic or infectious materials. And yet an animal house and a laboratory with highly sophisticated air-filtration systems were scheduled there. These design features were strongly indicative of plans to work on infectious agents and to experiment on animals with them.

- The al Hakam project imported a lot of equipment and materials that were not required for single-cell protein production but would be required for a biological weapons programme. These included four filling machines, which can be used for filling munitions with biological and chemical warfare agent; they have many other industrial uses, but none in a single-cell protein production plant. They had been ordered from a European company in 1989. Iraq's explanation of why the filling machines were at al Hakam, which it acknowledged having only after being specifically questioned on the issue by UNSCOM, was that they were purchased by TSMID for a 'biopesticide project', allegedly a backup project at Salman Pak – another link between al Hakam and Salman Pak. The first mention of these biopesticide activities at Salman Pak was made only when an explanation for their presence at al Hakam was required.

  (Had we been cynical, we would have recognised that this immediately gave away the fact that Iraq had made biological weapons. 'Pesticide' seemed to mean weapon: the State Establishment for Pesticide Production made Iraq's chemical weapons. Now there was a biopesticide project at the prime suspect site of the biological weapons programme.)

- The newly declared biopesticide project at Salman Pak was alleged to have imported a spray drier from another European company. This was also now at al Hakam. Spray driers are used to harvest the bio-mass product of fermentation from the rest of the fermentation slurry. The spray drier was capable of producing particle sizes of 10 microns – an ideal size for biological weapons but useless for biopesticides, undermining that alibi.

- In mid-1988 one of Dr Rihab Taha's colleagues had tried, in perhaps the biggest display of sheer nerve in the entire Iraqi biological weapons programme, to purchase the most virulent strain of anthrax (the world's number-one choice of biological warfare agent) from none other than Britain's Chemical and Biological Defence Establishment at Porton Down – David Kelly's and Bryan Barrass's home institution. Of course, the request had been turned down and the Iraqis now denied ever having placed such an order, but it was still on the records at Porton Down.

- A large part of the imported media was not suitable for growing the aerobic bacteria used in single-cell protein production, but was ideal for growing anaerobic bacteria. All three of the biological warfare agents that Taha had declared she studied at Salman Pak (anthrax, botulinum and gas gangrene) are anaerobic bacteria.

- Through its newly declared biopesticide activities, al Hakam was working on *Bacillus cereus*, a perfect simulant for growing anthrax, and *Bacillus thurengensis*, with which al Hakam staff had perfected the technique of one-step drying of bacterial culture to produce dried spores. This process used bentonite (known to biological weapons makers) and resulted in a particle size in the range of 1–10 microns – ideal for biological weapons purposes.

- TSMID placed numerous orders in 1989 to equip a high-quality laboratory at al Hakam. While much of the equipment was of general dual-purpose nature, some of it was clearly not required for the production of single-cell protein but would be required for the production, testing and research of biological weapons.

- TSMID had also placed orders in 1989 and 1990 with a number of companies to buy an inhalation chamber. Salman Pak already had an inhalation chamber, purchased, as Dick Spertzel had found out in January, some time before 1984. The indications were then that this new inhalation chamber was destined for a different site, the obvious candidate being al Hakam. Inhalation chambers have no use whatsoever in single-cell protein production, but are essential in conducting trials on infection by airborne pathogens – biological weapons were generally delivered by the air.

- TSMID ordered three large fermenters from yet another European company in 1989, allegedly for single-cell protein production at al Hakam. However, Iraq falsified the end-user certificate required by the government concerned to prove the use for which it was being bought and the location at which it would be installed. Iraq had stated that the fermenter would be installed at Latifiyah – a site some 40 kilometres south of Baghdad. Indeed, the company's representatives had been taken on a tour of Latifiyah before the contract was signed. This, together with the fact that Iraq had sought to buy the equipment for al Hakam from many different companies in many different countries, implied a conscious effort on the part of Iraq at the time to conceal the extent and purpose of the purchases.

- In 1988 TSMID had tried to buy spare parts from a fourth European company for a fermenter that had been transferred to al Hakam from the vast military camp at al Taji, just north of Baghdad. But in ordering the spare parts, Iraq falsely indicated to the company that the fermenter was still at al Taji – more evidence of attempts to conceal the existence of al Hakam.

- The entire al Hakam project had been shrouded in the most extraordinary levels of secrecy since its very inception. The Iraqis had employed different consulting engineers from different companies to design different aspects of the plant, rather than contracting the whole design to one consultant engineer and letting him sub-contract as necessary, which was normal practice. Iraq could show UNSCOM no plans that proved al Hakam had been conceived and designed as a single-cell protein plant. No foreign contractors were involved in the construction – indeed, no foreigners had ever visited al Hakam. There had been no public launch; the opening of a plant producing such ground-breaking technology as single-cell proteins had not even been announced. And the site was surrounded by double barbed wire fences, more reminiscent of Iraq's military facilities than an innocent civilian factory. In short, the secrecy at al Hakam was even higher than that imposed at Iraq's chemical weapons production plant or at its declared military biological warfare research laboratory at Salman Pak.

• The layout of the entire al Hakam site indicated a military plant. It covered 6 kilometres by 3 kilometres, was located in the desert far from the nearest water supply (water was essential for single-cell protein production), and its buildings were dispersed around the site in a manner that spoke of highly infectious agents, not single-cell protein. And why would a single-cell protein production plant need those ammunition bunkers?

The case against al Hakam was overwhelming. All the experts agreed with the UNSCOM assessment: Iraq had had a full-blown biological weapons programme. When they heard the case on weaponisation, they left believing that Iraq had probably also designed and filled weapons with biological warfare agents.

On the question of munitions, suspicion fell on two areas: the DB-0 and DB-2 bombs, long suspected of being intended for biological rather than chemical weapons; and the special SCUD missile warheads. UNSCOM had destroyed some seventy-five of these in the summer of 1991. But now it was known that in late 1988 or early 1989 – precisely when TSMID was making all its purchases for al Hakam – MIC (General Amer Rasheed's command) had approached three European companies in three different countries for parachute systems that could be deployed on missiles to slow their fall once the rocket motors had cut out.

Iraq did not just want a few parachutes, but a serial order of some fifty to one hundred systems per year, implying a combat application for the system. It was also known that there was a TSMID interest in this MIC operation. UNSCOM asked to interview the officials involved. Iraq pushed forward a Dr Issam Jassim, who explained this by saying that the Technical Reseach Council, through its Electronic Department at Salman Pak, was working on drone and remotely piloted vehicles (RPVs), both of which needed parachute systems.

This did not ring true and was cause for further alarm. The parachute systems were for 15–70kg loads – no drone or RPV would be that light. On the other hand, drones and RPVs would be an ideal way to deliver biological agent as a fine mist spread over the battlefield – the most effective way to cause maximum infection of enemy soldiers. That a facility, operated by the declared military research facility's parent organisation and co-located with that facility, should be working on an ideal way to deliver biological agents over the battlefield was extremely worrying.

Another area for concern here was that Dr Ahmed Murtada, director of the TRC, was a mechanical engineer and was also director of the Badr Scientific Establishment – Iraq's munition design and production centre. This strongly indicated that the biological programme had a weaponisation component.

Finally, Dick Spertzel had done his sums to see if General Wafiq al Samarra'i's claim that Iraq had 200 500lb germ bombs was possible with these imports. He calculated that each 250kg (500lb) bomb would contain about 100 litres of finished product, i.e. 140kg of fill at a specific density of approximately 1.4. Using the data that Dr Rihab Taha had provided on how the 'biopesticide' was to be delivered, the agent would be in a 1.2 per cent spores mix with bentonite, thereby requiring 1.68kg of dried anthrax spores per bomb.

On a very conservative estimate, Iraq could produce 1 gram of anthrax spores per litre of culture. This yield could go up to 10g per litre. Al Hakam had two fermenter lines: one transferred from al Taji and the other from al Kindi. The two 1850-litre fermenters from al Kindi could each produce 1.5kg of anthrax per run. The seven 1150-litre fermenters could each produce 1.15kg per run. Each fermenter could manage two runs per week, so in fifteen weeks the al Kindi fermenters could produce enough anthrax to fill the 200 bombs. Likewise, the combined working volume of the five fermenters from al Taji was 2150 litres, and so they could between them produce 2.15kg of anthrax per run. Using only these fermenters, it would take eighty weeks to produce the anthrax for 200 bombs.

With this preparatory meeting out of the way, it was time to brief the Council on Iraq's biological weapons programme. The UNSCOM written report of 10 April 1995 was explosive stuff. It concluded that:

> The Commission assesses that Iraq obtained, or sought to obtain, all the items and materials required to produce biological warfare agents in Iraq. With Iraq's failure to account for all these items and materials for legitimate purposes, the only conclusion that can be drawn is that there is a high risk that they had been purchased and in part used for proscribed purposes – the production of agents for biological weapons.

At the end of this review Gabriele Kraatz-Wadsack was asked to join the New York biological team on a semi-permanent basis. She happily accepted, but it would take a further – crucial – five months before the paperwork could be pushed through the German system. Her timing could not have been worse. By then, she had missed the dénouement of the Iraqi biological weapons saga.

Tariq Aziz returned to New York to see the release of this report and to lobby against UNSCOM. Again, he got a flea in his ear from the members of the Security Council, this time mainly about biological issues rather than VX. He was also forced into negotiations on the oil-for-food deal. The result was that Aziz negotiated a new oil-for-food deal, which was adopted under resolution 986 on 14 April 1995.

After Aziz's return to Baghdad Saddam Hussein rejected the deal outright. There were rumours that Aziz was out of favour for 'trusting' UNSCOM and falling for our strategy back in 1993 to get Iraq to accept monitoring in return for lifting the oil embargo. Indeed, some thought he was for the chop – but that may only have been Iraqi propaganda to soften us up for our next trip to Baghdad, and to strengthen the hand of Iraq's new, hard-line negotiating position.

Concerns had been growing as new supplier information came in that Iraq might be hiding large numbers of VX chemical munitions. There had always been a suspicion that Iraq had willingly yielded its chemical weapons to the inspectors in 1991 only because the weapons were old and dangerous, no longer suitable for use. There was a further suspicion that, should Iraq seek to rebuild its chemical arsenal in the future, it would not make these same mustard, sarin and tabun weapons, but concentrate on a VX programme. Iraq had always had problems with making mustard, sarin and tabun, with the result that weapons filled with these agents had a short shelf life before the agent degraded or polymerised into a gelatinous goo.

Another reason for suspicion was that chemical weaponry was the only area where Iraq willingly proffered 'all its weapons' in its 1991 declarations. It had denied any nuclear or biological weapons or superguns, and had declared less than half its SCUD force. Why had it declared all its chemical weapons? The news about imports of chemical precursors, special stainless steel production equipment (VX production produces some highly corrosive by-products that would eat away lower-spec equipment), and munitions were all reinforcing this worry that there might be a totally undeclared VX programme in Iraq.

To address this, Charles Duelfer, Horst Reeps and Igor Mitrokhin went to Baghdad, arriving on 14 May 1995. Charles was carrying a message for General Amer Rasheed from Rolf Ekéus: as many of the outstanding issues as possible needed to be clarified in time for the next formal written report to the UN Security Council, due in mid-June, he said. Unless UNSCOM could report progress, the chances of Iraq achieving its objective of getting the sanctions lifted would be much reduced.

The visit did not start well. There were no Iraqi Protocol officers waiting to meet Charles Duelfer at the airport – the normal procedure for someone of his rank within the UN. As Deputy Executive Chairman of UNSCOM he carried the rank of Assistant Secretary-General. Nevertheless, a meeting was set for eight o'clock that evening with General Amer Rasheed. During the afternoon the meeting was put back to 10 p.m. When he arrived at General Amer's office, Charles was informed by Hossam Amin that Amer might be fifteen minutes late. At 10.30 Hossam Amin suggested that they start the meeting in Amer's absence. Charles demurred, saying that his message was for Amer. Amer arrived at 11.30, fresh from a meeting at the Council on Agriculture and Health. Charles wondered to himself whether the council had been contemplating additional complex growth media purchases.

The essence of Charles's message was simple – Iraq's accounting for its VX-related activities did not make sense and sufficient precursor chemicals to make hundreds of tonnes of VX, which kills in milligram quantities, remained unaccounted for. The suppliers had made it clear that Iraq had imported these chemicals: they had to be accounted for. UNSCOM's analysis was that Iraq had succeeded in its VX programme to a much greater extent than hitherto admitted, and perhaps even to the point where it had made VX-filled weapons. Iraq's own best interests would be best served by declaring the programme and allowing UNSCOM to destroy all remaining assets. Then the matter could be put to rest and, if the biological issue were also dealt with, UNSCOM could report that the conditions for lifting the sanctions had been achieved.

Charles's report to New York provoked comparisons with the famous scene from *Casablanca*. Apparently, Hossam Amin was looking dapper in a white suit. General Amer Rasheed, on hearing the message, was 'Shocked, shocked ...' – not at the suggestion of gambling on his premises, but at the thought that UNSCOM could doubt the Iraqi story. He claimed to have lost all confidence in UNSCOM, which was clearly acting under US instructions to fabricate new issues just to block the lifting of sanctions. Nevertheless, he instructed his experts to hold further talks with Horst Reeps and Igor Mitrokhin to resolve outstanding issues.

The next day, however, Hossam Amin, in a heated debate with Igor on the munitions issues, noted that, at the political strategy level, Iraq was making a link between the two investigations – chemical and biological. Iraq would not issue any additional declaration on the biological programme until UNSCOM had 'closed the file' on the past chemical weapons programmes.

With this rebuff to his message, delivered through Charles Duelfer, Rolf Ekéus and his team, including me, were on our way back to Baghdad.

Tariq Aziz refused to allow his biological experts to talk to us during this trip. The new strategy was out. Iraq was playing for the end game. It would not talk about biological issues until there was a deal: the UN should commit to lifting the oil embargo and economic sanctions as soon as Iraq made its declaration on biological weapons, but this could not take place until UNSCOM had closed all the other files. Iraq was asking the UN to buy a pig in a poke: we were not to be given an opportunity to verify the story on biological weapons – the price for getting the statement sight unseen was the lifting of the sanctions. Iraq was trying to horse-trade.

Aziz said that the only reason Iraq was cooperating with UNSCOM was that it wanted to be reintegrated into the international community. Chief among the benefits was the lifting of the economic sanctions. If Iraq saw no prospect of reintegration, then it would be difficult to justify the expense and effort of cooperating with UNSCOM. For cooperation to continue, Iraq required statements from the IAEA confirming that the nuclear file was closed, and from UNSCOM confirming that the chemical and missile files were closed and the monitoring system was operational. If UNSCOM's next written report, due in mid-June, included these statements, and Iraq judged from the reaction of the Council that the prospects for reintegration were good, it would in late June address the one outstanding issue of significance, the biological programme. If the prospects were not good, Iraq would reassess the situation.

So, on the one hand Aziz was implicitly acknowledging that Iraq had some explaining to do on the biological side, but on the other he was trying to set the terms for Iraq coming clean – putting Iraq in judgement of the Council, not the Council in judgement of Iraq. The Council, of course, would have none of it.

CHAPTER 19

Chicken Farms and Treasure Troves: Defection of Hussein Kamal Hassan

'Round numbers are always false.'

SAMUEL JOHNSON

'Mordre wol out.'

CHAUCER (on the death of Chauntecleer the cockerel)

The Security Council was not amused by Iraq's antics. Rolf Ekéus had not acceded to Tariq Aziz's demands.* Stern warnings were issued by the US and the UK. France and Russia both had severe egg on their faces: in February and March they had taken sides with Iraq on the biological issue, trying to persuade UNSCOM that there really was nothing of significance to account for and suggesting that UNSCOM was being too pernickety; both now

---

* The June report, in fact, repeated the conclusions on biological weapons contained in the April report and, in addition, noted that Iraq was refusing to consider or discuss any question relating to its biological programme. While it did note that advances had been made in the VX area and even stated that 'The Commission is now confident that it has a good overall picture of the extent of Iraq's past chemical weapons capabilities and that the essential elements of it have been destroyed', it added that 'Remaining issues, which centre by and large on verification of Iraq's revised declarations, can be resolved satisfactorily given continued cooperation on the part of Iraq and assistance from supporting Governments on supplies to Iraq. These issues will be pursued until the Commission considers that all avenues for investigation have been exhausted.' Once again, it emphasised that all this had to be verified, and that Iraq was in large part responsible for ensuring that the story checked out.

placed severe political pressure on Iraq to come clean.

Iraq blinked, although Aziz would probably say that the lobbying from Russia and France had assured Iraq that the prospects of reintegration were good enough to make it worthwhile for it to 'continue its cooperation'. In any case, Rolf Ekéus was invited back to Baghdad to hear Iraq's account of its biological programme. We arrived on 30 June 1995 and were told by Aziz that while the report contained 'negative and positive elements, [Iraq] had concluded that the positive elements were such that Iraq would now address the issue of its biological weapons [sic] programme.'

The next day, 1 July 1995, was one of excitement and anticipation, mixed with a degree of scepticism and 'wait and see'. This was what we had all worked so hard for over the past four years – to hear Iraq admit that it had made biological weapons. We could still not quite believe that it might come to pass. And we wondered whether the Iraqis would in fact follow their old pattern of behaviour and – in the face of incontrovertible proof that they were lying – come up with a new lie that incorporated what they now knew we knew, but did not tell the whole story.

The sceptics won the day, but by the end of 1 July Iraq could no longer say it had never planned to build biological weapons. A short opening statement admitted that Iraq had an offensive biological weapons programme and had gone so far as to produce bulk quantities of biological warfare agent. However, Iraq denied having ever weaponised it.

The essence of the new story was as follows:

- Dr Rihab Taha was working on biopesticides at the Muthanna State Establishment but, towards the end of 1985, came to the conclusion that Muthanna did not have the expertise to succeed in this area. Aware of Muthanna's other activities, she suggested to the director-general of Muthanna, Dr Murthada, that she should conduct exploratory research into biological warfare agents.

- At the end of a four-month literature search, Taha reported that anthrax and botulinum should be explored further. Murthada sought the approval of his superiors, who agreed on condition that this was not done at Muthanna. Taha moved her work to Salman Pak, but in the meantime, Muthanna's procurement arm, SEPP, purchased culture stocks, complex growth media, antitoxin and various materials and equipment for a biological research laboratory.

- Taha completed the move to Salman Pak in April 1986. The first phase of the work was to prepare the labs and animal houses. This preparatory work continued until the director-general of the TRC visited in January 1987 and approved the project plan. Basic research then continued until the beginning of 1988. Success with anthrax and botulinum research resulted in a decision to produce these agents in bulk. Tariq Aziz, in a smaller meeting, confided that these were the dark days in the war with Iran, and everyone was desperate to stop the Iranian hordes from swamping the Iraqi lines. Iraq had to consider every weapon for its mere survival.

- Because Salman Pak was so close to residential areas, it was not suitable as a production facility. There was a search for another site. At the same time the Ministry for Industry and Military Industrialisation (MIMI, the precursor of General Amer's MIC) adopted the single-cell protein project. MIMI asked the TRC to implement it and planning for al Hakam was started. The site was chosen as it was close to another site, which would provide the raw materials for the single-cell protein production. Taha visited the site to ensure that it was suitable for biological agent production.

- Construction started in mid-1988. A search for fermenters that were not in use was conducted and the fermenter lines at al Kindi and al Taji were identified. These were transferred to al Hakam.

- In preparation for agent production, complex growth media orders were placed in the first quarter of 1988. As no one had any experience in production, the orders were based on gues-timates, without any particular reference to the installed fermenter capacity. Other equipment was ordered to improve the spec of the animal house and lab buildings to bio-hazard containment level two.

- Dr Nissar al Hindawi tried to operate the al Kindi and al Taji fermenters in trials covering three months in early 1989, but these trials failed as the fermenters were designed for aerobic, not anaerobic, bacteria. It was concluded that the 5000-litre anaerobic fermenter, for which Iraq had tried but failed to gain an import licence, was essential. Hence the renewed efforts to purchase the fermenter, and the lie that it was intended for Latifiyah, not al Hakam.

- With the end of the Iran–Iraq War, the matter was no longer urgent. The al Taji fermenters started producing botulinum in May 1989 and continued until August 1990. Fifty-five batches of 9000 litres were produced, each batch taking eight days. This consumed about 15 tonnes of complex growth media. The product was concentrated by a factor of twenty and stored in stainless-steel 5000-litre vats on site in the bunkers at al Hakam.

- Anthrax production started in October 1989 and continued until August 1990. Forty batches were made and concentrated. The total concentrate produced was 600 litres.

- In August 1990, given the threat of aerial strikes and the risk of contamination that would ensue, the order was issued to destroy all toxic and infectious materials. This was completed around September/October 1990.

Rolf Ekéus welcomed this new declaration, but pointed out that it was rather thin on detail. Such a major change in Iraq's de-clarations meant that it had to produce a new 'full, final and complete disclosure' for its past biological programme, with details of who was involved when, etc. Once UNSCOM had received this, it could go about verifying it. He pointed out that this new declaration did not address some of UNSCOM's concerns about the previous declarations, namely the starting date of the programme and the issue of weaponisation. Rolf requested that the full, final and complete disclosure address these issues. General Amer Rasheed assured Rolf that he would get the new disclosure in the latter half of July.

Even before we boarded the plane the next day to return to New York, Dick Spertzel was saying that the Iraqi story was non-sensical. With the media imported by Iraq, it should have made more anthrax than botulinum. The calculations of the number of batches made in the given time did not add up. It did not make sense to produce large quantities of bulk agent without having some idea of how it would be weaponised.

To help Iraq produce a revised full, final and complete disclosure quickly, an inspection team led by Dick Spertzel was sent to talk through the new declarations and advise on the additional explanations and clarifications required to satisfy UNSCOM. An Iraqi draft disclosure was discussed.

Analysis indicated that the 1 July statement was little more than a fairly careless attempt to come up with an accounting for the media, with no particular regard for the truth. The statement avoided making any link between the military and the biological weapons programme. It seemed to be designed to deny any information that might link the programme to weaponisation. Dick's team strongly urged Dr Rihab Taha not to submit this deficient disclosure, as it might be interpreted as yet more evidence that Iraq was seeking to conceal the true extent of its biological programme, damaging the prospects for lifting the sanctions.

On 17 July 1995, the anniversary of the accession to power of the Ba'ath Party in a bloody coup in 1968, Saddam Hussein made a speech declaring that cooperation with UNSCOM would end if no progress was made in lifting the sanctions. No deadline was given for cooperation. However, a few days later Mohammed al Sahaf repeated this threat in a speech in Cairo; the deadline for the lifting of sanctions, he said, was 31 August 1995.

Under this cloud, Rolf Ekéus and the team went back into Iraq on 4 August to seek clarifications on the 1 July statement and to receive the 'full, final and complete disclosure'. In spite of Dick Spertzel's advice to Dr Rihab Taha, Tariq Aziz formally handed over the deficient disclosure. It contained virtually nothing new. A quick glance showed that Iraq had ignored all the suggestions made by Dick's team and that no substantial new information had been added to the 1 July statement, and no clarifications given. Even so, Tariq Aziz warned Rolf Ekéus during a meeting on 5 August that Iraq would cease cooperation with UNSCOM if there was no progress by 31 August. He asked Rolf to convey this message to the Security Council. Rolf promised to do so, knowing that such threats would go down badly.

During this meeting Rolf noted that the MIC had played a big role in the biological weapons programme and that everything was reported through General Hussein Kamal Hassan. He asked whether, in the interests of putting the biological story to rest as quickly as possible, it might be possible to interview the general during his next visit. Aziz promised to pass this on to Hussein Kamal Hassan with a positive recommendation.

Rolf and his entourage left Baghdad on 6 August. After travelling virtually non-stop for twenty-four hours, we arrived back in New York mid-afternoon on 7 August. Shortly after returning to his office, Rolf received a phone call from Tariq Aziz, reminding him of his promise to tell the Council about the threat. Rolf reiterated his promise and did, in fact, brief the Council orally on 10 August.

By then, though, the entire game had changed.

* * *

On the evening of 7 August General Hussein Kamal Hassan sent some of his trusted henchmen on a series of bag runs. Over the past few days he had ordered the various state establishments under his command to draw out large amounts of dollars in cash and keep them in office safes. The bag men were collecting this hoard together. That night Hussein Kamal Hassan, his brother (Saddam Kamal Hassan), their wives (both daughters of Saddam Hussein) and a large entourage left Baghdad for Amman with some $25 millions in US bank notes. The man with the most influence in Iraq's government after Saddam Hussein had just defected.

As soon as this news broke, plans were made for an UNSCOM team to go to Amman to debrief him. Hussein Kamal Hassan had been in charge of all the weapons programmes. If this was a genuine defection, the cat was out of the bag as far as Iraq's lies were concerned.

Almost as soon as UNSCOM started making those plans, Rolf Ekéus received another phone call from a panicked Tariq Aziz, who told him that he must visit Baghdad before going to Amman. This was followed by a letter from General Amer Rasheed al Ubeidi, alleging that new information had come to light: Hussein Kamal Hassan had been responsible for hiding from UNSCOM important information on Iraq's banned weapons programmes by ordering Iraqi technical personnel involved in those programmes not to disclose this information and not to let either Tariq Aziz or General Amer know about these instructions. Aziz called Rolf again the next day to tell him that the 31 August deadline for cooperation was off.

In Baghdad again on 17 August, Rolf heard Tariq Aziz repeat that Hussein Kamal Hassan, unbeknownst to the highest levels of Iraq's government, had conducted a concealment programme. But now Iraq would disclose this information. Indeed, Iraq had decided on a policy of cooperation and full transparency with UNSCOM, without any time limits. It would also follow a policy of good neighbourliness with the states of the region and elsewhere, and devote its resources towards economic development in the future.

Over the next few days' discussions Iraq admitted that it had indeed made biological weapons, by filling 166 bombs and twenty-five missile warheads with biological warfare agent. (This figure of 191 munitions was remarkably close to the 200 germ bombs mentioned by Wafiq al Samarra'i in February 1995.) However, the discussions were still not providing UNSCOM with anything by way of supporting evidence to show that even this current, expanded Iraqi account of its full-blown weaponisation programme was accurate.

In the final meeting with Tariq Aziz, and then again in comments made to the press just before he left the hotel, Rolf Ekéus complained loudly about the lack of evidence. As he was getting into his car to go to Habbaniyah with his entire team of some fifteen experts, one of the Iraqi minders urgently spoke to him: Iraq, he said, had just found out that the defector, Hussein Kamal Hassan, had, unbeknownst to the Iraqi leadership, maintained a stash of documents about the weapons of mass destruction programme. These had just been found at a chicken farm owned by the defector.

The team were whisked off to this farm, which was on the way to Habbaniyah. It was more of a villa with some disused outhouses. In one of the sheds there were about forty crates of documents, microfiche, microfilm, video film and photographs, which UNSCOM would later estimate to include over 600,000 pages of text. The team spread out to examine, photograph and review this hoard.

The first thing that was noticed was that the crates were unnaturally clean – they had clearly just been moved to their new home. Secondly, the documents inside the crates showed signs of having been disturbed after they had first been put into the crates.

The suspicion was that they had been sanitised – that is, the most incriminating documents, or even documents logging items Iraq still wanted to keep secret from UNSCOM, had been selectively removed.

Even so, more or less the first document that John Scott picked up was a progress report on Iraq's biological weapons programme. At last, here was some real documentary proof which UNSCOM could use to make a full accounting for the biological programme.

The team did not stay in Baghdad. It had an appointment with the defector Hussein Kamal Hassan that it did not want to miss.

When he first arrived in Amman, Hussein Kamal Hassan was put up in one of King Hussein's guest palaces. It was here that Rolf Ekéus and a small UNSCOM team met him. He was holding court and clearly had high ambitions for himself. The meeting did not go quite as UNSCOM had hoped. Instead of a detailed question and answer session, the general launched into a wide-ranging exposé of the regime and the weapons programmes in general. However, he was able to confirm the command structure for the programmes and their overall aims and shape. He also had interesting things to say about how Iraq went about hiding the weapons and documents from UNSCOM. When told about the chicken farm and the archives found there, he expressed utter ignorance, and dismissed it as mere trickery on the part of Saddam Hussein. He had not kept any documents and he did not know about the farm.

On 22 August 1995, after a very rapid scan of these documents, Dick Spertzel led another team back into Iraq to try to straighten out Iraq's by now confused account of its biological weapons programme. The results of this inspection were so dramatic that they do not need any further comment. Here is the text of UNSCOM's October 1995 report to the Security Council, stating what had been revealed in that hectic month of August:

Map 7: Iraq's Biological Programme

In July 1995 Iraq admitted that it had an extensive programme to make biological weapons. In August 1995 it finally admitted having succeeded in making and testing biological weapons. Research had been conducted at Salman Pak, Muthanna and Taji; production of biological agent took place at al Hakam and al Fudhaliyah; special bombs and missile warheads were made at Muthanna; weapons were tested at Azziziyah and stored at Airfield 37, Camp Bani Sa'ad and Mansuriyah.

A summation of the most recent revelations of Iraq's biological weapons programme follows. It should be stressed that it is solely based on declarations made by Iraq since mid-August, which remain subject to verification. At this time, therefore, the Commission can give no assurances as to the correctness and comprehensiveness of that information:

(a) Iraq stated that, in 1974, the Government had adopted a policy to acquire biological weapons. In 1975, a research and development biological weapons programme was established under the al Hazen Ibn al Haytham Institute at a site located in Al Salman [Salman Pak]. The work was poorly directed. Coupled with a lack of appropriate facilities and equipment, it was said the Institute achieved little and it closed in 1978;

(b) The failure of the Al Hazen Institute was claimed to be a severe setback for the programme and the following years are alleged to be devoid of any biological weapons-related activity. In the early period of the Iran/Iraq war (perhaps 1982 or 1983), a prominent Iraqi microbiologist wrote a report expressing his concerns on scientific developments relating to biological warfare agents and suggesting that research in this subject be commenced in Iraq. It is still uncertain whether this report was followed up, but in 1985 the Muthanna State Establishment, Iraq's main facility for chemical weapons research and development, production and weaponization, recommended the commencement of a biological weapons programme. In May or June 1985, Muthanna sought and obtained endorsement from the Ministry of Defence for this programme. It was anticipated that the biological weapons research would be production-oriented and thus, in addition to the laboratory-scale equipment, a pilot plant in the form of one 150-litre fermenter was purchased by Muthanna. Throughout 1985, personnel were recruited by Muthanna and by the end of the year, a staff of 10 was working on biological weapons research;

(c) Initial work at Muthanna was said to focus on literature studies, until April 1986, when bacterial strains were received from overseas. Research then concentrated on the characterization of *Bacillus anthracis* (anthrax) and *Clostridium botulinum* (botulinum toxin) to establish pathogenicity, growth and sporulation conditions, and their storage parameters. (Anthrax is a acute bacterial disease of animals and humans that can be incurred by ingestion or inhalation of the bacterial spores or through skin lesions. It produces an infection resulting in death in days to weeks after exposure. Botulinum toxin produces an acute muscular paralysis resulting in death of animals and humans.) As claimed by Iraq, there was no production of agents and the imported fermenters at Muthanna were not used. However, Muthanna was still looking ahead to biological warfare agent production and wrote a report to the Ministry of Defence recommending that the former single-cell protein plant at Taji be taken over by Muthanna for the production of botulinum toxin. The Ministry of Defence agreed but, in early 1987, before the plan could be implemented, the proposal went into abeyance for a short time owing to administrative reasons;

(d) In May 1987, the biological weapons programme was transferred from Muthanna to Al Salman. The reason for this was said to be that the biological work interfered with the (presumably higher priority) chemical weapons programme at Muthanna. At Al Salman, the biological weapons group administratively came under the Forensic Research Department of the Technical Research Centre (TRC) of the Military Industrialization Corporation. After a slow beginning, it appeared that the programme flourished at Al Salman. Equipment, including fermenters, was transferred from Muthanna, new equipment was acquired, and new staff joined the biological weapons group to bring the workforce up to about 18. The research at Al Salman shifted to issues related more to the application of the agents as biological weapons. The effects on larger animals, including sheep, donkeys, monkeys and dogs, were studied within the laboratory and inhalation chamber, as well as in the field. Initial weapons field trials were conducted in early 1988. Studies of scale-up production were initiated on botulinum toxin and anthrax;

(e) The earlier proposal for the acquisition of a biological weapons production site was revived and the former single-cell protein plant at Taji was taken over by TRC in mid-1987. The plant was said to be in a run-down condition and it was not until early in 1988 that it was made operational. With a workforce of 8 people, and using one 450-litre fermenter, production of botulinum toxin commenced in February or March 1988 and continued until September/October of that year. Production of botulinum toxin also was carried out at Al Salman in flasks or laboratory fermenters;

(f) Initial production fermentation studies with anthrax at Al Salman used 7- and 14-litre laboratory-scale fermenters at the end of 1988. From the beginning of 1989, the 150-litre fermenter transferred from Muthanna was used to produce *Bacillus subtilis*, a simulant for anthrax as a biological warfare agent. After five or six runs of producing subtilis, anthrax production began at Al Salman around March 1989. About 15 or 16 production runs were performed, producing up to 1500 litres of anthrax, which was concentrated to 150 litres. Additional production with the laboratory fermenters was also accomplished;

(g) Towards the end of 1987, a report on the success of biological weapons work by TRC was submitted to MIC. This resulted in a decision to enter the full-scale production phase for a biological weapons programme;

(h) In March 1988, a new site for biological weapons production was selected at a location now known as Al Hakam. The project was given the designator '324'. The design philosophy for the Al Hakam plant was taken from the chemical weapons research and production facility at Muthanna: the buildings were to be well separated, research areas were segregated from production areas and the architectural features of Muthanna buildings was copied where appropriate. The plan for the new facility at Al Hakam envisaged research and development, production and storage of biological warfare agents, but not munitions filling. Construction of the production buildings at the northern end of the Al Hakam site was largely complete by September 1988 after which work commenced on erection of the laboratory buildings;

(i) In 1988, a search for production equipment for the biological weapons programme was conducted in Iraq. Two 1850-litre and seven 1480-litre fermenters from the Veterinary Research Laboratories were transferred to Al Hakam in November 1988. The 450-litre fermenter line at Taji, which was at the time used in the production of botulinum toxin, was also earmarked for transfer to Al Hakam and was relocated there in October 1988. From mid-1988, large fermenters were also sought from abroad, but after Iraq completed a contract for a 5000-litre fermenter, an export licence was not granted;

(j) At Al Hakam, production of botulinum toxin for weapons purposes began in April 1989 and anthrax in May 1989. Initially, much of the fermentation capacity for anthrax was used for the production of anthrax simulant for weapons field trials. Production of anthrax itself, it is claimed, began in earnest in 1990. In total, about 6000 litres of concentrated botulinum toxin and 8425 litres of anthrax were produced at Al Hakam during 1990;

(k) From the early period of the biological weapons pro-

gramme at Al Salman, there was interest in other potential
biological warfare agents beyond anthrax and botulinum
toxin. It became the policy to expand the biological
weapons programme into these other fields. Thus from the
design phase of Al Hakam as a biological weapons
research, production and storage facility, there were plans
for such diversification, including facilities to work on
viruses and laboratory space for genetic engineering
studies;

(l) In April 1988, in addition to anthrax and botulinum toxin,
a new agent, *Clostridium perfringens* (gas gangrene), was
added to the bacterial research work at Al Salman.
(*Clostridium perfringens* produces a condition known as
gas gangrene, so named because of the production of
gaseous rotting flesh, common in war casualties requiring
amputation of limbs.) In August 1989, work on perfringens was transferred from Al Salman to Al Hakam;

(m) In May 1988, studies were said to have be initiated at Al
Salman on aflatoxin. (Aflatoxin is a toxin commonly
associated with fungal-contaminated food grains and is
known for its induction of liver cancers. It is generally
considered to be non-lethal in humans but of serious
medical concern because of its carcinogenic activity.) Later
research was also done on tricothene mycotoxins such as T-
2 and DAS. (Tricothene mycotoxins produce nausea,
vomiting, diarrhoea and skin irritation and, unlike most
microbial toxins, can be absorbed through the skin.)
Research was conducted into the toxic effects of aflatoxins
as biological warfare agents and their effects when combined with other chemicals. Aflatoxin was produced by the
growth of the fungus aspergillus in 5-litre flasks at Al
Salman;

(n) In 1989, it was decided to move aflatoxin production for
biological weapons purposes to a facility at Fudhaliyah.
The facility was used for aflatoxin production in flasks

from April/May 1990 to December 1990. A total of about 850 litres of toxin in solution was declared as having been produced at Fudhaliyah;

(o) Another fungal agent examined by Iraq for its biological weapons potential was wheat cover smut. (Wheat cover smut produces a black growth on wheat and other cereal grains; contaminated grain cannot be used as foodstuff.) After small production at Al Salman, larger-scale production was carried out near Mosul in 1987 and 1988 and considerable quantities of contaminated grain were harvested. The idea was said not to have been further developed; however, it was only some time in 1990 that the contaminated grain was destroyed by burning at the Fudhaliyah site;

(p) Another toxin worked for weapons application was ricin. (Ricin is a protein toxin derived from castor bean plants that is highly lethal to humans and animals. When inhaled, ricin produces a severe breakdown of lung tissue resulting in a haemorrhagic pneumonia and death.) It appears that work started in 1988 at Al Salman. The first samples of ricin were supplied from the Samarra Drug Factory and, after some initial toxicological tests in conjunction with Muthanna, the quantity required for a weapons test was determined. Ten litres of concentrated ricin were prepared. A weapons trial was conducted with the assistance of Muthanna using artillery shells. The test was considered to be a failure. The project was said to have been abandoned after this;

(q) Work on virus for biological weapons purposes started at Al Salman in July 1990. Shortly thereafter, a decision was taken to acquire the Foot and Mouth Disease facility at Daura and it was taken over for biological weapons purposes, in addition to the continued production of vaccines. It was decided that the Daura plant within the biological weapons programme would include facilities for bacteriology, virology and genetic engineering. Three viral agents were obtained from within Iraq: haemorrhagic conjunctivitis virus, a rotavirus and camel pox virus. (Haemorrhagic conjunctivitis is an acute disease that causes extreme pain and temporary blindness. Rotavirus causes acute diarrhoea that could lead to dehydration and death. Camel pox causes fever and skin rash in camels; infection in humans is rare.) It was stated that very little work had been done on these viruses and none had been produced in quantity;

(r) Early in 1988, efforts began in the weaponization of biological warfare agents and some of the senior scientists involved in the biological weapons programme at TRC were sent to Iraq's munitions factories to familiarize themselves with this aspect. At about the same time, TRC first discussed with the Muthanna State Establishment weaponization of biological warfare agents and it was agreed that, because of Muthanna's experience in the weaponization of chemical agents, the Establishment would also provide the necessary assistance to the selection of weapons types for warfare agents and the conduct of field trials;

(s) The first field trials of biological weapons were said to have been conducted in March 1988 at Muthanna's weapons test range, Muhammadiyat. Two tests were done on the same day, one using the anthrax simulant, *Bacillus subtilis*, and the other using botulinum toxin. The munitions chosen for the tests were aerial bombs positions on adjacent stands. The effects were observed on test animals (for botulinum toxin) or on Petri dishes (for subtilis). The first tests of both agents were considered failures. The agents in both cases did not spread far enough. Later in March, the second field trial with the same weapons systems was said to have been conducted and it was considered successful;

(t) No further weapons field trials were claimed to have been carried out for the next 18 months. In November 1989, further weaponization trials for anthrax (again using subtilis), botulinum toxin and aflatoxin were conducted, this time using 122mm rockets, again at Muhammadiyat. These tests were also considered a success. Live firings of filled 122mm rockets with the same agents were carried out in May 1990. Trials of R400 aerial bombs with *Bacillus subtilis* were first conducted in mid-August 1990. Final R400 trials using subtilis, botulinum toxin and aflatoxin followed in late August 1990;

(u) After 2 August 1990, the date of Iraq's invasion of Kuwait, Iraq's biological weapons programme was drastically intensified: the emphasis was shifted to production and later to weaponization of produced biological warfare agents. The Foot and Mouth Disease Plant at Daura was converted to biological weapons production. The six vaccine fermenters with ancillary equipment at the plant were used for production of botulinum toxin from November 1990 until 15 January 1991, by which time about 5400 litres of concentrated toxin had been produced. It was decided that there was an additional requirement for anthrax production and the fermenters at Al Hakam that had been previously used for the production of botulinum toxin there were modified to meet the requirements for increased anthrax production. Production of perfringens for biological weapons purposes also began at Al Hakam in August 1990 using the 150-litre fermenter which had been relocated from Al Salman. A total of 340 litres of concentrated perfringens was produced;

(v) In December 1990, a programme was initiated to develop an additional delivery means, a biological weapons spray tank based on a modified aircraft drop tank. The concept was that tanks would be fitted either to a piloted fighter or to a remotely piloted aircraft to spray up to 2000 litres of anthrax over a target. The field trials for both the spray tank and the remotely piloted vehicle were conducted in January 1991. The test was considered a failure and no further effort towards further development was said to have been made. Nevertheless, three additional drop tanks were modified and stored, ready for use. They are said to have been destroyed in July 1991. The prototype spray tank used for trial was claimed to have been destroyed during the Gulf War bombing;

(w) Weaponization of biological warfare agents began on a large scale in December 1990 at Muthanna. As declared, the R400 bombs were selected as the appropriate munition for aerial delivery and 100 were filled with botulinum toxin, 50 with anthrax and 16 with aflatoxin. In addition, 25 Al Hussein warheads, which had been produced in a special production run since August 1990, were filled with botulinum toxin (13), anthrax (10), and aflatoxin (2). These weapons were then deployed in early 1991 at four locations, where they remained throughout the war;

(x) In summary, Iraq has declared the production of at least 19,000 litres of concentrated botulinum toxin (nearly 10,000 litres were filled into munitions), 8500 litres of concentrated anthrax (some 6500 litres were filled into munitions) and 2200 litres of concentrated aflatoxin (1580 litres were filled into munitions);

(y) Iraq declared that it had decided to destroy biological munitions and the remaining biological warfare bulk agent after the Gulf War. An order for destruction was claimed to have been given orally, and no Iraqi representative seems to be able to recall the exact date for the order or the dates of destruction operations. The order was said to have been given some time in May or June 1991. All filled biological bombs were relocated to one airfield and deactivation chemicals added to agent fill. The bombs were then explosively destroyed and burnt, and the remains buried. A similar disposal technique was used for the missile warheads at a separate site. In late August 1995, Iraq showed an UNSCOM team a location which it claimed to be a warhead destruction site. However, later on, Iraq changed its story and was unable to identify with any degree of certainty the exact location of warheads destruction operations;

(z) Of the bacterial bulk agent stored at Al Hakam, Iraq stated that a similar deactivation procedure had been adopted. The detoxified liquid was emptied into the facility's septic tank and eventually dumped at the site. About 8000 litres of concentrated botulinum toxin, over 2000 litres of concentrated anthrax, 340 litres of concentrated perfringens and an unspecified quantity of aflatoxin, according to Iraq's declarations, were destroyed at Al Hakam.

Iraq's biological weapons programme as described to the Commission embraced a comprehensive range of agents and munitions. Agents under Iraq's biological weapons programme included lethal agents, e.g. anthrax, botulinum toxin and ricin, and incapacitating agents, e.g. aflatoxin, mycotoxins, haemorrhagic conjunctivitis virus and rotavirus. The scope of biological warfare agents worked on by Iraq encompassed both anti-personnel and anti-plant weapons. The programme covered a whole variety of biological weapons delivery means, from tactical weapons (e.g. 122mm rockets and artillery shells), to strategic weapons (e.g. aerial bombs and Al Hussein warheads filled with anthrax, botulinum toxin and aflatoxin) and 'economic' weapons, e.g. wheat cover smut. Given the Iraqi claim that only five years had elapsed since its declared inception in 1985, the achievements of Iraq's biological weapons programme were remarkable.

The achievements included the production and actual

weaponization of large quantities of bacterial agents and aflatoxin and research on a variety of other biological weapons agents. A special dedicated facility, Al Hakam, for biological weapons research and development as well as large-scale production was under construction, with most of the essential elements completed at the time of the Gulf War and production and storage capabilities operational. A number of other facilities and establishments in Iraq provided active support for the biological weapons programme. The programme appears to have a degree of balance suggesting a high level of management and planning that envisioned the inclusion of all aspects of a biological weapons programme, from research to weaponization. It is also reasonable to assume that, given that biological weapons were considered as strategic weapons and were actually deployed, detailed thought must have been given to the doctrine of operational use for these weapons of mass destruction.

It appears that, until August 1990, the biological weapons programme had been developing at a steady pace, continuing to expand and diversify. In August 1990, a 'crash' programme was launched and the imperatives of production and weaponization took over.

The documentation on Iraq's biological weapons programme obtained by the Commission in August 1995 appears to represent a fraction of all the documents generated under the programme. For example, studies were described orally by Iraq to the Commission that are not included in any of the documentation. Some of the studies referred to in the documents differ significantly from those described to the Commission. Information available to the Commission from other sources does not correspond in important aspects to the information provided by Iraq.

In spite of the substantial new disclosures made by Iraq since mid-August, the Commission does not believe that Iraq has given a full and correct account of its biological weapons programme. The Commission intends to continue its intensive inspection, verification and analytical efforts with the objective of presenting to the Security Council, as soon as possible, its assessment of Iraq's compliance with the biological weapons-related provisions of Security Council resolution 687 (1991). Success will depend upon Iraq's cooperation with these efforts and its complete openness, including the provision to the Commission of all documentation and of a truly full, final and complete disclosure of Iraq's proscribed biological weapons programme.

Vindication! But more work left to do …

CHAPTER 20

Fall Out: The Lies Unravel

'Necessity makes honest men knaves.'

DANIEL DEFOE

'Nullumst iam dictum quod non dictum sit prius.' (Nothing has yet been said that has not been said before.)

TERENCE

The first thing to do was to send in an inspection team to talk through the new Iraqi declarations and question them for details. Dick Spertzel led this team (UNSCOM125/BW27), which included Rod Barton and Hamish Killip. The team arrived in Iraq on 19 August 1995 to delve deeper.

The new information received from both sources – the Iraqis and Hussein Kamal Hassan – then had to be checked against the situation on the ground and the sites now declared to have been a part of the programme. David Kelly was again recruited to lead this team (UNSCOM126/BW28), which entered Iraq on 27 September 1995 with a mission to inspect all the sites now declared by Iraq to have been part of the biological weapons programme and to verify as far as possible Iraq's new declarations. The sites were:

- Salman Pak (the home of the first programme at the al Hazem Ibn al Haitham site, now known to have operated the 150-litre fermenter after its transfer from Muthanna)

- Muthanna (where the modern programme was born)
- Al Hakam (the planned production centre for biological warfare agents)
- Taji single-cell protein production project (whose fermenters had been used for anthrax production)
- The al Dawrah Foot and Mouth Disease Plant (the only negative-pressure, high-containment PL-3 laboratory in Iraq, where evidence of additional wall partitions was still evident on the floors in 1991)
- The Agricultural Research Centre at Fudhaliyah, used to produce aflatoxin
- Airfield 37 (where tests of biological weapons were conducted)
- The Azziziyah firing range (also where tests of biological weapons were conducted)
- Camp Bani Sa'ad (where aerosolisation of biological warfare agents was tested)
- A railroad tunnel at Mansuriyah, where Iraq claimed to have hidden ten SCUD missile warheads filled with anthrax (later amended to botulinum toxin fill)
- A site on the Tigris canal (where Iraq buried some of the biological weapons it claimed to have detoxified and destroyed in the summer of 1991. The team found remnants of one R400 bomb and fifteen SCUD missile warheads, said to have been filled with either anthrax or aflatoxin).

David Kelly's team came to the conclusion that most aspects of the new Iraqi story tied in with the configuration of the facilities at the named sites, but others raised some doubts.

In September 1995 Gabriele Kraatz-Wadsack rejoined UNSCOM, this time as an analyst based out of New York. Her first mission was to lead UNSCOM127 as chief inspector to assess and inventory which elements of Iraq's biological programme needed to be destroyed.

Her team went to Baghdad in December 1995 and inspected al Hakam, the al Dawrah Foot and Mouth Disease Vaccine Plant, Taji, Fudhaliyah and the al Adile stores, where large quantities of complex growth media were still being kept. Her mandate was both straightforward and strict: to inventory all the equipment at these sites and to assess whether it had been used, or designed, for the production of biological weapons. If the answer to either was yes, then the equipment was slated for destruction.

The recommendation for al Hakam was simple. It had been designed and used for the production of biological warfare agents and therefore it all needed to be destroyed. The decision was a little more complex for those sites which had been designed and built for civilian purposes but which had subsequently been acquired by the biological weapons programme – at Fudhaliyah and al Dawrah. After some deliberation the recommendation was made to destroy all items Iraq had now admitted had been used in the programme. When the final tally was made, Gabriele instructed Dr Rihab Taha to dismantle and transfer all this equipment from the various sites, including the large 2650-litre fermenters at al Dawrah, to al Hakam pending destruction by a new team. These instructions also applied to the complex growth media from the al Adile stores.

Iraq, predictably, complained about the decision to destroy all these buildings and equipment. There were repeated appeals for Rolf Ekéus to permit Iraq to dismantle the equipment and reuse it in civilian applications. However, the ceasefire resolution was clear: items that had been used to produce biological weapons had to be destroyed. Rolf held firm.

So it was that, in May 1996, Terry Taylor found himself at the head of another inspection team, this one to demolish Iraq's biological weapons production facilities. His team included a structural engineer and explosive demolitions experts to destroy the equipment and complex growth media now assembled at al Hakam and to blow up the buildings there. Hossam Amin (by now promoted to major-general) and Dr Mohammed Mahmoud Bilal (a well-known Iraqi counterpart, formerly a middle-ranking official in the chemical weapons programme, now with the rank of brigadier) both showed a good deal of interest in the process.

It soon became clear that the Iraqis wanted to save as much as possible at al Hakam. They proposed that the team should exclude those dual-purpose items that Iraq admitted had been used in producing biological weapons, such as the animal house and central services such as heating. Terry pointed out that the animal house had been a central part of the weapons research and so should go. The Iraqis appealed over Terry's head to Rolf Ekéus in New York. Rolf backed Terry up and the team started with the animal house.

Terry gave Hossam Amin a list of things required for the destruction process – Iraqi personnel to operate bulldozers and cranes, etc., equipment, explosives and fuses. The first day was spent surveying the site and checking everything against the inventory prepared by Gabriele Kraatz-Wadsack's team. On the second day a few barely serviceable bulldozers and a workforce of very young teenagers turned up. There were no explosives or fuses. Hossam Amin claimed that Iraq did not have the items requested. Terry then suggested that, in this case, the HMX (a very high-quality explosive) from Iraq's former nuclear programme, now under IAEA supervision, could be used. This was neat because it would be double disarmament – removing biological weapons facilities with items required for building a nuclear bomb. Hossam Amin, once IAEA consent was given, could do nothing. Terry's team got all the HMX they needed.

Between 23 May and 10 June the team destroyed all the major structures at al Hakam. Fermenters and other key items of equipment were cut up with acetylene torches and the pieces placed in a pit; concrete was then poured on top. Less crucial equipment was crushed, cut up and buried. Every item on Gabriele's inventory was checked from the buildings, via the destruction process, into the pits.

The only items to escape this process were three large air compressors that formed part of the air-treatment plant for the unfinished single-cell protein production facility. Iraq asked if these could be taken to hospitals in and around Baghdad, where they were desperately needed. Terry doubted very much whether the items could be adapted to such use, but Rolf Ekéus, ever mindful of the PR angle, decided to let the Iraqis reuse them, so long as they were monitored. As it turned out, two were damaged *en route* from al Hakam, so only one survived. Gabriele later visited the hospital it was destined for as part of the monitoring process, and confirmed Terry's suspicion. The unit was not in use and the hospital manager said that there was no way it could be used in the hospital. Still, having sat out in the open, the unit is no longer much use for a renewed biological weapons programme.

The team then moved on to the Foot and Mouth Disease Vaccine Plant at al Dawrah and deactivated the negative pressure systems so that it could no longer be used for research into and production of lethal biological agents. This left the plant still in good shape – it still has three large fermenters that are under constant camera surveillance. The plant is still useful for many other purposes, including vaccine production. But Rolf's decision not to permit Iraq to retain all the equipment was proved wise: the Foot and Mouth Disease Plant, despite its ability to produce vaccines for a population Saddam Hussein insists is starved of medical supplies, has remained unused ever since it was rendered useless for weapons purposes.

Dick and Rod Barton's efforts to make sense of Iraq's new declarations were, in the meantime, getting bogged down. Nothing added up, the way the Iraqis told it. General Amer Rasheed was pushing for UNSCOM to declare that the conditions for lifting sanctions had now been fulfilled. So Rolf Ekéus decided that the only way around this problem was to ask the Iraqis to resubmit a brand-new 'full, final and complete disclosure' of their biological weapons programme. If the new story checked out, a line could be drawn under the biological file. General Amer agreed.

Various meetings were set up so that the UNSCOM experts could tell their Iraqi counterparts precisely what types of information should be included in the new disclosure to make it acceptable to UNSCOM. The Iraqis sagely nodded their heads to everything that was said and then proceeded to submit a disclosure that contained no new information and was just as muddled as before. Moreover, while it failed to remove the internal contradictions of the previous disclosure, it introduced new discrepancies with previous accounts. The situation was now even murkier. As a consequence of Rolf's determination that UNSCOM should not lay itself open to blame for the delays in lifting sanctions, no fewer than eleven biological inspection teams visited Iraq between October 1996 and March 1997, each aiming to elicit a full and consistent account of Iraq's biological weapons programme. None of them was able to do so.

Again, in the face of growing international sympathy with Iraq's impatience with the sanctions, Rolf sought to eliminate any possibility that UNSCOM would be saddled with the blame. He asked Dick Spertzel to convene a panel of biological experts from various countries. Dick, Gabriele, Rod and David Kelly sat down with them and went through the known facts, Iraq's declarations, and the various inconsistencies. They then asked the experts what conclusions they had drawn. They were the same as UNSCOM's – Iraq's account of its past programme made no sense. The only possible conclusion was that Iraq had still not told the full and true story.

On the basis of this seminar's analysis, Rolf Ekéus made another plea to Iraq in April 1997. He again told the Iraqis (now led by General Sa'adi following General Amer Rasheed's promotion to Oil Minister) that UNSCOM could not report the conditions for lifting sanctions fulfilled until the biological story made sense. Rolf suggested yet another redraft of the full, final and complete disclosure. Sa'adi refused, saying, 'No, never.'

* * *

'No, never' turned out to mean 'not until September'. Rolf Ekéus was preparing to leave UNSCOM and the job he had done for some seven long, exhilarating but exhausting years. General Sa'adi's 'no, never' had not been an isolated incidence of petulance. Iraq was again peddling the idea that, because UNSCOM had not recently found anything, everything had been declared and sanctions should therefore be lifted. It was also up to its old salami tactics.

Scott Ritter had been heading up a programme of inspections premised on the assumption that, if anything was still being hidden in Iraq, Saddam's most trusted state organisations would be in charge of the operation. This boiled down to the Republican Guard and the Special Security Forces (al Amn al Khaas). Scott's inspections had been increasingly subjected to denials of access, delayed access and general non-cooperation. Iraq was once again trying to establish that it, not UNSCOM, was the arbiter of how, when, where and by whom inspections could be conducted.

Rolf Ekéus started briefing Council members on this new, insidious threat to the health of the inspection and monitoring regimes. Member by member, he was convincing them of the need to put Iraq under additional pressure to come fully clean, so that the sanctions could, finally, be lifted. He wanted to make sure that Iraqi compliance remained inseparably linked with the prospect of sanctions being lifted in the near future.

A new Security Council resolution was slowly being drafted.

Meanwhile, Terry Taylor was about to give Rolf Ekéus something to work with.

Information from the documents found at the chicken farm and other sources suggested that Iraq had been working on ricin, a naturally occurring toxin found in castor beans and cherry pits, as another potential biological warfare agent. Dr Rihab Taha continued to deny this and so UNSCOM had to find other evidence in order to discover the truth.

Terry was trying to track down those scientists declared to be involved in the biological weapons programme but still not interviewed by UNSCOM, and also those suspected of being involved in the programme but not declared by Iraq. UNSCOM's information suggested that a Dr al Keedi fell into the latter category and had been the principal Iraqi researcher in this area. The team wanted to find Dr al Keedi and two other scientists. When he arrived in Baghdad, Terry was informed by Dr Rihab Taha that one of the scientists was dead and that the other was absent on maternity leave and uncontactable.

Dr al Keedi was a top-notch scientist. He had an international reputation in his field, having obtained his MSc in Pharmacology from Imperial College in London, and his PhD from Cardiff University. He had a good publications record in anti-cancer treatments – hence his knowledge of toxins such as ricin – and had worked for a while between 1983 and 1984 at the Centre of Applied Microbiological Research – the privatised part of the Porton Down home of David Kelly and Bryan Barrass. Furthermore, he was a member of Iraq's Scientific Research Council – which UNSCOM had long suspected was linked to the biological weapons programme, although it had been unable to prove any involvement.

Dr al Keedi worked at Baghdad University. His office was on the top floor of an outer building that housed the Pharmacology Department. He was not there, and so the team went to the main building, securing all the exits. The main building of Baghdad University forms a square with an internal courtyard overlooked by external corridors. The team started on the ground floor and worked upwards. By positioning himself on the external corridor, Terry could watch the progress of each of the four different sub-teams, one of them led by Gabriele Kraatz-Wadsack. The team members had been given a key word (just as David Kay's had in 1991) to use if they came across something of interest, so that they would not immediately alert the Iraqi minders to the fact. Terry had also arranged a 'code' with his UNSCOM translator: if there was something in Arabic that was a giveaway, the translator would nudge Terry in the back.

The inspection proceeded in orderly chaos. The team was well trained and disciplined, but it was PhD viva day at the university, so there were fraught students rushing around. The Iraqi minders had tried to block the inspection on the grounds that the exams should not be disturbed; they were very upset when Terry overruled their objections. Indeed, they claimed that UNSCOM was holding hostages, even though Terry had made it clear that the students could leave whenever they wanted.

As the team moved up to the second floor, Terry noticed that one of the minders was rushing up to the third floor. Terry immediately suspected that he might be going ahead to warn of the inspectors' impending arrival. Sure enough, a few moments later he noticed a short, distinguished-looking gentleman in a neat, double-breasted suit coming down the stairs holding a transparent plastic file jacket. On a hunch, Terry called out, 'Dr al Keedi,' and the man acknowledged the greeting. Terry gave the key word into his radio to inform the others that Dr al Keedi had been found and then went up to al Keedi to introduce himself as the chief inspector. He asked to see the documents in the doctor's hand and was told that it was just his wife's driving licence application. However, Terry noticed that the front and back pages were copies of the same application form – the doctor was using them to hide the other documents.

Terry took the folder from Dr al Keedi and started to leaf through it, his translator at his side. All of a sudden the translator nudged Terry in the back so hard it nearly knocked him over. The document was a progress report on research into ricin. It showed that Dr al Keedi had been asked to examine its potential as a biological warfare agent, and reported the results of experiments on various animals, from guinea pigs to donkeys. It concluded that ricin was a viable biological warfare agent that could be developed entirely within Iraq.

By now, Gabriele's sub-team had joined them. Because of the chaotic situation, Terry had become separated from his minders.

He seized the opportunity and ordered Dr al Keedi, 'Take me to your office, now!' The doctor obeyed without hesitation. Gabriele and her team crowded in too, effectively preventing the minders from entering. Together, they turned over the doctor's office, finding several handwritten notes about ricin research, about meetings with military officers, and other documents recording the names of others involved in the programme. Terry then took the doctor into the laboratory to talk through the entire programme. Amazingly, the minders were more concerned about the search going on in the doctor's office than about Terry's debriefing.

At another site the team found a handbook from the al Hazem Institute, dating back to the 1970s. This explained why UNSCOM had never been able to find the institute, despite reliable intelligence that it had been involved in the early days of Iraq's biological weapons programme. The institute had been disbanded. However, the document contained the names of the instructors and those in charge, and standard operating procedures for handling hazardous biological materials. Furthermore the Iraqis referred to this institute variously as al Hazen and Ibn al Haitham, adding to the confusion.

Finally, at the Serum and Vaccine Institute at Amariyah, the team found a letter from General Amer Rasheed al Ubeidi, dated 1992, telling all managers of such institutes to hide incriminating evidence from inspectors. At the time the letter was written, General Amer was telling Rolf Ekéus, John Scott and me that he had sent out instructions to destroy all such evidence, not hide it. This find was also interesting from another perspective – to this day, Iraq insists that the Serum and Vaccine Institute was never involved in the biological weapons programme, despite UNSCOM's suspicions about it. Why, then, had it received such instructions to hide things from the inspectors?

This inspection demonstrated what was needed for a successful find in a no-notice inspection: good information and analysis on which to base the inspection; a well-trained and disciplined team to spot the moment and take advantage of it; plans to disguise a find and ruses to prevent the minders from interrupting the inspection before it is complete; and good old luck.

The inspection also demonstrated how difficult it must be for top scientists to live under a regime like Saddam Hussein's. Dr al Keedi's first response to being caught with the documents was concern about how it would affect his reputation. Here was a man who had dedicated most of his working life to researching medical cures and training young scientists. Who knows what pressure he was put under to join Iraq's biological weapons programme?

Resolution 1115 was adopted by the Security Council on 21 June 1997. Its main thrust was that the regular sanctions reviews (the ceasefire resolution back in 1991 had stipulated that these reviews should be held every sixty days) would, in response to Iraq's growing recalcitrance, be suspended until UNSCOM next reported to the Council in October 1997. There was also a threat: if Iraq did not move within that time to resolve the outstanding issues, particularly those relating to the biological weapons programme, then the Council might take additional, unspecified measures against Iraq.

Rolf Ekéus used this new resolution with General Sa'adi to show that: (a) there was advantage to Iraq in clearing up the biological weapons story as the Council had clearly reiterated that principle that compliance would result in lifting the sanctions, regardless of what Madeleine Albright and others in the US administration might have been saying in public; and (b) non-cooperation was not a cost-free option. Under this pressure, Sa'adi agreed to the drafting of yet another full, final and complete disclosure.

This was delivered in September 1997 – so that UNSCOM, under its new chairman, Richard Butler of Australia, could take it into account when making its October report to the Council. There was nothing new in it.

CHAPTER 21

The End of UNSCOM? What's Left to Do

'The demand was for constant action; if you stopped to think you were lost.'

RAYMOND CHANDLER

'There must be a beginning to any great matter, but the continuing unto it be thoroughly finished yields the true glory.'

SIR FRANCIS DRAKE

'Ils n'ont rien appris, ni rien oublié.' (They have learnt nothing, and forgotten nothing.)

CHARLES-MAURICE DE TALLEYRAND

In July 1997 Rolf Ekéus left UNSCOM to take up his new position with the Swedish Diplomatic Service as ambassador to the United States. His hand-picked successor was Richard Butler – a bluff Australian diplomat who, like so many at UNSCOM, had paid his dues at the Conference on Disarmament in Geneva, where he was Australian ambassador from 1983 until 1989. Richard knew his disarmament law well. Like Rolf, he had also played a leading role in the chemical weapons negotiations and had a keen interest in nuclear weapons issues. Many credited him with success-fully intervening with the non-aligned at the ill-fated Review Conference of the Non-Proliferation Treaty in 1993. Following Richard's eleventh-hour intervention, an indefinite extension of the treaty beyond its initial term of twenty-five years was agreed.

However, Richard's first year at UNSCOM was to be a rough ride. Events conspired to threaten the very existence of UNSCOM no less than three times. This situation was brought about by a number of factors, none of which was Richard's fault: the stage of the disarmament and inspection process, the Richard Butler–Rolf Ekéus comparison and Iraq's opportunistic mischief-making on any pretext.

Throughout late 1996 and early 1997 Iraq had been at its salami tactics again. By now, Scott Ritter was concentrating not on missiles inspections but on trying to fathom Iraq's counter-measures. The logic was that, if UNSCOM could find out what measures the Iraqis were taking to hide their weapons, it could then plan other inspections to catch them in the act of moving or hiding the evidence. This was an approach that applied to all the weapons categories.

However, because of the nature of Iraq's concealment activities, this took Scott Ritter's teams close to the very heart of Saddam Hussein's regime. It had soon become clear that Saddam's personal secretary was responsible for coordinating all the counter-measures. He was based in the Offices of the Presidency, but a proposal to inspect these was bound to trigger a confrontation. Saddam's most trusted personnel, the Revolutionary Guards and various security services, were entrusted with the task of physically moving the evidence around. This had been confirmed by both General Wafiq al Samarra'i and Hussein Kamal Hassan. If the Presidency and presidential palaces were too sensitive to inspect without a fight, that left the Revolutionary Guards barracks and the offices of the security services.

These inspections had led to a series of stand-offs between January and March 1996, with Iraq denying or delaying access to the sites Scott Ritter wanted to inspect. As usual, Rolf Ekéus reported these to the UN Security Council as breaches of the ceasefire terms. However, since Iraq's dramatic admission of nuclear and biological weapons programmes in August 1995, the Council no longer had the stomach for making dramas out of each instance of denied access. Iraq was allowed to get off with verbal admonitions and little more.

This pattern continued into 1997. By now, UNSCOM was certain that Iraq had still not come clean about its VX programme. Some 200 tonnes of VX precursor chemicals remained unaccounted for – sufficient to make over 100 tonnes of VX, enough for some 400 SCUD missile warheads.

And, despite all the information gained in 1995, the biological story still did not make sense. With new information in from suppliers, the amount of complex growth media unaccounted for now stood at 20 tonnes. This is more than enough to make 200 of the 250kg bombs mentioned by General Wafiq al Samarra'i back in February 1995. These quantities were horrifying – they could do serious damage to fifty leading cities if delivered under optimal conditions.

Nikita Smidovich's efforts had also shown that Iraq might well have developed the ability to make all the components for ballistic missiles. If that were the case, then there could be an unknowable number of Iraqi-made missiles hidden from UNSCOM.

Evidence was also coming in that Iraq was actively working on re-establishing its banned weapons activities. As early as 1995 UNSCOM had intercepted an Iraqi attempt to import gyroscopes for its ballistic missiles programme. These were found in Amman, Jordan, awaiting shipment into Iraq. All this evidence left the uncomfortable suspicion that Iraq was hiding all that was unaccounted for and was maintaining operational weapons systems: missiles to deliver warheads filled with VX and anthrax.

Rolf Ekéus had hoped to stay with UNSCOM until the monitoring system was operational and UNSCOM had satisfactorily accounted for all Iraq's holdings of biological, chemical and nuclear weapons, and ballistic missiles, and the means for their maintenance, testing, production and repair. The

monitoring system was in good shape. In March 1996 the UN
Security Council had put in place the last plank of the system – the
export/import monitoring regime.

But in 1997 Rolf Ekéus could not in good faith claim that the
past programmes had been accounted for satisfactorily. Nor could
he see any prospect that they would be in the near future. After six
long years of living and breathing UNSCOM, to the detriment of
himself and his family, it was time for him to move on. However,
he did not want to leave Richard Butler with a situation where Iraq
had the upper hand, with UNSCOM's inspection rights continuously being eroded, to the point where finding the remaining
weapons and materials was impossible.

Rolf's parting gift to Richard Butler was to push through the
UN Security Council resolution 1115, which had condemned
Iraq's pattern of obstructionism. This resolution was clearly
intended to strengthen UNSCOM's hand in what would necessarily be a vulnerable handover period. Iraq had, since 1991,
demonstrated its opportunism in seizing any chance to get away
with not complying. One ruse, of course, was to denigrate those
charged with policing it. However, Rolf Ekéus, because of both his
early successes and his assiduous preparation of the members of
the Security Council for each looming crisis, had a personal
integrity that remained undented by Iraq's numerous attempts at
character assassination. And, because of his insistence on being the
sole interlocutor with Iraq on weapons issues, the Iraqis knew
that, at the end of the day, they would have to deal with him. This,
too, had a muting effect on their criticisms. Even so, he had
suffered vicious personal attacks.

Any new Executive Chairman of UNSCOM could not, by
definition, bring to the table that reservoir of goodwill with the
Security Council that Rolf had been able to accumulate. It was
predictable that the Iraqis would seek to exploit this. And they did.

They did so in two ways. First by mounting a challenge to
UNSCOM that would test Richard's mettle, and then by attacking
his character.

Rolf's parting gift to Richard provided the vehicle for the challenge. Iraq clearly had no intention of complying with demands for access to the sensitive sites. Instead, it launched a diplomatic offensive, repeating the tired mantra that Iraq had fully complied, that UNSCOM was a tool of the US and was dragging its feet, and that the time had come to lift the sanctions.

The result was that, when October 1997 came and UNSCOM reported that Iraq had not complied with the demands of resolution 1115, the sponsors of that resolution were compelled to impose new sanctions on those responsible for the non-compliance. The US and UK put forward a draft resolution with suitably strong language, but this immediately hit opposition in the Council. It became clear that the tough language would not survive and so the US and the UK watered it down. Eventually, on 23 October 1997, they had to force a vote – the first on an UNSCOM-related resolution since the ceasefire resolution itself six and a half years earlier – but could get only ten votes for and five abstentions. Iraq had achieved one of its long-standing objectives, splitting the Security Council. And the split was extremely significant – three of the permanent members of the Council (France, Russia and China) had abstained, breaking with the US.

This emboldened Iraq to test the situation on the ground. The week after the split vote in the Council, on 29 October 1997, Iraq wrote a letter claiming that there were too many Americans on the inspection teams, accusing them of being CIA spies, and demanding that all US staff be withdrawn from UNSCOM operations. It was accompanied by a long list of Americans who would no longer be acceptable as inspectors. My name, despite my British nationality and the fact that I had left UNSCOM some two years earlier, was on that list. In fact, amongst UNSCOM inspectors, it was something of a badge of honour to be on the list. Clearly the Iraqis were trying to stop many of the effective inspectors being involved in future inspections.

UNSCOM's response was, in my view, a massive strategic

blunder. Richard Butler withdrew all except a skeleton staff from the Baghdad Monitoring and Verification Centre and cancelled his own planned trip to Baghdad in protest because Iraq would not allow Americans in his team. While I can see the logic behind this position (stand together or not at all), it brought about a situation that Rolf Ekéus had always tried to avoid at all costs. The road was now clear for a non-UNSCOM interlocutor to be sent to Baghdad to discuss UNSCOM issues. Inevitably, this happened. The Secretary-General, Kofi Annan, dispatched 'three wise men' to Baghdad to discuss the matter with the Iraqis. Fortunately, the situation was recoverable as the visit did not produce a solution. But it had proved to the Iraqis that they might be able to circumvent Richard Butler and UNSCOM in future dealings and hence demote them from the top table.

However, the situation was then compounded by the fact that in November 1997 the Russians sent their own envoy, separate from any UN action, to negotiate a deal. In the past the UN had declined to negotiate on the terms of the ceasefire – they had been held to be non-negotiable. The Russian envoy, being there as a representative of his country, was not bound by such consid-erations. Of course, equally, he could not speak for the UN, only Russia. Against the background of massive US and UK military preparations for a strike on Iraq, this envoy obtained a deal. The details were never made public, but to judge from Iraq's later actions, my best guess is that Russia played up the split in the Council, and suggested that, if Iraq played ball, Russia would be able to rein in UNSCOM's intrusive inspections, even bringing UNSCOM under tighter political control, and broker some relief on the sanctions front. In any event, UNSCOM was back at work at full strength on 21 November.

There will be endless debates about whether it was the skill of Russian diplomacy or the credible military threat mounted by the US and the UK that brought the situation back from the brink. In my mind, there is no doubt: without the military threat, Iraq would have had no reason to negotiate. Indeed, I believe that, with the seriousness of the military threat at that time, the Russian envoy probably underplayed his hand and promised more than was either deliverable by Russia or required to obtain Saddam's retreat. Russia's inability to deliver was underscored by the fact that the sanctions regime remained unchanged and that Russian efforts to restructure UNSCOM failed entirely in an emergency session of the Special Commission (the meeting of the twenty-one government-appointed members of UNSCOM), held on 21 November 1998. The net effect was entirely predictable. This was not a solution to crisis but merely the crisis in abeyance.

Soon after the inspectors were withdrawn from Iraq, the cameras monitoring the fermenters at the al Dawrah Foot and Mouth Disease Vaccine Plant showed the Iraqi workers blatantly removing tagged equipment from the room and out of sight of the cameras. UNSCOM now had no means of knowing where these fermenters were or what they were being used for. The worst-case scenario was that Saddam Hussein had decided to make a complete break with UNSCOM and was now using these fermenters to use whatever hidden stocks of complex growth media he might still have to make biological weapons. At about this time William Cohen, the US Secretary of Defense, went on national television holding a 2lb bag of sugar: that much anthrax, he said, could wipe out the world's population. The world was right to be scared.

Exclusion from Iraq for any period of time will always mean a setback for UNSCOM in its efforts to get to the stage where it can, in good conscience, report that Iraq is sufficiently in compliance for the Council to lift sanctions. Time away means that UNSCOM cannot know how all the monitored equipment has been used in its absence. This was compounded in October 1997 by the fact that Iraq had blacked out some of the monitoring cameras – so that

UNSCOM could not even be sure that the equipment had remained at its usual site, let alone what it had been used for – and had moved some of the tagged and sealed monitors away from their declared locations.

This was a bad sign. Under the terms of the monitoring regime, Iraq is required to notify UNSCOM of the relocation or reconfiguration of any monitored equipment. Failure to do so has to be taken as bad faith. Iraq's explanation was that it was dispersing the equipment in case of air attacks by the US and UK. UNSCOM needed to start its monitoring all over again, beginning with baseline inspections of all the monitored sites and the inventorying, tagging and sealing of the equipment. Gabriele Kraatz-Wadsack led two such inspections back into Iraq in December 1997 and January 1998. She also asked why equipment had been moved, and to where, and why cameras had been blacked out.

Iraq's explanation was characterised by the black sense of humour already seen in some of the Iraqi minders. At one missile test stand it was clear that the Iraqis had simply hung a jacket over the camera. At another missile site, it was claimed that the power had gone off when a cable had been cut. When she asked how the cable had been cut, Gabriele was told that a psychopath had cut it in a fit brought on because he did not have his usual medicines. He did not have the medicines because of the sanctions which were still in place because UNSCOM had not reported that Iraq's biological programme was fully accounted for.

On 17 December 1997 the brief interlude of plain sailing ended. Richard Butler, returning from another trip to Baghdad, reported to the Council that Iraq had created a new category of sites – presidential and sovereign – from which it claimed UNSCOM inspections were barred. The ceasefire foresaw no such limitation on UNSCOM's inspection rights. Indeed, this was the old Ministry of Agriculture chestnut raising its head again, five years later.

* * *

During her second repeat baseline inspection in January 1998 Gabriele's team linked up with another of Scott Ritter's teams. This team was acting on information that Iraq had conducted biological weapons experiments on humans between 1994 and 1995, taking as its experimental subjects inmates at the Abu Ghuraib prison on the western outskirts of Baghdad. This followed a series of different reports, all indicating that human experimentation had taken place within the biological weapons programme. It was claimed that there were human burial sites near Salman Pak, and that animal experimentation cages were 'human-sized'. UNSCOM had no firm evidence to back up these persistent reports, but obviously could not ignore them. The joint team that went to Abu Ghuraib was looking for documents about these experiments. Nothing was found and, in the absence of a coherent and consistent Iraqi accounting for the biological weapons programme, the case remains open.

The crisis erupted again on 13 January 1998, when Scott Ritter tried to conduct an inspection of a sensitive site, assumed to be involved in Iraqi countermeasures to hide weapons materials – the type of site that Iraq was now calling presidential and hence off limits.

Another visit to Baghdad by Richard Butler failed to resolve the issue. On 22 January 1998 he reported to the Council that Iraq had refused to allow UNSCOM inspectors access to eight 'presidential sites'. Some of these sites were in fact massive complexes.

The US and UK, wearied by the events of October and November, were slow to mobilise another military force. Furthermore, the voices against military action were becoming strident. In Moscow Yeltsin claimed that US and UK action could spark a Third World War. Charitably, that remark should be ascribed to vodka. But, more seriously for the US and UNSCOM, none of the Gulf Arab states, save Kuwait, would countenance the use of military bases on their territories for launching strikes against

Iraq. That meant that any action would essentially be carrier based, which limited the duration and scope of the action, if only for resupply reasons.

The US and UK were, despite their tough words, clearly shaken by the severity and breadth of this opposition. Deep into the crisis, in late February 1998, there was the pathetic sight of President Clinton's entire national security team at an Ohio town hall unable to articulate the reasons why military action was not only justified but also necessary, should Iraq not back down.

No one wanted to go to war, but no one seemed to know how to avoid it. Into this breach stepped Kofi Annan. He dispatched a survey team to Baghdad on 15 February to ascertain the locations and sizes of the presidential palaces – which implied that UNSCOM itself could not be relied on to conduct the survey. On 20 February he launched an eleventh-hour diplomatic mission to Baghdad to seek a peaceful solution. This intervention spelt the end of UNSCOM I – UNSCOM as it had been from 1991 to 1997. It confirmed that it was no longer the sole interlocutor with Iraq on weapons issues; the Iraqis now knew that they could always appeal over the head of its Executive Chairman, Richard Butler, and did not have to listen too seriously to what he said. UNSCOM and Richard were no longer players; their roles had been usurped by Kofi Annan and the bickering senior members of the Security Council.

This new fact was compounded by the nature of the 'agreement' secured by Kofi Annan. I use the term 'agreement' as that is what it was called by both Iraq and Kofi Annan's team. In fact, it agreed only to agree on the details of how inspections should be conducted at a some later date. It did not specify who should be responsible for that agreement, or who should have an input; however, there would be a new UN bigwig to oversee the conduct of UNSCOM inspections of sensitive sites – a sort of ombudsman to whom Iraq could appeal if it did not like UNSCOM's behaviour. Furthermore, Kofi Annan was to appoint his own representative to Iraq to discuss political issues. This 'agreement' was endorsed by the Security Council on 2 March 1998.

I have nothing against Kofi Annan (indeed, I have the highest regard for him – he is a man of great integrity), nor against either of the men appointed to the new positions. Ambassador Jayantha Dhanapala, who was appointed to the ombudsman position, was an inspired choice, given the circumstances. He was well-versed in disarmament issues (another Geneva veteran), well-respected in the US and the Security Council, and a personal friend of Richard Butler's. Prakash Shah, who took up the personal representative position, was also an experienced diplomat. What I objected to was the overall result: UNSCOM, not Iraq, was now on trial, and its status had been so diminished that there was no longer any reason why the Iraqis should take it seriously. Kofi Annan's agreement was a band-aid to the immediate problem, but it was applied at the expense of entirely predictable damage to UNSCOM, and hence to longer-term prospects for peace and stability in the region.

Others clearly disagreed. Kofi Annan was greeted back in UN headquarters as the conquering saviour by UN staffers. UNSCOM personnel were notably absent.

In March 1998 Dr Nissar al Hindawi was arrested by the Iraqi authorities. They claimed that he had a false passport in his possession, implying that he had intended to defect. A search of the offices at his private diagnostics business revealed, they claimed, that he had kept various documents about the past biological programme. These Iraq handed over to UNSCOM as part of their documentary corroboration of their account of the past programme. In fact, there were few documents that were not already in UNSCOM's possession from the chicken farm hoard found in August 1995. The one surprise document looked, upon analysis, like a recent forgery designed to support Iraq's current story, rather than an authentic original.

* * *

In the aftermath of this crisis Richard Butler visited Baghdad yet again. Talks centred around how to conclude UNSCOM's work satisfactorily in the shortest possible time. At General Sa'adi's insistence, Richard agreed to a series of joint Iraqi–UNSCOM seminars, attended by experts from outside UNSCOM's usual coterie, to review UNSCOM's evidence in each of the weapons areas, check Iraq's accounts and come to a verdict on whether everything was accounted for. Iraq hoped that by stuffing the seminars with non-UNSCOM personnel it might get a more favourable verdict. Chemical and missiles seminars were held in Baghdad, with the external experts agreeing with the UNSCOM conclusions.

In the biological area, the result was the same. A seminar of nineteen UNSCOM and international experts and some ten Iraqis, led by General Sa'adi, was held in Vienna. Sa'adi claimed that everything would be explained. He was accompanied by Dr Mohammed Mahmoud Bilal from Muthanna. Absent were Dr Rihab Taha (now with a two-year-old baby by General Amer Rasheed) and Dr Nissar al Hindawi (now in Abu Ghuraib prison following his alleged attempt to defect). UNSCOM invited the international experts to New York for a two-week briefing before the meeting, so that they were armed with sufficient knowledge to question the Iraqi experts. They then moved to Vienna and meetings between the two sides took place between 24 March and 2 April 1998.

The seminar split its work into three groups, dealing with research and development, production, and weaponisation. They sought to address such thorny issues as the still hazy history of the programme's origins, accounting adequately and in a verifiable way for the complex growth media, and the reasons behind Iraq's concealment of its biological weapons programme from UNSCOM for the first four years of its operations.

General Sa'adi's strategy did not work, largely because he mishandled the meeting. Instead of buttering up the newcomers on the UNSCOM side of the table, he refused to answer 'questions that have been asked and answered before'. As most of these questions came from the newcomers, he succeeded only in irritating his intended allies. In addition, he insisted on answering the bulk of the questions himself, rather than letting his biological experts field them. The result was that most of the answers were political and not technical. When the Iraqi experts were allowed to answer a question, they did so by merely reading out a passage from the rejected full, final and complete disclosure.

The result was a foregone conclusion – the international experts agreed entirely with UNSCOM's earlier conclusion that Iraq still had a lot of explaining to do. All concluded that they could not 'determine when and whether the programme stopped'.

In mid-June 1998 Richard Butler returned to Baghdad. His strategy was the same as Rolf Ekéus's in the past – to be proactive in order to ensure that UNSCOM could not be blamed for delaying the disarmament process. Richard put forward the idea of a road map of how to get from the current position to one where UNSCOM could report its work done (save ongoing monitoring efforts), so that sanctions could be lifted. It specified what Iraq would need to provide and showed how it could be achieved in a six-week period.

The strategy failed. At the end of the road map's six weeks, on 3 August 1998, Richard Butler and his experts returned to Baghdad to review the status of each programme. Instead, they heard a lecture from Tariq Aziz. Aziz asked Richard point-blank whether he would tell the Council that the biological file was now closed. Richard said that, in view of the evidence, he could not. Aziz replied that, in that case, there was nothing left to discuss. He suspended the talks. Two days later, on 5 August 1988, Iraq announced that it would stop cooperating with inspections (that is, efforts to account fully for the past weapons programmes) but would, as a gesture of goodwill, continue to allow monitoring efforts. The implication was that, if the Council did not lift sanctions at its next review in October 1998, Iraq would cease all cooperation with UNSCOM.

The Council's response to this latest challenge from Iraq was merely to suspend the sanctions reviews indefinitely, until Iraq resumed 'cooperation' with UNSCOM inspections. Once again, UNSCOM was staring into the abyss and feared that its operations would be permanently halted before the biological programme was fully explained.

The weakness of UNSCOM was undermined by another incident on 9 August 1998. Scott Ritter, a veteran from 1991 and the person heading up UNSCOM's efforts to use Iraq's own concealment measures to help him to uncover the still hidden secrets, resigned from UNSCOM. He went public with his reasons. Apparently, since the October 1997 crisis, the US had been advising UNSCOM not to push too hard with its intrusive no-notice inspections. The US was unsure of its ability to mount credible military threats to respond to Iraqi obstruction of such inspections, and wished to avoid confrontations with Iraq. It counselled Richard Butler to rein in Scott's inspections.

Worse still, from Scott's point of view, he had set up an inspection to take place during Richard's August 1998 trip to Baghdad only to find that Sandy Berger, the US National Security Adviser, upon hearing of the plans, had insisted that Butler cancel the inspection and confine Scott to UN offices in Baghdad until the team left Iraq.

Scott accused the US and UK of failing to support UNSCOM. He did not want to be part of an organisation that no longer had the teeth to do the job entrusted to it, and he refused to continue going through the motions of inspections for the sake of it. Unless inspections could be done properly, in his view, they would achieve nothing useful. Worse still, they would give the appearance of being useful, but would in fact provide Iraq with the perfect cover to resume its weapons programmes. What could be better for Saddam than an ineffectual monitoring regime that gave him an official clean bill of health from one of the UN's most respected organs which would, in fact, be unable to detect new clandestine programmes?

Iraq noted the weakness of the Security Council's response and Scott's remarks about the new ineffectiveness of UNSCOM and went on the attack against Richard Butler, claiming that Iraq could no longer trust him or those American elements in UNSCOM behind him, and that therefore Iraq saw no reason to resume cooperation with UNSCOM until things changed. Remarkably, this entirely specious argument found fertile ground both in the Security Council and within the UN permanent staff. Instead of backing their own against a known serial liar cynically attacking the character of Richard Butler for its own political purpose, many in the UN system, to their shame, opted to believe Iraq.

Incredibly, Iraq also managed to impugn the US itself. In its efforts to track down the true story of the missing VX precursor chemicals, UNSCOM managed to locate the facility at which Iraq destroyed various chemicals, equipment and munitions associated with its VX programme. Iraq maintained that it had not put VX into weapons. To test this assertion, UNSCOM removed fragments of SCUD missile warheads found at this site for detailed analysis at a certified chemical laboratory in the US. This laboratory had been used previously by the US and the results then, which had confirmed certain aspects of the Iraqi VX story, were happily accepted by Iraq. However, the analysis indicated that the Iraqis were lying and that VX had indeed been filled into SCUD missile warheads. This time around the Iraqis were far from happy to accept the results, accusing the US of doctoring the results. In response, UNSCOM sent other samples to laboratories in France and Switzerland.

When I visited the UNSCOM offices in New York in the first week of October 1998 as part of my fact-checking for this book, I called in to see some of my former colleagues in the UN press corps. I was staggered to discover that most of them believed the Iraqi allegations. Two weeks later experts from the three laboratories and from seven countries met to review the results from the laboratories and unanimously concluded that the initial US results were correct. This story, unlike the Iraqi allegations that the US had doctored its results, did not make the news.

Whatever the reasons, the situation for UNSCOM, and hence for the prospects of fully disarming Iraq, looked bleak. The Security Council was hopelessly split, to the point of inaction in October 1998. The credibility of the US was so low that even Iraq could challenge it. There was no strategy for how to deal with the new situation, other than to leave ineffective sanctions in place indefinitely. UNSCOM and Richard Butler had lost their positions at the high table, and were excluded from the real power-bargaining. Iraq's ambitions for its weapons of mass destruction remained unchanged and, increasingly, unchallenged.

In fact, Iraq seemed to be the only hope. Never one to let a good crisis fester, on 31 October Saddam Hussein announced that Iraq would cease cooperation with UNSCOM's monitoring activities (although it would allow the IAEA to continue its monitoring).

The US and UK could not ignore Iraq's actions now. Nor could Iraq's erstwhile friends in the Council defend its actions and block US and UK military threats. Another massive military buildup ensued. Saddam probably calculated that he had some weeks in which to wheedle a back-down agreement out of the UN that would result in yet more concessions to him. But the US surprised him – it launched a large part of the attack direct from US territory, not from the Gulf as he had expected. Someone tipped him off, and with the aircraft in the air on their way to Baghdad, laden with Tomahawk missiles programmed to hit a large number of military sites, Saddam panicked and backed down totally. UNSCOM was to be allowed to resume all its activities in Iraq, as per the ceasefire resolution and the Annan agreement of February 1998.

However, within days, Iraq was refusing to answer UNSCOM's

requests to hand over documents about its missile, chemical and biological programmes. The true nature of the Iraqi problem could not be more clearly stated: cooperation is not merely allowing inspectors in and saying to them 'Catch us if you can' – it involves Iraq working with UNSCOM to clear up the murky elements of its past programmes. Iraq's refusal to hand over documents that might help in this task – documents that UNSCOM had seen at one stage or another but had never been allowed to examine – showed that Iraq was not interested in cooperating with UNSCOM, but rather in preserving what was left of its knowledge base so that it could resume its weapons programmes as soon as UNSCOM was off its back.

By December 1998, a month after UNSCOM resumed operations in Iraq, Richard Butler was required to report on Iraq's cooperation with UNSCOM. The US and UK had threatened, in calling off the airstrikes in November, that anything short of full cooperation would lead to immediate military strikes against Iraq without further warning. Butler's report, when it came, left them no option – it stated that, given Iraq's attitude, UNSCOM was unable to perform its disarmament mandate.

Operation Desert Fox was launched – four days of aerial bombardment by the US, with support from the UK. The targets hit were well-chosen: Iraq's dual-purpose factories (to indicate that if UNSCOM were not permitted to do its job, then other means would be used to prevent Iraq from rebuilding its weapons); Saddam's palaces (to show that areas declared by Iraq to be 'off-limits' to UNSCOM could be removed); the Ba'ath Party, the security and internal intelligence apparatus and Saddam's praetorian guard – the Special Republican Guards (to undermine Saddam's regime and show that non-cooperation came with a price-tag); the Republican Guard (to reduce Saddam's ability to suppress his own people and threaten his neighbours); and Saddam's air defences (to reduce the threat to US and UK aircraft).

While militarily a limited success, however, Desert Fox has not (yet) been a political success. Iraq remains unbowed. Indeed,

Saddam is more defiant, not only refusing to let UNSCOM back in but kicking out all UN operations until sanctions are lifted. For the moment, the UNSCOM strategy is dead, with nothing to replace it. The only check on Saddam's ambitions to rebuild his weapons of mass destruction is the threat of resumed bombing of the sites concerned. But this is not a practical policy to prevent his reacquisition of these terrifying weapons. That can only be done by either getting effective inspections going again or removing the ambitions to acquire those weapons – i.e. removing Saddam himself.

Iraq has still not accounted for 20 tonnes of complex growth media, 200 tonnes of precursor chemicals for VX production, and the full extent of its capabilities to produce long-range missiles indigenously. In short, it could have an unknowable number of SCUD-type missiles, with sufficient anthrax and VX to cause immense damage. This represents an impressive power projection capability in the hands of a regime that has amply shown the political will to use it.

That should be enough to scare anyone into action. It scares me.

What scares me more is that the Security Council seems to have learnt nothing, and the Iraqis to have forgotten nothing.

Democracy versus Dictatorship: Some Unwelcome Lessons

'The rain it raineth on the just
And also on the unjust fella;
But chiefly on the just, because
The unjust steals the just's umbrella.'

LORD BOWEN

'It is necessary only for the good man to do
nothing for evil to triumph.'

EDMUND BURKE

'When society requires to be rebuilt, there is no
use in attempting to rebuild it on the old plan.'

JOHN STUART MILL

The Challenge

History regularly throws up regimes like Saddam Hussein's –
regimes that do not play by the established rules of international
relations and good neighbourliness; regimes that challenge the
established order, not for the common good, but for their own self-
aggrandisement. Such states have recently become known as
'rogue states'.

Precisely because regimes like Saddam's are ruthless and are not
constrained by humanitarian or human rights considerations, they
pose particular problems for liberal democracies: how can they be

confronted without compromising democratic principles? How do you force someone to be good?

The Context

In civil society there are inducements and rewards for being good, and punishments for being bad. In liberal democracies, we generally have separate bodies for making laws, policing compliance with them, judging those accused of infringements of the law, and punishing those found guilty. Efforts are also made to convert the offender into a law-abiding citizen.

International law does not have the same structures. Rather, the world is made up of sovereign states which, effectively, have the power to do what they want. Yes, there is an international law, and this is generally written by all those countries with an interest in being involved. Traditionally, though, international law only applies to those countries that have chosen to sign up to it. It does not generally apply to those which have not ratified or acceded to international treaties and conventions.

Even those that do sign up have no independent international police force to apprehend suspected law-breakers, and there is nothing that the general public would recognise as an independent judiciary. While there is the International Court of Justice (the UN's judiciary, located in the Hague and set up to arbitrate between states), nations can choose not to be bound by its findings, as the US has done. And there is no international prison where offenders are locked away. The ultimate recourse for a state that considered it had been wronged was to declare war on the wrongdoer.

Before the League of Nations was created in the embers of the First World War, that was it. The League was the brainchild of US President Woodrow Wilson and the South African General Smuts. Its centrepiece was the concept of collective defence, whereby any state that broke the rules would have to account to the serried ranks of the international community. However, the US never joined the League of Nations and the League failed to respond to its first three challenges – Japan's invasion of China (1932), Italy's of Abyssinia (1935–6) and the Soviet Union's of Finland (1939) – pointing up a fundamental flaw in the concept of collective defence: in a world of blocs and alliances, there is no monolithic international community to side with the victim against the aggressor. Furthermore, those states criticised by the League tended simply to leave it, as Brazil did in 1929.

The world made a second try towards the end of the Second World War, creating the United Nations and its Security Council. The Council is a body comprising fifteen members, five of which are permanent members (the US, UK, France, Russia and China) with the power to veto any decision or resolution. It is the sole body within the UN system which is charged with maintaining and restoring international peace and security. Effectively, it ignores the general rule that international law applies only to those who sign up to it and extends its judgments to all countries, regardless of their membership of the UN.* On matters relating to inter-national peace and security, it is judge, jury and executioner. It is empowered to judge what constitutes a threat to international peace and security, to decide who is to blame, and to take whatever measures it chooses to rectify the situation. There are no restrictions on what these measures might be, save the implicit one that the measures and their objectives should be consistent with the spirit of the UN Charter. In practice, the UN Charter also limits this power through two assumptions: that states should not interfere in the internal affairs of other states (in particular in the way and by whom they are governed), and that conflicts should, wherever possible, be resolved peacefully.

Until the late 1980s the Security Council did not exercise its powers to the fullest extent. Shortly after the end of the Second World War the Allies fell out and the Cold War set in. The Soviet

* In fact, few countries (Switzerland and Taiwan are the most significant) are not UN members.

Union always had the veto to stop the West from imposing its will through the Security Council, and the US, the UK and France had the veto to stop the Soviet Union from getting the Council to do its bidding.

The result, in the new bipolar world, was a Council that was incapable of action and a United Nations that was not the guardian and promoter of liberal democratic ideals the founders had hoped for. Korea was an exception, brought about by a tactical blunder on the part of the Soviet Union. In the fifties China was represented at the UN by Taiwan, not the People's Republic of China, and so had no veto against Western action. But the Soviet delegation, which did have the veto, stormed out of the meeting and were not there when the vote on the Korea resolution was called. Thus they lost their chance to veto the UN operation in Korea. This was a mistake the Soviet Union never repeated.

The Western nations assumed that the Charter gave them the right to intervene wherever there was a gross violation of human rights or a humanitarian crisis. But, as more and more countries gained independence in the post-colonial era, the non-aligned countries, together with the Warsaw Pact, came to out-number, and so out-vote, the West on such issues; the prevailing view was now that the UN should not interfere in internal matters even where there were massive human rights violations (South Africa and Rhodesia being the exceptions to this general rule).

The New World Order

Fortunately, international law is not static; it is constantly evolving. The old concept of sovereignty is slowly dying. States voluntarily hand over bits of it each time they sign up to a new international treaty. Europeans have conceded whole chunks of it to the European Union. Every state that joins the UN submits to the tyranny of the Security Council. And each state that joins an existing treaty makes that treaty stronger.

This is called the normative process. What starts off as a voluntary agreement between consenting parties becomes, over time and with a growing number of signatories, the universal standard. Laws such as those prohibiting slavery or piracy, or the rules of war governing the treatment of prisoners, are now deemed to be universal laws from which no nation or person can opt out – they form the corpus of 'customary international law'. This category includes the Universal Declaration on Human Rights, proclaimed by the UN General Assembly on 10 December 1948, which is why the West considers massive breaches of human rights and dire humanitarian situations as legitimate reasons for overriding the principle of non-interference. Genocide and torture also fall into this category – hence the detention of General Pinochet in London in October 1998 pending consideration of a warrant for his extradition to Spain. Western states are hoping to make the conventions prohibiting the proliferation of weapons of mass destruction similarly part of customary international law through the normative process. If this becomes so, then taking military action against rogue states that pursue nuclear, biological or chemical weaponisation programmes will be much easier.

In short, the world is moving into a much more interventionist mode, where the sanctity of the sovereign state counts for less and the leaders of states (except of those states that are too powerful to be brought to book) are held ever more accountable to the international community for their behaviour. This is why former leaders in Rwanda and Bosnia are being brought before international courts to stand trial for their crimes against humanity. This situation gives us hope that the international community might be better able to deal with rogue states in the future.

The UN's response to Iraq's invasion of Kuwait was ground-breaking, opening up the prospect of what George Bush coined the 'New World Order'. Here the international community could come together to respond decisively to aggression and breaches of conduct.

UNSCOM was a key part of that response to the threat to peace from Iraq. The world community saw that the winning of the war to liberate Kuwait would not be enough to remove the threat to international peace and security posed by Saddam Hussein unless Iraq were also forced to give up its weapons of mass destruction and the means of delivering them long-range; unless Iraq were forced to give up its ability to project its military power in the region and beyond.

That being the case, the successes and failures of the UNSCOM process should hold valuable lessons for future crises that might face the Security Council.

The Lessons of UNSCOM

UNSCOM's success stemmed from a large number of simultaneously propitious factors. If any one of them had been missing, UNSCOM would not have been the success that it was.

UNSCOM had a clear mandate set by the Security Council. Because of both the clarity of the mandate and the fact that UNSCOM was a single-issue organisation, there was never any clouding of the mission or diversion of attention and resources elsewhere from within UNSCOM. The result was a clear and effective active strategy for achieving the stated objectives, coupled with a dedication and determination to see it through to the end. It is important to note that this was an active strategy, not a passive one. UNSCOM did not simply accept the political environment within which it had to operate: it acknowledged that it required a certain political environment in order to be effective and went about proactively trying to ensure that that political environment prevailed. In order to achieve this, UNSCOM had to be truly independent – and perceived as such by observers. Without this, it would not have had the credibility necessary for it to work in such a political environment.

Another factor was that UNSCOM was given the powers it

needed to do the job. While the powers might at first have seemed excessive, UNSCOM's experience showed that, at one time or another, every single one of the powers had to be exercised in the search for Iraq's undeclared capabilities.

UNSCOM received unstinting support from the Security Council in the early years. This enabled it to exercise its powers to the full in the knowledge that, if Iraq tried to challenge them, the big battalions could be called up to force Iraq to back down. This created a virtuous circle – the more UNSCOM could exercise its powers, the more it could achieve; the more it achieved, the more willing the Security Council was to back it up in the face of Iraqi challenges.

But UNSCOM's success was largely due to the quality of its staff. Because it was backed strongly by key Security Council members, it could call on the world's very best experts in the appropriate disciplines. The more successful UNSCOM was, the more these experts wanted to be associated with it. By 1998, however, some senior UN officials were claiming that the problems between UNSCOM and Iraq were due to the fact that UNSCOM's personnel were all short-termers on loan from governments, not career international civil servants like themselves. This is disingenuous on two levels. First, when UNSCOM was formed, there was a freeze on UN recruitment, with no long-term contracts on offer; no budget was set aside for UNSCOM, so it had to borrow personnel from governments. Second, there were no career international civil servants within the UN system with the expertise required to do the job. If existing UN staff had been reallocated, regardless of their lack of appropriate knowledge, they would not have known where to start. Either nothing would have been achieved, or worse – Iraq would have pulled the wool over their eyes and obtained a clean bill of health without its past programmes being uncovered and destroyed.

The UN has to be able to incorporate both career international civil servants and shorter-term experts. Insisting on full-time career recruitment would discourage the world's best from ever participating in UN operations – they would merely seek better and more fulfilling careers elsewhere. And the longer any expert was with the UN and away from the cutting edge of science and technology, the less useful that person would become to the UN. For an operation like UNSCOM to succeed, you need people who are current experts, not those who were ten years ago. These experts are in high demand, and can at best offer a limited amount of their time to the UN. Giving short-term contracts is the only way the UN can get the best in the world. Of course, this concept frightens some career UN officials.

Culture was also important. The more UNSCOM was a success, the more it developed its own distinct culture – distinct from the cultures of the experts' own national governments, and distinct from the bureaucracy of the UN. This was a 'can do' culture, which many old UN hands, ever fearful of upsetting a member state to the extent of second-guessing themselves into a state of inaction, preferred to see as a 'cowboy operation'. But this culture was for real. Many of the inspectors became so 'UNSCOM' that they got themselves into trouble with their own governments. Scott Ritter's was by no means the only government career that has been curtailed by a refusal to do his government's bidding rather than remain true to UNSCOM and to UNSCOM's mandate. Such dedication to UNSCOM would make laughable Iraq's claims that UNSCOM is a nest of spies, were it not for the fact that many senior officials at the UN and many member states seem all too inclined to believe such allegations.

The culture was one of total dedication to the task of eliminating Iraq's banned weapons of mass destruction and long-range missiles – nothing more, but, importantly, nothing less. It was personified in the quiet, polite insistence of veteran inspectors like Dick Spertzel, David Kelly, Gabriele Kraatz-Wadsack and Terry Taylor. These are remarkable people who refused to let issues lie. They were prepared to find new ways of doing things if the first route did not succeed or was blocked by Iraq. In the process, they developed new applications for technology to the disarmament task, they developed new sources of information that the UN had previously rejected, they developed new methodologies for weapons inspections, established new legal precedents, and brought to bear thorough and systematic analysis. Without a successful grand strategy, as put in place by Rolf Ekéus, these people could not have done their work. But equally, without their application and attention to the minutest detail of Iraq's declarations and the findings of their own investigations, the grand strategy would have produced nothing.

In short, the success of UNSCOM came from having a clear strategy based on a clear mandate and being given the tools to achieve it, coupled with excellent people bound by a strong culture of achievement through innovation and attention to detail, all backed up by the implacable support of the Security Council in times of need.

Of course, there are those who would dispute UNSCOM's success. Some will, for political reasons, declare UNSCOM a success and move on. Russia and France, for commercial reasons as much as anything else, seem to be in this camp. In early October 1998 the US, having failed to find a new strategy to replace the ceasefire resolution, also appeared to be sliding into this camp. But, following Saddam's overplaying of his hand by putting an end to all inspections, the US got its nerve back. The old 'carrot-and-stick' strategy was revamped by raising the price of non-cooperation, with threats to undermine Saddam's regime if he refused to play ball. Saddam raised the ante further by kicking out UNSCOM again, leaving the US with options to remove him, contain him or negotiate with him.

Others will insist that UNSCOM was, after initial successes, ultimately a failure. They will point out that UNSCOM did not force Iraq to cooperate and that, despite its awesome powers, it was unable to uncover 100 per cent of Iraq's banned weapons programmes.

But a debate at that level would obscure the real issue. UNSCOM was a technical body, albeit one operating in a highly politically charged environment, mandated to achieve a technical task. This it did beyond its creators' wildest expectations. The failure, such as it is, is not to do with UNSCOM, but with the Security Council's reluctance to address the fundamental underlying political dilemmas posed by the continued existence of Saddam's regime.

Saddam, simply put, has not given up his ambitions to possess weapons of mass destruction. That is why Iraq has not come clean and why issues such as biological weapons remain unresolved – not because of some presumed incompetence on UNSCOM's part. And it was the inaction of the Security Council in the autumn of 1997 and again in the spring and summer of 1998, the failure of political will to enforce the very law it had itself enacted (the ceasefire resolution), that undermined the effectiveness of UNSCOM. In early 1999, it is again failing.

While much can be learned from UNSCOM about how to search out and destroy weapons of mass destruction, the real lessons of the UNSCOM experience must come from this political level. The symptoms of collective failure of political will are all too familiar:

- **Lack of a political solution.** All too many UN operations are based on a technical, humanitarian or military 'solution' to what is fundamentally a political problem; no effort is made to sort out the political issues in parallel with the application of the technical palliative. In UNSCOM's case, no strategy exists for addressing Saddam's unerring desire to acquire weapons of mass destruction once UNSCOM's inspections have been rendered ineffective. The ceasefire resolution made the reasonable assumption that Iraq would act as a defeated nation or, failing that, decide to give up its weapons and its secrets, once faced with the loss of $25 millions a day in forfeited oil revenues. That assumption has proved false, and no other political solution to the problem has been offered. Indeed, the US policy adopted in response to Iraq's latest challenge is premised entirely on the false assumption that Iraq will give up its secret weapons for resumed oil sales and in the face of vague, unsupported threats.

- **Crisis fatigue.** This often sets in once the issue begins to appear intractable or once memories of the horror fade. Not only are the world's institutions incapable of dealing with too many crises at the same time, but they seem incapable of staying the course. The Inter-Allied Commission of Control, established by the Versailles Treaty to oversee Germany's disarmament after the First World War, operated for seven years and eight months before Hitler's regime kicked them out. There was the merest of whimpers from the world community then. UNSCOM lasted seven years and six months before Saddam's regime kicked out the intrusive inspections. The world's reaction was reluctantly to accept a British resolution suspending reviews of sanctions against Iraq until it resumed 'cooperation'. Seven years and eight months into UNSCOM's operations, and Iraq announced the end of all 'cooperation', even on monitoring. The parallels are staggering. The Council has not heeded Francis Drake's words – 'the continuing unto it be thoroughly finished yields true glory'.

- **Impatience with sanctions.** Sanctions are at the best of times a blunt weapon. They inevitably inflict genuine suffering on the weakest members of the sanctioned country's population and are slow to work. But they do have a place as part of a clear, coherent strategy to push recalcitrant leaders in the desired direction. Ironically, it is usually those who are most keen to avoid military responses to international crises who propose sanctions as an alternative, and the same people who then agitate for the lifting of sanctions before they have had a chance to work. But sanctions are not merely an alternative to military options – they can only be useful if they are imposed in tandem with an overall political strategy. This does not always happen. And their effect is not always as intended. Indeed, the imposition of sanctions can strengthen the regime they are aimed at, and thus have the opposite effect from that desired. On their own, sanctions are useless and pointless. And pointless sanctions – sanctions that have no chance of achieving a desirable effect – are immoral in that they punish the weak, not those responsible for the situation. Too often it is the impatience of those who first moot sanctions as an alternative to military action who undermine their effectiveness: the transgressors read this impatience to mean that the sanctions have a time limit and that they can merely sit them out rather than complying. In short, impatience with sanctions is the best way to ensure that they will not work. In contrast, increasing support for sanctions over time, as was the case with Rhodesia and South Africa, will convince a regime of the hopelessness of resisting. The situation with Iraq is now clear: Iraq believes that sanctions will not last, and therefore sees no point in complying with the terms for lifting them.

- **Policy drift.** Policy objectives, such as the disarmament of Iraq stipulated in the ceasefire resolution, are put in place in a particular historical context and strategies for achieving them are developed. However, while the political context quickly changes, policies and strategies remain unchanged until some crisis brings the matter to the world's attention again. Adjustments are then made to some aspects of the policy and strategy, but other components remain unchanged or unchallenged. Over time, policies and strategies lose their coherence. For most of its two terms the Clinton administration merely left the Bush Iraq policy on auto-pilot. Consequently, the policy drift has been immense. There is now no coherent, well-articulated US policy towards Iraq and hence no coherent Security Council policy. Such a policy vacuum can only encourage a rogue state, such as Iraq, to believe it can get away with its rogue behaviour.

- **The 'Alice in Wonderland' syndrome.** In the absence of discoveries by UNSCOM of new hidden caches of weapons and weapons-making equipment, the international community seems to be accepting that whatever Iraq tells it 'three times is true'. I should rather Bertrand Russell's injunction not to believe a proposition until there were grounds to believe that it might be true. The preponderance of evidence shows that Iraq is still lying.

Future Options

The starting point for international responses to breaches of peace and security has to be to seek long-term political solutions. For many crises, such as those in the Middle East, Kashmir or Cyprus, the situation may not be ripe for a longer-term political solution. You can bring the horses to the water but you cannot make them drink. All the international community can do in such cases is to try to talk sense into both sides, offer its good offices in any attempts to end the tension, and take palliative action to minimise the suffering.

The situation with rogue states is different. Here, it is the regime itself that is the threat to international peace and security. In these situations, the international community does not need to constrain itself to mere exhortation – it can threaten, as it did in Somalia, Iraq and Kosovo. Ultimately, the options are: to walk away from the problem; to contain the problem; to engage in constructive dialogue; or to respond militarily.

Walking away from the problem can be a real option. If there are no strategic interests at risk, the international community might decide merely to let the crisis fester, so long as there is no risk of it spreading beyond the region. The price of intervention of any sort might be deemed too high. Containment represents the next level of involvement, but is much the same as walking away – it implies active measures to ensure that the problem does not spread beyond its region, but no effort to resolve the problem itself.

Constructive engagement does attempt to solve the problem. The logic is that, by engaging the recalcitrant party in trade, diplomatic relations or cultural exchanges, you can either educate and persuade the rogue state into acceptable behaviour (as propounded by the US and UK with the apartheid regime in South Africa, and practised by the US in Japan following the Second World War), or buy their good behaviour through lucrative trade and aid programmes (the US tried, unsuccessfully with Pakistan and successfully with Brazil and Argentina, to wean them away from their nuclear ambitions).

Finally, military action can be taken, either with a view to enforcing compliance (as was the case with Iraq until August 1998) or with a view to removing the cause of the problem by removing the rogue regime. Recent experiences, not least Desert Fox, argue that, if the military option is to be pursued, then the force deployed should be overwhelming. The deployment of overwhelming forces means that it is much less likely that force will have to be used at all. The Bosnian experience showed that the Serb forces feared the threat of military action. However, once this action was shown to be negligible (it came in a piecemeal fashion as part of a misguided policy of graduated and escalatory response) the fear of the threat was removed and the challenges to the NATO forces increased. Had the first response been overwhelming, I doubt very much whether a second one would have been required. And had an overwhelming force been deployed, even the first challenge might have been avoided.

The Iraqi Case

In Iraq's case, as noted above, the policy drift has been monumental. The initial strategy of the ceasefire was premised on the belief that Iraq would give up its weapons of mass destruction if given the proper incentives and if threatened appropriately. The carrot was the lifting of the oil embargo upon compliance; the stick was the threat of renewed military action; and the compliance bar was set at the complete elimination of Iraq's banned weapons. In other words, the aim was to make the costs of non-compliance too high to consider.

This was an eminently reasonable strategy to adopt in 1991. However, Saddam decided that the cost, most of which falls on the Iraqi population for whom he has such contempt, was bearable – his own people, those upon whom he relies to stay in power, were not suffering unduly and some were benefitting handsomely. And so he remains in defiance of the international community. We should, by now, be able to read the writing on the wall.

No Security Council member seems willing to admit the obvious. The threat to international peace and security comes not from the dual-purpose materials and equipment in Iraq, or even from its military capabilities. It comes from the ambitions of the regime, embodied in the person of Saddam Hussein. The threat to international peace and security will not be removed until the regime's ambitions have been removed or changed. After seven years of trying to persuade the leopard to change its spots (at great expense) it is time to realise that he won't.

Given the stakes involved, this is not a problem the international community can walk away from. It has to be resolved, which also rules out the policy of containment. Military enforcement action has proved too expensive both politically and financially. And it is not working – Saddam is simply dodging the punches.

That leaves two options for removing the threat posed by Saddam's weapons ambitions: remove his regime by force or engage in constructive dialogue with him. Dialogue, culture and education seem unlikely candidates for making Saddam change his intentions. Buying his vote might be a short-term solution. But once the oil money starts to flow, why should he need the bribe?

The obvious and only real solution is for the international community to take concerted action to remove the regime of

Saddam Hussein. This would not be an illegal action, inconsistent with the UN Charter's injunction not to interfere in the internal affairs of member states. Saddam, by his actions and ambitions, is a threat to international security and hence forgoes the protection of that injunction. The obligations of the Security Council to 'take all measures' to maintain international peace and security and remove threats to it take precedence.

This would be a brave new step for the UN, but not a departure from the trend in international law. The Council has stated that the proliferation of weapons of mass destruction is a threat to international peace and security, bringing into play Chapter VII of the Charter. Ratifications of the various arms control treaties are bringing their provisions ever nearer to the status of Customary International Law. The concept that a government can do what it likes within its own borders is increasingly under attack. There are limits to what dictators can do to their own people or threaten to do to their neighbours. Intervention against those who overstep those limits should be more commonplace.

Unfortunately, there is no sign of a policy of the aggressive pursuit of peace. While there have been hints of supporting efforts to remove Saddam's regime, the US and its closest allies appear to be more bent on a strategy of containment, regardless of the evidence that such strategies always ultimately fail. That cannot last for ever. Saddam will break out of the box Madeleine Albright claims he is in. The rest appear to have opted for acquiescence and appeasement. Neither of these policies, nor ridiculous optimism, will change Saddam's ambitions.

Ostrich-like, the world appears to be hoping that the problem of Saddam's ambitions will simply go away. But sooner or later, unless Saddam's regime is removed, Iraq will go about rebuilding its military might. And then the countdown will commence to the next major confrontation with Saddam, on the scale of the Gulf War. But next time, Saddam may well be armed with those weapons

UNSCOM strove to eliminate: chemical and biological weapons on long-range missiles. He may even have nuclear weapons. And who, then, will defend the world? I should like to hope it would be France and Russia, who so carelessly broke the international consensus on how to deal with Iraq. But I doubt it.

Brixton, 11 January 1999

Chronology

July–August 1932
Iraq and Kuwait, at the instigation of the British government, confirm the Iraq–Kuwait boundary.

19 June 1961
Kuwaiti independence from the United Kingdom.

14 May 1963
Kuwait becomes the 111th United Nations member state.

4 October 1963
After a period of tension, with Iraq making claim to Kuwait, Iraq accepts the boundaries as defined in 1932.

May–July 1990
In statements by President Saddam Hussein of Iraq and other Iraqi officials, Iraq advances political, territorial and financial claims against Kuwait.

2, 5, 6 and 7 July 1990
The Security Council considers the dispute between Iraq and Kuwait. No action taken.

Late July 1990
Iraqi troops deploy on the Kuwait border.

31 July 1990
Talks in Saudi Arabia between Iraq and Kuwait fail.

2 August 1990
Iraq invades Kuwait. The Security Council demands the immediate and unconditional withdrawal of all Iraqi forces.

6 August 1990
The Security Council imposes comprehensive mandatory sanctions against Iraq and occupied Kuwait.

7 August 1990
The United States and the coalition begin to deploy military forces to the Gulf region.

8 August 1990
Iraq announces the 'comprehensive and eternal merger' of Kuwait with Iraq.

12 August 1990
Kuwait requests military assistance for the liberation of Kuwait.

25 August 1990
The Security Council authorises maritime forces in the Gulf to enforce the sanctions against Iraq.

29 November 1990
The Security Council authorises the use of 'all necessary means' to liberate Kuwait unless Iraq withdraws on or before 15 January 1991 – the war enabling resolution 678 (1990).

9 January 1991
The United States Secretary of State, James Baker, and the Deputy Prime Minister and Minister for Foreign Affairs of Iraq, Tariq Aziz, meet in Geneva. According to later repeated statements by Aziz, Baker threatens to bomb Iraq into the 'pre-industrial age' and makes veiled threats to use the nuclear bomb in retaliation for any Iraqi use of chemical weapons.

12–13 January 1991
The UN Secretary-General, Javier Perez de Cuellar, meets President Saddam Hussein and Tariq Aziz to urge Iraq to withdraw from Kuwait.

16 January 1991
Iraq fails to withdraw from Kuwait. Coalition forces begin the air war, bombing Iraq.

21–22 February 1991
Iraq ignites some 500 Kuwaiti oil wells.

24 February 1991
Coalition forces begin the ground war, moving into both Kuwait and Iraq.

27 February 1991
Kuwait City is liberated. The coalition declares the end of the ground war. Iraq states that it will comply fully with relevant Security Council resolutions, but sets conditions. Iraq later informs the UN that all Iraqi forces have been withdrawn from Kuwait.

28 February 1991
Hostilities are suspended at midnight, EST. Iraq states that it will comply with all relevant Security Council resolutions.

2 March 1991
The Security Council takes note of the suspension of all offensive combat operations.

3 March 1991
Iraq agrees to comply with the terms of Security Council resolution 686.

3 April 1991
The Security Council adopts resolution 687, the ceasefire resolution. Its terms require, *inter alia*, the destruction of Iraqi weapons of mass destruction and long-range ballistic missiles under supervision of a Special Commission (UNSCOM) and the International Atomic Energy Agency (IAEA) and the establishment of a system of future ongoing monitoring and verification of Iraq's compliance with the ban on these weapons and missiles.

4 April 1991
Kuwait accepts resolution 687.

5 April 1991
The Security Council demands that Iraq cease repression of its civilian population.

6 April 1991
Iraq informs the UN that it has no choice but to accept the terms of resolution 687.

11 April 1991
The President of the Security Council acknowledges Iraq's acceptance of the terms of resolution 687. A formal ceasefire comes into effect.

18 April 1991
The Secretary-General submits a plan for the establishment of a United Nations Special Commission (UNSCOM); the Council approves the plan on 19 April.

18 April 1991
Iraq submits its first declaration of its holdings of weapons of mass destruction and ballistic missiles. It denies having weapons-grade nuclear material, a nuclear weapons programme, a biological weapons programme or any superguns. It does declare holdings of ballistic missiles and chemical weapons.

27 April 1991
Iraq amends its declaration regarding nuclear weapons, admitting to having additional nuclear materials and facilities to those declared to the IAEA under the Safeguards Agreement.

15–21 May 1991
The first IAEA inspection inventories Iraqi nuclear facilities.

16 May 1991
Iraq amends its declarations about chemical weapons and ballistic missiles, increasing the number of items declared, and declares a small amount of dual-use biological equipment and facilities.

17 May 1991
UNSCOM and the IAEA submit their plans for immediate on-site inspections and for the destruction, removal or rendering harmless of weapons of mass destruction and of the facilities for their production, maintenance, testing and development.

18 May 1991
Iraq formally accepts the Status Agreement detailing the facilities,

immunities and privileges to be afforded UNSCOM and the IAEA in implementing their mandates. This agreement is retroactive from 14 May, the date of Iraq's oral agreement to its terms.

June 1991
The coalition impose a 'no-fly zone' above the thirty-sixth parallel in Iraq, barring flights of Iraqi military aircraft over the Kurdish 'safe haven'.

2 June 1991
The Secretary-General submits guidelines for observing the arms embargo against Iraq.

9–15 June 1991
UNSCOM's first chemical inspection inventories Iraq's chemical weapons and production facilities at Muthanna.

17 June 1991
The Security Council approves the plan for eliminating Iraq's banned weapons programmes and decides that Iraq must pay the costs of doing so.

23–28 June 1991
Iraq obstructs David Kay's team (IAEA2) from gaining access to prohibited items. Iraqi soldiers fire at inspectors.

28 June 1991
The Security Council condemns the shooting incident and sends a high-level mission to Baghdad to obtain assurances that the government will not in any way prevent UNSCOM or IAEA from carrying out their duties.

30 June–3 July 1991
The high-level mission reports Iraq's inadequate response.

30 June–7 July 1991
UNSCOM's first ballistic missile inspection inventories Iraqi stocks and begins destruction of launchers and missiles.

7–18 July 1991
IAEA3 finds large stocks of natural uranium and 15kg of highly enriched uranium, and forces Iraqi admissions about the existence of various uranium-enrichment programmes.

7 July 1991
Iraq insists that its uranium-enrichment programmes are for peaceful purposes.

15 July 1991
The Secretary-General recommends an oil-for-food deal whereby Iraq can sell some oil to pay for food and medicine imports and to cover the costs of UN operations in Iraq.

18–20 July 1991
UNSCOM's second ballistic missile inspection discovers and destroys undeclared decoy missiles and equipment.

27 July–10 August 1991
David Kay leads IAEA4, which concludes that Iraq had a nuclear weaponisation programme.

2–8 August 1991
David Kelly leads UNSCOM's first biological inspection and uncovers an undeclared biological programme. The team removes seed stocks of various biological warfare agents.

5 August 1991
Dr Rihab Taha admits that Iraq conducted bacteriological research for military purposes from 1986 to August 1990.

8–15 August 1991
During UNSCOM's third ballistic inspection, Iraq admits the existence of a 'supergun' and other banned missile items.

11 August 1991
The US, on behalf of UNSCOM, begins high-altitude reconnaissance flights over Iraq – the U2 flights.

15 August 1991
The Security Council, in its resolution 707 (1991), *inter alia*, demands that Iraq halt all nuclear activities of any kind, that it move no nuclear materials without UNSCOM's prior consent, that it provide full, final and complete disclosure of its past weapons programmes and that it allow UNSCOM and IAEA inspection teams immediate, unconditional and unrestricted access to all sites duly designated by UNSCOM.

16 August 1991
Iraq states its objections to resolution 707.

18–20 August 1991
UNSCOM's third ballistic missile inspection reports that Iraq resisted efforts to inventory dual-purpose equipment.

3 September 1991
Iraq reiterates its objections to resolution 707.

6–13 September 1991
Iraq denies UNSCOM's fourth ballistic inspection its right to use UN helicopters to inspect sites in western Iraq.

14–20 September 1991
IAEA5 finds 2.2 tons of heavy water.

20 September–3 October 1991
David Kelly, at the end of UNSCOM's second biological inspection, concludes that Iraq had a biological weapons programme and that it must have included plans for weapons development and production.

21–30 September 1991
David Kay and Bob Gallucci lead IAEA6. They are held at gunpoint in a parking lot for four days after having found documents describing Iraq's plan to build nuclear weapons.

23 September 1991
The Security Council demands that Iraq abide by resolution 707 of 15 August.

24 September 1991
The Security Council condemns Iraq over the parking-lot incident.

4–6 October 1991
Rolf Ekéus, the Executive Chairman of UNSCOM, visits Baghdad. Iraq acquiesces to UNSCOM's use of helicopters for inspections. Germany starts flying helicopters in Iraq on behalf of UNSCOM.

1–9 October 1991
UNSCOM's fifth ballistic missile inspection destroys Iraq's fixed-missile

launchers, destroys the supergun at Jabal Hamran, and starts destruction of the components for four other superguns.

11 October 1991
The Security Council approves the UNSCOM and IAEA plans for the ongoing monitoring and verification of Iraqi compliance with its obligations not to reacquire weapons of mass destruction and long-range missiles.

11–22 October 1991
IAEA7 supervises the destruction of uranium enrichment and reprocessing equipment.

14 October 1991
Iraq finally acknowledges that it had researched how to build a nuclear bomb.

11–18 November 1991
IAEA8 removes stocks of un-irradiated nuclear fuel from Iraq.

18 November–1 December 1991
UNSCOM's first joint chemical and biological inspection discovers some 100 chemical bomb-making items at a Mosul sugar factory, along with undeclared missile items.

19 November 1991
Iraq objects to the UNSCOM and IAEA ongoing monitoring and verification plans.

20 November 1991
Iraq makes its first 'full, final and complete disclosure' of its nuclear, chemical, biological and missile programmes under resolution 707.

27 November 1991
Iraq and the UN sign a second Memorandum of Understanding for the provision by the UN of humanitarian assistance to the population of Iraq. This extends the programme until 30 June 1992.

1–9 December 1991
UNSCOM's sixth ballistic inspection supervises the destruction of the remaining supergun components and discovers that Iraq has welded

together parts of a missile transporter destroyed in a previous inspection. Further missile equipment and transporters are destroyed.

11 December 1991
Iraq gives the IAEA further information on its nuclear programme.

27–30 January 1992
The John Gee and Peter von Butler mission goes to Iraq to elicit Iraqi acknowledgement of its obligations under resolutions 707 and 715 (1991) and to urge Iraq to amend its 'full, final and complete disclosures' of its past programmes so that they are indeed full, final and complete.

31 January 1992
The Security Council meets at the level of heads of state or government for the first time ever. It demands that Iraq comply with all pertinent UN resolutions. It further states that the proliferation of weapons of mass destruction is a threat to international peace and security, implying that responding to such proliferation falls within the Council's competence under Chapter VII of the UN Charter.

14 February 1992
Rolf Ekéus informs Iraq of UNSCOM's plans to destroy Iraq's missile production and repair facilities and equipment.

18 February 1992
Rolf Ekéus informs the Security Council of the results of the John Gee and Peter von Butler visit to Baghdad, i.e. that Iraq rejects certain aspects of Security Council resolutions 687, 707 and 715, and objects to the destruction of prohibited missile-related facilities and equipment.

19 February 1992
The Security Council finds Iraq in material breach of resolution 687 for its refusal to acknowledge its obligations under resolutions 707 and 715, its rejection of the ongoing monitoring and verification plans and its failure to provide full, final and complete disclosures of its past nuclear, chemical, biological and missile programmes.

21–23 February 1992
Rolf Ekéus visits Baghdad to secure Iraq's unconditional compliance with all aspects of resolutions 687, 707 and 715.

21–28 February 1992
Christopher Holland, with UNSCOM's eighth ballistic missile inspection, is sent to supervise the destruction of missile production and repair facilities and equipment but Iraq refuses to destroy the specified missiles and components. The team is withdrawn and the Security Council informed.

21 February–24 March 1992
The first chemical destruction team destroys 463 122mm rockets, containing some 2.5 tonnes of sarin, at Khamissiyah.

24 February 1992
Iraq claims to be in full compliance with resolution 687. Iraq states that it does not reject an ongoing monitoring and verification regime, but that it objects to the nature of the privileges, immunities and facilities granted to UNSCOM and the IAEA and the infringement of Iraqi sovereignty, national security and territorial integrity they represent.

27 February 1992
Rolf Ekéus, following his visit to Baghdad, reports that Iraq refused to give the required assurances that it would fulfil all its obligations.

28 February 1992
Iraq questions the authority of UNSCOM to determine the items to be destroyed and seeks arbitration by the Security Council. The Council reaffirms that it is for UNSCOM alone to determine which items are to be destroyed and warns Iraq of the serious consequences of its refusal to comply with UNSCOM's requests.

11–12 March 1992
The Security Council debates Iraq's compliance with relevant resolutions. The Council issues two presidential statements to the effect that the government of Iraq is not yet in compliance. It demands Iraq comply immediately.

19 March 1992
Iraq, in the face of photographic evidence in UNSCOM's possession, declares the existence of eighty-nine additional ballistic missiles. It makes additional declarations about chemical weapons and material. Iraq avers that most of these items were unilaterally destroyed in the summer of 1991. Iraq says it is willing to accept additional destruction of items.

21–29 March 1992
UNSCOM's ninth ballistic inspection supervises the destruction of the missiles facilities and equipment Iraq refused to destroy in February. The team starts to verify Iraqi claims to have unilaterally destroyed 89 ballistic missiles and associated equipment in 1991.

25 March 1992
The IAEA presents Iraq with a list of buildings and equipment to be destroyed at the al Atheer-al Hatteen site.

7–15 April 1992
IAEA11 supervises the destruction of equipment and facilities at al Atheer, Iraq's nuclear weaponisation research and development centre.

9 April 1992
Following the incursion of an Iranian aircraft into Iraqi airspace, Iraq calls for a halt to UNSCOM's U2 aerial surveillance flights, stating that the safety of the pilots and aircraft could be in danger.

10 April 1992
In response to the Iraqi statement of 9 April, the Security Council reaffirms the right of UNSCOM to conduct aerial surveillance over Iraq, demands that Iraq ensure that its military forces do not threaten the safety of the commission's aircraft and personnel and warns Iraq of serious consequences if it does not.

12 April 1992
Iraq responds that it does not intend to threaten UNSCOM surveillance activity.

13–21 April 1992
UNSCOM teams supervise the destruction of more missile production equipment – forty-five items and ten buildings.

15 April 1992
The IAEA tells Iraq of its plans for the dismantling of uranium enrichment facilities at Tarmiya and Ash Sharqat.

15–29 April 1992
UNSCOM's eighth chemical inspection verifies the destruction of chemical weapon items which Iraq claimed to have destroyed unilaterally.

14–22 May 1992
UNSCOM's eleventh missile inspection supervises the destruction of the additional chemical warheads and ballistic missiles revealed in Iraq's declaration of 19 March 1992. It starts to inventory Iraq's missile production facilities.

26 May 1992
Iraq informs UNSCOM that it was ready to disclose its full nuclear, chemical, biological and missile programmes and to reach a practical solution to the ongoing monitoring and verification issue.

26 May–4 June 1992
IAEA12 supervises destruction activities at al Atheer and removes the remaining highly enriched uranium from Iraq.

18 June 1992
UNSCOM's Chemical Destruction Group starts its operations at Muthanna, destroying Iraq's bulk stocks of mustard and nerve agents, filled munitions and precursor chemicals.

June 1992
Iraq refuses to renew the Memorandum of Understanding governing the humanitarian aid programme operated by the UN in Iraq. France and the UK pressure UNSCOM not to create waves with Iraq while negotiations over a new MoU are ongoing.

21 June 1992
UNSCOM starts using its helicopters for aerial inspections in Iraq.

26 June–10 July 1992
UNSCOM's second joint chemical and biological inspection supervises the destruction of chemical bomb-making equipment. On 5 July Iraq blocks the team from entering the Ministry of Agriculture.

6 July 1992
The Security Council demands Iraq grant UNSCOM immediate entry to the Ministry of Agriculture.

6–29 July 1992
UNSCOM maintains a watch on the entrances to the Ministry of Agriculture building, pending access to the site. On 22 July there is an

attack on an inspector maintaining this watch. The team is withdrawn from outside the Ministry but stays in Iraq. Access is finally gained on 28–29 July. Inspectors' observations suggest the recent removal of items from the Ministry.

14–21 July 1992
IAEA13 supervises destruction of items at the uranium enrichment plants in Tarmiya and Ash Sharqat.

16 July 1992
A UN guard is murdered at Dohuk.

July 1992
A nine-month Inter-Agency Humanitarian Programme for Iraq is launched without a new MoU.

August 1992
A 'no-fly zone' over southern Iraq, south of the thirty-fourth parallel, is created by coalition states to protect the Marsh Arabs and dissidents finding refuge in the southern marshes from a renewed Iraqi military offensive against them.

31 August–7 September 1992
IAEA14 takes samples from Iraqi water courses as a part of its monitoring plan.

5–12 September 1992
UNSCOM commissions the hydrolysis plant which will be used to destroy Iraq's bulk stocks of nerve agent and various precursor chemicals at Muthanna. This is the converted Iraqi pilot plant for nerve agent production. Full-scale operations commence on 24 September.

19 November 1992
Iraq gives the Security Council a detailed account of its 'compliance with' resolution 687 (1991).

2 January 1993
Some 200 Iraqis soldiers enter the former Iraqi naval base at Umm Qasr in the demilitarised zone without UN authorisation and retrieve various items, including missiles.

7 January 1993
Iraq stops UNSCOM aircraft from transporting personnel and equipment into and out of Iraq from Bahrain.

8 January 1993
The Security Council demands that Iraq allow UNSCOM to operate its aircraft.

10 January 1995
Iraqi forces again muscle their way into Umm Qasr and take away most of the contents of six ammunition bunkers, including weapons awaiting destruction.

10 January 1993
Iraq maintains the ban on UNSCOM's use of the Habbaniyah airfield.

11 January 1993
The Security Council condemns Iraq actions *vis-à-vis* both UNSCOM and the crossing into the DMZ.

12 January 1993
Iraq states that the items taken from its former naval base at Umm Qasr were Iraqi property and that the property retrieved did not include any item prohibited under resolution 687. Iraq also states that banning UNSCOM was a temporary measure resulting from the danger posed to all foreign aircraft from a possible Iraqi retaliation to military action threatened by the US and UK.

13 January 1993
The US, the UK and France stage air raids on Iraqi air defence bases which the US stated that Iraq was building inside the southern no-fly zone.

17 January 1993
An Iraqi fighter is shot down in the northern no-fly zone by a US fighter. The US launches large-scale missile attacks on Iraqi sites at Zaafaraniyah and al Rafah.

19 January 1993
Iraq accepts that UNSCOM flights should resume under agreed procedures.

22–23 January 1993
US aircraft conduct further raids on Iraqi air defence installations in the no-fly zones.

February 1993
Iraq threatens to shoot down an UNSCOM helicopter providing overhead surveillance during a missile inspection. The helicopter is forced to leave the area.

February 1993
Iraq submits to UNSCOM updated declarations required for monitoring, but these are not in the format required by UNSCOM's monitoring plan or by resolution 715.

17 June 1993
Iraq blocks Mark Silver from installing monitoring cameras at two rocket test sites at Yawm al Azim and al Rafah. Iraq also refuses to move chemical weapons equipment and precursor chemicals located at Fallujah to Muthanna for destruction under UNSCOM supervision.

18 June 1993
The Security Council demands that Iraq accept the installation of cameras at the rocket test sites and move the chemical weapons equipment and precursors from Fallujah to Muthanna. It warns Iraq of the danger of refusing to comply.

15–19 July 1993
After visiting Iraq, Rolf Ekéus reports to the Security Council that Iraq had removed all chemical weapons equipment and precursor chemicals to Muthanna where it had been destroyed under UNSCOM supervision. He also reports that Iraq agreed to allow installation of cameras, but not to their operation.

July 1993
Iraq provides UNSCOM with a third set of monitoring declarations.

25 September 1993
Iraq agrees to the operation of the monitoring cameras at rocket test stands. The cameras are activated.

26 November 1993
Iraq accepts resolution 715 (1991), and so the UNSCOM and IAEA plans
for the ongoing monitoring and verification.

January 1994
Iraq makes its first monitoring declarations under resolution 715 (1991)
and notifies the commission that previous declarations should now be
considered as having been submitted under resolution 715 (1991).

12 March 1994
The IAEA completes the removal of all irradiated nuclear fuel from Iraq.
The fuel is sent to Russia for reprocessing.

March–May 1994
UNSCOM starts baseline inspections of dual-purpose facilities to be
monitored.

19 April 1994
Iraq gives UNSCOM detailed information on its imports of precursor
chemicals and equipment for its past chemical weapons programme. This
is important for creating a material balance for the chemical programme.

28 May–7 June 1994
UNSCOM inventories, photographs and tags biological dual-purpose
equipment as part of the baseline inspections.

July 1994
Iraq updates its monitoring declarations to UNSCOM once again.

22 August 1994
IAEA starts its ongoing monitoring and verification plan.

2 October 1994
UNSCOM announces that its ongoing monitoring and verification plan
is provisionally operational, thus starting a period to test its effectiveness.

6 October 1994
Iraq threatens to end 'cooperation' with UNSCOM and the IAEA and
moves troops towards the Kuwaiti border.

8 October 1994
The Security Council declares unacceptable Iraq's suggestion that it might withdraw cooperation from UNSCOM. In response to the Iraqi troop movements, the US deploy an additional 50,000 troops to Kuwait.

14 October 1994
Iraq withdraws its troops to their previous positions and says it is ready to recognise Kuwaiti sovereignty.

15 October 1994
The Security Council condemns Iraq's deployment of troops to the Kuwaiti border and demands that Iraq not redeploy them to the south. It also demands Iraq's full cooperation with UNSCOM.

10 November 1994
By Revolution Command Council decree and a National Assembly declaration, Iraq confirms its recognition of the State of Kuwait and of the international boundary between Iraq and Kuwait.

16 November 1994
The Security Council welcomes Iraq's recognition of Kuwait.

March 1995
A seminar of international biological weapons experts convened by UNSCOM in New York agrees with the UNSCOM conclusion that Iraq had in the past an as yet undeclared full-scale biological weapons programme.

10 April 1995
UNSCOM announces that its plan for ongoing monitoring and verification is operational.

14 April 1995
The Security Council offers Iraq new terms for an oil-for-food programme to meet the humanitarian needs of Iraq.

1–3 May 1995
UNSCOM convenes a seminar of international chemical weapons experts to assess evidence about Iraq's VX programme. The panel concludes that Iraq has not fully disclosed its VX activities.

15 May 1995
Iraq rejects the latest oil-for-food offer.

1 July 1995
During a visit by Rolf Ekéus to Baghdad, Iraq admits it had a full-scale biological weapons programme and that it produced large quantities of anthrax and botulinum.

17 July 1995
Saddam Hussein threatens to throw out UNSCOM and the IAEA if sanctions are not lifted. A few days later in Cairo, the Iraqi Foreign Minister sets a deadline of 31 August.

4 August 1995
Iraq gives UNSCOM a written account of its past biological weapons programme but denies it ever filled munitions with biological warfare agents.

7 August 1995
Hussein Kamal Hassan, the former director of MIMI and responsible for Iraq's weapons of mass destruction and ballistic missile programmes, defects to Jordan.

17 August 1995
Iraq makes new declarations about all its past weapons programmes. It admits that it filled weapons with biological warfare agents (anthrax and botulinum) and that it had a crash programme to acquire nuclear weapons. Other revelations were made about its VX programme and about its ability to produce ballistic missiles indigenously. Iraq claims that Hussein Kamal Hassan concealed this information from others in the Iraqi government. The threat to throw out UNSCOM and the IAEA is rescinded.

20 August 1995
Iraq gives UNSCOM and the IAEA some 680,000 pages of document-ation about its past weapons programmes.

November 1995
The government of Jordan intercepts a large shipment of missile com-ponents destined for Iraq in violation of sanctions, the arms embargo and UNSCOM's monitoring and verification plan.

7 December 1995
The Sanctions Committee forwards to the Security Council a proposal for a mechanism to monitor Iraq's exports and imports, once sanctions are lifted, of dual-purpose capabilities. This mechanism was devised by UNSCOM and approved by the IAEA.

March 1996
Iraq blocks access to sites, delaying access at five sites by up to seventeen hours.

19 March 1996
The Council issues a presidential statement condemning Iraq's blocking of access.

27 March 1996
The Council adopts the import/export monitoring mechanism.

May–June 1996
UNSCOM supervises the destruction of the al Hakam biological weapons production facility and other biological weapons production equipment.

June 1996
An inspection team led by Scott Ritter to investigate sites involved in Iraq's countermeasures against UNSCOM to hide incriminating evidence about banned weapons is denied access to a number of sites.

12 June 1996
The Security Council demands that Iraq grant immediate access.

13 June 1996
Iraq blocks Scott's team access to another site. The Council sends Rolf Ekéus to Baghdad to secure access.

19–22 June 1996
Rolf Ekéus visits Baghdad, and agrees with Iraq a joint programme of action to conclude investigations into Iraq's past programmes, and establishes inspection modalities for 'sensitive sites' in order to take into account Iraq's legitimate security concerns whilst allowing UNSCOM the access necessary for its inspection activities.

22 June 1996
Iraq provides its fourth 'full, final and complete disclosure' of its past biological weapons programme.

November 1996
Iraq blocks UNSCOM from removing missile components for off-site analysis. UNSCOM is finally able to remove the items in February 1997.

May 1997
Iraq admits that large quantities of equipment and materials that it had previously denied were part of its chemical weapons programme were in fact used for the production of VX.

June 1997
Iraq starts to systematically interfere with the operations of UNSCOM's aerial inspections.

21 June 1997
Iraq blocks access to sites designated for no-notice inspection.

21 June 1997
The Security Council demands that Iraq give access to the sites and suspends reviews of sanctions until UNSCOM's October report.

September 1997
Iraq submits its fifth version of its 'full, final and complete disclosure' of its past biological weapons programme.

17 September 1997
Iraq is seen burning documentation at a 'sensitive site' while the UNSCOM team is kept waiting at the gates. The events are videotaped by UNSCOM.

Late September/early October 1997
UNSCOM is denied access to three sites on the spurious grounds that they are presidential sites and hence out of bounds to UNSCOM.

23 October 1997
The Council splits (ten for, five abstentions) for the first time on UNSCOM issues since April 1991, when it adopts resolution 1134, demanding Iraq give access to the sites.

27 October 1997
Richard Butler sends Tariq Aziz a letter proposing the agenda for their upcoming talks. He sets discussion of the VX programme and adequate access to 'sensitive sites' high on the agenda.

29 October 1997
Tariq Aziz informs the UN that it will no longer accept US personnel in UNSCOM teams and demands the end of U2 flights. The Security Council rejects both demands as unacceptable and threatens serious consequences.

12 November 1997
The Security Council condemns Iraq's failure to comply, and imposes new sanctions on Iraqi officials in the form of travel restrictions.

13 November 1997
Iraq demands the departure of US personnel in UNSCOM from Iraq within twenty-four hours. UNSCOM withdraws all but a skeleton staff from Baghdad in response. The Security Council condemns Iraq.

20 November 1997
Iraq reaches a deal with a Russian envoy. UNSCOM returns to Baghdad with its US personnel.

21 November 1997
The Special Commission meets in emergency session to discuss ways to make UNSCOM more effective.

17 December 1997
Richard Butler reports on his visit to Baghdad, and Iraq's refusal to allow UNSCOM access to 'presidential and sovereign sites'. No exceptions to the right of access are made in any of the resolutions.

22 December 1997
The Security Council demands Iraq allow access to all sites.

13 January 1998
Scott Ritter's inspection team is barred access to a site. Iraq states that the team has too many Americans and Britons.

14 January 1998
Iraq continues to refuse to work with Scott's team, which is consequently withdrawn by UNSCOM.

22 January 1998
Richard Butler reports on his visit to Baghdad, and on Iraq's refusal to allow access to eight 'presidential sites'.

Early February 1998
Technical evaluation meetings, comprising experts from Iraq and UNSCOM and other international weapons experts, meet in Baghdad to review the status of knowledge of Iraq's past chemical and missile programmes. The conclusion of the UNSCOM and international experts is that Iraq has yet to reveal the full extent of its programmes.

15–18 February 1998
The Secretary-General sends a survey team to assess the size and scope of the eight 'presidential sites' unilaterally declared off limits to UNSCOM by Iraq.

20–23 February 1998
The UN Secretary-General visits Iraq, meets Saddam Hussein and Tariq Aziz. Comes away with an 'agreement' that permits access to these sites. It requires the appointment of a new commissioner by the Secretary-General to head a special group to oversee inspections of these sites. Jayantha Dhanapala is appointed to this position on 2 March 1998.

9 March 1998
The Security Council endorses the agreement.

20–27 March 1998
A second technical evaluation meeting, this dealing with biological weapons issues, is held in Vienna. The UNSCOM and international experts agree that Iraq's account of its past biological weapons activities is incomplete and inadequate.

4 April 1998
Access to the presidential sites is obtained.

May 1998
Nissar al Hindawi, one of the founders of Iraq's biological weapons

programme, is arrested and imprisoned by Iraq for being in possession of a false passport. The implication is that he was on the point of defecting. Iraq gives UNSCOM various documents that it claims were taken from Hindawi's offices. These documents are suspected to be compiled purely to support Iraq's current account of its biological weapons activities. The authenticity of some of them is doubted.

14 June 1998
In a visit to Baghdad, Richard Butler lays down a 'road map' for getting Iraq to a position of full compliance. This envisages six weeks of intensive work on Iraq's part.

3 August 1998
Richard Butler returns to Baghdad to review implementation of the 'road map'. Before he can start, Tariq Aziz insists that Butler report to the Security Council that Iraq is in full compliance and asks whether Butler will do so. Butler says he cannot, in the face of the evidence. Aziz suspends the talks.

5 August 1998
A joint meeting of Iraq's Revolutionary Command Council and the Ba'ath Party Command decide to halt 'cooperation' with UNSCOM and the IAEA, ending no-notice inspections. Monitoring activities are allowed to continue.

6 August 1998
Richard Butler reports the situation to the Security Council, which condemns Iraq's actions as totally unacceptable.

9 September 1998
The Security Council condemns Iraq and suspends reviews of sanctions until UNSCOM is permitted to resume full operations.

End September/Early October 1998
Tariq Aziz visits New York, holds meeting with the UN Secretary-General, and demands a full review of sanctions against Iraq. He also demands the restructuring of UNSCOM and the move of its headquarters away from New York.

26 October 1998
Richard Butler presents to the Security Council the results of a review by

experts from seven countries and UNSCOM of the findings of analyses conducted in three laboratories (in the US, Switzerland and France) of fragments from SCUD missile warheads. These results proved, against Iraqi protestations to the contrary, that Iraq had filled missile warheads with VX. This infers that Iraq's VX account needs to be retracted and replaced with an accurate and true account.

31 October 1998
Saddam ends all cooperation with UNSCOM.

14 November 1998
With US aircraft in the air to strike at Iraq, Saddam backs down, agrees to allow UNSCOM back in. The US and UK warn that anything less than full cooperation will result in immediate strikes without warning.

15 December 1998
Richard Butler reports that, given Iraq's attitude to UNSCOM, his team is unable to perform its disarmament mandate.

16–19 December 1998
Operation Desert Fox – four days of aerial bombardment – hits many military and political targets in Iraq.

December 1998
Iraq states that UNSCOM in its current configuration is dead. It will never be allowed back into Iraq.

December 1998–January 1999
Iraq challenges the no-fly zones by firing at US and UK aircraft patrolling them and sending its own aircraft into the zones.

10 January 1999
Iraq's Parliament calls for an end to all cooperation with the UN until sanctions are lifted.

List of Abbreviations

ACDA: Arms Control and Disarmament Agency (US)
BMVC: Baghdad Monitoring and Verification Centre
BW: Biological Weapons or Warfare
CAM: Chemical Agent Monitor
CD: Conference on Disarmament
CFE: Conventional Forces in Europe
CNC: Computer numerically controlled – machine tools that are run by computers
CSCE: Conference on Security and Cooperation in Europe
CW: Chemical Weapons
EMIS: Electromagnetic Isotope Separation
G77: Group of Non-Aligned Nations at the UN (formerly of 77 nations)
GPS: Geo-positioning satellite.
HEPA: High Efficiency Particulate Air filter
HEU: Highly Enriched Uranium
HMX: a very high-quality explosive
IAEA: International Atomic Energy Agency
IAEC: Iraqi Atomic Energy Commission
IAU: Information Assessment Unit
INF: Intermediate-range Nuclear Forces (Treaty)
MIC: (Iraqi) Military Industrialisation Corporation
MIMI: (Iraqi) Ministry of Industry and Military Industrialisation
NAM: Non-Aligned Movement
NATO: North Atlantic Treaty Organisation
NPT: Non-Proliferation Treaty
OMV: Ongoing Monitoring and Verification
OPCW: Organisation for the Prohibition of Chemical Weapons
P3: The P4 less Russia (i.e. US, UK and France)
P4: The P5 less China (i.e. US, UK, France and Russia)
P5: Group of five permanent members of the UN Security Council

RPV: Remote Piloted Vehicle

SCDMAM: (Iraqi) State Company for Drugs and Medical Appliances Marketing

SEPP: (Iraqi) State Establishment for Pesticide Production

START: Strategic Arms Reduction Talks/Treaty

TRC: (Iraqi) Technical Research Centre

TSMID: (Iraqi) Technical and Scientific Materials Import Division

UN: United Nations

UNSCOM: UN Special Commission (for Iraq)

UNSCR: UN Security Council Resolution

WMD: weapons of mass destruction

Glossary

Aerial inspections: Periodic helicopter overflights of sites subject to monitoring in which still and video photographs are taken and changes to the layout of the site reported.

Aerial surveillance: Periodic U2 overflights of Iraq in which photographs are taken and date and GPS coordinates of items photographed recorded. Together with the aerial inspections, provides the films used by UNSCOM's photographic interpreters to plan inspections and prepare line diagrams.

Aerobic bacteria: Bacteria that grow in environments containing oxygen.

Aerosol: A suspension of liquid droplets in air.

Aerosol generator: A machine that generates aerosols. Can be as innocent as a perfume dispenser, or as deadly as a crop sprayer.

Aerosolisation chamber: Chamber used in laboratories to measure the effects of different types of aerosols on experimental animals or subjects.

Aflatoxin: A mildly toxic and carcinogenic substance produced by a fungus. One of Iraq's chosen biological warfare agents.

Anaerobic bacteria: Bacteria that grow in environments with no oxygen, for oxygen which is poisonous. Botulinum is an anaerobic bacterium.

Anaerobic chamber: A cabinet constructed for creating anaerobic environments – ones with no oxygen – in which to conduct experiments or to manipulate materials that are harmed by contact with oxygen.

Anthrax: The disease caused by the bacterium *Bacillus anthracis*, or the bacterium itself. The bacterium is capable of both aerobic and anaerobic growth.

Anthrax spores: The suspended life form of the *Bacillus anthracis* bacterium. Extremely resistant to heat and pressure.

Autoclave: An autoclave is like a pressure cooker. It is used in biological laboratories to sterilise equipment.

Bacillus anthracis: See 'anthrax'.

Bacillus cereus: A non-toxic simulant for anthrax.

Bacillus megaterium: A non-toxic simulant for anthrax.

Bacillus subtilis: A non-toxic simulant for anthrax.

Bacillus thurengensis: A non-toxic close relative of anthrax, used as a bio-pesticide.

BADR-2000: Iraqi missile project based on the Argentinian Condor II project. A two-stage ballistic missile with a planned range of 2000 kilometres.

Ballistic missiles: Rockets, with guidance and control systems, which follow a ballistic trajectory.

Baseline inspections: The first monitoring inspections, designed to inventory all items and activities at a site that need to be monitored (thus creating the baseline for monitoring), and to determine how the site should be monitored.

Bentonite: A grist used in many milling operations. Used in biological weapons programmes to grind bacteria to the right size for effective aerosols.

Biological warfare agent: Any living organism or product of a living organism intended for use in a weapon in such a way that it will cause harm to humans or animals through its physiological effects – bacteria, viruses, fungi and toxins.

Biological weapons: Weapons that deliver biological warfare agents to a target.

Biopesticide: A bacterium or other living creature that is used to kill another biological pest.

Blister agent: Chemical weapons that work by causing chemical burns on the skin.

Calutrons: Large electromagnetic inducers used to separate U235 from U238 in EMIS – electromagnetic isotope separation.

Ceasefire: The terms for ending the Gulf War, set out in resolution 687.

CH-53g: Large military transport helicopter.

Chapter VII: The chapter of the UN Charter that deals with maintaining and restoring international peace. It also lays down the methods that the UN may deploy to restore peace. These include economic sanctions, blockades and military action.

Chemical weapons: Weapons that rely on chemicals.

Chief inspector: The Status Agreement states that UNSCOM should nominate one inspector in each inspection team to be the main interlocutor with the Iraqi authorities – the chief inspector.

Clostridia botulinum: The anaerobic bacterium that produces botulism poisoning.

Clostridium perfringens: The anaerobic bacterium that causes gas gangrene.

Complex growth media: Any combination of organic substances on or in which bacteria grow, such as agar or broth.

Cruise missiles: Missiles that do not follow a ballistic trajectory. They are generally designed to hug the terrain to escape detection by enemy radar.

CS: A particular type of riot gas.

Culture stocks: Laboratory strains of bacteria for scientific research.

Dual-purpose: An item of equipment or material that can be used for one purpose or another. In this book, one that could be used for the production of weapons of mass destruction or long-range missiles, but also has other, non-proscribed uses.

Dual-use: See dual-purpose

Electromagnetic isotope separation: One of many ways of separating weapons-grade uranium from naturally occurring uranium. Uses calutrons.

Enrichment: Separation of weapons-grade uranium from natural uranium.

Exchange of letters: The Status Agreement.

Explosive lens: The lining of explosives wrapped around the nuclear core in an implosion type nuclear bomb. The explosive lens forces the nuclear material in on itself, focusing it as a lens focuses light.

Fermentation: The chemical process whereby bacteria and fungi turn sugars into alcohols, thereby releasing energy for themselves. In biological weapons programmes, the process whereby biological warfare agents are produced.

Full, final and complete disclosures: The declarations required of Iraq under resolution 687 and specifically mentioned in resolution 707. These should give a full account of each of its weapons programmes from initiation to final dissolution.

Gas centrifuge: A means of isolating weapons-grade uranium.

Gaseous diffusion: A means of isolating weapons-grade uranium.

Genetic engineering: The process of inserting DNA from one organism into another to change the genetic characteristics of the recipient of organisms.

Glove boxes: Laboratory equipment used for handling hazardous materials, such as pathogenic bacteria, toxic materials, or radioactive materials. The dangerous material is kept inside a box, with glass windows. The box has two holes in which there are gloves so that the operator can insert his or her hands into them and so manipulate safely the material inside the glove box.

GPS: Global-positioning satellite. A system of navigation satellites that allow one to fix one's position on earth to within a few metres.

GPS coordinates: Map coordinates taken from GPS.

Gun device: A design of the nuclear bomb that relies on firing a bolt of plutonium into a mass of weapons grade uranium. Alternative to implosion bomb.

Gyroscopes: A component of guidance and control systems used in missiles, aircraft, tanks and other vehicles.

Highly enriched uranium: Uranium containing more than 90 per cent of the U235 isotope.

al Hussein: An Iraqi adaptation of the Russian SCUD missile, with an extended range and reduced payload.

Immunities and privileges: The rights given to inspectors to enable them to disarm Iraq without fear of retaliation.

Implosion device: A nuclear bomb that relies on an explosive lens to initiate the chain reaction that constitutes a nuclear explosion. See gun device for comparison.

Inhalation chamber: See aerosolisation chamber.

Initial declarations: Declarations required from Iraq about its holdings and recent imports of dual-purpose items. These form the baseline information from which ongoing monitoring and verification activities start.

INMARSAT: The international marine satellite. A private enterprise satellite similar to the GPS, but also used for satellite telephony.

Line diagram: A map of a site to be inspected, showing each of the buildings at the site with lines showing the walls, roads, rivers and boundary fences.

Long-range: For the purposes of UNSCOM's mandate, more than 150 kilometres.

Machine tools: Lathes and metal-forming machines.

Maraging steel: A high-quality steel used in high-precision gyroscopes and centrifuges.

Material balance: An accounting for all the materials used in a weapons programme. Items imported + items produced in Iraq = items used + items destroyed + items used + items monitored.

Minders: The Iraqi officials who accompanied UNSCOM inspection teams.

Mycotoxin: A toxin produced by a class of fungi.

Nerve agent: A chemical which blocks the transmission of nerve impulses. Victims die of suffocation and a general shutdown of the body's vital organs.

PL4 laboratory: Designation given to biological laboratories with the highest levels of containment.

PL3 laboratory: Biological laboratories with the second highest level of containment.

Plutonium: Artificial element used in gun device nuclear bombs.

Precursors: Chemicals which, when reacted together, make chemical weapons.

President of the Security Council: Chairmanship of the Security Council. This rotates between the Council's fifteen members on a monthly basis.

Resolution 687: The resolution that set out the terms for ending the state of war that existed between Iraq and the UN coalition. It was passed on 3 April 1991.

Resolution 707: Resolution that authorised the U2 flights and barred Iraq from any nuclear activities. It demanded full, final and complete disclosure of all aspects of Iraq's past programmes.

Resolution 715: Resolution that adopted the plans for ongoing monitoring and verification.

Resolution 986: The second oil-for-food deal.

Resolution 1151: Resolution that adopted the export/import monitoring mechanism.

Ricin: A naturally occurring toxin found in castor beans.

Safwan Agreement: The meeting held by military leaders of Iraq and the UN coalition at the end of the Gulf War to make practical arrangements for ending hostilities.

Sarin: A 1930s vintage nerve agent.

SCUD: Vintage ballistic missile, developed by the Soviet Union from von Braun's Second World War V2.

Seed stocks: Collections of scientifically defined bacteria.

Shear force: A shear force occurs when two slightly offset forces act in opposite directions upon an object – e.g. a finger trapped in a door.

Single-cell protein: Protein produced by single-cell organisms such as bacteria.

Site protocol: The document produced at the end of a baseline inspection of a site that describes what needs to be inspected and how it should be inspected.

Spore: An highly resistant, suspended animation form of a bacterium.

Spray drier: A piece of equipment used to harvest bacteria from a fermenter.

Status Agreement: The agreement between the UN and Iraq which sets the inspection rights of UNSCOM and IAEA teams and the obligations of Iraq to facilitate them.

Sulphur mustard: A chemical warfare blister agent.

Supergun: A large-calibre gun designed to deliver large shells long distances, or to lob satellites into orbit.

Tabun: A 1930s vintage nerve agent.

Tear gas: A riot control agent that irritates the eyes, nose and throat.

Tomahawk: US cruise missile operated by both the US Navy (surface ships and submarines) and Air Force.

Toxin: A poisonous substance produced by bacteria, viruses and fungi.

Transall: A military transport aircraft (designation C-160).

U235: Uranium of the isotope used in making nuclear bombs.

U238: Uranium of the naturally occurring isotope.

U2: High-altitude surveillance aircraft, of 1960s vintage.

UNSCOM: UN Special Commission for Iraq, set up in the ceasefire resolution to eliminate Iraq's biological and chemical weapons and its long-range missiles. Used in this book to denote the permanent staffers, as opposed to the Special Commission, which is used to describe the twice-yearly meetings of the government-nominated members of the commission.

UN Security Council: The part of the United Nations responsible for maintaining and restoring international peace and security.

VX: A highly toxic nerve agent developed in the 1940s.

Weaponisation: The process of designing and filling weapons for chemical or biological warfare agents, or the engineering of a nuclear weapon.

Bibliography

Most of the documents listed below dated before December 1995 are contained in the book, *The United Nations and the Iraq–Kuwait Conflict 1990–1996* published by the UN's Department of Public Information as part of its Blue Book series. ISBN 92 1 100596 5, United Nations, New York 1996. All UN Security Council documents are available in depository libraries around the world. Alternatively, the UN's and UNSCOM's web sites both contain many of the documents and other information about the UN's activities in Iraq and Kuwait.

UN Security Council Resolutions
S/Res/687 (1991) adopted 3/4/91
S/Res/699 (1991) adopted 17/6/91
S/Res/706 (1991) adopted 15/8/91
S/Res/707 (1991) adopted 15/8/91
S/Res/712 (1991) adopted 19/9/91
S/Res/715 (1991) adopted 11/10/91
S/Res/778 (1992) adopted 2/10/92
S/Res/949 (1994) adopted 15/10/94
S/Res/986 (1995) adopted 14/4/95
S/Res/1051 (1996) adopted 12/6/96
S/Res/1115 (1997) adopted 21/7/97
S/Res/1134 (1997) adopted 23/10/97
S/Res/1137 (1997) adopted 12/11/97
S/Res/1154 (1998) adopted 2/3/98
S/Res/1194 (1998) adopted 9/9/98

Key Security Council Documents
relevant to the mandate and establishment of UNSCOM
ST/SGB/238 of 5/4/91
S/22508 of 18/4/91

S/22614 of 17/5/91
S/22615 of 17/5/91
S/22660 of 2/6/91
S/22792 of 15/7/91
S/22871/Rev. 1 of 2/10/91
S/22872/Rev. 1 of 20/9/91
and Corr. 1 of 2/10/91
S/23673 of 4/3/92
S/25863 of 27/5/93
S/1995/208 of 17/3/95
S/1995/215 of /3/95
S/1996/805 of 30/12/96

UNSCOM Reports to the Security Council

S/22761 of 5/7/91
S/23165 of 25/10/91
S/23268 of 4/12/91
S/23514 of 25/1/92
S/23606 of 18/2/92
S/23643 of 26/2/92
S/23687 of 7/3/92
S/23801 of 10/4/92
S/23993 of 22/5/92
S/24108 of 16/6/92 (Corr. 1)
S/24443 of 14/8/92
S/24661 of 19/10/92
S/24984 of 17/12/92
S/25172* of 2/3/93
S/25620 of 21/4/93
S/25960 of 16/6/93
S/25977 of 21/6/93
S/26127 of 21/7/93
S/26451 of 16/9/93
S/26571 of 12/10/93
S/26684 of 5/11/93
S/26825 and Corr. 1 of 1/12/93
S/26910 of 21/12/93
S/1994/151 of 10/2/94
S/1994/341 of 24/3/94
S/1994/489 of 22/4/94
S/1994/520 of 29/4/94

S/1994/750 of 24/6/94
S/1994/860 of 20/7/94
S/1994/1138 and Corr. 1 of 7/10/94
S/1994/1422 and Add. 1 of 15/12/94
S/1995/284 of 10/4/95
S/1995/494 of 19/6/95
S/1996/258 of 11/4/96
S/1996/848 of 11/10/96
S/1997/152 of 24/2/97
S/1997/301 of 11/4/97
S/1997/774 of 06/10/97
S/1997/922 of 24/11/97
S/1997/987 of 17/12/97
S/1998/58 of 22/1/98

IAEA Reports to the Security Council
S/22788 of 15/7/91
S/22837 of 25/7/91
S/22986 of 28/8/91
S/23112 of 4/10/91
S/23122 of 8/10/91
S/23215 of 14/11/91
S/23283 of 12/12/91
S/23295 of 17/12/91
S/23505 of 30/1/92
S/23514 of 25/1/92
S/23644 of 26/2/92
S/23813 of 15/4/92
S/23947 of 22/5/92
S/24036 of 29/5/92
S/24110 of 17/6/92
S/24223 of 2/7/92
S/24450 of 16/8/92
S/24593 of 28/9/92
S/24722 of 28/10/92
S/24981 of 17/12/92
S/24988 of 17/12/92
S/25013 of 24/12/92
S/25411 of 13/3/93
S/25621 of 19/4/93
S/25666 of 26/4/93

S/25982 of 21/6/93
S/25983 of 21/6/93
S/26333 of 20/8/93
S/26584 of 14/10/93
S/26685 of 3/11/93
S/26897 of 20/12/93
S/1994/31 of 14/1/94
S/1994/355 of 25/3/94
S/1994/490 of 22/4/94
S/1994/564 of 13/5/94
S/1994/650 of 1/6/94
S/1994/793 of 5/7/94
S/1994/1001 of 26/8/94
S/1994/1151 of 10/10/94
S/1994/1206 of 22/10/94
S/1994/1443 of 22/12/94
S/1994/1438 of 22/12/94
S/1995/287 of 11/4/95
S/1995/481 of 13/6/95

UN Security Council Statements

S/22509 of 19/4/91: Council's agreement to set up UNSCOM
S/22746 of 28/6/91: Statement about shooting incident
S/23070 of 25/9/91: Council's position on aircraft rights
S/23305 of 6/3/92: Council's position on 'no objection'
S/23517 of 5/2/92: Council's position on compliance
S/23609 of 19/2/92: Council's position on rejection of 715
S/23663 of 28/2/92: Invitation of Iraq to the Council
S/23699 of 11/3/92: President's opening remarks
S/23709 of 12/3/92: Statement at end of Aziz visit
S/23803 of 10/4/92: Reaction to Iraqi threat to U2s
S/24240 of 6/7/92: President's note on Ministry of Agriculture
S/24836 of 23/11/92: President's opening remarks
S/24839 of 24/11/92: Statement at end of Aziz visit
S/25081 of 8/1/93: Response to Iraq's ban on flights
S/25091 of 11/1/93: Response to Iraq's failure to respond
S/25970 of 18/6/93: Cameras and chemical production equipment
S/PRST/1994/58 of 8/10/94: Response to Iraqi troop movements
S/PRST/1994/68 of 16/11/94: Welcome of Iraqi recognition of Kuwait
S/PRST/96/11of 19/3/96: Iraq's denial of access

S/PRST/96/28 of 14/6/96: Iraq's denial of access
S/PRST/96/36of 23/8/96: Iraq's denial of access
S/PRST/96/49of 30/12/96: Iraq's refusal to allow removal of missile remnants
S/PRST/49 of 29/10/97: Iraq's ejection of US inspectors, refusal of U2 flights
S/PRST/51 of 13/11/97: Iraq's expulsion of inspectors
S/PRST/54 of 3/12/97: Iraq's refusal to allow access
S/PRST/1 of 14/1/98: Demand for full cooperation

UNSCOM Press Releases
IK/18 of 22/4/91: Appointment of Ekéus and Gallucci
IK/19 of 1/5/91: Appointment of members of UNSCOM
IK/21 of 22/5/91: IAEA1/UNSCOM
SC/5283 of 17/6/91: SC approves guidelines for arms embargo
IAEA/1164 of 18/6/91: Preparations for IAEA2
IK/27 of 24/6/91: Initial exploration of Muthanna
SC/5284 of 26/6/91: SC comments on denial of access, IAEA2
IK/28 of 28/6/91: Denial of access, shooting incident
SC/5287 of 28/6/91: SC demands on access and mission
IK/29 of 1/7/91: IAEA review of inspection activities
IK/30 of 1/7/91: High-level delegation's Baghdad visit
IAEA/1171 of 5/7/91: IAEA3's arrival in Baghdad
SG/1890 of 5/7/91: S-G's report on high-level mission
SG/T/1673 of 5/7/91: S-G's personal message to Saddam
IK/31 of 8/7/91: Iraqi declaration on nuclear programme
IK/32 of 8/7/91: IAEA's reaction to Iraq's new story
IK/33 of 10/7/91: UK and France agree on nuclear fuel removal
IK/35 of 18/7/91: IAEA condemnation of Safeguards breach
IK/36 of 19/7/91: EMIS discoveries
IK/38 of 22/7/91: IAEA3 report – EMIS
IK/40 of 25/7/91: IAEA4's departure for Iraq
IK/43 of 5/8/91: Iraqi declaration on defensive BW R&D
IK/44 of 6/8/91: Iraqi declarations on plutonium
IK/46 of 14/8/91: Biological weapons inspection
SC/5298 of 15/8/91: SC votes on resolutions 705-707
IK/48 of 23/8/91: Talks on chemical weapons destruction
IK/50 of 11/9/91: Fourth chemical weapons inspection team
IK/51 of 17/9/91: Third chemical weapons inspection team
IK/51/Rev.1 of 18/9/91: Ditto
GA/8197 of 18/9/91: Comments of GA President on UNSCOM

IK/52 of 18/9/91: Fourth ballistic missiles inspection team
IK/54 of 23/9/91: SC President's comments on nuclear programmes
IK/55 of 23/9/91: Discovery of documents at PC-3
IK/56 of 23/9/91: Documents confiscated - IAEA6/UNSCOM16
IK/57 of 24/9/91: Iraqi refusal to allow removal of documents
IK/58 of 24/9/91: Parking lot (IAEA6/UNSCOM16)
IK/59 of 24/9/91: Documents missing from those returned
IK/60 of 24/9/91: Detention of IAEA6 continues
IK/61 of 24/9/91: Presidential statement - IAEA6/UNSCOM16
IK/62 of 24/9/91: Iraqis on the commission helicopters
IK/6? of 30/9/91: Iraq set to release IAEA6
IK/63 of 30/9/91: Arrival of IAEA6 in Bahrain
SC/5318 of 11/10/91: SC demands compliance, adopts 715
IK/68 of 24/10/91: Second plenary session of the commission
IK/69 of 31/10/91: Second biological weapons inspection team
GA/8257 of 13/11/91: GA supports IAEA actions in Iraq
IK/70 of 15/11/91: Sixth chemical weapons inspection team
IK/71 of 15/11/91: Removal of highly enriched uranium
IK/72 of 20/11/91: Fifth chemical weapons inspection team
IK/74 of 26/11/91: CW destruction fact-finding team
IK/76 of 11/12/91: CBW inspection team
IK/77 of 11/12/91: IAEA release of data on suppliers
IK/79 of 18/12/91: Sixth ballistic missiles inspection team
IK/81 of 17/7/92: IAEA9 verifies centrifuge part stocks
IK/82 of 27/1/92: Incident at the Sheraton Hotel (CW7)
IK/83 of 27/1/92: Special mission (Gee/von Butler)
IK/84 of 3/2/92: Results of special mission
IK/86 of 10/2/92: Seventh chemical weapons inspection team
SC/5381 of 28/2/92: SC condemns Iraq's non-disclosure
IK/89 of 4/3/92: Eighth ballistic missiles inspection team
IK/91 of 13/3/92: Talks between Iraq and the commission
IK/92 of 20/3/92: New Iraqi disclosures
IK/93 of 23/3/92: Verification of Iraqi disclosures (BM9)
IK/94 of 25/3/92: Destruction of missile production equipment
IAEA/1214 of 25/3/92: IAEA calls for destruction of al Atheer
IK/95 of 26/3/92: Verification of destroyed missiles
IK/97 of 31/3/92: Chemical destruction inspection team
IK/98 of 3/4/92: Update on the commission's activities
IK/100 of 10/4/92: SC warns Iraq not to threaten U2
IK/102 of 16/4/92: Second chemical weapons destruction team
IK/103 of 27/4/92: Tenth ballistic missiles inspection team

IK/104 of 4/5/92: Eighth chemical weapons inspection team

IK/105 of 7/5/92: Special Commission third plenary session

IK/106 of 2/6/92: Eleventh ballistic missiles inspection team

IK/108 of 1/7/92: 'Full, final and complete report' and start of helicopter surveys

IK/110 of 6/7/92: Denial of access to Ministry of Agriculture

SC/5434 of 6/7/92: SC demands access to Ministry of Agriculture

IK/112 of 22/7/92: Withdrawal of UNSCOM team from Ministry of Agriculture

IK/113 of 27/7/92: Modalities for the inspection of Ministry of Agriculture

IK/117 of 5/8/92: Result of the inspection of Ministry of Agriculture

IK/118 of 7/8/92: UNSCOM agrees to delay next inspection

IK/119 of 25/8/92: Twelfth ballistic missiles inspection team

IK/120/Rev.1 of 3/9/92: IAEA's position on Iraqi nuclear programme

IK/121 of 16/9/92: commissioning CW destruction plants

IK/123 of 24/9/92: Destruction of nerve agent

IK/125 of 15/10/92: Security Council statement on UNSCOM45

GA/PS/2923 of 23/9/92: Iraq condemns selective enforcement

IK/127 of 5/11/92: Fourth plenary session of the commission

IK/128 of 5/11/92: Iraq's account of its 819 SCUD missiles

IK/129 of 12/11/92: CW incinerator commissioned

SC/5505 of 23/11/92: SC debate on Iraqi compliance

SG/SM/4880 of 14/12/92: S-G on members' help with suppliers

SC/5534 of 8/1/93: SC demands re UNSCOM flights

SC/5536 of 11/1/93: SC warning of serious consequences

IK/137 of 4/2/93: Initiation of interim monitoring

IK/139 of 24/2/93: Destruction of nerve agents and rockets

IK/143 of 22/4/93: CW10 – destruction of POCl3/PCl3 plant

IK/144 of 22/4/93: Sarin destruction complete

IK/145 of 3/5/93: Completion of the destruction of DF

IK/149 of 21/5/93: Return of second interim monitoring team

IK/150 of 2/6/93: Destruction of POCl3, PCl3 and SOCl2

IK/151 of 2/8/93: Observation of missile tests

IK/152 of 23/8/93: Destruction of D4 complete

IK/153 of 27/8/93: Destruction of tabun starts

IK/154 of 24/9/93: High-level mission to Baghdad

IAEA/1251 of 1/10/93: General Conference resolutions

IK/155 of 5/11/93: UNSCOM63

IK/156 of /11/93: UNSCOM65 (CW use) - launch

IK/157 of 22/11/93: UNSCOM65 - results of on-site tests

IK/158 of 13/12/93: Destruction of 155mm mustard shells
IK/160 of 16/12/94: Second gamma survey
IK/162 of 10/1/94: Shot fired at UNSCOM convoy
IK/163 and IAEA/1254 of 15/2/94: Removal of nuclear fuel
IK/164 of 23/2/94: CW13 – equipment tagging, etc.
IK/165 of 28/2/94: CW use – results of lab analyses
IK/166 of 8/3/94: BM21 – monitoring methods for missile sites
IK/167 of 25/3/94: Destruction of mustard complete
IK/168 of 28/3/94: Attack on UNSCOM helicopter
IK/169 of 18/4/94: Completion of destruction of precursors
IK/171 of 22/6/94: Closedown of Chemical Destruction Group
IK/172 and IAEA/1278 of 12/7/94: Joint statement – Baghdad talks
IK/173 of 15/7/94: SG says Iraq should comply with resolutions

Iraqi Letters
S/22456 of 6/4/91: Iraqi response to UNSCR 687
S/22673 of 5/6/91: Iraqi complaints at air violations
S/22682 of 10/6/91: Costs of 687 Section C
S/22689 of 11/6/91: Compliance
S/22749 of 29/6/91: Iraqi response to UNSC message
S/22762 of 5/7/91: Saddam Hussein's letter
S/22780 of 10/7/91: Complaint about sanctions reviews
S/22786 of 13/7/91: Compliance – uranium enrichment
S/22803 of 16/7/91: Nuclear sites
S/22826 of 24/7/91: Response to IAEA governors
S/22899 of 6/8/91: Reconnaissance aircraft
S/22912 of 8/8/91: Response to IAEA3/UNSCOM5 report
S/22939 of 14/8/91: Objection to U2
S/22957 of 16/8/91: Iraq's position on 705 and 707
S/22998 of 3/9/91: Position on 707
S/23064 of 24/9/91: Agreement to UNSCOM helicopters
S/23065 of 24/9/91: Iraqi protest about David Kay
S/23102 of 1/10/91: Iraqi allegations that David Kay is a CIA agent
S/23110 of 4/10/91: Conduct of inspectors/Kay
S/23115 of 7/10/91: Israeli violation of Iraqi airspace
S/23123 of 10/10/91: Bush statement on Saddam and embargo
S/23139 of 14/10/91: Israeli violation/helicopter flight
S/23140 of 14/10/91: US passing of weapons of mass destruction data to
     Israel
S/23168 of 25/10/91: Aziz on Iraqi research
S/23197 of 5/11/91: Allegation that US inspectors work for CIA not

UNSCOM
S/23472 of 24/1/92: Compliance
S/23636 of 24/2/92: Iraqi report of Ekéus visit – seminars
S/23806 of 13/4/92: the commission's response to U2 letter
S/24002 of 26/5/92: Sahaf letter of 26/5/92 on full, final and complete disclosures, etc.
S/24276 of 13/7/92: SG's letter on Ekéus visit
S/23421 of 20/7/92: Invitation to non-aligned to inspect Ministry of Agriculture
S/24336 of 22/7/92: Iraqi Ministry of Information on Ministry of Agriculture
S/24339 of 23/7/92: Hussein letter on Ekéus visit
S/24339* of 7/8/92: Ditto
S/24384 of 5/8/92: Al Anbari letter on David Kay
S/24475 of 21/8/92: Sahaf letter on no-fly zone
S/24551 of 12/9/92: Sahaf letter on Sanctions Committee
S/24726 of 29/10/92: Sahaf letter to the SG on UNSCOM
S/24822 of 13/11/92: Sahaf letter – request to address UNSC
S/24829 of 20/11/92: Iraqi 'factual report' on compliance
S/24964 of 14/12/92: Iraqi response to Corden's letter to the Council
S/25064 of 8/1/93: Information bulletin
S/25086 of 10/1/93: Response to 8/1/93 Council statement
S/25093 of 14/1/93: U2 flights over southern Iraq
S/25097 of 13/1/93: Response to 11/1/93 Council statement
S/25111* of 21/1/93: 16/1/93 letter to UNSCOM on flights
S/25128 of 19/1/93: Revolutionary Command Council statement
S/25276 of 11/2/93: U2 protest
S/25387 of 10/3/93: Israel's plans to kill Saddam - U2 info
S/25391 of 10/3/93: Information bulletin
S/25391* of 17/3/93: As above reissued for technical reasons
S/25523 of 5/4/93: Iraqi response to P4 démarche
S/25535 of 6/4/93: Information bulletin
S/25548 of 7/4/93: Iraqi disposal of munitions
S/25758 of 12/5/93: Information bulletin
S/25761 of 12/5/93: Complaints about Sanctions Committee
S/25815 of 21/5/93: Response to third monitoring report S/25620
S/25836 of 25/5/93: Complaints about Sanctions Committee
S/25865 of 29/5/93: Iraqi statement on the border
S/25915 of 9/6/93: Attack on fifth plenary session
S/25928 of 11/6/93: May 1993 bulletin
S/25979 of 21/6/93: Sahaf letter on S/25970

S/26004 of 27/6/93: Iraqi letter on US attack on intelligence HQ
S/26072 of 13/7/93: Sahaf letter on sealing mission
S/26204 of 2/8/93: Complaints about Sanctions Committee
S/26302 of 13/8/93: Information bulletin on June
S/26380 of 30/8/93: Complaints about Sanctions Committee
S/26424 of 10/9/93: Iraqi response on human rights
S/26427 of 11/9/93: Information bulletin on August
S/26811 of 26/11/93: Iraq's acceptance of 715
S/26826 of 1/12/93: Complaints against Sanctions Committee
S/26849 of 7/12/93: Iraq's complaint at U2 flights
S/26867 of 10/12/93: Complaint against US propaganda
S/26882 of 16/12/93: Complaint against US propaganda
S/1994/219 of 25/2/94: Complaint against US/UK/Kuwaiti propaganda
S/1994/348 of 26/3/94: Complaint against use of frozen assets
S/1994/464 of 19/4/94: Complaints – Clinton's State of Union
S/1994/771 of 28/6/94: 'Malaysian declaration' on sanctions
S/1994/973 of 15/8/94: Complaint against US propaganda
S/1994/997 of 26/8/94: Complaint against US propaganda
S/1994/1149 of 10/10/94: Sahaf statement on troop movements
S/1994/1173 of 15/10/94: Joint Iraqi–Russian communiqué
S/1994/1207 of 24/10/94: Complaint against US/UK interpretation of
    949
S/1994/1288 of 14/11/94: Letter transmitting recognition of Kuwait

Proces Verbales

S/PV.2977 Parts I and II (resumptions 1–5) of 13, 14, 16, 23, and 26
    February and 2 March 1991: Discussions on the air war and efforts to
    bring about a ceasefire
S/PV.2981 of 3/4/91: Adoption of SCR 687 (1991)
S/PV.2996 of 28/6/91: Denial of access to IAEA2/UNSCOM4
S/PV.3004 of 15/8/91: Adoption of SCRs 705/706/707 (1991)
S/PV.3008 of 19/9/91: Adoption of SCR 712 (1991)
S/PV.3012 of 11/10/91: Adoption of SCR 715 (1991)
S/PV.3058 of 28/2/92: Iraq's non-acceptance of 707 and 715
S/PV.3059 and resumption 1 and 2 of 11 and 12/3/92: Aziz's visit to New
    York
S/PV.3139 and resumption 1 and 2 of 23 and 24/11/92: Aziz's visit to New
    York
S/PV.3161 of 8/1/93: Iraq's blocking of UNSCOM aircraft
S/PV.3242 of 18/6/93 and Corr. 1 of 2/7/93: Cameras
S/PV.3245 of 27/6/93: US attack on intelligence HQ

S/PV.3435 of 8/10/94: Adoption of presidential statement
S/PV.3438 of 15/10/94: Adoption of SCR 949
S/PV.3439 of 17/10/94: Kozyrev/Aziz
S/PV.3519 of 14/4/95: Adoption of SCR 986

Other Documents
S/22739 of 26/6/91: Denied access at Abu Gharaib
S/22743 of 28/6/91: Denied access at Fallujah – shooting
S/23449 of 21/1/92: German letter on German suppliers
S/24056 of 3/6/92: Ekéus's letters to Sahaf and General Amer
S/24985* of 17/12/92: Corden's note to Council President
S/25384 of 9/3/93: Kuwaiti letter – Iraqi territory claims
S/25465 of 23/3/93: Kuwaiti letter – Iraqi press items
S/25790 of 18/5/93: Kuwaiti letter – Iraqi non-compliance
S/25865 of 29/5/93: Kuwaiti on adoption of SCR833 (border)
S/26003 of 27/6/93: US letter on attack on intelligence HQ
S/26449 of 16/9/93: Kuwaiti letter – Iraqi non-compliance
S/26841 of 5/12/93: Council acknowledgement of Iraq's 715 acceptance
S/1994/25 of 11/1/94: Kuwaiti letter – Iraqi non-compliance
S/1994/338 of 24/3/94: Kuwaiti letter re sanctions renewal
S/1994/545 of 6/5/94: Kuwaiti letter re sanctions renewal
S/1994/812 of 11/7/94: Damascus Declarations summit meeting
S/1994/814 of 11/7/94: Kuwaiti letter – Iraqi non-compliance
S/1994/980 of 17/8/94: Kuwait/Saudi rebuttal of Iraqi complaints
S/1994/1036 of 8/9/94: Kuwaiti letter Iraqi compliance
S/1994/1126 of 4/10/94: Kuwaiti letter on return of property
S/1994/1137 of 6/10/94: Kuwaiti letter - RCC statement
S/1994/1162 and A/49/523 of 14/10/94: GCC statement on Iraq/Kuwait
S/1994/1165 of 14/10/94: Kuwaiti reaction to I/RF communiqué
S/1994/1297 of 16/11/94: Council letter to Iraq welcomes its recognition
    of Kuwait
S/1995/300 of 13/4/95: P5 letter on sanctions

The Special Commission's Status, Immunities and Privileges

The Convention on the Privileges and Immunities of the United Nations
of 13 February 1946.

The Agreement on the Privileges and Immunities of the International
Atomic Energy Agency of 1 July 1959.

SCRs 687, 707 and 715 (1991) as above, and the plans for ongoing monitoring and verification contained in documents S/22871/Rev. 1 and S/22872/Rev. 1/Corr. 1.

The exchange of letters of 6 and 17 May 1991 between the Secretary-General and the Minister for Foreign Affairs of Iraq, constituting the status agreement for the Special Commission in Iraq.

The exchange of letters of 1 and 28 September 1991 between the Secretary-General of the United Nations and the director-general of the IAEA on the one part and the Minister for Foreign Affairs of Bahrain on the other part, constituting the status agreement for the field office in Bahrain. This agreement has been extended on a six-monthly basis by subsequent exchanges of letters.

Index